Presidents, Prime Ministers and C

Also by Ludger Helms

INSTITUTIONS AND INSTITUTIONAL CHANGE IN THE FEDERAL REPUBLIC OF GERMANY (*editor*)

PARTEIEN UND FRAKTIONEN: Ein Internationaler Vergleich (*editor*)

POLITISCHE OPPOSITION: Theorie und Praxis in westlichen Regierungssystemen

POLITISCHE THEORIE UND REGIERUNGSLEHRE (*co-editor with Uwe Jun*)

REGIERUNGSORGANISATION UND POLITISCHE FÜHRUNG IN DER BUNDESREPUBLIK DEUTSCHLAND (*forthcoming*)

WETTBEWERB UND KOOPERATION

Presidents, Prime Ministers and Chancellors

Executive Leadership in Western Democracies

Ludger Helms
Heisenberg Fellow and Academic Visitor
Department of Government
London School of Economics and Political Science

First published 2005 by
PALGRAVE MACMILLAN
Houndmills, Basingstoke, Hampshire RG21 6XS and
175 Fifth Avenue, New York, N.Y. 10010
Companies and representatives throughout the world

PALGRAVE MACMILLAN is the global academic imprint of the Palgrave
Macmillan division of St. Martin's Press, LLC and of Palgrave Macmillan Ltd.
Macmillan® is a registered trademark in the United States, United Kingdom
and other countries. Palgrave is a registered trademark in the European
Union and other countries.

ISBN 1–4039–4250–1 hardback
ISBN 1–4039–4251–X paperback

This book is printed on paper suitable for recycling and made from fully
managed and sustained forest sources.

A catalogue record for this book is available from the British Library.

Library of Congress Cataloging-in-Publication Data
Helms, Ludger.
    Presidents, prime ministers, and chancellors : executive leadership in
    western democracies / Ludger Helms.
        p. cm.
    Includes bibliographical references and index.
    ISBN 1–4039–4250–1 (cloth) — ISBN 1–4039–4251–X (pbk.)
    1. Executive power—Cross-cultural studies.   2. Political leadership—
    Cross-cultural studies.   3. Heads of state—Cross-cultural studies.
    4. Democracy—Cross-cultural studies.   I. Title.

    JF251.H45 2005
    352.23′6—dc22
                                                           2004056901

10   9   8   7   6   5   4   3
14   13   12   11   10   09   08   07   06

Printed and bound in Great Britain by
Antony Rowe Ltd, Chippenham and Eastbourne

For Niken
with love and gratitude

Contents

List of Tables and Figures

Tables

Figures

Acknowledgements

In the course of writing this book, I enjoyed invaluable support from various sources, and of various kinds. Generous financial support was provided by the Thyssen Foundation and the German Research Foundation. The intellectual support and feedback I received on previous drafts and versions of this work included kind advice from a large number of senior colleagues, most of whom could not reasonably be expected to be prepared to share their knowledge with me. As there is, unfortunately, no room here to express my sincere gratitude in more proper terms, I just list those I feel particularly indebted to, in alphabetical order: Klaus von Beyme (Heidelberg), Terri Bimes (Harvard), Bruce E. Cain (Berkeley), Gert-Joachim Glaessner (Berlin), Peter A. Hall (Harvard), George W. Jones (London), Morton Keller (Brandeis), Anthony King (Essex), Peter Lösche (Göttingen), Stephen Padgett (Strathclyde), Gillian Peele (Oxford), Richard Rose (Strathclyde) and Cindy Skach (Harvard). Needless to say, all possible remaining errors are my responsibility alone.

A note of gratitude is also due to the anonymous referees who read, and commented on, an earlier draft of this manuscript, and to my publisher, Alison Howson, at Palgrave Macmillan for her much appreciated ability to reconcile this author's fancies and ambitions with the increasingly tough laws of global publishing.

LUDGER HELMS

List of Abbreviations

BBC	British Broadcasting Corporation
BdL	Bank deutscher Länder
BHE	Bund der Heimatvertriebenen und Entrechteten
BVerfGE	Entscheidungen des Bundesverfassungsgerichts
CDU	Christlich-Demokratische Union
CIA	Central Intelligence Agency
CPRS	Central Policy Review Staff
CSU	Christlich-Soziale Union
D	Democrat
DP	Deutsche Partei
ECB	European Central Bank
ECHR	European Convention of Human Rights
EEC	European Economic Community
EOP	Executive Office of the President
EMS	European Monetary System
ERM	European Exchange Rate Mechanism
EU	European Union
FDP	Freie Demokratische Partei
FDR	Franklin D. Roosevelt
Fed	Federal Reserve Board
FTSE	Financial Times Stock Exchange
GDR	German Democratic Republic
GOP	Grand Old Party
HEW	(Department of) Health, Education and Welfare
IG Metall	Industriegewerkschaft Metall
IMF	International Monetary Fund
INF	Intermediate-Range Nuclear Forces
JCC	Joint Constitutional Committee
MORI	Market and Opinion Research International
MP	Member of Parliament
NATO	North Atlantic Treaty Organization
NEC	National Executive Committee
NHS	National Health System
NSC	National Security Council
OMB	Office of Management and Budget
PDS	Partei des Demokratischen Sozialismus
PLP	Parliamentary Labour Party

R	Republican
RPM	Resale Price Maintenance
SES	Senior Executive Service
SPD	Social Democratic Party
TUC	Trades Union Congress
UK	United Kingdom
US	United States

Part I
Introduction

1
Studying Executive Leadership

This book is about executive leadership in Western democracies. Focusing specifically on the leadership performance of twenty-nine political 'chief executives'[1] in three major advanced democracies, it seeks to explore the emergence, development and impact of different leadership styles and strategies under different constitutional, political and historical conditions. In doing so, it tries to overcome the limitations of most of the available literature on the subject, which has either centred on historical comparisons of different leaders within a single country or ventured to compare whole countries without paying due attention to the considerable variations between different office-holders acting within a given country. However, while the focus of this study is considerably broader than that of many other works in the field, it is neither meant to be another general inquiry into the nature of political leadership[2] nor a full-scale comparison of three governmental systems.

Executive leadership can be understood as a specific subcategory of political leadership in the broader sense. Whereas political leadership in its most general form is not dependent on any specific institutional preconditions, executive leadership refers to forms of political leadership to be exerted by the office-holders in the executive branch of a given political system. In this general sense, executive leadership is by no means confined to democratic forms of leadership, or leadership in democratic regimes, though only the latter will be considered in this study. Another important distinction relates to the political/administrative divide that characterizes the structural features of executives as institutions in democratic political systems. While the relationship between the political and the administrative part of the executive – between politicians and civil servants – is occasionally touched upon, the key focus of this study is on the political executive; that is, the elected and politically responsible

3

power-holders in the executive branch. Irrespective of its more specific manifestations, executive leadership in modern democracies comprises two different dimensions of leadership; namely, policy leadership (which is concerned with the actual contents of public policy), and political leadership (which is about mobilizing a sufficient amount of political support for a given policy). Though leadership styles of chief executives cannot be studied in complete separation from policy issues, the primary focus of this book is on the second dimension; that is, on the politics of executive leadership.

Needless to say, the premise from which this study starts is that national executives and executive leadership matter, and matter significantly for the overall performance of contemporary democracies. For most of the period on which this study focuses – from the end of the Second World War until the very early twenty-first century – the significance of national governments as core political players in liberal democracies has been beyond question. By contrast, in the more recent political science literature, the central role of national executives and executive leadership in the decision-making process of advanced democracies has come to be questioned from different angles. As even a brief consideration of the arguments put forward reveals, however, executive leadership continues to be one of the prime subjects for contemporary comparative political research.

The significance of national executives as key actors and decision-makers has been called into question by arguments relating to both the national and the international arenas of politics. More recent perspectives on the role of national executives in a changing world have centred primarily on the specific limitations of executive leadership resulting from the increasing denationalization of politics. While the increasing role of international organizations and supranational decision-making arenas cannot seriously be denied, the 'negative' effects of internationalization and globalization on the role of national governments and executive leadership are easily exaggerated. As Robert Dahl (1999: 926-7) has rightly pointed out:

> after all, until the First World War, the United States and most European countries were even more integrated into the international economy than they are today: yet the functions of national and local governments were far from trivial. Indeed, today people in democratic countries may want more governmental action, not less, simply in order to counter the adverse effects of international markets. Thus the

quality and performance of democratic governments in these national and sub-national units will continue to be a matter of prime importance.

Similar qualifications have been made by leading scholars of public policy research who have argued that the 'net room for manoeuvre' that national governments enjoy has become larger rather than smaller since the 1950s because of the evolution of the welfare state and an increase in public revenues (Schmidt, 2000: 306).

Another bunch of arguments challenging the traditional notion of the executive's dominant role in the political decision-making process has focused on the continuing fragmentation of modern societies and the dramatically increased number of other political players, which are seen as severely constraining the room for manoeuvre of national governments. While the normative-ideological interpretations of these phenomena show a great deal of variation among different authors – stretching from conservative scenarios of 'ungovernability' to sociological theories of post-modern 'self-governance' of society – the empirical assessments offered are stunningly similar. In the more recent works of many political scientists, even the term 'government' has been replaced widely by 'governance' – a change in terminology meant to acknowledge the development away from hierarchical concepts of political authority to a much more open and less centrally co-ordinated structure of the public policy-making process (Rhodes, 2003; Mayntz, 2003). A somewhat closer look suggests, however, that the *relative* superiority of the executive over other, non-public, political players has by no means withered away. Governments may, as much as ever, draw on a number of resources, such as, in particular, the formal authority to make laws, which interest groups and other social actors lack (Blondel, 1992: 267). Largely the same holds true for the executive's position towards other public political institutions. Neither the often-criticized tendency towards a 'judicialization of politics', nor the notable efforts to strengthen the policy-making capacities of parliaments by increasing their staff, which may be observed in many Western countries, has sidelined the executive in the public policy-making process. In parliamentary democracies, the strong position of the executive towards parliament has been documented empirically in surveys measuring the proportion of governmental bills among the total of bills initiated and the considerably better chances of the former to secure parliamentary approval (von Beyme, 2000a: 93). Moreover, in the bulk of both parliamentary and presidential democracies, executives have been increasingly successful in circumventing parliament altogether by making excessive use of executive orders or statutory instruments (Carey and Shugart, 1998).

There has been a host of other developments, all of which have strengthened rather than weakened the role of the executive in the political system, as well as (and in particular) that of the head of government. To begin with, the chief executive's position within the executive branch has been strengthened by the increasing demands of policy co-ordination which, in turn, may be considered the result of an increased sectorization of policy-making, increasing budgetary pressures, and the rise of more complex policy agendas that require increased public expenditure and core executive co-ordination (Peters *et al.*, 2000: 9–10).

Moreover, the chief executive's position within the executive branch and in relation to other political players in the wider political process has been upgraded as a result of the effects of the modern mass media, which favour a high degree of personalization of politics. In many countries, media reporting on politics and political leaders has in fact become more or less part of the 'celebrity industry'. Whereas the dramatically increased exposure of political leaders in the media does not enhance their respective influence over other actors directly, being a political celebrity undoubtedly adds to the resources a leader has at his or her disposal in the decision-making arena. As will be further substantiated later in this book, the specific effects of personalization vary from country to country, and in particular between parliamentary and presidential systems of government. In the United States one of the most prominent effects of a president's popularity are his (supposed or real) 'coat-tails' at congressional elections and the more indirect repercussions of these in the legislative decision-making process.[3] In parliamentary democracies, rather than having a strong impact on executive–legislative relations, a high amount of prime ministerial prominence is more likely to have a significant effect on the prime minister's position within the cabinet and within his or her party.

With the rise of 'summit politics' in the international arena, there is at least one other major factor that has worked to strengthen the position of the executive in the political system, and that of the chief executive in particular. Prima facie, international summitry may seem to be just another factor increasing the visibility of the political leaders in the media and in the competitive arena. However, recent research on the European Union (EU) and its individual member states has demonstrated that 'summit politics' has in fact added to the decision-making power of the executive and its chief actors (Moravcsik, 1997). While the position of the head of government as a country's 'chief executive' in the international arena has long become a highly familiar feature, the establishment of such de facto prerogative powers of the chief executive in international relations in fact marks a rather recent historical occurrence. As Richard Rose (1991a: 21) has pointed out, until the early twentieth century not a single American president had ever travelled abroad while in office, and it was even argued that presidents lacked the legal authority to do so. Even in Britain, arguably the European country one would consider the least restrictive of the prime minister's room for manoeuvre in the international arena, foreign policy was very much perceived to be the task of the foreign secretary alone before the Second World War. Churchill's lengthy and unsuccessful battle with his cabinet for permission to go to Russia to ease East–West tensions suggests that, even in the first decades after 1945, personal involvement of the prime minister in foreign affairs was still far from being generally accepted (Thomas, 1997: 103–4).

Given the counter-evidence available, it would seem hardly convincing to argue that national executives, and their top representatives in the office of head of government or head of state, have gradually been deprived of their capacity to act. The negation of this popular assumption can even be carried a step further. As Carnes Lord has argued in his recent work on the nature of political leadership (2003: 10), 'one of the most striking things about outstanding leaders in any historical period is the extent to which the failed or incomplete aspects of their political projects may be traced to flaws in their personalities rather than to any inexorable constraints imposed by the age'. This is a stark contention, which is neither to be supported nor to be dismissed here, though it will be addressed later on.

A key question for any comparative study regards the choice of countries to be covered. The concentration of this study on a comparatively small number of major Western countries – the United States, Britain and Germany – reflects, to be sure, the author's limited expertise on most other liberal democracies. At the same time, however, keeping the number of countries covered small in number should be seen as a deliberate attempt at placing this study in a specific tradition of comparative politics, which considers individual countries to be more than mere 'cases' needed to test competing theoretical hypotheses. Instead, special emphasis is being laid here on grasping the fundamentally different functional working logics of the American, British and German governmental systems.

In order to justify our choice of countries it is necessary to take a look at the classifications of contemporary executives in political science and the different levels of executive activity, which serves the additional purpose of highlighting the subject's wider boundaries.

Classifications of Modern Executives

Historically, the main divide between early models of constitutionalist government related to the alternative models of constitutional monarchy and presidential republicanism (Lane, 1996: 63–86). The acknowledgement of a specific presidential form of democratic government by the theoretically-orientated school of modern constitutional history dates back only to the mid-nineteenth century. Outside the United States the presidential system was first conceived of as a specific model of government by Walter Bagehot and Robert von Mohl. The overwhelming majority of contemporary institutional classifications of modern liberal democracies focus on the relationship between the executive and the legislature, thereby constructing a dualism between presidentialism and parliamentarism.[4] Since the early 1980s, an increasingly sophisticated debate has developed concerning the usefulness of Maurice Duverger's (1980) concept of 'semi-presidentialism', in which the principle of parliamentary responsibility of the government (prime minister and cabinet) is combined with the existence of a powerful and directly elected president (Elgie, 1999). In an influential attempt at getting a firmer analytical grip on systems combining the requirements of parliamentary responsibility of the government with a directly elected president, Matthew Shugart and John Carey (1992: 55–75) have suggested a difference between two sub-categories of 'semi-presidentialism' – namely, 'premier-parliamentary systems' and 'president-parliamentary systems'. While in premier-parliamentarism, the cabinet is responsible only to parliament, in president-parliamentarism it is jointly responsible to the (popularly elected) president and parliament. These analytical refinements of categorizing liberal democracies have proved to be particularly useful in studying the new democracies in East Central Europe.

This being said, the basic separation between presidential and parliamentary systems of government remains the most important analytical concept for classifying the established Western democracies. The criteria suggested by different scholars are marked by a large degree of variation (Lijphart, 1992). The most extensive catalogues of criteria can claim validity only as a description of the two prototypes of presidential and parliamentary systems; that is, the United States and Britain. If there is a primary criterion for distinguishing presidential government from parliamentary government – and there appears to be a growing consensus that it is in fact useful to base comparative classifications on a primary criterion (Steffani, 1995; Siaroff, 2003) – it must be seen in the constitutional provision of parliamentary responsibility of the government in parliamentary democracies, which cannot be found in any genuinely presidential system. There are, however, other major defining criteria of presidential and parliamentary government. First of all, in presidential systems the offices of head of state and head of government – which Harold Laski (1925: 340–56) referred to as the 'constitutional executive' and the 'political executive'– are merged institutionally and held by a single incumbent. By contrast, virtually all parliamentary democracies are characterized by a 'double-headed' executive. They may be differentiated by whether there is a monarch or a president serving as the country's head of state.

However, the formal distinction between parliamentary republics and parliamentary monarchies provides rather poor empirical guidance when it comes to gauging the constitutional power of the head of state. Examples can be found of both monarchs and presidents who are weak in terms of the constitution, though it is true that constitutionally strong monarchs in Western Europe have largely died out since the early twentieth century (Heywood and Wright, 1997). Formally, presidential heads of state in parliamentary democracies can further be distinguished with regard to their method of selection (direct popular election versus indirect election by an electoral college). As Table 1.1 indicates, the majority of presidential heads of state in West European parliamentary democracies is selected through direct popular election. The alternative of selecting the head of state through an electoral college marks an exception to be found only in Germany, Italy and Greece.

Whereas indirect election by the legislature may be considered a key feature of the parliamentary government model[5], there are different devices for electing the head of government in the West European parliamentary democracies. West European prime ministers can be separated into two groups according to whether or not there is a parliamentary vote of investiture forming part of the official government-building process. The explicit constitutional requirement of a candidate to secure a majority vote of parliament before being appointed exists only in Germany, Ireland and Spain. There are, however, a number of West European countries in which a candidate either needs the 'tacit approval' of parliament (Sweden) or a real parliamentary vote is to be taken as soon as the new government has been formed and its programme

Table 1.1 Selection methods of heads of state and heads of government in sixteen West European countries and the United States

Country	Head of state	Method of election	Title of head of government	Formal parliamentary election of head of government
Austria	President	Universal suffrage	Bundeskanzler	No
Belgium	Monarch	Heredity	Eerste-minister	No
Britain	Monarch	Heredity	Prime minister	No
Denmark	Monarch	Heredity	Statsminister	No
Finland	President	Universal suffrage	Pääministeri	Yes
France	President	Universal suffrage	Premier ministre	No
Germany	President	Electoral college	Bundeskanzler	Yes
Greece	President	Electoral college	Prothypourgos	No
Ireland	President	Universal suffrage	Taoiseach	Yes
Italy	President	Electoral collage	Presidente del Consiglio	No
Luxembourg	Grand duke	Heredity	Premier ministre	No
Netherlands	Monarch	Heredity	Minister-president	No
Norway	Monarch	Heredity	Statsminister	No
Portugal	President	Universal suffrage	Primeiro ministro	No
Spain	Monarch	Heredity	Presidente de Gobierno	Yes
Sweden	Monarch	Heredity	Statsminister	No
United States	President	Universal suffrage	President	No

Sources: Adapted from Heywood and Wright (1997: 80) and Steffani (1999: 238); revised and updated by the author.

introduced to parliament (Italy, Greece, Belgium and Portugal; see de Winter, 1995: 133–4).

There is at least one other major institutional difference between the parliamentary and presidential types of democratic government which has a significant effect on the executive. In presidential systems, members of the executive are not allowed to hold a seat in the legislature during their incumbency. In the large majority of West European parliamentary democracies the compatibility of a governmental office with a seat in the parliament – which emerged historically as an attempt to prevent the monarch from imposing hostile ministers on the parliamentary majority – is not just legally permitted but also politically welcomed, for a number of reasons. First, as members of government can, and often do, participate in the internal decision-making process within their given parliamentary party group, the necessary co-ordination between the government and its parliamentary supporters is eased to a significant extent. Second, parliamentary control of the executive is made more effective by the insider knowledge that former ministers may contribute to parliamentary deliberations and questioning. Finally, compatibility can be considered to have an overall positive impact on a system's capacity for recruiting political elites, as committed and able politicians do not have to make a choice between the branches in which they want to serve.

Levels of Executive Activity

Whatever specific institutional arrangements are in place within a given country, it is necessary to make a clear distinction between the central executive territory, the so-called 'core executive' – defined by Patrick Dunleavy and R. A. W. Rhodes (1990: 4) as 'all those organizations and structures which primarily serve to pull together and integrate central government policies, or act as final arbiters within the executive of conflicts between different elements of the government machine' – and a system's overall governance structure. Scholars of executive politics have not always made sufficiently clear to which level their judgements and conclusions relate. A large scope of action of the head of government within the inner executive territory does not necessarily have to be accompanied by an equally strong position of the chief executive and the executive as a whole in the wider political system, and vice versa (see Table 1.2).

Generally speaking, a constitutionally strong position of the prime minister within the core executive would include the possession of

Table 1.2 Position of the head of government within the core executive, dominant forms of government and cabinets, average cabinet life, and institutional barriers against majority rule in seventeen West European countries and the United States

Country	Strength of the head of government within the core executive	Dominant form of government after 1945	Dominant type of cabinets after 1945	Average cabinet life (1945-96, in years)		Institutional barriers against majority rule
				I	II	
Austria	Medium	Coalition government	Majority	8.42	2.53	Medium
Belgium	Medium	Coalition government	Majority	2.29	1.68	Medium
Britain	Strong	Single-party government	Majority	8.49	2.55	Weak
Denmark	Medium	Mixed	Minority	2.81	1.75	Weak
Finland	Medium	Coalition government	Majority	1.31	1.18	Weak
France	Medium	Coalition government	Majority	2.88	2.08	Weak
Germany	Strong	Coalition government	Majority	3.60	2.03	Strong
Greece	Strong	Single-party government	Majority	3.60	2.16	Weak
Ireland	Strong	Mixed	Mixed	3.72	2.42	Weak
Italy	Weak	Coalition government	Mixed	1.28	0.99	Medium
Luxembourg	Medium	Coalition government	Majority	5.62	3.16	Weak
Netherlands	Weak	Coalition government	Majority	2.94	2.50	Weak
Norway	Weak	Single-party government	Minority	4.22	2.11	Weak
Portugal	Strong	Mixed	Majority	2.32	1.86	Weak

Table 1.2 continued

Country	Strength of the head of government within the core executive	Dominant form of government after 1945	Dominant type of cabinets after 1945	Average cabinet life (1945-96, in years)		Institutional barriers against majority rule
				I	II	
Spain	Strong	Single-party government	Minority	6.35	2.38	Weak
Sweden	Medium	Single-party government	Minority	4.77	2.07	Weak
Switzerland	Weak	Coalition government	Majority	16.19	0.99	Strong
United States	Strong	Single-party government	Mixed	7.07	1.83	Strong

Notes: Institutional barriers against strong executive leadership and majority rule to be found in a given system have been judged as 'weak' if none, or only one, of the devices mentioned in the text exist; as 'medium' if two or three criteria qualify; and as 'strong' if four or five institutional barriers against majority rule exist. The dominant form of government in a given country was classified as 'coalition government' or 'single party government' if this form prevailed for at least two-thirds of the post-war period; all other cases were classified as 'mixed'; and the same measures were applied for assessing the dominant type of cabinets. For Portugal, Spain and Greece the data presented cover the period from the mid-1970s to date only. As column 3 relates only to the modus of party control within the executive branch, the United States has been classified as 'single party government'. 'Average cabinet life I' is based solely on changes of party composition of the cabinet; 'average cabinet life II' takes into account four criteria: changes in party composition, prime ministership and coalitional status, as well as new elections.

Sources: Column 1 based on King (1994a: 153) and Heywood and Wright (1997: 80); columns 2, 3 and 4 based on Müller and Strøm (2000a: 2; 2000b: 561) and Woldendorp *et al.* (2000); columns 5 and 6 adapted from Lijphart (1999: 132–3); column 7 adapted from Schmidt (2002: 177–8); all figures updated by the author on the basis of data from *Keesing's Contemporary Archive*, various issues.

most or all of the following devices: the right to decide upon appoint-ments and dismissals of members of the cabinet as well as on the major political appointments below the cabinet level; the right to determine the number and terms of reference of ministerial departments; a super-ior position within the cabinet; and the unconditional right to dissolve parliament (through an official proclamation of the head of state) with-out the need to secure the cabinet's approval. Moreover, the position of the head of government in parliamentary democracies is significantly strengthened if he or she is the leader of the (dominant) governing party, though this has not become part of the formal constitutional provisions regarding the office of prime minister outside the United Kingdom. Some other institutional devices often mentioned in this context – such as the existence of a so-called 'constructive' vote of no-confidence (to be found in Germany, Spain and Belgium) – regard the prime minister's position towards parliament rather than his or her position within the core executive, although a strong position in the parliamentary arena is likely to have a positive effect on the prime minister's standing and leeway in the core executive.

The overall position of the head of government within the core executive is also influenced by a number of structural variables reaching beyond the constitutional powers of office. The single most important genuinely political variable may be seen in the prevailing type of govern-ment, which can be either single-party government or a coalition. Other things being equal, the structural capacities of chief executives to exert strong policy leadership tend to be larger in single-party govern-ments than in coalitions (however, with significant variations to be duly considered in the latter category). One of the most important character-istics influencing the role of the head of government within the cabinet relates to the number of parties participating in a given government. *Ceteris paribus*, the internal decision-making costs of a cabinet depend on the number of parties involved, and tends to be highest in a multi-party coalition government, though 'grand coalitions' (involving two more-or-less equally strong major players) may restrict the chief executive's leeway even more. Furthermore, the quality of auxiliary institutions at the prime minister's (exclusive) disposal, which are nor-mally not provided for specifically by the constitution, may be considered to have a major impact on the chief executive's chances of dominating the executive decision-making process.

The overall governance structure varies no less significantly among individual countries than the constitutional rules and political parameters defining the core executive. The continuum here stretches from the highly centralized leviathan-like state to forms of liberal democracy marked by a complex system of checks and balances, and strong power-sharing devices. The assessments offered in column 7 of Table 1.2 are based on the respective number and strengths of what may be considered the six most important institutional barriers to majority rule and unfettered executive power in the consolidated democracies. These include (i) the degree of centralization of state structures; (ii) the difficulties of amending constitutions; (iii) strong bicameralism; (iv) central bank autonomy; (v) a strong position of the constitutional court, and (vi) the existence of referenda in a given polity. These six components of modern political systems can be seen as the most important institutional barriers to majority rule and unfettered executive power that governments may face once they have been elected to office. Those among them that are real actors (including second chambers, central banks, and constitutional courts) have been classified in many more recent works as potential 'veto players' of governments (Schmidt, 2002: 177–8).[6]

Again, formal characteristics such as these should not be viewed in isolation from the wealth of additional factors influencing a government's capacity to govern. In parliamentary democracies, the most important single political variable at the level of executive–legislative relations may be seen in the difference between majority and minority status of the government. While majority cabinets represent the dominant type of government in Western Europe, virtually all the countries included in Table 1.2 have experienced periods of minority government. In Denmark and Sweden, more than two-thirds of all post-war cabinets were minority governments. Together with the average number of governing parties, the proportion of minority governments also has a strong impact on the average cabinet life (particularly if the latter is defined as accounting for changes in party composition, in the office of 'chief executive' or the coalitional status, as well as new elections), though the overall explanatory power of the average number of parties is stronger than that of minority governments.

The Choice of Countries

As Tables 1.1 and 1.2 indicate, the three countries placed at the centre of this study represent different forms of liberal democracy with, in particular, rather different kinds of executive structure. If one were to restrict a comparison of the United States, Britain and Germany to the aspect of parliamentary versus presidential government, the two latter systems would appear to be rather similar. The bulk of institutional arrangements to be ignored by this general systemic classification show clearly, however, more differences than similarities. Similarities are largely confined to the notably strong position of the head of government in the core executive. Even within the wider executive territory of both countries, a couple of very different institutional arrangements, such as the rules of (s)election for the British prime minister and German chancellor, may be identified. The most striking differences though, clearly relate to the character of each country's wider governance structure. Whereas the British system looks in fact like 'a set of arrangements facilitating governance' (Jordan, 1994: 196), German governments have been described as being 'semisovereign' (Katzenstein, 1987) because of the extremely tight network of institutional counterweights to majority rule.[7] In fact, within the group of West European parliamentary democracies with a constitutionally and politically strong head of government, Britain and Germany represent the two most different cases that could have been chosen. At the same time, the British and the German political systems are very different from the US polity, which combines a highly complex separation-of-powers system with a 'single-headed' executive structure, in which a (de facto) directly elected president is the only player enjoying constitutional responsibility.

Put in the theoretical terms of modern comparative political research, this choice of countries may be described as a combination of the most-similar-cases design and the most-different-cases design (Przeworski and Teune, 1970). While all our countries belong to the group of regimes in which executives are held to be politically responsible, and executive leaders use peaceful means to pursue their goals – separating the United States, Britain and Germany from various forms of non-democratic regimes – they still represent a wide spectrum of contemporary forms of liberal democracy.

To specify the perspective on executive leadership developed in this study, it is necessary to take a closer look at the main currents of executive research, which serves the additional purpose of highlighting the key aspects of the broader subject.

Main Currents of Executive Leadership Research

Research into executives can be separated into at least two major areas. A significant body of research has dealt with *executives as institutions*, analysing the constitutional and organizational features of the political executive, including more specific aspects of executive politics, such as the determinants of cabinet stability or the relationships between ministers and mandarins. In the second major area of executive research, the *process dimension of executive politics*, including the leadership performance of individual office-holders, lies at the heart of scholarly interest. Given the specific focus of this study, the sections that follow are confined to highlighting the most relevant threads in the second area.

Whereas the institutional school of executive research has been dominated by political scientists, scholars dealing with the phenomenon of political leadership come from a much broader canon of disciplines, including philosophy, history, sociology, psychology or even psychoanalysis (Kellerman, 1986). Moreover, in contrast to the predominantly empirically-orientated research on institutional aspects of executive politics, the modern study of political leadership builds on a venerable normative tradition dating back to Platonic philosophy. Democratically transformed normative concepts of 'good government' have survived until the present day. They stretch from rather modest normative demands, such as the decentralization of government, to more specific concepts which, for example, emphasize the task of governments to provide clear symbolic directions in the choice and formulation of policies, and guarantee effective policy implementation. Even approaches focusing more specifically on the moral dimension of 'good government' have secured their place in modern political science, most obviously in the field of assessing leadership styles of chief executives. Many studies of the American presidency in particular tend to display a normative preference for a specific leadership style, to be embodied by the historical record of the presidency of Franklin D. Roosevelt. A normative bias, while normally less obviously related to the behaviour of any specific incumbent, may, however, also be found in the bulk of more recent empirical studies on manifestations of political leadership in parliamentary democracies which emphasize the desirability of democratic responsiveness and transparency of the executive decision-making process.

Turning to the field of empirical approaches to studying executive leadership, three main currents of research may be distinguished. The first focuses on individual leaders, their performance and their impact on the political decision-making process within a given system. Although the 'great man' approach to understanding politics and history has been dismissed as 'reductionist' in more recent works, it has maintained a rather prominent position in works studying manifestations of undemocratic political leadership, such as the role of Adolf Hitler or Joseph Stalin for twentieth-century world history. The potentially strong impact of individual leaders has also been stressed in studies focusing on the innovative potential of different leaders on policy outcome in modern democracies, or the role of leaders in the process of regime building.

A focus on individual political leaders, their personal characteristics and styles has, however, not necessarily to be based on the conviction that individual leaders mark the most important single variable in the political decision-making process. There is a large number of works dealing with political leaders that do not make an explicit claim to a superior or dominant position of incumbents within the decision-making process, though it seems reasonable to suggest that scholars focusing specifically on the nature and performance of individual leaders are inclined to consider them to have a major impact. Leader-centred approaches of this kind – owing much to the classic works of Max Weber – have held a particularly prominent position in studies on presidential leadership in the United States. It was also in the American context that more sophisticated approaches, including psychoanalytical concepts centring on the personality of political leaders, first gained a prominent status in the 1970s. The popularity of leader-centred executive research in the United States may to a considerable extent be seen as a reflection of the specific structural conditions of executive leadership in the American republic, the monocratic structure of the executive and, in particular, the (de facto) direct election of the president.

More sophisticated concepts for studying specific leadership styles did not evolve before the introduction of Richard Neustadt's extremely influential behavioural approach to American executive research (Neustadt, 1960) whose focus was on the ways that presidents exercise informal power through persuasion and bargaining. Again, the bulk of the relevant concepts for studying leadership styles of chief executives have been developed in the United States and are identified easily as being tailored towards analysing leadership styles under the conditions of American presidential government. By contrast, more sophisticated works on prime ministerial leadership styles, in particular those trying explicitly to develop an internationally comparative perspective, have remained rather thin on the ground.

Needless to say, leader-centred perspectives on the decision-making process and its social preconditions have never been the only, not even always the dominant, approach to studying political leadership. For much of the nineteenth century and the early decades of the twentieth century, approaches focusing on the social and institutional structures of the state dominated the field. This perspective was accompanied by a notable pessimism regarding the possible impact of individual political leaders. As Jean Blondel (1987: 47) has concluded:

Hegel, Ricardo, Comte and later Marx, among many others, had attempted to divest political leaders of their real decision-making capabilities and turn them increasingly into mere mouthpieces for the deeper developments that were transforming the social and economic fabric of the nations of the world. Whatever 'romantic' views some literary figures may have had about the role of Napoleon or other great 'heroes', the 'scientific' analysis of society seemed to suggest – and, indeed, in the eyes of some seemed to prove – that in reality leaders scarcely mattered and that they were replaceable or interchangeable: they were symbols of historical trends, not the engines of history.

Albeit for other reasons, the classical legal or constitutional concept of studying political leadership – being particularly prominent among continental-European scholars – also left precious little room for leaders' personalities to be included. By contrast, in more recent decades, there have been only two groups of scholars questioning systematically or even denying the importance and possible impact of leaders in the political process – namely, the shrinking group of neo-Marxist writers and scholars representing the autopoietical paradigm in modern sociology.

Authors advocating an 'enlightened' institutionalism acknowledge that there is a certain amount of leverage for chief executives in modern democracies. In the bulk of more recent works the key question relates to the effects that different forms of government, namely presidential and parliamentary government, have on the scope of action chief executives enjoy under different institutional conditions. Scholars, being aware of the large institutional variations among different parliamentary democracies have been careful not to draw over-ambitious generalizations. As Bert Rockman (1997: 60) has argued, a system's degree of centralization of power might be more relevant with regard to the latitude provided for top political leadership than the difference between the presidential and parliamentary form of government. There is a more general tendency in the recent study of comparative executive leadership to dismiss any kind of institutional determinism. In fact, most authors are likely to subscribe to Rockman's judgement that 'institutions shape much but, in the end, determine little' (ibid.: 55). This brings us to the third and final main approach in executive leadership research, which may be called the 'interactionist' approach to understanding political leadership.

The 'interactionist' approach to the study of political leadership is characterized by the attempt to account for both personal and systemic variables that have an impact on the overall character of executive leadership, and stresses the dynamic character of the relationship between the two (groups of) variables. From this perspective, political leaders operate within an environment that both constrains their freedom of action and shapes their ambitions and behaviour. However, leaders are not considered to be hostages of the system. Rather, they are seen as being able to influence their environment and leave their specific mark on the system.[8]

The conditions and circumstances leaders face can be differentiated into several areas, any one of which constitutes a major field of executive leadership research in its own right. As to the area of political institutions, the relationship between political executives and administrations, between executives and legislatures, and between executives and parties, have been considered to be of particular importance in shaping the overall character of executive leadership in a given system and/or over a given period of time. More recently, the relationship between executives and the mass media has come to enjoy a particular amount of attention, including a wide range of different perspectives in which either political leaders or the media are considered as the independent variable.

However, most authors belonging to the 'interactionist' school of executive studies consider that the 'environment' leaders find themselves in includes more than the institutional parameters of executive leadership in a given system. There is first of all the specific brand of political culture – widely understood to be composed of the attitudes, beliefs, emotions and values of society that relate to the political system, both its structures and the interaction of different political players within this system, and to political issues (Kavanagh 1972: 9–19) – which has a crucial impact on the strategic choices of political leaders. Societies in Western countries are characterized by rather different patterns of basic orientations towards political actors and institutions, and different forms of political action. These differences include specific expectations regarding the behaviour of political leaders and the interaction of political actors, such as government and opposition parties, which may be described as the 'cultural parameters' of executive leadership in a given system.

Institutional and political cultural factors usually generate a combination of highly specific conditions of executive leadership, which are often marked by a notable degree of historical persistance. This does not, however, mean that there can be no significant change over time. In particular, internationally comparative studies tend to neglect the dimension of historical change in the prevailing conditions and manifestations of political leadership. From an American or a continental-European perspective, the general features of executive leadership in the British Westminster system may appear as a fixed pattern of institutional and political cultural parameters, which has hardly changed between, say, the early 1950s and the early 1990s – an assessment that, obviously, would be untenable even for a considerably shorter period of time.

The historical dimension includes the leadership conceptions of individual office-holders, which cannot be thought of meaningfully in a historical vacuum. The formative years in politics invariably have an impact on a leader's general understanding of politics, and the 'art of politics'. Interestingly, the established patterns of elite recruitment in the consolidated democracies – the fact that most people achieve highest political office at middle or slightly-beyond-middle age – tend to 'neutralize' the impact of generation-related differences between individual leaders. Normally, both leaders and their most likely challengers are products of their times. The historical dimension of a leader's personal profile becomes a more independent variable when he or she is 'a leader from a different age', not fully sharing the common background of the current generation – for example, Winston Churchill during his last term in 10 Downing Street.

Needless to say, the overall performance of a political leader will always be influenced by the concrete political circumstances her or she encounters. There is a wealth of factors to be considered, including the leader's relationship with his or her party, the majority constellations in parliament or the legislature, the strength of potential political opponents both within and outside the leader's 'camp', the state of the economy, or major events in the international arena – to name just a few. 'Political circumstances' constitute the 'random variable' within any realistic concept of political leadership. In fact, it is the contingency of circumstances that has largely undermined any efforts at building coherent and reasonably realistic 'interactionist' theories of executive leadership.

Still, it is the 'interactionist' school of leadership research that has produced the most inspiring perspectives on executive leadership in contemporary liberal democracies. Among the more recent debates in the field, the 'presidentialization' paradigm – devoted to discussing various manifestations of 'presidentialization' in many of the major parliamentary democracies – would appear to mark the most interesting approach to be considered in a study like this. To keep this introduction reasonably short, the different contributions to the 'presidentialization' debate will be addressed in the context of assessing the empirical dimension of 'presidentialism' in Britain and Germany in Chapter 8.

Key Questions and Plan of the Book

For a book on executive leadership in the United States, Britain and Germany, it would seem a decent starting point to recognize the specific virtues of the rather different research traditions in the three countries under scrutiny. With the large majority of American scholars, we acknowledge the enduring relevance of Richard Neustadt's understanding of the leadership process, focusing on the informal powers of a chief executive resulting from persuasion and bargaining (Neustadt, 1960). Neither British nor German political science has produced a single book even approaching the strong impact of Neustadt on a whole generation of scholars of political leadership. Apart from this, different orientations of more recent British and German executive research may be identified. In Germany, as in many other continental-European countries, the interest of political scientists in constitutional aspects of leadership has remained stronger than in the Anglo-Saxon world. A due consideration of the constitutional parameters of executive leadership seems, however, by no means justified only as a mark of respect for the continental-European tradition. It is also in line with the focus of an emerging literature in the United States that redirects attention to formal sources of presidential authority (Mayer and Price, 2002: 371–3; Howell, 2003). While not marking an exclusive British contribution to the study of leadership, the idea that political science inquiries into the world of governments have to pay due attention to the 'network dimension' of the leadership process has been particularly prominent in the more recent major works of British scholars on Westminster and Whitehall (Rhodes, 2000). Although we do not share the belief of some British scholars that the question as to whether there is cabinet or prime ministerial government (or 'presidentialism') is irrelevant, we do acknowledge that it is reasonable to conceive of the leadership process as an exchange of resources among different players.[9]

Drawing on such an 'intercultural' and 'interactionist' approach to analysing executive leadership, the study places four questions, or group of questions, at its centre:

- How may substantial differences in leadership performance within a single country be explained? What is the impact of changes among individuals in the office of president, prime minister or chancellor compared with changes in the party composition of the government, the state of the economy, or even broader structural changes in society and the international arena?

• Are there any common tendencies regarding the development of executive organization and leadership to be observed in the three countries considered,[10] and how do the three systems rank with regard to the chief executive's room for manoeuvre during different stages and at different levels of the leadership process?

• What impact have the different variables distinguished above – personalities, institutions and circumstances – had on the overall performance of chief executives within individual and among different countries?

• And, finally, how much empirical evidence do the case studies gathered in this volume provide in support of the 'presidentialization' thesis in comparative executive leadership research?

Part II of this book focuses on the manifestations of core executive leadership, including both the internal structures and working mechanisms governing the core executive, and the relationship between chief executives and other players within the executive branch. Each country chapter starts with a brief overview of the political profiles of the individual chief executives from 1945–9 to the present time. Part III broadens the focus to include the manifestations of executive leadership in the wider political process. Here, the nature of 'executive–legislative relations'[11] and the various manifestations of public leadership will be accorded special attention. And, the role of other major players at the political system level – such as interest groups, central banks or the courts, all of which have the potential to challenge and restrict the executive's room for manoeuvre in the political system – will be examined. Part IV, finally, offers a comparative assessment of the various aspects tackled in the previous chapters.

Part II

Patterns of Core Executive Leadership

2
The United States: Variations of Presidential Predominance

The Political Profiles of American Post-war Presidents

There is no other major Western democracy in which the chief executive's personality is more central to the overall conception of executive leadership than in the United States. From the early days of the republic, personalities have tended to have a stronger hold on the American public imagination than specific policy issues. While this may be considered part of the general American understanding of politics, the constitutional parameters of executive leadership in the United States have worked in the same direction. Both the quasi-direct election of the president and the whole constitutional construction of the political executive, in which the president is the sole representative of executive power, underline the centrality of those occupying the Oval Office. In the more recent political science literature on the American presidency, even leading proponents of the neo-institutionalist paradigm have maintained that 'the incumbent is the institution' (Rockman, 1992: 100).

There are remarkably few explicit constitutional qualifications for the office of president. From a West European perspective, the eight-year maximum term limit for presidents, as established by the Twenty-second Amendment (1951), marks the most notable feature of the constitutional presidency. The most dramatic transformation of the original constitutional provisions regarded the selection system for presidential candidates. The steady proliferation of primaries since the late 1960s has not only led to a dramatic loss of influence of the political parties (or at least the party leaders), but has also been responsible for the emergence of more 'personal candidates' running for the presidency.

Despite the decreasing role of the political parties, all incumbents who occupied the Oval Office between the end of the Second World War and 2002 were affiliated to either the Democratic or the Republican Parties. Ronald Reagan is the only post-war president to have changed his party identification (from Democrat to Republican) at an earlier stage of his political career. Third-party candidates have never come close to winning the presidency.[1]

The peculiarities of the American electoral system, which distinguishes a popular and an electoral college vote, make the calculation of the overall electoral support basis of different presidents more complicated than in most other countries. The average difference between the popular and the electoral vote for successful presidential candidates in the post-war period has been about 20 percentage points, though there have been a number of more spectacular results in the more recent past, such as in 1984 when Ronald Reagan received a 97.6 per cent share of the popular vote based on only 59.2 per cent of the electoral vote. There have been six occasions since 1945 when presidents have been elected with less than 50 per cent of the popular vote (Harry S. Truman in 1948, John F. Kennedy in 1960, Richard Nixon in 1968, Bill Clinton in 1992 and 1996, and George W. Bush in 2000). However, George W. Bush – having been elected with a 47.9 per cent share of the popular vote and 50 per cent of the electoral college vote – was the only twentieth-century president to achieve a smaller share of the popular vote than his chief contender for the office.[2]

A closer look at the political background of incumbents suggests that there is no specific body of political experience that candidates have to possess. There have been significant variations with regard to the length of elective political experience as well as the legislative and party experience of incumbents (Jones, 1994: 42–8): whereas Dwight D. Eisenhower had no specific elective political experience whatever when he gained the presidency in 1953, Johnson commanded no less than twenty-seven years of experience in elected offices. All other office-holders of the post-war period fell between these two extremes. George W. Bush's elective political experience, being confined to six years as governor of Texas, was among the most modest records of American post-war presidents.

There is also a wide variation regarding the eleven presidents' amount of legislative experience. Among the first six post-war presidents (Harry S. Truman to Gerald Ford), Eisenhower was the only one not to have been elected to either the House or the Senate. By contrast, among the five most recent presidents (Jimmy Carter to Bush Jr), George H. W. Bush was the only one who had been a member of Congress. Lyndon Johnson and Ford had by far the most extensive experience in Congress (in fact, both served for almost a quarter of a century), but Kennedy was the only post-war president to be elected to office directly from a position in Congress.

Since the 1970s, it has become much more typical of presidents to have experience as former state governors than as members of Congress. While none of the six presidents from Truman to Ford had been governor before becoming president, all but one of the last five post-war presidents (Carter, Reagan, Clinton and Bush Jr) had formerly held this post. Finally, post-war presidents also had very different bodies of experience within their respective political parties. Most of them held one or more party positions at state, local or national level. Nixon, Reagan and George H. W. Bush had the closest and most diverse ties with their party. Johnson and Ford had lengthy experience as party leaders in Congress but did not work for the national party organization. Eisenhower, Kennedy and George W. Bush were the only post-war presidents who never held any formal party position. Among the latter, Eisenhower was special for not even declaring his party preference before entering the presidential race.

Even a very brief discussion of the political background of American post-war presidents has to include the office of the vice-president, which has proved to be a springboard to the presidency since 1945.[3] Both Truman and Johnson gained office as a result of a president's death, and were later confirmed in office by winning the next presidential election. George H. W. Bush stands out as the only twentieth-century vice-president (alongside three earlier candidates) who proved able to capitalize on his public standing gained during his vice-presidency in the presidential race. Nixon had eight years of experience as vice-president, but only gained the presidency eight years after losing the vice-presidency. Ford marks a special case among those vice-presidents advancing to the presidency, as he was not elected to the position of vice-president but appointed by Nixon under the provisions of the Twenty-fifth Amendment after the elected vice-president, Spiro T. Agnew, resigned over charges of financial corruption.

Since Harry Truman assumed the office of president on 12 April 1945, only three incumbents (Eisenhower, Reagan and Clinton) have held the office for the maximum period of eight years. Truman and Johnson, who combined a first incomplete term with a second full term, served for almost eight years and slightly more than five years, respectively.

Whereas both were eligible for another term, both decided on the basis of rather unfavourable re-election prospects not to run again. Nixon, although being one of the four post-war candidates winning two presidential elections, served for only about five-and-a-half years before resigning on 9 August 1974 in the face of impeachment. By mid-2004, George H. W. Bush and Carter were the only two candidates holding the office for a full single term and losing it through electoral defeat. With less than three years in office, Kennedy's and Ford's were the shortest terms of office during the post-war period.

Staffing the Cabinet and the White House Office

The president's appointment power dwarfs the patronage powers of the head of government in most parliamentary democracies.[4] However, while it is possible to distinguish different areas or levels of political appointments that are relevant in both presidential and parliamentary systems, the two most important levels – cabinet appointments on the one hand and other appointments within the 'core executive' on the other – are of very different weight in the United States and in Western Europe. To a large extent, these differences spring from the fundamentally different construction of the executive branch in presidential and parliamentary systems.

Richard Fenno (1966: 5) has famously described the US cabinet as a 'secondary political institution', that 'lives in a state of institutional dependency to promote the effective exercise of the president's authority and to help implement his ultimate responsibilities'. The institutional weakness of the cabinet is further fostered by the fact that it does not exist as a truly collective body in constitutional practice. Cabinet unity does not even really exist as a normative value. Even occasional demands for strengthening the collegial dimension of American 'cabinet government' have been based on functional rather than normative arguments (Campbell, 1998: 51, 87).

The formal aspects of the cabinet-building process have been the subject of much debate, both in the political arena and among presidential scholars. Whereas the president's right to choose his cabinet secretaries independently – that is, free from any legal restrictions (apart from the need for confirmation by the Senate) – has never been seriously challenged, the president's removal power has been contested more than once. The (politically motivated) Tenure of Office Act (1867) even forbade explicitly the removal of department heads without the consent of the Senate. However, both before and after that date, presidents *have* dismissed cabinet officers at their discretion. In 1926, the Supreme Court confirmed the president's removal power that Congress had recognized for the first time as early as 1789 (Redlich *et al.*, 1995: 130).

A serious restriction of the president's discretionary powers in organizing his cabinet must be seen in the fact that the reorganization power – that is, the power to shift duties from one department to another, to shift responsibilities from one agency within a department to another, and to create new departments and agencies – lies with Congress.[5] These restrictions (from the president's point of view) have come to be reflected in the remarkably high degree of organizational stability at cabinet level. Not only has the overall number of cabinet departments remained rather stable; there has also been notably little change with regard to the assigned responsibility of existing departments.

In 1947, Truman cut the number of cabinet departments from ten to nine by combining the departments of Navy and War into the newly created Department of Defense. Under Eisenhower, the number of cabinet departments rose to ten again with the establishment of the Department of Health, Education and Welfare. The next two departments (Housing and Urban Development, and Transportation) were set up in the mid-1960s during the Johnson years. Under Nixon, in 1971, the Post Office Department was abolished as a cabinet department and became a separate government entity, the United States Postal Service.[6] While there was no change at all under Ford, Carter was the most active reformer of the cabinet department structure of the post-war period. The Department of Energy and the Department of Education were newly created in 1977 and 1979, respectively; and in 1980 the Department of Health, Education and Welfare became the Department of Health and Human Services. The Department of Veterans Affairs (1988–9) and the Department of Homeland Security, created in late 2002, were the only new cabinet departments to be established since the early 1980s.[7]

Only a small proportion of departments were originally created as cabinet departments; many others existed decades before they achieved cabinet rank. This tendency has become the dominant pattern of the post-war period. As Bert Rockman (2000: 251) has emphasized, '[b]y the middle of the twentieth century, when new cabinet departments came into being, the aim was not to create new functions but consolidate old ones...The creation of a cabinet department is [now] a sign of policy and programme legitimation.' Even more so than in the bulk of parliamentary democracies, where the creation of new cabinet departments often results from 'coalition arithmetic', the elevation of a department to a cabinet department usually marks a success of key clientele groups. However, as the reorganization power lies chiefly in the hands of Congress, such demands are likely to be fulfilled only during periods of 'unified government'. Thus it is hardly surprising that the Department of Veterans Affairs in 1988–9 marks the only clear-cut case of a new post-war cabinet department having been created under the conditions of 'divided government'. The case of the recently established Department of Homeland Security, widely considered to mark a major achievement of the Bush administration in its war against terrorism,[8] was different. For much of the 107th Congress (2000–2), Republicans and Democrats accused each other of obstructing the legislative process on the Homeland Security Bill. A compromise was only found during the lame duck session of Congress – that is, after the Republicans' sweeping victory in the November 2002 congressional elections (*Washington Post*, 13 November 2002).

The approaches to staffing the core executive have been as different as the personal and political profiles of the eleven post-war presidents. Arguably the most remarkable feature of Truman's approach to staffing his cabinet was the strong representation of former members of Congress. Moreover, the share of former federal executives among his cabinet officers was considerably higher than in any other previous administration. In contrast to his predecessor, Eisenhower devoted little attention to the process of finding suitable candidates for his cabinet. Indeed, practically all important decisions were at least prepared by two close friends of the president-elect (Herbert Brownell and General Lucius Clay), whereas sub-cabinet appointments in the departments were left to the respective cabinet officers. Eisenhower's first cabinet team became famous as a gathering of 'eight millionaires and one plumber'. The 'millionaires' were all well-off professionals, while the 'plumber' was Martin P. Durkin, head of the Plumbers and Pipe Fitters Union. With the nomination of the latter, Eisenhower obviously tried to appease the unions. The selection of the other cabinet members bore witness to the president's firm belief that people successful in their respective professional fields would be equally successful as members of the national government. What drew most attention in certain quarters, however, was the fact that the first Republican cabinet in twenty years did not include any nationally well-known members of the Republican Party, and no conservative party heavyweights in particular – a fact that was apt to underline Eisenhower's notably unpartisan understanding of presidential leadership.

The cabinet-building process under Kennedy became the first post-war example of the tendency to respond to an extremely narrow presidential election victory with the selection of a cabinet team representing a large number of different political and social forces. In Kennedy's case, this included the nomination of two members of the opposition party as well as representatives with very different religious, regional and professional backgrounds. In an attempt to maintain a high degree of government stability in the aftermath of Kennedy's assassination, Johnson left the Kennedy cabinet completely unchanged for the first ten months of his term. Later nominations were mainly inspired by Johnson's wish to recruit experienced former government officials, though there was also a notable willingness to consider genuine political criteria, including the promotion of minorities. Johnson was the first president to appoint a black cabinet secretary (Robert C. Weaver in the Department of Housing and Urban Development).

If most of his predecessors had tried to win a number of strong personalities and well-known public figures to serve in the cabinet, Nixon's first cabinet was remarkable for the lack of any prominent figures. One observer described Nixon's original team as 'a grey-flannel cabinet...not very exciting but comfortable' (Bennett, 1996: 48). Nixon's later cabinets included more prominent figures, especially high-profile academics, but were also less comfortable for the president, which manifested itself in the extremely high number of replacements (31 nominations in 66 months). The rather limited amount of minority representation remained a key characteristic of the cabinet's composition throughout the Nixon years. In contrast to his predecessor, Ford was keen to recruit as many representatives of different social groups as possible. His choice of suitable candidates was, however, restricted significantly by the unfavourable background conditions of the nomination process, including the overall loss of reputation of the executive branch because of the Watergate scandal and the relative proximity of the 1976 presidential election.

Carter started first preparations for the nomination process as early as during the late stages of the presidential race. Many of his early cabinet appointments disappointed those who had supported Carter during the presidential campaign and who had expected an exceptionally strong representation of women and social minorities. Particular emphasis was laid on finding candidates who had some working experience in or with Congress in an attempt to make good Carter's own inexperience in dealing with the legislative branch. To a certain extent, this strong orientation to functional criteria had the effect of de-politicizing the selection process (Warshaw, 1996: 127).

Whereas Carter had changed the rules of the nomination process by his very early engagement in staffing matters, the cabinet-building process under Reagan meant a break with the past for the drastically reduced role of the president's party. For the first time, applications for political appointments went directly to the White House (Bledsoe and Rigby, 1996: 1166). Reminiscent of the Nixon years, virtually no attempts were made to enlarge the new administration's basis of support by including opposition forces, such as the unions or environmentalists, or social minorities. Most of the nominations went to candidates who were not personally known to the president but shared his conservative core beliefs, and to those who had supported Reagan's presidential campaign.

Under George H. W. Bush, pragmatism and professional qualifications of candidates became the most important criteria in the nomination process. Another remarkable feature of Bush's team of cabinet officers was the unusually high share of confidants and friends of the president, which in most other administrations were to be found only at the level of White House advisers to the president. As Dilys Hill and Phil Williams (1994: 6) have specified, about two-thirds of his cabinet officers had known Bush for ten years or more, making the administration more than any other in recent memory 'a gathering of friends'.

Clinton went out of his way to make the cabinet a true mirror of American society. Potential members of the cabinet had to pass the so-called 'egg-test' – considering a candidate's ethnicity, gender and geographical background. Indeed, this sophisticated procedure resulted in a cabinet more diverse with regard to the social background of its members than any previous cabinet in American history. This does not mean, however, that Clinton was able to satisfy all demands of fair social representation in his cabinet. Rather, it produced allegations of tokenism, or forceful demands for even more fairness and equality.

The cabinet choices of George W. Bush combined a large proportion of ethnic and racial diversity, which equalled that among the Clinton cabinet, with a strong element of conservatism. As three women, two African Americans, one Hispanic, and one Democrat (a Clinton holdover) were offered seats at the cabinet table, even the Democrats commended Bush for inclusiveness. At the same time, most figures chosen for the most critical domestic policy posts clearly represented the Republican's conservative wing (or, if drawn from different quarters of the party, were at least acceptable to the latter). Despite its reputation as a gathering of 'competent conservatives', the proportion of Washington insiders – defined as those who had a primary career in the national government, had entered the cabinet directly from the sub-cabinet, or had been transferred from another cabinet post – in Bush's first cabinet was even slightly below the average of initial appointments from Ford to Clinton.[9] According to an assessment by MaryAnne Borrelli (2002a: 49), there were also no policy specialists in the first Bush cabinet. Rather, Bush's team was split almost evenly between generalists and liaison secretaries (defined by strong relationships with their departments' traditionally dominant clients or issue networks).

The centrality of the cabinet as a group of key political appointees and its role within the core executive decision-making process have been diminished gradually by the rise of the White House Office. This was established in 1939 as the first sub-division of the Executive Office of the President (EOP), which was created the same year.[10] Within the wider environment of the executive branch, the White House Office has been considered as performing three main functions – policy co-ordination; outreach and communications; and internal co-ordination (Hart, 1995: 143) – all of which have contributed significantly to strengthening the president's resources for strong executive leadership.

The degree of continuity among personnel within the 'presidential branch' tends to be low, and membership of the units typically changes with each presidency, or even during an administration. About a third of the staff at the sub-cabinet level leave within eighteen months, and less than a third remain longer than three years (Pious, 1998: 475). The Office of Management and Budget (OMB) and the Office of the US Trade Representative are the only units to have a considerable 'institutional memory' by occupying a sizeable career civil service staff. In all other agencies there are now staff structures in place designed to provide the president with what has been called 'responsive competence' (Moe, 1985: 239).[11]

The most obvious difference between appointments of cabinet secretaries on the one hand and members of the president's White House team on the other relates to the significantly greater leeway presidents have in choosing their White House staff. The latter do not require Senate approval (and normally also do not have to appear before the congressional committees to answer questions and testify).[12] In comparison with the wide range of different staffing approaches of individual presidents characterizing the cabinet-building process, variations between different administrations at the level of White House staffing have remained fairly modest.

Typically, the White House staff is composed largely of people who have surrounded the candidate during his campaign, who enjoy his trust, and whose primary qualifications are in the art of politics rather than governance. All presidents since Kennedy, with the notable exception of George H. W. Bush, have had a higher share of close associates in the EOP and among their White House staff than in the cabinet. This difference was largest under Carter, whose White House staff was made up of more than 80 per cent of close associates, whereas there were fewer than 10 per cent among cabinet members falling into this category (King and Riddlesberger, 1996: 501).

Clinton's personnel selection to fill the senior positions in the White House was rather similar to that of Carter. Instead of compensating for his lack of national government experience with Washington-experienced staff, Clinton relied heavily on outsiders from his campaign team, acquaintances from Arkansas and 'friends of Bill'. Among the four most recent administrations, the Clinton administration was the only one in which working in the executive branch was not among the top two former occupations of senior office holders in the EOP – a phenomenon that has been explained by the long dearth of Democratic presidents before Clinton's takeover (Tenpas and Hess, 2002: 583).

George W. Bush's 'A' team in the EOP, as of 2001, has been remarkable for at least two reasons. First, the Bush administration was the only one in twenty years in which former members of the campaign team represented a majority alongside members with different professional backgrounds. Second, Bush appointed a larger proportion of minorities than any of his predecessors, including Clinton. Also, at 28 per cent, the proportion of women in Bush's 'A' team was just slightly lower than in Clinton's, and twice as large as in his father's administration. Particularly remarkable was the exceptionally large proportion of women among Bush's inner circle of advisers (ibid.: 582–3).

Styles of Presidential Core Executive Decision-making

The conventional notion about President Truman has long been that of a 'little man' without charisma, surrounded by a selection of mediocre 'cronies'. However, more recent research has been able to draw a more balanced picture of decision-making in the White House during the Truman years, which has been less biased by unfavourable comparisons with the legendary Franklin D. Roosevelt. Still, a certain tension between different principles of Truman's leadership approach cannot be denied. On the one hand, Truman was superb at delegating authority.

One of his administration's most outstanding achievements in foreign policy was, tellingly, labelled the 'Marshall Plan' (acknowledging the leading role of Secretary of State George Marshall in developing the project) – not the 'Truman Plan'. Also, Truman relied much more on the cabinet than, say, Roosevelt or Hoover. But, on the other hand, he left no doubt that he wanted the final decision-making authority and responsibility for his administration's policies to rest with the Oval Office.

The differences in White House organization between the Truman and Roosevelt administrations reflected to a large extent the crucial differences in the two presidents' overall ideas of management. What Roosevelt had found pragmatic, seemed chaotic to Truman. By mid-1946 a more or less coherent staff system emerged in the Truman White House, which has been described as 'structured decentralisation' (Hamby, 1988: 58), combining a clear definition of responsibilities with a remarkably open access to the president. For the first three years of Truman's administration, the newly created National Security Council (NSC) functioned essentially as an information-gathering and policy co-ordinating agency. The NSC's overall role increased even further later on, though it barely became an independent policy-making institution.

Any attempts to create coordinating bodies that could have narrowed this organizational focus on the Oval Office – such as early suggestions to create a 'cabinet secretariat' or plans to increase the decision-making powers of the NSC – were firmly dismissed by the president. Nevertheless, Truman appreciated the principle of organizational burden-sharing. Despite the intensive involvement of the president in many details of decision-making and the strongly president-centred organization of the executive branch, it has rightly been remarked that 'the presidency, under Harry Truman, was becoming as much an institutionalized as a personal office' (McCoy, 1984: 164).

No other post-war president's leadership style has been as fundamentally misjudged by observers as that of Dwight D. Eisenhower. Until the publication of Fred Greenstein's masterpiece on 'the hidden-hand presidency' in 1982, public assessments of the Eisenhower years were governed by the belief that the president was in fact incapable of exercising any sort of efficient leadership. Even though Eisenhower's overall involvement in the details of the policy-making process did remain relatively modest, especially in most areas of domestic policy, such assessments could not have been more off the mark.

The key to the Eisenhower system was a smoothly operating White House Office. Eisenhower – regarded by many as 'the father of the modern White House' (Patterson, 1994: 277) – developed a model of White House organization that has come to be viewed as the prototype of the so-called 'pyramidal system'. The White House staff was organized on the basis of specific areas of responsibility and functional specialization. A key motive behind this approach was the president's unwillingness to become involved in every detail of organizational or policy deliberation. At the top of the organizational White House pyramid was Eisenhower's charismatic chief of staff, Sherman Adams. Whereas presidency watchers at the time saw Adams as the 'de facto president', who appeared to be more in charge than the president himself, his decision-making role was in fact much more limited (Greenstein, 1982: 138–50).

From a historical perspective, one of the most remarkable features of the Eisenhower presidency was the strong role of the cabinet. During his two terms, Eisenhower convened the cabinet more than 230 times, and chaired the majority of meetings himself (Edwards and Wayne, 1990: 166). Although the cabinet did not serve as a real decision-making body, it was an important place where presidential decisions were deliberated and sometimes prepared. Individual cabinet officers had the opportunity to present their ideas and programmes, which then often became the basis of later presidential decisions in a given field of public policy. The 'aid to education' programme of 1959 and the renovation of the National Park system under the 'Mission 66' programme mark two important examples within this category of cases. Moreover, cabinet meetings became a valuable forum for bringing the departments into line with the president's expectations regarding the federal budget (Henderson, 1988: 51, 59). The cabinet as an institution also profited from the creation of a cabinet secretariat. The latter served primarily as an important catalyst for the development and presentation of agenda items for the cabinet, yet also played a role at the implementation stage. Formal meetings of the cabinet were often followed by a meeting with the cabinet secretary and the assistant secretaries of departments.

Throughout the Eisenhower years, the cabinet remained in a more powerful position than the White House staff. Members of the president's White House team played an important part in co-ordinating policy initiatives and facilitating communications with the individual executive departments and Congress, but lacked any genuine policy-making role.

Kennedy was the first post-war president under whom it became apparent that the White House staff was about to replace the cabinet as the most important advisory body to the president. White House aides were deployed as 'critics of departmental performance and as emergency repair crews when departmental undertakings went awry' (Koenig,

1972: 9). Kennedy's inclination to let his staff maintain close supervision over the departments manifested itself particularly in domestic affairs. There were few exceptions to this general policy of White House supervision of the departments. The two most important ones related to Douglas Dillon at the Treasury and Arthur Goldberg in the Department of Labor, whom the president regarded as particularly able thinkers and decision-makers.

In stark contrast to his predecessor, Kennedy had no regard for rules and procedures, and little desire to rely on institutionalized committees. More than a dozen executive office agencies created under Eisenhower, were abolished. Instead, a circular staff structure was set up in the White House Office with no chief of staff and almost equal opportunities for all of his advisers to meet with him. Kennedy's personal involvement in the policy-making process, while varying from one issue to another, was quite intense by comparative standards. It was particularly manifest in foreign policy, where the president became to an exceptional degree his own secretary of state, and Secretary of State Dean Rusk was not even made part of Kennedy's inner circle of advisers (Yoder, 1986: 89).

It was hardly surprising, then, that Kennedy's reliance on personal relationships and such pronounced emphasis on personal loyalty generated specific problems. As one observer has remarked, 'loyalty to Kennedy often became a substitute for good government' (Paper, 1975: 149). That is, when Kennedy made his wishes clear about a particular matter, staff members usually accepted his decision without further questioning. Moreover, 'the staff was prone to confuse Kennedy's political fortunes with principles of good leadership' (ibid.: 150). Indeed, the civil rights issue may be seen as a good example of many advisers arguing against strong presidential action, mainly for fear of lacking support among the American mainstream electorate rather than because of reservations in terms of policy.

When Johnson succeeded Kennedy in the Oval Office, he adhered to the tradition of convening the full cabinet on a regular basis. Even so, the Johnson cabinet clearly did not advance to become a central presidential advisory body (Pfiffner, 1986: 676–7). Some observers used stronger language to describe this. According to one member of Johnson's White House staff, 'the Cabinet became a joke' (cited by Cronin, 1980: 186), never being used even for presidential consultation, let alone presidential decision-making. The decision-making centre of the Johnson presidency was clearly located in the White House. Although Johnson kept many of his predecessor's staff and stuck to the circular staffing structure, the atmosphere was quite different. Johnson's assistants were expected to remain anonymous. The president watched jealously to ensure that none of his staffers gained too much publicity or attention. Even Johnson's decision to operate the White House without a chief of staff must be seen against the background of his unwillingness to let anyone in his administration become too powerful. Johnson's approach was based on the principle of strong personal loyalty and was marked by the expectation that the president's top advisers were to be multi-functional generalists.[13]

Even though it was the White House staff who formed the centre of presidential decision-making, individual cabinet members were sometimes made part of the presidential advisory system. The existing department-centred system was supplemented by a White House-centred system. Moreover, a series of task forces, working in secrecy, was created, which played a prominent role in preparing many core measures of Johnson's 'Great Society' programme. During Johnson's five years in office, no fewer than 145 of such task forces were convened (Lammers and Genovese, 2000: 79). The increasing prominence of the Vietnam issue in the field of national security policy gave rise to a rather specific presidential consultation body. While the NSC continued to meet regularly, its deliberations effectively lost clout. Key decisions in this field were made by the so-called 'Tuesday Cabinet', a weekly meeting of the president with the secretary of state, the secretary of defence, the special assistant for national security affairs, the director of the CIA, the chairman of the Joint Chiefs of Staff, and the president's press secretary (Hess, 1976: 102–7). The overall direction in foreign policy was, however, clearly determined by the president. So eccentric and dominant was his role that some observers suggested that, under the conditions of parliamentary government, Johnson would probably have been seriously challenged by his peers in the government (Yoder, 1986: 104).

Many scholars found that Johnson's 'character, political style, and personal makeup were ill suited to the presidential environment' (Berman, 1988: 144). Several features of Johnson's behaviour – such as his legendary preoccupation with his public image – may pass as a manifestation of his uneasiness about being compared incessantly with his exceptionally popular predecessor. Several other features of his style, such as his extreme sensitivity to criticism, his preoccupation with secrecy, and not least his ruthless treatment of members of his staff, seem, however, to have been deeper reflections of Johnson's personality.

To an even greater extent than most other office-holders of the post-war period, Nixon was convinced that the president's primary responsibilities lay in the field of foreign policy. Consequently, he set out to leave the bulk of domestic policy decisions to his cabinet officers, which seemed to signal a return to a more cabinet-based domestic presidency. The responsibility of individual cabinet secretaries included programmatic decisions as well as decisions regarding personnel matters in the departments. No less importantly, Nixon was accessible to cabinet members, especially the Secretary of Labour George Shultz, HEW Secretary Robert Finch, and Attorney General John Mitchell. During the first months of Nixon's incumbency, the cabinet met regularly every fortnight to give cabinet officers the opportunity to be briefed on major current issues. Nixon also revitalized the cabinet secretariat in the White House, which had been dormant in the Kennedy and Johnson administrations. However, Nixon's determination to establish strong 'cabinet government' lasted for less than a year.[14]

Disappointed at the extent to which individual cabinet members became absorbed by the interest group clientele, and in particular the bureaucracy within their respective departments, Nixon ordered the dismissal of the whole cabinet in 1972. All his really influential top advisers were placed in the strictly hierarchically organized White House, and were instructed to keep cabinet officers away from him. Nixon also contributed to the declining status of the cabinet in the American executive branch by introducing a number of structural innovations. Most importantly, in 1970 he created the Domestic Policy Council (and the somewhat less important Urban Affairs Council) in the White House, thereby institutionalizing the role of the domestic policy adviser. For the first time, the White House became the centralizing mechanism for major domestic policy development and management (Warshaw, 1996: 65).

At least three other crucial characteristics of presidential leadership style within the Nixon White House are worth highlighting. The first relates to Nixon's marked inclination to decide things alone, often without consulting even his most senior advisers. Meetings between the president and his staff were used to air and sort out ideas rather than to decide things or reach a consensus. Recommendations on specific issues were usually demanded in writing, which allowed the president to analyze them in his own mind without interference from his aides. Most observers have been inclined to consider Nixon's decision-making style as being closely affected by his personality needs, which included a strong emphasis on control, secrecy and loyalty, as well as a deep-rooted distrust of his environment.

A second principal feature of Nixon's leadership approach may be seen in the president's marked self-perception as a 'crisis manager'. As

Joan Hoff-Wilson (1988: 167–8) has put it, 'Nixon's management style as president arose in reaction to an assortment of crises – some actual; others invented by him or his staff. This real and pseudo-crisis atmosphere was the natural by-product of consensual breakdown, but it was reinforced by the fact that Nixon operated most effectively in it'. The same author has emphasized a third notable feature of Nixon's performance in the White House; namely, the peculiar repercussions of the president's mania for establishing orderly procedures on the overall character of his policy programme. There was a marked tendency from the early days of the administration for process and organizational reform to become a substitute for substantive policies, and often effectiveness seemed to be judged more highly than morality and constitutionality (ibid.: 181).

The structural conditions of the Ford presidency would have weakened any candidate in the Oval Office. The negative impact of the deep public mistrust of the post-Watergate executive branch on the president's room for manoeuvre can hardly be overestimated. As a senior member of the former administration, Ford lacked the aura of an 'anti-Nixon', which was later to become part of Carter's political capital. Moreover, and more importantly, Ford had been elected neither president nor vice-president, a fact that he readily acknowledged.[15]

These background conditions alone would appear sufficient to explain why Ford tried to practice a more collegial style of core executive decision-making, giving cabinet members the feeling of being an important part of the presidential team. 'Cabinet government' seemed to be 'an ideal way to go slowly and rebuild the presidency' (Warshaw, 1996: 99). The historical circumstances suggesting the pursuit of a more collegial style were strongly supported by Ford's personality, which valued collegiality and the ability to compromise over hard-edged leadership. The substitution of the president's somewhat taller chair in the cabinet room by a chair having exactly the same size as those of all other members of the cabinet (Gergen, 2000: 141) may seem a trivial matter, but it symbolized the new administration's spirit very well.

This notwithstanding, the overall degree of 'cabinet government' as a decision-making modus remained fairly limited, for various reasons. To begin with, the slightly upgraded position of the cabinet (towards the 'presidential branch') was only a secondary effect of the chaotic conditions in the White House. There was constant infighting among senior members of Ford's White House staff, producing serious gridlock at the very centre of the system. As discipline in the White House improved (which was the case after Ford appointed a formal chief of staff and established a more pyramid-like system in late 1974), the cabinet's role within the decision-making process diminished. Another reason for the limits of 'cabinet government' in the Ford presidency was the rather restricted freedom the individual departments were granted. Whereas the heads of departments enjoyed free access to the president, individual departments were not authorized to develop innovative programmes independently.

As Roger Porter (1988) has shown, Ford applied rather different decision-making styles in different policy fields. In foreign policy, he used a variant of centralized management that to a large extent may be seen as a reflection of his unique relationship with Henry Kissinger, who made up for the president's inexperience in foreign policy. In domestic policy, an *ad hoc* approach prevailed, reflecting both Ford's lack of interest in a continuing inter-agency apparatus that would raise large numbers of possible initiatives for his decision, and his inclination to delegate much responsibility in this area to the vice-president. In economic policy, to which he devoted a great deal of time and energy, he developed a 'multiple advocacy approach' marked by collegial discussions among a wider range of advisers.

No other post-war president appeared to be as determined to install 'true cabinet government' as Carter during the early stages of his incumbency. Individual cabinet officers were granted a maximum of discretionary power both with regard to sub-cabinet appointments within the departments and policy formulation in their respective areas. Although Carter was certainly much more interested in facing issues and solving problems than in managing executive decision-making processes, the central role of the cabinet and its individual members cannot be explained fully by a lack of interest in administrative matters on the president's part. Rather, Carter seems positively to have been convinced that 'policy development based on the principle of home-work would be a unifying and motivating force in his administration'; he 'believed that people of goodwill who had learned to work together would develop the right policies' (Hargrove, 1988: 25, 31). This collegial style also characterized Carter's initial approach to managing his White House. Not only did he try to revive the circular staff system operated by his more recent Democratic predecessors, but he also became the last president of the twentieth century to try to run the White House without a chief of staff.

Despite the prominent position the cabinet enjoyed for much of the late 1970s, most scholars hesitate to refer to Carter's presidency as a period of true 'cabinet government'. There was, in fact, not even a symbolic sense of collegiality among the individual cabinet secretaries and the president. Rather, many cabinet members used their experience in dealing with Congress (which Carter himself lacked) in order to mobilize congressional support against legislative proposals of the president whenever this seemed expedient from a departmental view (Warshaw, 1996: 115–8). During the second half of his term, Carter completely abandoned his initial plans of institutionalizing a cabinet-centred decision-making system, and relied heavily on his circle of advisers in the White House. In 1979, four cabinet ministers were dismissed and about fifty or so sub-cabinet officials in the departments were replaced by White House-approved appointees. Moreover, Carter appointed a White House chief of staff (Hamilton Jordan) and, a year later, a staff director (Alonzo McDonald), who came to symbolize a considerably more hierarchical staff structure in which most informal gatherings were replaced by formal staff meetings.

There is at least one other characteristic of Carter's leadership style well worth mentioning; namely, his obsession with even the most minute details of policy decisions, which often prevented him from linking particular decisions to the wider political and policy context. Erwin Hargrove (1988: 171) has explained this phenomenon with a deep-rooted predisposition in Carter's personality: 'At the core of Jimmy Carter's political personality was the imperative for mastery. His life was to be a testing ground on which he would prove himself, and he was to do it alone. This was the source of his strength and his weakness as a political man.'

The effects of the change in the office of president from Carter to Reagan were obvious in almost any field of presidential leadership, reaching beyond the fundamental differences in the two administrations' public policies. Most of the structural features of the Reagan White House and cabinet were innovative enough not to stand out only in direct comparison with the Carter administration. Reagan's White House staff was separated into different units, each headed by a senior member of staff who enjoyed ready access to the president. The joint authority to co-ordinate all major decisions was left to the so-called 'troika', including the chief of staff, James Baker, special counsellor to the president, Edwin Meese, and special counsellor to the president for special events, Michael Deaver.

This arrangement was not without its problems, though. As Dom Bonafede (1997: 507) has argued, 'it clogged policy-making channels. Every high-priority issue had to be routed to the Big Three, who collectively debated it. This invited delay, private outside lobbying, and decision by consensus before offering their group-think recommendation to Reagan.' The original pattern remained in place for slightly more than a year. After having been expanded to a system of the 'Big Four', including NSC director William Clark, the whole arrangement was eventually replaced by a much more hierarchical structure at the beginning of Reagan's second term. The position of chief of staff, occupied by former business executive and chief executive officer, Donald Regan, turned out to be an institution with an enormously centralizing effect. Even after Regan's forced resignation in 1987, following the devastating report of the Tower Commission that blamed him for failing to control his subordinates and to protect the president's interests, there was no return to a significantly less hierarchical structure in Reagan's White House.

Reagan's core executive decision-making style was particularly notable for the establishment of a highly specialized system of cabinet committees. According to the administration's official proclamations, the creation of seven cabinet committees in 1981–2 was designed to strengthen the role of the cabinet by institutionalizing policy deliberations between individual members of the cabinet and senior White House staff.[16] While Reagan's cabinet committee system initially generated some kind of integrative core executive decision-making, the whole system soon became dominated by the president's White House staff. The influence of cabinet members within the committees decreased gradually, as did the number of occasions on which the president was present. The cabinet councils' real impact on the administration's major decisions remained, however, questionable. Many core decisions in the field of domestic policy seem to have been prepared by the OMB, and in informal meetings in the chief of staff's office (which rarely included any cabinet members), rather than in the cabinet councils (Benze, 1987: 83–4; Hill, 1990: 163–4).

During Reagan's second term, all, apart from two committees in the field of domestic policy and economic policy – the Economic Policy Council and the Domestic Policy Council – were abolished. However, this did not mean that the cabinet completely lost clout. The immediate result of scrapping most of the committees was the further centralization of power in the White House. But, just as in the Ford presidency, the cabinet was to profit from the paralysis in the White House that surrounded (and indeed caused) the Iran-Contra affair.

Another key feature of Reagan's leadership style in the core executive was his penchant for delegating the details of policy-making. While all presidents delegate a certain amount of decisions, Reagan carried delegation to excess. Journalists and scholars have been deeply divided over the reasons and effects of this hands-off approach.[17] There can be no doubt that the large-scale delegation of policy matters had much to do with Reagan's uninformedness and lack of interest in more specific aspects of policy, which made him significantly more dependent on his aides than most of his predecessors had been. The Iran-Contra affair has often been cited as the prime example of the dangers of such an approach. However, one has to be careful not to consider Reagan's marked inclination to delegate as synomymous with being out of control. In most major areas of public policy, while not caring about the details of a decision, Reagan had a clear sense of where he wanted to go. Looked at from a distance, Reagan appears in fact to have been 'another hidden-hand Ike' (Greenstein, 1990), inviting friends and foes alike to underestimate him.

While some of the most recent judgments of the presidency of George H. W. Bush have been, on balance, slightly more favourable than the bulk of assessments produced during or in the immediate aftermath of the 1989–92 period (Maggs, 2002), this Bush presidency is unlikely ever to be considered an outstanding success. Part of the overall mixed performance of the George H. W. Bush administration may be attributed to the historical circumstances. William Lammers and Michael Genovese (2000) considered Bush (alongside Nixon, Carter and Clinton) as a 'low-opportunity president' who faced many challenges and had few opportunities, particularly on the domestic front. However, they also found Bush (together with Carter) the least effective president within this very category. To a certain degree, such an assessment is obviously influenced by the authors' chosen evaluation criteria, which focus on the overall amount of policy change a president achieved. Bush, in fact, saw himself as a guardian of the political status quo rather than as a reformer. This notwithstanding, he did seem to have more difficulty in setting his administration's overall course than did many other post-war presidents.

Bush's limited grip on the core executive decision-making process may have been favoured by his unique record as an 'heir apparent', which marked a big difference from other former vice-presidents, in terms of both experience and style. As Bob Woodward (1999: 223) has emphasized, from the early 1970s, Bush 'had built his career as the patron of other Republican presidents, turning setbacks into opportunity . . . He had not acquired the political skills that many politicians develop through struggle and adversity.'

Dilys Hill and Phil Williams (1994: 6–8) have singled out four major aspects of Bush's leadership style in the executive branch: a good deal of informality resulting from the president's good personal relationship with many of his cabinet officers and chief advisers in the White House; a strong preference for agreement and accommodation; a pragmatic approach to handling matters, with a preference for competence over ideology; and, though seemingly contradictory, an emphasis on hierarchy.

Bush's emphasis on collegiality and informality governed his contacts with White House assistants as much as his relations with cabinet secretaries. Whereas he continued to operate the small-scale cabinet committee system of Reagan's second term, the committees were used as a means of developing informal interaction between the president and individual cabinet members, rather than integrating the cabinet and White House staff. Bush's social skills were considered to be particularly valuable by many senior figures within the core executive, who often found formal channels of communication blocked by the president's first White House Office chief of staff, John Sununu. However, Bush's informal style and pragmatic approach also had obvious negative consequences. Informality sometimes prevented a systematic consideration and careful scrutiny of options, glossing over differences among advisers, while the president's pragmatic style contributed to a lack of consistency in approach, fostering accusations that the administration was essentially reactive. Traces of hierarchy were still to be found, especially in the area of foreign policy, where Bush established a system of 'restricted collegiality' marked by a narrower policy advice net and even a certain amount of secrecy (Burke, 2000: 169–72). In the end, however, neither informal nor more hierarchical structures of decision-making could compensate for what many observers considered to be the president's serious lack of policy leadership capacity.

Bill Clinton's leadership style in the core executive – especially his chaotic White House management and his perfectionist approach to decision-making – had more in common with that of his Democratic predecessor, Jimmy Carter, than could reasonably be explained by party affiliation. There were, however, also major differences. Despite the highly publicized cabinet-building process, the cabinet took a back seat in Clinton's decision-making system virtually from the start. This is particularly true for the role of the cabinet as a collegial body. Early on, the most important issues were dealt with in a powerful 'kitchen cabinet' including special White House counsellor David Gergen, Vice-President Al Gore, Hillary Clinton and Thomas 'Mack' McLarty, Clinton's first White House chief of staff. Formal cabinet meetings were soon replaced by so-called 'cabinet briefings' which were attended only rarely by the president and, from 1994 onwards, chaired by Clinton's White House chief of staff. After only three years, Clinton stopped convening the full cabinet almost completely. In mid-1999 it was reported that Clinton had held no more than two cabinet meetings over the past one-and-a-half years (*National Journal*, 22 May 1999: 1387). The freezing-out of the full cabinet did not mean, however, that individual secretaries had no chance to see the president. Some cabinet members, such as Clinton's two secretaries of state, Warren Christopher and Madeleine Albright, enjoyed remarkably easy access to the Oval Office.

The policy-making system of so-called 'working groups', including individual cabinet members and White House staff on an *ad hoc* basis, gained its particular character from the president's widely-noticed obsession with even the most minor details of policy and personnel matters, which in most other administrations were delegated to the sub-cabinet level. Added to this obsession with detail came a marked degree of indecisiveness – a feature of Clinton's personality that may help to explain the president's inclination to have advisers with strong personalities and clearly defined political and policy goals – for example, Leon Panetta or Dick Morris. Until the end of his second term, the whole leadership process within the executive branch remained deeply influenced by Clinton's liking for inclusiveness and deliberation.

Early in his administration, in particular, Clinton received much criticism from scholars for his obvious attempt to revert to the old inclination of Democratic presidents to operate the White House on the basis of a more-or-less circular staffing structure. This approach was judged to be old-fashioned and inadequate because of its lack of internal organizational coherence and administrative efficiency (Campbell, 1996: 75). Although Clinton appointed a formal chief of staff immediately after inauguration, he acted essentially as his own chief of staff during the first months of his incumbency. The system was designed to allow for maximum flexibility and to institutionalize the capacity to produce policy alternatives quickly, but in practice, it resulted all too often in disorganization and inefficiency. Reforms of the White House decision-making system, intended to strengthen the organizational hierarchy, started with the appointment of Leon Panetta, Clinton's second chief of staff, in 1994, and were consolidated under Panetta's successors, Erskine Bowles (1996–8) and John Podesta (1998–2001). Still, many observers found that the Clinton White House remained one of the most disorganized, even chaotic administrations of the whole post-war period.

Two other major characteristics of presidential leadership during the Clinton years relate to the prominent role of the first lady and the vice-president. Whereas the increased role of the latter had long been foreshadowed in previous administrations,[18] the prominent position of Mrs Clinton in the policy-making process was virtually unique. Hillary Clinton was delegated responsibility for devising a national health care system within the first few months after inauguration, and remained highly influential as a close adviser to the president in the nomination of federal judges and key administrative posts. It has even been suggested that her position was 'at least as important as most cabinet posts' (Burns *et al.*, 1995: 395).

The influential position of the first lady and the vice-president's prominent role in the administration could have been foretold by the end of the presidential race. Choosing Al Gore as his running mate, Clinton replaced the established 'balancing the ticket' approach to selecting a vice-presidential candidate by a clear focus on the candidate's qualities as a co-governing actor and potential successor in the Oval Office. Gore played a central role in directing the administration's National Performance Review Project and had considerable influence in a number of policy areas, such as environment and high technology, although he also served as a prominent personal representative of the president in foreign affairs. Gore developed a sophisticated technique of building 'virtual departments', a gathering of experts from various executive agencies that were involved in dealing with an issue. There were frequent crossovers between the presidential and vice-presidential staff, which further strengthened the vice-president's role in the core executive decision-making process (Patterson, 2000: 308–9).

The prominent role of the vice-president marked one of the few parallels between the inner workings of the Clinton administration and that of George W. Bush. In fact, from the beginning, Vice-President Dick Cheney enjoyed an unusually influential role within the core executive and beyond that dwarfed even Gore's position in the Clinton White House. No sooner had the administration taken up its business than Cheney was chosen to chair the president's budget review board as well as a task force designed to undertake a major review of US energy policy. Moreover, he was assigned a seat on a select committee of the NSC established to make final decisions regarding national security policy. Yet there were numerous other, partly more informal, roles the vice-president performed. Not only did Cheney attend the weekly and separate meetings between Bush and his two foreign policy heavyweights on the cabinet, Secretary of State Colin Powell and Secretary of Defense Donald Rumsfeld, but he also joined the president's weekly economic and domestic policy meetings and was more often than not present when Bush met foreign leaders. Cheney also met weekly for lunch with Powell, Rumsfeld and Condoleeza Rice, Bush's high-profile national security adviser. Another key area for the vice-president lay in the legislative arena, where he attended Republican leadership meetings and established regular meetings with congressional fellows. The clearest demonstration of Cheney's very special position came on 26 August 2002, when the vice-president rather than the president himself delivered the administration's key speech on Iraq that set the tone for many weeks. As the Bush presidency went on, the vice-president's role was gradually transformed into 'a popular adminstration ambassador to heartland conservatives' and a part-time fund-raiser for Bush's re-election campaign, though he remained an important counsellor to the president (Allen, 2004). There has been widespread consensus among White House aides and external observers that the secret behind Cheney's key role – apart from his undivided loyalty, competence and valued experience as a former White House chief of staff (in the Ford White House), cabinet officer (under George H. W. Bush) and congressman – was the fact that he had no presidential ambitions of his own.

Among the many contrasts between the Clinton and Bush administrations the dramatically reduced role of the first lady was one of the most obvious, if not one of the most relevant.[19] More crucial was Bush's principal approach to organizing the core executive, which was marked by a strong orientation towards discipline and loyalty, to be combined with a notable and widely criticized penchant for secrecy that characterized White House relations with the outside world. Whereas the unusual amount of popularity that Bush enjoyed among his aides may have played a part in making major leaks an extremely rare occurrence, it seems more reasonable to consider the highly disciplined White House atmosphere to be a direct result of Bush's heavily loyalty-focused staffing approach. Examples supporting this view were neither confined to the transition period nor to presidential appointments in the core executive territory. The selection of Bush's close confidant, Tom Ridge, in early 2002 to head the White House Office of Homeland Security, and later become the administration's secretary of homeland security, was fully in line with Bush's staffing approach shown in the immediate transition period. The replacement of James Gilmore III, who was said to have no close relationship with the president, as the Republican national chairman by Bush's long-term friend Marc Racicot in late 2001 marked another case in point.

Right at the beginning of his term, Bush created two new units in the EOP: the first was the Office of Strategic Initiatives, designed to advise the president on long-term political strategy. It was headed by one of the president's closest confidants, Karl Rove.[20] The second, the Office of Faith-Based and Community Initiatives was intended to demonstrate Bush's commitment to what had figured large in his campaign as 'compassionate conservatism'. The overall structure of relationships in the Bush White House resembled the 'spokes-of-a-wheel' configuration, with a strong chief of staff, that had characterized the Reagan years. Some observers even identified parallels between the leadership arrangements in the Bush White House and Reagan's 'troika'. The counterparts of Baker, Meese and Deaver under Reagan were Bush's chief of staff Andrew Card, chief adviser Karl Rove, and Karen Hughes, a long-term trustee of Bush in the post of counsellor to the president, who left the administration in April 2002 (Walcott and Hult, 2003: 151). While Bush soon acquired the reputation of being an unusually laid-back chief executive,[21] with a strong emphasis on team-spirit that many thought to be a reflection of Bush's former experience as a former baseball entrepreneur, he nevertheless fostered 'a culture of dignity' (Berke, 2001) in the White House. In internal conversations, and even e-mail messages, White House aides were reported to refer to Bush as 'the president'.

As a notable parallel to the Reagan years, the strong element of hierarchy in the Bush White House was combined with a marked inclination on the president's side generously to delegate decisions.[22] Even more so than under Reagan, the president's prevailing focus on the big picture was grounded in a deeply moral view of politics that tried to sort out complex issues by distinguishing 'good' and 'evil' motives, aims or actors. Different explanations have been put forward for this phenomenon. To some, Bush's desire to find moral clarity on almost any major issue marked an attempt to distance himself from his father's tendency to have positive views about almost everyone and everything. Others judged Bush's way as a reflection of his Western Texas background, which has been associated with a penchant for viewing things with a black-and-white approach. However, most believed there was some connection between Bush's tendency to develop clear-cut choices and stick to them, and his tough personal decision in 1986 to stop drinking from one day to the next (Duffy, 2002).

While it was the terrorist attacks on 11 September 2001 that came to mark the true watershed in the organization of the core executive decision-making process, Bush's initial leadership conception, based on a strong element of 'cabinet government', displayed signs of change before that date (Nakashima and Milbank, 2001). As with most earlier presidents, Bush set out to restore some clout to the cabinet. Monthly cabinet meetings were reinstated and attempts were made to establish more contact between cabinet members and the White House staff. The White House chief of staff, Andrew Card, had lunch weekly with a different cabinet member, while the White House secretary of cabinet affairs, Albert Hawkins, hosted monthly meetings with department staff chiefs. Still, neither the cabinet as a whole nor its highly credited individual members lived up (or were allowed to live up) to the expectations that had developed during the transition stage. Although cabinet members enjoyed a certain amount of managerial leeway, the key policy issues, especially in the major domestic areas including education, tax and health policy, were clearly decided in the White House (Kumar, 2002: 36). The frequency of cabinet meetings later fell to about once every two-and-a-half months.

At no time in Bush's adminstration did individual departments function as think tanks producing innovative ideas in their respective areas of responsibility, let alone for the administration's more general policy direction. Some observers found the most important functions of cabinet officials to be related to the area of public communication, rather than the core executive decision-making process. The secretaries of state and defence, Colin Powell and Donald Rumsfeld, were the only members of the cabinet who had regular time to talk with the president. All others had to make appointments with the White House chief of staff or another senior Bush aid to see the president alone. The dominant form of communication between the president and all members of his cabinet remained oral communication, either face-to-face or, more often, over the telephone. As in some other recent administrations, individual cabinet officers were integrated through a system of policy councils, which included top executive branch officials, to be supported by a presidential adviser and significant numbers of staff. Every cabinet member was a member of one, or several, of the four policy councils (Domestic Policy, National Security, National Economic Policy, and Homeland Security), and each was chaired by the president (*National Journal*, 25 January 2003: 232–41).

Whereas Bush's heavily 'delegation-orientated' leadership style could have hardly contrasted more with Clinton's detail-focused approach to decision-making, the president's degree of involvement in single decisions varied among policy fields. At the beginning of the administration, education was certainly an issue on which Bush spent a considerable amount of time and energy. By contrast, global environmental policy was left almost completely to the discretion of other forces in his administration. However, there was not always a nice fit between substance and appearance. For example, Bush's much publicized effort at producing a decision on genetic research involving embryonic stem cells was considered by some observers primarily as a carefully crafted public relations exercise, designed to *present* the president as being 'deliberative', seriously interested, and personally involved (Bruni, 2002: 250–1).

It is hard to say to what extent, if at all, the terrorist attacks of 11 September 2001 altered the president as a private person. While he stuck to his general habits in the private sphere (ibid.: 246–63), many thought that he had become more serious, less self-interested and more self-confident. However, others have argued that this was just a changed perception among many journalists and the public at large through to a projection on to the president of the transformation they wanted to see in themselves (Beinart, 2002). Whatever is believed to be correct, there can be no doubt that the events of 11 September 2001 changed the presidency. While this became most obvious in the areas of public leadership and presidential–congressional relations (see Chapter 5), there were also significant elements of change within the core executive territory.

In the immediate aftermath of the attacks, daily meetings of the NSC, lasting for about an hour, were established. They included the president and vice-president, Chief of Staff Andrew Card, Secretary of State Powell, Defense Secretary Rumsfeld, and Bush's national security adviser, Condoleeza Rice. The frequency of meetings attended by the president was later reduced to three times a week. Even before the start of these meetings, Bush was briefed each weekday at 8 am by the CIA director, George Tenet, another key member of the 'war cabinet'. In addition, a 'domestic consequences' group, chaired by Deputy Chief of Staff Joshua Bolton, was established to meet every morning at 10.30. It included several cabinet members and discussed anti-terrorism legislation and related issues.

The establishment of the 'war cabinet' strengthened the role of some cabinet members – most notably of Secretary of State Powell, who in the days and weeks before the September 2001 attacks was widely considered to have become almost 'invisible'. As Bob Woodward (2002) has revealed, Powell's breakthrough as a key political player within the administration did not come before the summer of 2002, however.

Until well after the September attacks he enjoyed little more than an arm's-length relationship with the president. The first, more private, meetings between Powell and Bush, having been arranged by the president's national security adviser at Powell's request, took place in the late spring of 2002. His single most important achievement was that he managed to persuade the president of the advantages of pursuing a less unilateral and more flexible strategy on Iraq – an achievement, though, that deepened the split among Bush's foreign policy team into a conservative wing (led by Cheney) and a faction of pragmatists (led by Powell) that had been visible virtually from the beginning of the Bush presidency. In contrast to Powell, Defense Secretary Rumsfeld was a highly influential and visible figure well before the evolution of a crisis management system at the White House. Within the latter, Rumsfeld and Cheney soon emerged as the key figures enjoying unrestricted access to the president.

However, arguably the most remarkable career in the post-9/11 White House related to Bush's national security adviser, Condoleeza Rice. Not only did she emerge as a crucial voice in the meetings of the 'war cabinet' and a key figure in other gatherings. She was also often the only senior adviser present with the president on weekends at Camp David, thereby gradually transforming her role of troubleshooter into one of little less than a genuine co-decision-maker, outperforming even the prominent role of Henry Kissinger in the Nixon White House (Sanger and Tyler, 2001). Her influence on the president was not even confined strictly to the key areas of foreign policy. There were signs, for example, that Rice had been the central force behind Bush's much-noticed efforts early in 2003 to condemn publicly the race-conscious admissions policies of American universities (*Washington Post*, 17 January 2003). But Rice's authority was shaken when it emerged later in the same year that she had not read in its entirety the most authoritative assessment of pre-war intelligence on Iraq's weapons programmes. However, the criticism directed against her by many White House officials centred more on her general style of managing the decision-making process within the NSC. There was a widespread perception that Rice did not resolve enough issues before they reached the president, which in the eyes of many led to an overall weakening of the NSC's role as an adjudicator between agencies. Moreover, in foreign policy briefings of the president, she reportedly rarely bothered to forge a common position and rather preferred to save her advice for the president alone (Kessler and Slevin, 2003).

Conclusion

The post-war period in American politics has witnessed an enormous variety of presidential leadership styles in the core executive. From the appointment process to the organization of the White House Office and the use of the cabinet, individual presidents have differed from each other to a very significant extent. If one looks for pairs or groups of incumbents adopting a similar style, probably Carter and Clinton, and Reagan and George W. Bush spring to mind first. However, on watching more closely, even seemingly similar incumbents turned out to have been rather different. Moreover, presidential leadership styles do not only vary between presidents but also between policy fields. This has been particularly notable in the case of Gerald Ford, but it also applies to the patterns of core executive decision-making under Richard Nixon or George H. W. Bush. In a number of policy areas, such as tax policy or defence policy, even 'chief delegator' Reagan showed a certain willingness to be involved in the policy-making process.

The overall picture is made still more complex by the changes of style that occurred within the term of a single incumbent. Most presidents discussed in this chapter increased their emphasis on hierarchy and efficiency in the core executive decision-making process as their term went on, and relied to a growing extent on the White House Office rather than the cabinet. This said, even towards the end of their respective terms, individual presidents displayed rather different leadership styles in terms of accessibility, informality, policy expertise, or the degree of involvement in the policy-making process.

Even though some of the most obvious 'pair cases' of presidents, such as Carter/Clinton or Reagan/Bush Jr, would seem to fit the party affiliations of individual office-holders, the party factor alone seems to explain very little. Perhaps its impact has been strongest in the field of White House organization.[23] Generally, Republican presidents have tended to create 'pyramidal' staff structures in the White House, whereas virtually all Democratic incumbents have preferred to create circular models of White House organization. Bert Rockman (1996: 353) has offered a number of possible explanations for this phenomenon, including a natural inclination of Republicans to hierarchy and fixed responsibilities, and the larger pool of experienced staff personnel, advisers and White House managers that Republicans have had at their disposal.

A set of more important questions relates to the broader historical developments of the post-war period. Because of the creation of the 'institutional presidency' or, as some prefer to call it, a 'presidential branch', in the late 1930s and its gradual expansion, all post-war presidents faced significantly different conditions of core executive leadership than had their historical predecessors of the pre-war period.[24] In fact, with regard to the administrative resources available to the president, the Truman and Eisenhower years (1945–61) had more in common with any of the later presidencies than with the pre-Roosevelt presidency. While many of the most important effects of the 'institutional presidency' on the president's leverage relate to the area of executive–legislative relations and the various aspects of public leadership (see Chapter 5), the emergence of a 'presidential branch' within the wider executive branch has also had a crucial impact on the nature of core executive leadership in the American system. The parties and the cabinet were among the most obvious losers of this gradual transformation. Whereas the president's party played a major role within the core executive before the First and Second World Wars, its traditional role as the president's central organization for advice and strategy while in office was largely lost to the White House Office (Milkis, 1993). At the same time, the cabinet evolved into an institution that now matters primarily in terms of political representation.

The development of the 'presidential branch' has been accompanied by more latent and ambiguous changes. As personnel resources in the White House increased, so did the danger of presidents becoming overly dependent on their staff. Moreover, the growing complexity of the White House Office generated serious problems such as internal competition, empire building and divided loyalties among the staff. In one of his last articles, the late Richard Neustadt (2001: 8–9) specifically highlighted the steady increase of presidential staff, and its inherent dangers, as a key reason for a structural weakening of presidential power in the political system.

The more recent past witnessed the emergence of at least one new influential political player within the contemporary presidency. Whereas the future of the first lady as a genuinely political actor within the presidency remains unclear, after Laura Bush has shown virtually no intention to follow in the steps of Hillary Clinton,[25] the office of vice-president was transformed under Gore and Cheney to an extent that makes it unlikely that future presidents will cut it back to the rather modest role it played for most of the twentieth century. Apart from the personal relationship between more recent presidents and their vice-presidents, which undoubtedly had a major impact on the development of vice-presidential power, there have been structural reasons for this recent transformation. These are similar to those that can explain the rise of the 'institutional presidency'. The 'new vice-presidency' fills a functional gap that has been opened up as presidents have encountered an ever-more-demanding job with Congresses being more divided, policy issues becoming more complex, and the task of public leadership placing more burdens on the president than ever before.

3
Britain: Prime Ministers, Cabinets and the Struggle for Supremacy

The Political Profiles of British Post-war Prime Ministers

The office of the British prime minister is not to any similar extent an autonomous position, as is the office of the American president. Whereas the supremacy of the prime minister over other actors in the British core executive has increased significantly, both politically and constitutionally, over recent decades, British politics, even in the core executive territory, remains very much a team game. Thus, it seems only natural that many of the constitutional and political qualifications for the office of prime minister have to be acquired within the other institutions of British politics, such as parliament, the cabinet and the political parties.

There is neither a formal election of the prime minister by parliament nor a parliamentary confirmation of the newly formed government as a whole, although more recently the introduction of such a procedure has been suggested by one of the most prominent commentators on the constitutional process in Britain (Riddell, 2000: 234). The most essential constitutional requirement for becoming British prime minister is the need first to become a member of parliament.[1] During the course of the twentieth century the requirement that eligible candidates must sit in the Commons or the Lords has been refined. Prime ministers are now expected to hold a seat in the House of Commons rather than the House of Lords.[2] In effect, a candidate has not only to hold a seat but must command a majority in the Commons, which means, more specifically, that he or she has to be the official leader of the strongest party in the Commons. It is this constitutional requirement, together with the existence of mostly clear-cut parliamentary majorities, that has been responsible for the near absence of any discretionary power of the monarch in the appointment process since 1945.[3]

There have been eleven different post-war prime ministers in Britain, with one incumbent, Harold Wilson, holding the prime ministership twice (1964–70 and 1974–6). Seven of the incumbents had an affiliation with the Conservative Party, while four were representatives of the Labour Party. On average, as of April 2004, British post-war prime ministers held office for slightly less than five years, with a very significant range between the longest (Margaret Thatcher, 11.6 years) and the shortest term (Alec Douglas-Home, 1 year).[4] As there has been no significant difference between the average length of terms of Conservative and Labour candidates, the larger number of Conservative prime ministers has also been reflected in the overall duration of Conservative and Labour rule between 1945 and early 2004, which amounted to thirty-five years and twenty-four years, respectively.

While all post-war prime ministers – apart from Douglas-Home[5] – have been drawn from the House of Commons, there are marked differences regarding the parliamentary experience of individual incumbents, with a range from just eleven years (John Major) to thirty-eight years (Winston Churchill). The average parliamentary experience of the eleven post-war prime ministers was twenty-three years. The two most recent prime ministers, John Major and Tony Blair, were notable for their rather modest body of parliamentary experience (eleven and fourteen years, respectively), which may partly be explained by the young age at which they gained the premiership (although Major was also the oldest newcomer in parliament among prime ministers since Clement Attlee). Douglas-Home's parliamentary career was exceptional for a different reason: he was a member of the House of Commons for fourteen years until he lost his seat in 1945; he then re-entered the Commons in 1951 and finally inherited an earldom the following year, which took him to the House of Lords (Shell, 1995a: 12–15).

Furthermore, post-war prime ministers differed significantly with regard to their previous experience as government ministers. Even though it is not required by the constitution, government experience clearly marks a typical feature of the political biography of British prime ministers. James Callaghan was the only candidate who had extended experience in all the great offices of state (the Exchequer, the Home Office and the Foreign Office) before succeeding to the prime ministership. This was in direct contrast to Tony Blair – the first candidate in more than seventy years who had held no ministerial office at all before gaining the prime-ministership.[6] Having entered the Commons in 1983, he served as a

Labour spokesman in five different policy fields before being elected party leader in 1994. Even though each career is unique, a certain historical pattern can be identified. Thatcher and Major, Blair's immediate predecessors, lacked any particularly impressive experience as cabinet ministers. Thatcher held only one cabinet post before becoming prime minister (secretary of state for education and science), which cannot even be regarded as a particularly prestigious one. Major had more diverse experience as a cabinet minister, including the very senior position of chancellor of Exchequer, but gained his first cabinet experience just three years before achieving the premiership.

As all British prime ministers are expected by the constitution to hold the leadership of the majority party, there has been less variation among post-war incumbents regarding their formal party ties than among chief executives in many other Western democracies. Still, as to the succession of events leading to a candidate's appointment to prime ministerial office, different patterns can be distinguished. Historically, many Conservative prime ministers gained the prime ministership first and secured the position of party leader only later (Barber, 1991: 6). The case of Edward Heath in 1970 marked the first occasion since 1922 that a Conservative candidate was made party leader before becoming prime minister. After 1945, the longest interval between the moment of becoming prime minister and that of being confirmed as party leader was a three-and-a-half-week period in the case of Douglas-Home in 1963. James Callaghan and John Major each assumed the offices of party leader and prime minister almost simultaneously, whereas all other British prime ministers of the post-war period were the leader of their respective parties *well before* assuming the prime ministership.

On seven occasions, new prime ministers gained the office on the basis of a general election victory. This was the case with Attlee (1945), Churchill (1951), Wilson (1964 and 1974), Heath (1970), Thatcher (1979) and Blair (1997). On five occasions, new prime ministers succeeded outgoing premiers of the same party (Anthony Eden in 1955, Harold Macmillan in 1957, Douglas-Home in 1963, Callaghan in 1976 and Major in 1990). Douglas-Home and Callaghan stand out as the only post-war prime ministers who were neither elected to nor confirmed in office by a public vote. Callaghan was also special in being the only post-war prime minister to be toppled by a parliamentary vote of no-confidence. More than half of British post-war prime ministers lost office because of a defeat at a general election. Among those who stepped down during a parliament – Churchill (1955), Eden (1957), Macmillan (1963), Wilson

(1976) and Thatcher (1990) – Wilson is usually seen as the only clear-cut case of a voluntary resignation, while all the others faced more-or-less severe opposition from their parties, who considered them to have become a major electoral liability.

Staffing the Cabinet and the Administrative Core Executive

When setting up the basic organizational structure of the government and appointing the governing personnel, British prime ministers face few formal obligations or constraints. From a legal point of view, the prime minister is free to create and dissolve departments of state and distribute them among the candidates who have been chosen to hold ministerial office.[7] There are also few constitutional provisions to be considered in the selection process of potential ministers. As with the prime minister himself, ministers must hold a seat in parliament, which normally means in the Commons (though only a small proportion of them, such as the Treasury team, in fact always have to be members of the House of Commons). There are also some statutory provisions restricting the overall number of people who may be paid ministerial salaries (though these may be changed to fit a government's political will). The Ministerial and other Salaries Act 1975 set the total number of salaries that may be paid at 110. Another restriction relates to the total number of ministers that may be drawn from the ranks of the House of Commons (whether scheduled to receive a ministerial salary or not).[8] The House of Commons Disqualification Act 1975 provides that 'no more than ninety-five persons being the holders of offices specified in Schedule 2 to this Act (in this section referred to as Ministerial offices) shall be entitled to sit and vote in the House of Commons at any one time'.

In constitutional practice, the prevailing political circumstances and the personalities involved have played a more crucial role than the formal rules mentioned, however. Labour's sweeping election victory of July 1945 enabled Clement Attlee to form the first Labour majority government in British history. Attlee's cabinet included representatives of the various ideologies and interests in the party. While the left remained under-represented, the number of union-sponsored MPs in the cabinet exactly matched their number in the Parliamentary Labour Party (PLP). There was a large number of cabinet members with a high and independent standing in the party (including Herbert Morrison, Ernest Bevin, Sir Stafford Cripps and Hugh Dalton). The narrow victory of the Labour Party in the 1950 general election was followed by extensive changes in the administration, though there were few changes in the major offices. The most significant alterations to the late Attlee cabinet – the replacement of Ernest Bevin (who died in 1951), and the resignations of Sir Stafford Cripps and Aneurin Bevan (through ill-health in 1950 and 1951, respectively) – were all out of the prime minister's control, and contributed significantly to making Attlee a more aloof figure in the cabinet.

The general election of 1951 produced a change of government and provided Winston Churchill, who had led the war cabinets (1940–5), with another opportunity to form a Conservative government. Churchill was intent on forming a broad-based administration, and even offered the Liberals formal participation in his government. As the Liberals declined this offer, Churchill appointed a number of respected person-alities from outside politics (such as Lord Ismay – a general, and Lord Cherwell – an Oxford scientist). The first Conservative post-war cabinet was also highly specific for the appointment of co-ordinating ministers ('overlords') – aimed at cutting down the need for cabinet committees – who, with the exception of the prime minister himself, were all peers. In party political terms, the cabinet was carefully balanced, albeit with a slight leaning towards the more liberal Conservatives (including such members as Harold Macmillan, Peter Thorneycroft, David Maxwell Fyfe and R. A. Butler). This mixture was retained throughout Churchill's post-war premiership, which witnessed six minor reshuffles, and a major one in October 1954 (Seldon, 1987: 68).

Churchill's heir apparent, Anthony Eden, emphasized continuity when he eventually became prime minister on 6 April 1955. The immediate ministerial appointments – the single most important one was Macmillan taking over the Foreign Office from Eden – were marked by a minimum of change, signalling that a general election was imminent. The 1955 general election, which for the first time in almost 100 years brought considerable gains for a governing party, was followed by a rather extensive reshuffle of the government, which reached down to lower ministerial ranks. Butler leaving the Treasury to become Lord Privy Seal and leader of the House of Commons, Macmillan transferring to the Treasury, and the appointment of Selwyn Lloyd as foreign secretary marked the most important changes ordered by a prime minister, who soon acquired the reputation among senior cabinet fellows for poor judgment in selecting the right man for a given job, and poor timing of changes of the ministerial team.

In January 1957, Macmillan succeeded Eden at 10 Downing Street. Macmillan ordered a sweeping reconstruction of the government, though the principal cabinet appointments were marked by a high degree of continuity. The resignation of the entire Treasury team (Peter Thorneycroft, Enoch Powell and Nigel Birch) in protest at the cabinet's opposition to the Treasury's proposed cuts in expenditure, only about one year into the administration, marked by far the single most important cabinet-personnel-related event of Macmillan's first term. There were few new names to be introduced after the 1959 general election, especially in the key departments. However, the best was yet to come. Macmillan's cabinet reshuffle of 13 July 1962 – remembered as the 'Night of the Long Knives' – became the most spectacular purge in British post-war history. No fewer than seven cabinet ministers, including such senior figures as Selwyn Lloyd and Lord Kilmuir, were dismissed without any previous warning. Macmillan's primary objective was to respond to a dramatic slide in the government's popularity by appointing a breed of significantly younger ministers.[9] While the new cabinet did enjoy a considerably more vigorous image, which had a (moderately) positive effect on the Conservative's public standing, the July 1962 reshuffle marked a turning point in Macmillan's public reputation as prime minister (Alderman, 1992).

When Sir Alec Douglas-Home succeeded Macmillan as prime minister in 1963 he was significantly constrained in his choice of available cabinet ministers by the fact that he had not been the favourite candidate among large parts of the Conservative Party, facing severe reservations especially among many of the most senior party figures (Bogdanor, 1994: 75–80). Thus the whole cabinet-building process was marked by two principal aims: not letting divisions among the Conservatives grow deeper, and securing a reasonable representation of party heavyweights in the cabinet. While some very senior party figures (including Iain Macleod and Enoch Powell) refused to serve under Douglas-Home, some of those who could be persuaded eventually to accept ministerial office enjoyed the rare privilege of virtually writing their own job descriptions, as was most evidently the case with Edward Heath. Still, some of those who accepted ministerial office under Douglas-Home, such as Reginald Maudling, later more-or-less publicly regretted having done so (Gilmour and Garnett, 1997: 209).

The 1964 general election brought the prime ministership of Douglas-Home to an early, if not unexpected, end. With a parliamentary majority of just four seats, the new Labour prime minister, Harold Wilson, had to be very careful to keep his troops together. As Graham Thomas (1997: 22) has observed, 'Wilson tended to make ministerial appointments for various reasons besides ability and fitness for the job. These included simple patronage, that is to ensure loyalty and support in Parliament and on Labour's National Executive Committee (NEC), to keep the unions happy and to balance the various factions in the party.' With twenty-three members Wilson's first cabinet was the largest British post-war cabinet until the mid-1990s. Having been confirmed in office by Labour's 1966 general election victory, Wilson disappointed those who had hoped that he would feel free to cut down the unusually high number of cabinet members. The later Wilson cabinets, formed after the premiership of Edward Heath (1970–4), shared few similarities with his earlier ministerial team. Unlike 1964, when only two ministers had cabinet experience, in 1974 there were thirteen members who had previously served in the cabinet. At the centre of the 1974 cabinet were six heavyweights (James Callaghan, Roy Jenkins, Barbara Castle, Denis Healey, Anthony Crosland and Tony Benn), with Callaghan in the special position of chancellor of the Exchequer and a particularly close confidant of the prime minister.

The first cabinet of Edward Heath, introduced on 20 June 1970 following a Conservative victory at the polls, reflected almost perfectly the left and right wings of the party: 90 per cent of the shadow ministers went into the cabinet, virtually all of them taking up exactly the post they had been shadowing when in opposition. This situation notwithstanding, Heath's ministerial team has been described as 'one filled with political lightweights' (Rose, 1980: 44). Another key characteristic of the various Heath cabinets relates to the prime minister's peculiar reshuffling practice. Even though Heath did not dismiss a single cabinet minister during his whole incumbency (and there were also no resignations over policy disagreements), he made considerable use of his right to move ministers from one department to another. By 1974, fewer than half of the members of the original cabinet team were still serving in the same post (Kavanagh, 1987: 219).

James Callaghan, taking over from Wilson in March 1976, changed the composition of the cabinet only modestly. The bulk of changes were confined to moving members of the former Wilson cabinet to other offices. The most strongly debated decision related to Callaghan's offering the Foreign Office to Anthony Crosland, as many observers had expected the much more internationally experienced Roy Jenkins to be nominated as foreign secretary. This was mainly because of the rather lukewarm pledge to Europe that Crosland shared with the prime minister, which was in stark contrast to the clearly pro-European beliefs of Jenkins. The most problematic cabinet member Callaghan 'inherited' from his predecessor was Tony Benn who, to an increasing degree, became 'a leader of the opposition in the very Cabinet room' (Whitehead, 1987: 250). While Callaghan, as any prime minister, had to pay due attention to the complex structure of power within his party when composing his cabinet team, he evinced an exceptionally strong inclination to make appointments a matter of friendship and personal trust (Redhead, 1978: 230–1).

When Margaret Thatcher gained the prime ministership in May 1979, an inexperienced prime minister met an experienced cabinet. Thatcher's first cabinet team included few surprise appointments. In fact, she seemed keen on including every strand of the party, in a calculated attempt to deflect intra-party criticism. Nevertheless, key economic positions were filled by candidates deemed to be particularly supportive of the prime minister's neo-liberal policy preferences. It has even been argued that 'there were two parallel Cabinets, one Thatcherite, running the economic ministries, and one Tory running everything else' (Vincent, 1987: 284). There were few spectacular reshuffles in the immediate aftermath of the two re-elections of Thatcher in 1983 and 1987. Rather, Thatcher worked steadily to increase the proportion of ministers she considered fit for office, leaving herself by 1990 the sole survivor of the original cabinet formed in 1979. Many sackings were about fundamental policy disagreements rather than incompetence, which marked a new pattern of personnel policy at cabinet level (King, 2002b: 447). Added to frequent sackings came a string of resignations. The spectacular resignation of Sir Geoffrey Howe in November 1990 (the last in a line of others who had resigned in protest at Thatcher's uncompromising style and policy programme, including Michael Heseltine in 1986 and Nigel Lawson in 1989) worked as a catalyst to the parliamentary party's ousting of Margaret Thatcher later that same month.

Thatcher's successor, John Major, tried to use his first cabinet appointments to heal the wounds within the Conservative Party, and to fight off charges that he was merely a 'mark 2 Mrs Thatcher'. Still, there were very few changes in the immediate aftermath of Thatcher's leaving No. 10. Major's single most remarkable appointment was Heseltine's return to the cabinet, as secretary of the environment, which signalled the prime minister's willingness to consider radical changes, notably on the poll tax. The most extensive reshuffle occurred in the summer of 1995, after Major had stepped down in protest at persistent intra-party criticism. Having been reconfirmed as party leader, he strengthened the left-of-centre faction of the party and appointed Heseltine deputy prime minister.

Tony Blair's first cabinet, formed after Labour's landslide victory in May 1997, was the least experienced new government for over seventy years. John Morris, the attorney general, was the only member of the government who had previously sat in a Labour cabinet, and only four other members of the cabinet had previous junior ministerial experience. Blair's early appointments included representatives from virtually all intra-party factions, though there was no complete transfer of the shadow cabinet to the first Blair cabinet. There were essentially three heavyweights in Blair's original cabinet team: Gordon Brown as chancellor, Robin Cook at the Foreign Office, and John Prescott as deputy prime minister and secretary of state for the environment, transport and the regions. Blair's early inclination to build an 'inclusive' government and seek inter-party compromise manifested itself in the creation of a Joint Cabinet Committee (JCC) in 1997 to include representatives of Labour and the Liberal Democrats.[10] The appointment of Peter Mandelson (in the summer of 1998), his first resignation (in December 1998), his return to the cabinet (in October 1999), and his second resignation (in January 2001) became the most remarkable incidents of Blair's first term.[11]

The single most important change in the aftermath of the 2001 election was the replacement of Robin Cook by Jack Straw at the Foreign Office, a decision Blair justified publicly as his desire to avoid an alleged split between the Foreign Office and the Treasury over the euro. The heavy-handed style of this reshuffle became a symbol of Blair's ruthlessness in dealing with even his closest allies. Later key incidents of Blair's second term included the resignation of several government ministers, including Robin Cook and Clare Short at the cabinet level, over the administration's decision to go to war against Iraq in the spring of 2003. The reshuffle of June 2003 – the fifth in about twelve months – was especially remarkable for its far-reaching constitutional consequences. Blair used the departure of Lord Irvine to announce the abolition of the post of Lord Chancellor and the creation of a new Department for Constitutional Affairs, which aroused a storm of controversy. There were other constitutionally relevant changes, including the downgrading of the posts of secretaries of state for Scotland and Wales, as well as further personnel changes, which by the summer of 2003 made Chancellor Gordon Brown the only cabinet minister remaining in the same post as in 1997.

Before inquiring into how these different cabinets have worked in practice, it is both useful and necessary to glance briefly at the basic patterns of core executive appointments beyond the cabinet. For decades, the two most important administrative powerhouses of the British machinery of government have been the Prime Minister's Office and the Cabinet Office. Both perform functions which have (for the most part) historically been carried out by the Treasury. The Cabinet Office, established during the First World War, became a separate part of the governing machine in 1968. In contrast to the more recently established Cabinet Office, the first historical precedents of the Prime Minister's Office can be traced back to the very early nineteenth century, when in 1806 parliament provided for the first time public funds for a private secretary to aid the prime minister. However, with the notable exception of the Private Office, which had been properly established by the 1920s, all major parts of the contemporary Prime Minister's Office were created only after the Second World War. Under Blair, the Prime Minister's Office initially comprised five different main sections: the Private Office, the Political Office, the Press Office, the Strategic Communications Unit and the Policy Unit. There was, however, a whole series of reforms that changed the face of the organizational core executive. A few months after Blair's second election victory in June 2001, the prime minister's Private Office was merged with the Policy Unit to form the Policy Directorate. The Whitehall post of the prime minister's principal private secretary was abolished and replaced by a policy adviser. The position of chief press secretary was also scrapped and replaced by two prime minister's official spokesmen, while a new position of director of communications and strategy was created, whose key role was to oversee the Strategic Communication Unit, the Downing Street Press Office and the Whitehall Information Strategy.

From an American perspective, as Richard Neustadt (1969) pointed out several decades ago, the most important thing to note is the rather limited power British prime ministers enjoy when it comes to staffing the Cabinet Secretariat and the Prime Minister's Office (the two institutions in the British core executive which come closest to the EOP). While this British/American difference largely persists, the prime minister's room for manoeuvre in the appointment process has been enhanced significantly since the 1970s. Not only has there been a marked increase in the overall number of staff at No. 10, but also a gradual introduction of a larger political element via political appointments. As in many other areas, the Blair premiership marked a sea-change in the evolution of the British civil service.[12]

The story of the prime ministerial advisory system started not long before the premiership of Harold Wilson. Until the early 1960s, constitutionally, prime ministers were expected to receive policy and political advice from their cabinet colleagues or from traditional policy advisers from the civil service (Pryce, 1997: 6–21). When Wilson came to office in 1964 he made efforts to change the traditional advisory system by appointing a number of personal political aides who would deliver the kinds of policy and political advice that the prime minister considered necessary. This led to the creation of the Political Office, an institution that all succeeding incumbents have worked with since. Heath's single most important innovation in the core executive was the creation of the Central Policy Review Staff (CPRS) in 1971, a small, multi-disciplinary unit located in the Cabinet Office. The CPRS was designed initially to serve the cabinet as much as the prime minister, advising on issues of both strategy and policy. Although it has been maintained that the CPRS worked chiefly for the prime minister, rather than the cabinet (Jones, 1987: 40), Wilson considered it necessary on returning to Downing Street in 1974 to set up the Policy Unit, a body designed specifically to provide policy and political advice to the prime minister alone. His successor, Callaghan, was not particularly interested in developing, let alone fundamentally reforming, the organizational core executive, and so there was little change until the late 1970s. Thatcher, who abolished the CPRS in 1983, significantly extended the role of the Policy Unit and personal advisers, thereby advancing the institutionalization of a policy role for the prime minister (Smith, 1999: 173). Nevertheless, the Thatcher years may barely be classified as a period of expansion. The overall number of special advisers in Whitehall was reduced, and after eight years in office Thatcher still employed fewer staff than Labour had in 1979 (Kavanagh and Seldon, 2000: 298).

While there was little 'machinery change' under John Major, Tony Blair became the most determined 'modernizer' of the post-war period, enforcing significant changes both in the area of responsibilities of departments and at the level of administrative support structures. Blair's reforms included the creation of several special units with an explicit focus on cross-cutting issues in the Cabinet Office (such as the Performance and Innovation Unit), the appointment of a chief of staff in the Prime Minister's Office, and a dramatic increase in the overall number of special advisers. It was the latter two factors – the appointment of a chief of staff,[13] and the growing number of special advisers – that marked the most tangible elements in a process many believed would lead to the emergence of a Prime Minister's Department (in all but name).[14] The creation of cross-cutting special units in the Cabinet Office should not be underestimated in its effects on changing the British core executive, though. Whereas previous attempts at establishing 'joined-up government' tended to focus on institutional or procedural devices (Kavanagh and Richards, 2001), the reforms of the Blair government also emphasized meaningful cultural change and aspired to mitigate the obvious strength of departmentalism (Flinders, 2002).

It remained difficult, however, to identify a clear direction of institutional reform in the administrative core executive. During an early stage of the Blair premiership much energy was focused on strengthening the overall role of the Cabinet Office within the machinery of government, making it 'more of a policy-oriented and a proactive co-ordinating body', in fact 'something of a corporate headquarters over-seeing government strategy' (Kavanagh and Seldon, 2000: 309–10). More recent stages of machinery change have been directed towards reducing the role of the Cabinet Office, which was slimmed down significantly in May 2002 with most of its personnel resources being transferred to a newly created Deputy Prime Minister's Department.[15] It was also, for the first time in a decade or so, the situation that the Cabinet Office was not run by a cabinet minister. There were two main sides in the remaining Cabinet Office. Marking an important innovation, a position of 'crisis manager' (filled by Sir David Omand) was created, to co-ordinate security and intelligence, and deal with risks and major emergencies. The other side, being under the direct control of the cabinet secretary, has been in charge for the whole area of reform and delivery. The Performance and Innovation and Forward Strategy Units were merged, while the Delivery Unit, created in June 2001, has been given a wider remit over the main domestic goals.

From early on, the Political Office and the Policy Unit have been the two units providing prime ministers with the largest opportunity to bring in genuinely political personnel. The Political Office is completely staffed by political appointees, and the salaries of those employed there are traditionally paid for by whichever party is in power. The various heads of the Policy Unit since 1974 have been drawn from rather different professional backgrounds. Bernard Donoughue, the first head of the Policy Unit and the only person to serve under two prime ministers (Wilson and Callaghan), was a political scientist and former journalist. Under Thatcher there were no less than four successive heads of the Policy Unit with rather different professional experiences, including an ex-soldier and computer consultant, a journalist, a former merchant banker and a professor of economics. Major worked for five years with Sarah Hogg, a financial journalist, and after her resignation appointed the management consultant Norman Blackwell. Blair faced stunning problems in finding a suitable head for his Policy Unit until David Miliband was eventually appointed. The logic of appointments to the Policy Unit has varied with different prime ministers. Wilson's Policy Unit was very much a group of staff who had all already been involved with Labour in opposition. No party affiliation was required among members of the Policy Unit under Thatcher and Major, who both relied on the political empathy of appointees. Early in his term, Blair focused heavily on recruiting representatives of 'New Labour', though later replacements of his No. 10 team, following a series of organizational reforms, brought in more long-established Labour figures who could not reasonably be described as genuine 'Blairites'.

Core Executive Leadership in Britain

From a constitutional point of view there is no stronger head of government in Western Europe than the British prime minister.[16] His or her constitutional powers within and towards the cabinet – as well as those already mentioned above – include the exclusive right to call and chair cabinet meetings to decide the cabinet's agenda, to 'sum up' the discussion at cabinet meetings and to create, abolish and chair the cabinet committees.[17] This set of well-established constitutional powers of office may provide some useful guidance when it comes to comparing the leadership performance of different office-holders. However, marking a major difference to the situation in the United States and on the Continent of Europe, there is little sense in contrasting constitutional provisions and practice in Britain. The British constitution reflects rather than circumscribes or restricts the actual room for manouevre that individual actors enjoy within the political system. Thus, as Richard Rose (2001: 15) reminded us, accusing 'prime ministers such as Margaret Thatcher and Tony Blair of behaving unconstitutionally is to miss the point; they are not violating explicit rules or conventions but unaware of them'. In fact, the history of core executive leadership in Britain is very much a story about altering old and generating new constitutional rules and conventions without the legal fuss that tends to accompany similar processes in the United States and on the Continent.

The exceptional degree of flexibility that characterizes British constitutional provisions facilitates a strong impact of other factors, including personalities and circumstances, on a given prime minister's performance in office. This is at least what a historical perspective on governing the core executive in Britain would appear to suggest.

Although more recent historical research on the Attlee years has partly challenged, and revised, the popular picture of Labour's first post-war prime minister as a perfectly calm and elegant cabinet manager (Pearce, 1997: 125–7), Clement Attlee's premiership remains very much a revered role model of a prime minister being firmly in command of decision-making in the core executive. His grip on the cabinet and the party was facilitated significantly by the collective memory among his party fellows of the party's 1931 split, which reduced Labour's parliamentary represen-tation at the ensuing general election from 289 to 52 MPs. However, there can be no doubt that much of the administration's favourable performance, especially in terms of core executive decision-making, rested on Attlee's superb managerial talents. Among the key features of prime ministerial leadership of this period was Attlee's remarkable ability to encourage, and generate, compromise, which was above all a reflection of his eminently practical, almost 'apolitical' understanding of politics and leadership. This was to be accompanied by the prime minister's commitment to achieving the highest possible degree of coherence among the administration's policies.

It took some time, however, before the government eventually found its feet. Until 1947, when several senior ministers were moved and a more rational cabinet structure with a stronger concentration on economic power put in place, the government machine was just too ponderous to allow the operation of a truly efficient form of cabinet government. The prime minister was often dragged in to mediate between committees or to make decisions (Dowse, 1978: 52–5). Cabinet meetings under Attlee tended to be short, and many important issues were discussed by the full cabinet only in very general terms. Early on, an 'inner cabinet' was formed, which included Ernest Bevin (the foreign secretary), Sir Stafford Cripps (the chancellor), and Herbert Morrison (the leader of the House of Commons). It was here (and in the committees), rather than in the full cabinet, where the bulk of decisions were made. However, even the inner cabinet did not really represent the inner core of the administration's core executive. Instead, it was the exceptionally close relationship between the prime minister and his foreign secretary – the so-called 'Attlee–Bevin entente' – that became the true driving force behind many of the administration's major initiatives (ibid.: 57). Unlike the first Attlee government, which had not only set new standards of executive management but also enacted a wide range of landmark legislation in domestic policy (including far-reaching nationalization measures), the 1950–1 government was a troubled one which suffered from a whole series of defects. These included serious internal rifts over the economic implications of Britain's military participation in the Korean War, politically motivated resignations of several key figures, poor health among many of its remaining protagonists, and an obvious lack of new political ideas and initiatives.

Churchill's return to No. 10 marked a notable change in core executive leadership. He was a firm believer in traditional cabinet government. Unlike many other post-war prime ministers, Churchill did not rely on an inner circle or an inner cabinet, but rather attempted to restore the position of the cabinet as the major forum for policy discussion and co-ordination. Even cabinet committees, a major decision-making device of Attlee's governing machinery, were considered with great suspicion. Their number was kept to a minimum, as they were seen as elements that possibly undermined the central position of the full cabinet. The weirdest institutional feature of all, however, remained the awkward system of 'overlords'. It was clearly inspired by Churchill's experience as war leader, and there were signs that its reinstatement was more than just an institutional reverence to a once successful part of the governing machine. As Peter Hennessy (2000: 194) has pointed out, 'Churchill, in his own mind at least, believed that to some degree Britain was once more in warlike circumstances, thanks to Korea, the associated fear of more general war and the huge rearmament programme the Conservatives had inherited from Labour.'[18]

The large amount of independence that cabinet ministers under Churchill enjoyed was largely owed to the prime minister's lack of interest in the bulk of policy details. Ministerial discretion was greatest in the various fields of domestic policy. By contrast, foreign affairs remained the area in which the prime minister's interest and actual involvement was particularly pronounced, leaving little room for independent initiatives from ministers or collegial decision-making. The autumn of 1953 marked a sea-change in Churchill's grip on his government. Having suffered a severe stroke in June 1953, he never recovered completely. Cabinet meetings turned more and more into lengthy monologues with few, if any, decisions being arrived at by serious debate. During the administration's last year, several cabinet meetings were chaired by Churchill's heir apparent, Foreign Secretary Anthony Eden, rather than by the prime minister himself. Churchill also developed a growing reluctance to read any documents. His waning physical and political energy had a tangible effect on the administration's policy record. Whereas the first years of the government were marked by several successes, centring on a series of measures designed to consolidate the post-war consensus, there were few, if any, tangible results after 1953. As Roy Jenkins (2001: 846) has argued, '[w]ith the exception of one issue which increasingly dominated [Churchill's] mind, the saving of the world from destruction in a reciprocal holocaust of H-bombs, his struggle to prolong his life in office became more important than any policy issue'.

Under Churchill's successor, Eden, the cabinet never really represented a forum of true discussion among the top members of the government. Much of the business was handled on a one-to-one basis between the prime minister and the involved cabinet minister, or was dealt with in small cabinet committees. The Suez crisis, by far the single most important political issue of the Eden years, was to a significant extent tackled by a 'war cabinet', the so-called 'Egypt Committee' (brought into being by a cabinet decision of 27 July 1956). Being characterized by a flexible membership structure to be chaired by the prime minister, the 'Egypt Committee' made, in fact, most initial decisions on Suez, which were then often only rubber-stamped by the full cabinet (Seymour-Ure, 1984: 191–3). This is not say, however, that the cabinet was bypassed by the 'Egypt Committee'. In fact, the sheer number of people involved at various occasions (amounting to more than 60 per cent of the cabinet team) ensured that the cabinet was well-informed throughout the months of crisis. Although more detailed research into Eden's handling of the Suez problem has concluded that the basic criteria of successful crisis management were largely ignored (Brady, 1997), the core executive decision-making processes in this field probably still belonged to the better aspects of Eden's overall leadership performance.

It seems fair to say that the Eden government was, after all, not only characterized by rather poor co-ordination and insufficient internal communication, but also lacked strong overall leadership from the prime minister. The exceptionally high degree of prime ministerial interference in the work of individual departments, which marked much of Eden's performance in the core executive, may not be accepted at face value to indicate a reasonable amount of leadership capacity. Most ministers complained about Eden's leadership style, which seemed to combine overly tight supervision with a minimum of policy expertise. Eden's political experience (being confined largely to the area of foreign policy) was simply too modest to enable him to set out clear guidelines for the major areas of public policy, let alone to direct more specific policy decisions in various fields. Moreover, Eden had obviously become used to concentrating his attention and energy on a single major issue for a long period of time while serving in the Foreign Office. This led inevitably to major problems after his move to No. 10, as directing and co-ordinating decision-making processes in different areas simultaneously marks an inescapable task for any prime minister (Rothwell, 1992: 165, 188).

Added to major shortcomings in policy competence came the somewhat unfavourable international political circumstances of the mid-1950s, and the very brevity of Eden's term in office. The combination of all these factors was responsible for a perception of the Eden years as a – largely failed – 'single-issue premiership', focusing on Britain's ill-fated involvement in the Suez conflict. However, while the height of the Suez crisis undoubtedly marked the moment of truth for the Eden premiership, observers who described the administration as 'an unhappy ship' with persisting rivalry among senior ministers, budget problems and an unfavourable press long before it finally got into deep international water in 1956 (Kavanagh and Seldon, 2000: 58), can hardly be charged for unfairness or serious misjudgement.

Macmillan brought to office many qualities of leadership that were missing under his predecessor. This paid off both in terms of prime ministerial control of the core executive decision-making process and the overall policy achievements of the Macmillan administration. Macmillan kept his eye on most major areas of public policy, with foreign affairs and economic policy occupying a special place on his agenda. With few exceptions, the cabinet played a major role in determining the broad lines of policy. In contrast to the Eden government, the overall degree of prime ministerial intervention in departmental business remained rather modest: 'He knew what he wanted but he was a believer in delegation and he did not bother his colleagues with detailed supervision' (Blake, 1985: 280). Also, the increasing use of cabinet committees was intended to reduce the burden on the full cabinet, rather than to bypass the latter. Few cabinet committees were chaired by the prime minister, although there were close contacts between the prime minister and the committee chairpersons. Macmillan contributed to the structural development of the cabinet system by establishing a small Ministerial Action Group on Public Expenditure in 1960 (Hennessy, 1986: 63), which pointed early in the direction of Thatcher's more famous 'Star Chamber'.

Whereas Macmillan did not establish an inner group within his cabinet, several senior members of the government (including Edward Heath, Peter Thorneycroft, the Earl of Home and Reginald Maudling) enjoyed a rather close relationship with the prime minister. There were, however, no fixed patterns of contacts between individual ministers and the prime minister. During the second half of Macmillan's incumbency, 'autocratic' tendencies of prime ministerial leadership – symbolized in his sweeping cabinet reshuffle of 1962 – increased. Informal decision-making gained in importance,[19] and the prime minister's temptation to interfere in the work of departments grew, though few commentators are likely to go as far as Peter Hennessy (2000: 256), who described Macmillan as 'a shameless intervener in the business of his ministers'.

Douglas-Home's record of core executive leadership was influenced to a very significant extent by the rather unusual, and unfavourable, conditions under which he had become prime minister. The forces that kept the cabinet together during Douglas-Home's short incumbency remained largely negative in character, centring on the awareness among the Conservatives that if this government failed, the party would be defeated in the next election. The exceptionally limited authority that Douglas-Home enjoyed as party leader was translated directly into his opportunity structure as leader of the cabinet. Many of those who reluctantly joined the cabinet demanded an unusually large amount of freedom in conducting their departmental policies, and were less than willing to take any advice from No. 10. Still, Douglas-Home's rather weak leadership performance cannot be explained convincingly as a mere side effect of his ministers' strength. The notable extent to which responsibility was delegated to individual ministers was at least partly related to the prime minister's – readily conceded – lack of experience in domestic affairs, and economic policy in particular. This was to be combined with a stunning lack of ideas for political initiatives. Therefore, it rather appeared as though his ministers were forced to compensate for his inability to lead.

Rather unsurprisingly, Douglas-Home has been assigned a unique position in comparative assessments of British post-war prime ministers, representing a combination of 'weak leadership' and 'strong collegiality' (James, 1999: 94). A more subtle, yet similar, assessment was formulated by his biographer:

> As Prime Minister Home did things that were expected of him con-scientiously and accurately, though without a feel for the wider imaginative role. He was clear-sighted in Cabinet, but without the philosophical flair that so characterised the Macmillan era...To a great extent, Alec Home was a lonely political figure in Downing Street. There was no inner circle, such as Macmillan enjoyed in the company of John Wyndham; no 'Kitchen Cabinet', in the manner of the incoming Prime Minister, Harold Wilson. (Thorpe, 1996: 320, 376)

When Wilson came to office in late 1964, he dominated his cabinet for the first two or three years like few other incumbents had after 1945. The prime minister's strong role was greatly favoured by both the inexperience of most of his party fellows represented in the cabinet, and the cabinet's unusual size, making it more difficult for individual ministers to close ranks on a given issue. It has remained a moot point whether, or to what degree, there was an inner cabinet during the early Wilson years. Whereas Peter Mackintosh (1978: 206) has maintained that 'Wilson never had an inner Cabinet', most authors agree that there was at least 'a semi-formed inner Cabinet' (Walker, 1987: 197) which – ironically enough – became known as the Parliamentary Committee.[20] In 1968, the Parliamentary Committee comprised the prime minister and nine senior members of the cabinet; the number was later reduced to seven. It met twice weekly to discuss all major issues. In 1969, the Parliamentary Committee was replaced by a new, informal gathering, the so-called Management Committee, which included only Wilson's closest associates within the cabinet. Throughout Wilson's first term, most major issues – among them industrial relations, devaluation of the pound and economic sanctions against Rhodesia – were carefully considered, if only rarely finally decided, by the so-called 'Wilson–Callaghan–Brown triumvirate' (including the prime minister, the chancellor, and the minister for economic affairs).

The creation of a more informal decision-making system under Wilson was accompanied by a reduction of meetings of the full cabinet from twice to once a week (Brazier, 1999: 88–9), a practice that was to be followed by all later prime ministers. In the later years of Wilson's incumbency, bilateral negotiations between the prime minister and individual ministers gained a greater weight, as did decision-making in informal small groups and cabinet committees. While cabinet committees had been used before, it was Wilson, in 1970, who established the convention that matters settled in cabinet committees would be brought before the full cabinet only if explicitly demanded by the committee's chairperson (ibid.: 117–18).

During much of his second term, stretching from March 1974 to April 1976, Wilson appeared to be little short of paralyzed. There was little, if any, sign of political or policy leadership from No. 10. Martin Burch and Ian Holliday (1996: 144) have assessed the degree of intervention by the prime minister during Wilson's second term as 'low' – a grade assigned to only one other incumbent after 1945 (Douglas-Home). Others have judged Wilson's workload and effectiveness as 'less than those of any premier since 1945', to be 'matched only by Churchill from the time of his severe stroke in 1953' (Ballinger and Seldon, 2004: 175). There was a strong element of informality and signs of power-sharing with Callaghan, who had a particularly close working relationship with Wilson in the area of European policy and to many became a sort of de facto deputy, or even 'alternative prime minister'. Wilson's growing detachment from the world of power was symbolized in his decision not to make 10 Downing Street his home when he returned to office in 1974.

What caused Wilson's drastically altered performance after returning to No. 10 in 1974 remains a mystery. There are essentially three possible explanations for this phenomenon, which are not mutually exclusive. Many blamed Wilson's weakness on matters of personal exhaustion, an obvious explanation in an assessment of a leader's second term in office. As Ballinger and Seldon (2004: 175) have pointed out, Wilson's personal state was not confined to exhaustion, but included signs of the early onset of Alzheimer's disease. Yet there were other, additional factors, largely absent during Wilson's first term, that restricted the prime minister's room for manoeuvre. Not only did Labour have an extremely small majority in the House of Commons, but there was also a rather left-wing Labour manifesto (about which Wilson had major reservations) and a 'social contract' with the unions, both of which limited severely the government's potential for bold initiatives in large areas of public policy. Third, as close Wilson watchers of the time have emphasized, he may simply have had a radically different blueprint of leadership for his second term. In Wilson's own words, drawing on the vocabulary of his passion, football, his role would be one of a 'sweeper' in the defence rather than one of a 'striker' in the attack (Donoughue, 1987: 48).

Edward Heath never left a doubt about his determination to go down in history as a 'strong' prime minister. He not only dominated his cabinet throughout his term, but also left a significant mark on the administrative face of the British core executive. Heath's dominant position in the cabinet was certainly eased by the small number of heavyweight ministers in his administration. However, what was probably more important was his impressive expertise in many major fields of public policy. Heath played a very active role in developing major new policy initiatives (such as the application for membership of the EEC, or the imposition of direct rule in Northern Ireland), and also exercised close control over the Treasury (Kavanagh, 1987: 220).

More recent assessments of the Heath premiership, particularly those focusing on the prime minister's leadership style in the core executive, have tended to revise the older notion of an 'autocratic' leader of the cabinet. According to Simon James (1994: 496), 'Heath...was in fact extremely solicitous about ministerial collegiality, and ran the most harmonious Cabinet of recent decades.' Indeed, neither his style of

chairing cabinet meetings nor the frequency of interventions in departmental decision-making appear to be spectacular in comparison with
the record of Margaret Thatcher in particular. Most minor decisions
were taken in cabinet committees, and many major issues were at least
thoroughly considered, if not always finally decided, by an inner cabinet
which included Lord Carrington, Jim Prior, William Whitelaw, Francis
Pym, Peter Walker and Robert Carr. The intensive use of mixed committees
(including ministers and civil servants) by the Heath administration has
led some observers to speak of 'a task-force approach to Cabinet government' (Hennessy, 1986: 79).

Perhaps the most notable feature of Heath's performance as prime
minister was the unusual degree to which he relied on his senior
administrative staff, especially on Sir William Armstrong (who was
referred to openly as 'the deputy prime minister') and Sir Burke Trend,
the head of the Home Civil Service and the cabinet secretary, respectively. While most former members of the Heath government have
dismissed the view that he was overly dependent on policy advice by
senior civil servants,[21] the least that may be said is that there was a
strong mental affinity between the prime minister and some senior
members of the civil service. As Lewis Baston and Anthony Seldon
(1996: 55) have maintained, 'Heath was in some ways not interested in
"politics" at all. He was interested in reaching the right, rational,
decision. Once he had done so, he regarded anyone who did not agree
with him, including Conservative MPs, as obstructive.' It is thus small
wonder that Heath's overall performance in the parliamentary arena
(see Chapter 6) was considerably less impressive than his record in the
core executive.

James Callaghan, taking over from Wilson in March 1976, faced a rare
mix of factors shaping his term in No. 10. In terms of former political
experience, Callaghan was 'the sweatiest of old political sweats' (Hennessy,
1986: 88) – the only candidate to have held all three great offices of
state before succeeding to the prime ministership. This greatly paid off,
not only in terms of political authority that Callaghan enjoyed among
his cabinet fellows. In particular, the relationship between the prime
minister and the key permanent secretaries in the major Whitehall
departments was entirely free of mutual suspicion and ignorance. This
was even more remarkable for an incoming Labour prime minister than
it would have been for a Conservative leader. The most influential
source of advice to the prime minister, during his first two years, was
Kenneth Stowe, the principal private secretary in No. 10.

'Solitary decisions' by the prime minister – such as his decision not to hold a general election in 1978 – marked a rare exception rather than the rule,[22] even though they continue to shape scholarly assessments of the Callaghan years to a considerable extent. Normally, much centred on the close relationship between Callaghan and two colleagues, Anthony Crosland (at the Foreign and Commonwealth Office) and Michael Foot (the leader of the House of Commons), who proved indispensable in keeping the party together. Cabinet meetings were marked by a reasonable degree of collegiality, which did not, however, challenge the prime minister's superior role as the genuine leader of the cabinet. A number of more sensitive issues in the area of economic policy were not brought to the cabinet, but rather dealt with by the so-called 'economic seminar' – a secret body that included Callaghan, Denis Healey (the chancellor of the Exchequer), Harold Lever (the chancellor for the Duchy of Lancaster), as well as a number of officials. As during the last year of the Wilson government, economic policy, especially broad strategic issues, was to a large extent under the active control of the prime minister.

The IMF crisis of 1976 became a case study of Callaghan's capacity for strategic leadership (Dell, 1991: 225–33). It remains a remarkable achievement that Callaghan managed to solve the crisis without any resignations from his cabinet, although personnel continuity had to be paid for by granting individual ministers unusually generous room to voice their starkly differing opinions on the issue. The integration, or more often the effective isolation, of Tony Benn proved a more permanent challenge during the Callaghan years, as it had done during Wilson's second term. Judged by Benn's overall effect on the government's course between 1976 and 1979, Callaghan was reasonably successful in neutralizing his influence (Whitehead, 1987: 249–50).

While it was the March 1979 election defeat that marked the start of Labour's extended period of deprivation of power, the internal demise of the Callaghan government began well ahead of the election. The so-called 'winter of discontent', by far the most bitter public disputes with the unions in the history of post-war Labour governments, almost paralyzed the prime minister and his cabinet. Bernard Donoughue, an insider, has spoken of 'a deathly calm in No. 10, a sort of quiet despair', continuing: '[t]he Prime Minister was for a time worryingly lethargic. He was clearly very tired, both physically and mentally...Ministers were clearly demoralised. Moving among them as they gathered for Cabinet in the hallway outside the Cabinet room, their sense of collective and individual depression was overwhelming' (Donoughue, 1987: 176–7).

Margaret Thatcher was by any standards the most ruthless prime minister in British post-war history. As Anthony King (2002b) has argued in a recent article, Thatcher displayed many aspects of a social and psychological outsider, and eventually chose to adopt the political role of an outsider. This included, in the first place, radical policy preferences that survived her own term as a leader in the much-debated concept of 'Thatcherism', but also manifested itself in a highly specific leadership style to be observed both inside and beyond the core executive territory.

Combining an iron self-discipline and a passion for hard work with the deep conviction that she was by far the most able person in her government to deal with any major political problem, Thatcher must have felt there was little room for a collegial institution such as the cabinet. While at an early stage of her premiership, traditional manifestations of cabinet government were at least maintained in the form of inner cabinets and the use of cabinet committees – although accompanied and increasingly challenged by the additional use of special policy advisers, especially in the area of economic policy[23] – the feeling of a teamspirit among members of the cabinet vanished almost completely in later years. Cabinet meetings gradually turned into events providing the prime minister with opportunities to deliver extended monologues. Cabinet deliberations were functionally substituted by bilateral meetings between the prime minister and individual ministers, or meetings involving a small number of ministers and/or special advisers.

It has often been argued that Thatcher, despite her disregard for institutions and conventions, did not aim to abolish the traditional rules of British cabinet government, but rather worked to ignore and circumvent them. As Anthony King (2002b: 448) has put it, 'she established her own parallel government within the traditional system. She ran, in effect, an outsider's government inside the existing government'. Moreover, the transformation of core executive decision-making during the Thatcher years did not follow a strictly linear course. As late as the mid-1980s, leading scholars of the British executive identified 'a revival of collegiality in the Cabinet Room' (Hennessy, 1986: 122), which was, of course, not bound to last. Also, as Dennis Kavanagh and Anthony Seldon (2000: 165) have pointed out, very early in her incumbency Thatcher seems to have had a notable hostility to special advisers – only to contrast sharply with her later practice of undermining the roles of government ministers by the excessive use of external, unofficial advisers, such as Sir Alan Walters in the key area of economic policy.

Perhaps the most important question about the 'Thatcher phenomenon' at the level of the British core executive relates to the reasons for

Thatcher's exceptional degree of domination of the executive decision-making process. Her largely undisputed personal leadership capacity was certainly supported by an impressive record as an election winner, and a scarcity of internal challengers within her party. But there were also more subtle factors at work. As more recent historical assessments of the Thatcher administration suggest, other structural advantages were magnified by inaccurate assessments of her personality among many of her colleagues. During the first years of her incumbency there were many ministers who seriously underestimated her, believing that her 'conviction' statements were little more than blustering political propaganda. Moreover, it has been argued that Thatcher also made 'calculated use of femininity with men, most of whom came from single-sex public-school backgrounds which equipped them poorly to deal on equal terms with a determined, professional woman' (Evans, 1997: 42–3).

Margaret Thatcher's legacy in British politics was clearly not confined to the changes at the level of the 'politics of leadership'. Whereas scholars have remained divided over the question whether the administration's policies were sufficiently coherent to allow the subsuming of different measures under the label 'Thatcherism', Britain under Thatcher's rule undoubtedly experienced a very considerable amount of policy change – from economic policy via trade union and law and order policies, to central–local government relations – the greater part of which clearly reflected the prime minister's personal policy preferences (Savage and Robins, 1990).

John Major, succeeding Thatcher in the office of prime minister after so many years of uninterrupted Tory rule, was clearly among those prime ministers of the twentieth century facing particularly unfavourable conditions for effective leadership. This was not just because of a combination of negative trends in the economic sphere (including rising interest rates and inflation, and decreasing consumer confidence) and worrying structural developments at an international level; there were genuine political problems on the domestic front as well. Part of these related to the internal condition of the Conservative Party, which appeared to be split more deeply than ever. Across the country, the policies of the Thatcher government, in particular the infamous 'poll tax', had alienated much of the party's popular support.

Major reintroduced a system of core executive leadership that centred on the principle of reaching consensus through extended discussion in cabinet, though as he emphasized in his memoirs, he much preferred to let his views be known in private and see potential dissenters ahead of a meeting (Major, 1999: 209). There was no inner cabinet working behind the scenes. Instead, so-called 'political cabinets' (gatherings of cabinet members, influential party figures and advisers to the prime minister) soon emerged as a key structure in the administration's decision-making system. They were popular among ministers and produced a considerable amount of integration (Hennessy, 2000: 445). There was, however, also a moderate degree of continuity from Thatcher to Major. Early in his premiership, Major chaired exactly the same seven cabinet committees as Thatcher had done, and while there was a very different atmosphere in the cabinet room, meetings did not last longer than they had under Thatcher (Kavanagh and Seldon, 2000: 223–4). Moreover, despite the upgraded role of the cabinet, the Policy Unit in the Prime Minister's Office retained an important position during Major's incumbency, being responsible for many of the government's key policy initatives, including the Citizen's Charter and the 'Back to Basics' campaign.

Early scholarly assessments of Major's leadership style tended to be rather positive (Seldon, 1994), and this corresponded closely with the wider public perception of the prime minister and his cabinet. During his first years in No. 10, Major benefited from being different from Thatcher – if not so much in his policies, certainly in his leadership style. This early impression seemed to be confirmed by the Conservatives' fourth consecutive election victory in the spring of 1992. But 1992 also marked a turning point. Britain's forced suspension of its membership of the European Exchange Rate Mechanism (ERM) in September of the same year damaged the government's public standing in a serious, and permanent, way. From that time onwards, 'Major's "niceness" came to be seen as a weakness, and his preference for consultation to be seen as dithering' (McAnulla, 1999: 193).

More recent accounts of the Major premiership have been dominated by more negative assessments. Among the most obvious negative aspects of Major's 'collectivist' leadership style was its immensely time-consuming character. Often, decisions were delayed until differences had been settled. The non-existence of an inner cabinet facilitated the emergence of a large amount of conflicting advice, which weakened the prime minister's position in the core executive. Moreover, to many observers, the remarkable cohesiveness of Major's (early) cabinet could hardly be attributed to his specific leadership qualities, but were basically generated by the difficult circumstances in which he took over the prime-ministership after Thatcher's sudden fall from power. In the second half of the 1990s, when Major came more and more under pressure from his own party, the strategy of 'collectivist' leadership finally collapsed. There were hardly any ministers in the post-1995 reshuffle cabinet who felt a reasonable amount of loyalty to the prime minister (Brady, 1999: 222–3).

In many ways, Tony Blair looked on Major as a negative role model for his own premiership, relating to different positions in a wide range of fields, over both politics and policy. In an early assessment, Blair's leadership strategies and tactics were described as 'directive', marked by a determined use of the Prime Minister's Office and the Cabinet Office to develop strategic direction (Smith, 1999: 88, 93). This seemed, however, to include a rather modest amount of prime ministerial intervention and oversight. In fact, senior allies of the prime minister were reported to be seriously worried that Blair did not know what was going on in individual departments, and had too little, rather than too much, control over initiatives being planned (*The Times*, 16 March 1998). Assessments such as these, by journalists and those involved more closely, continued well into Blair's second term, with much criticism centring on the absence of adequate institutional devices of leadership and delegation.

The role of the full cabinet has been rather limited from the very beginning of the Blair premiership, and it appeared to be a matter of time when the cabinet was going to lose even its residual role as a court of appeal or clearing house for issues not having been settled elsewhere in the system. Civil servants described cabinet meetings under Blair as 'perfunctory, lasting between 30 and 40 minutes', with the prime minister often not sticking to the agenda, or sometimes even being absent (*The Sunday Times*, 31 January 1999; *The Times*, 9 November 1999). Significantly more efforts were being directed to developing a bilateral system of dealing with ministers. During the first twenty-five months of his premiership, Blair held no fewer than 783 meetings with individual ministers, compared with just 272 such sessions held under Major over a similar period of time (Kavanagh and Seldon, 2000: 279).

The role of the cabinet committees within the executive decision-making process has also remained open to debate. Whereas the committees were clearly more active than the full cabinet, most commentators have maintained that neither the full cabinet nor the committees were the real centres of decision-making. According to one observer, what really mattered were the regular stock takes by the prime minister and his domestic ministers, held every six to eight weeks. This system was based on the obligation of individual departments to set targets and expected trajectories towards them that were monitored closely by the Delivery Unit and the Treasury. Problems at this stage were to be tackled at four different levels of central intervention. At the first stage, an adjustment would have to be made by the relevant department. Second, there would be a joint 'problem-solving exercise' including the department and the Delivery Unit. Third, 'a major-problem solving exercise involving commitment of Prime Ministerial Time', and finally, 'a high-intensity drive' led by the prime minister (Riddell, 2002).

As in previous administrations, however, cabinet government under Blair has remained very much a dynamic concept. Early in 2004 it emerged, through a series of statements by the cabinet secretary, Sir Andrew Turnbull, before the Public Administration Committee of the Commons, that discussion in cabinet appeared in fact to have expanded rather than declined since late 2002. Cabinet proceedings included regular reports and discussions regarding different areas of policy or major forthcoming announcements by individual departments. As Sir Andrew, who attended cabinet meetings as principal private secretary to the prime minister during the Thatcher years, also emphasized, there was more discussion under Blair than during the final stages of the Thatcher premiership (*The Times*, 5 March 2004). Blair's surprising U-turn, in mid-April 2004, concerning a possible referendum on a European constitution, marked another occasion that nourished perceptions of a prime minister who was too weak not to give in to the mounting pressure of forces in the cabinet. His later apology over not having discussed the issue properly in cabinet before announcing it, indicated, however, that the driving force behind Blair's decision was powerful individual ministers, such as Gordon Brown, Jack Straw and John Prescott, rather than the full cabinet (*The Times*, 21 and 29 April 2004).

The exceptionally large number of special advisers, and their unprecedented influence at the very heart of the governing machine marked another, indeed for many *the* hallmark of the Blair administration. The prominent role of special advisers was by no means confined to the work of the major sections of No. 10, though many of the most powerful ones have been attached to Downing Street. Early in Blair's administration, a highly sophisticated system of policy advisers, covering all major departments, was put in place, with its members holding regular meetings on Friday mornings to plot the next moves of the government. By 2001, the overall number of special advisers had grown to eighty, with twenty-nine alone working at No. 10 (*The Times*, 28 April 2001). Even though talk about setting a legal limit on the maximum number of spin-doctors, which was to be included in a Civil Service Act, was prominent from mid-2000, neither the government nor the cabinet secretary appeared to be in a rush to impose a cap on special advisers. Long before the end of Blair's second term, the unusually high turnover rate among special advisers and members of the civil service team in the core executive became an issue in its own right. By mid-2004, Jonathan Powell, the chief of staff in the Prime Minister's Office, represented one of the very few survivors of the original Blair team that had worked together since 1994.

The extremely close and complex relationship between the prime minister and his chancellor, Gordon Brown, undoubtedly marked another key feature of the Blair premiership. From the start, it has been much more than just another part of Blair's sophisticated bilateral system of core executive decision-making. Daily meetings between the prime minister and the chancellor, covering all issues facing the government, were at the very heart of the core executive decision-making process. However, the Blair–Brown connection became more difficult with almost every year they were in office. By 2001 at the very latest, tensions had infected the whole governing machine as there were few, if any, 'intermediaries' left in the government team. There were several factors governing the special relationship between No. 10 and the Treasury, which was complicated and conflict-prone at the best of times. To begin with, there were notable ideological differences between Blair's version of New Labourism and Brown's more social democratic approach to most policies. These were complemented by different stances on key issues – such as taking Britain into the euro – not to be discussed reasonably in terms of 'new' or 'old' Labour, which, however, were no less fundamental in character. There were, furthermore, the ambitions of two men who had both aspired to the office of prime minister when Labour was still in opposition. Even after this conflict had been decided with Blair's nomination as Labour leader in mid-1994 and Labour's election victory in May 1997, a serious conflict persisted about who should in fact be leading the government, especially in the key areas of domestic policy. This conflict was aggravated by the open question of if and when Brown would be allowed to succeed Blair in the office of prime minister. By late 2002, the conflict between the prime minister and the chancellor had reached a level that led some observers to compare the Blair–Brown row to the deep rift between Margaret Thatcher and Nigel Lawson in 1989 (Hutton, 2002). While by mid-2004 the Blair–Brown relationship appeared to have become more settled – with Brown having gained considerable ground, especially in terms of influence within the PLP, but also with regard to important policy decisions, such as Britain's (non-)joining the euro – it seemed clearly to be built on a feeling of mutual dependence, rather than friendship and trust.

The international challenges since 11 September 2001 that transformed the Bush presidency also had significant repercussions on the premiership of Tony Blair. Immediate responses included the creation of a war cabinet, which held its first formal meeting on 9 October 2001. Its full membership comprised, alongside the prime minister, the deputy prime minister (John Prescott), the foreign secretary (Jack Straw), the chancellor (Gordon Brown), the defence secretary (Geoff Hoon), the home secretary (David Blunkett), the leader of the Commons (Robin Cook), the international development secretary (Clare Short), and the chief of the defence staff (Admiral Sir Michael Boyce). Other officials attending included Blair's foreign affairs adviser (Sir David Manning), his chief of staff (Jonathan Powell), his then communications director (Alastair Campbell) as well as the attorney general, Lord Goldsmith (*The Times*, 9 October 2001). The size of the war cabinet, being considerably larger than, for example, Thatcher's Falklands committee, invited the suspicion that key decisions were to be made by the prime minister and a small inner group of advisers. According to an assessment by Peter Riddell (2001), the core decision-making group, led by the prime minister, included just three or so cabinet ministers and some key players from Downing Street, such as Sir David Manning (an American-style national security adviser serving as the key link to the White House), Sir Stephen Wall (European adviser), and Jeremy Heywood (Blair's principal private secretary).

Considerably more important than the immediate, and temporary, institutional repercussions of the challenges in the post-9/11 international arena has been their obvious impact on the behavioural dimension of prime ministerial leadership. At first it seemed as if the changing circumstances were to bring out the very different character of Blair's leadership approaches in the areas of domestic and foreign policy. Blair's commitment to a tough line in the war against terror, and later his unwavering determination to go to war against Iraq, contrasted sharply with his cautious, conflict-avoiding and often indecisive leadership to be observed in the bulk of domestic policy areas. However, it soon became clear that Blair's unexpected rebirth as a 'conviction leader', sticking to his guns in the teeth of fierce public opposition, was not confined to the area of foreign policy. The long-raging battle over the introduction of variable 'top-up fees' at British universities, and the creation of 'foundation hospitals' as a major piece of NHS reform became the most important examples of Blair's new leadership style on the home front. These threatened to break his premiership as much as the aftershocks of Britain's involvment in the war against Iraq.[24]

Conclusion

The development of the British core executive since the end of the Second World War has been immensely complex. Each administration represents a micro-cosmos of its own, which makes it difficult to formulate any generalizing conclusions that would do justice to the performance of individual administrations, and individual prime ministers in particular. This having been said, there are some notable similarities between some prime ministers and their administrations. For example, Thatcher and Blair certainly stand out among British post-war prime ministers in terms of 'ruthlessness'; some would even describe both as 'conviction leaders'. As to their inclination to act as 'cabinet managers', Attlee and Heath could be grouped together, whereas the premierships of Douglas-Home and Wilson in his second term were marked by an almost eerie absence of prime ministerial leadership. Callaghan and Heath shared a particularly impressive policy expertise, whereas Blair's early move to allow the Liberal Democrats to participate in the intra-governmental decision-making process was (if only remotely and superficially) reminiscent of Churchill's attempts at building an inclusive post-war 'national government'.

Ultimately, however, comparisons such as these seem only to underscore the limits of meaningful comparisons between two different prime ministers – especially if the party affiliations of incumbents are considered as major guide lines. In fact, as the previous observations clearly indicate, most pairs of prime ministers sharing key features of leadership style include incumbents from different parties.[25] Even the more sensible distinction put forward by Richard Rose (2001: 3–6) between 'old-school' and 'new-style' prime ministers would appear to be more valuable in the field of public leadership (dealt with in Chapter 6), than for studying leadership styles in the core executive. Still, Rose's approach points to some basic structural developments that have come to characterize the British core executive in the post-war period.

Looking for the two most important structural developments within the British post-war executive, the first to be noted is the changing role of the cabinet. Generally, the role of the full cabinet as a true decision-making body has declined since the end of the Second World War, although it took some time after 1945 before this trend became fully manifest, and there have been temporary revivals of collegial government under individual prime ministers, such as Churchill or Major. The frequency of regular cabinet meetings was reduced from twice to once a week in the late 1960s (Brazier, 1999: 88), and the length of meetings has declined virtually constantly ever since. The Attlee administration may be considered to represent a crucial turning point in the history of the British cabinet system, as it marked the beginning of a development towards an ever more sophisticated system of cabinet committees. From the late 1940s onwards, the bulk of items of business would go initially to committee rather than to cabinet. Since the mid-1970s, issues tackled by a cabinet committee have only been referred to the full cabinet with the committee chair's explicit approval. Treasury ministers have been in a special position, as they were granted an unconditional right of appeal, not subject to the chairman's permission, under Callaghan – a privilege to be confirmed by successive prime ministers.

As the role of the cabinet committees increased, the cabinet became a more reactive body serving mainly as a 'court of appeal' approving or, less often, rejecting decisions taken in committee. By the mid-1980s, the extensive use of cabinet committees had also left their mark on the constitutional conventions governing the core executive. Ever since then, committees have been seen to constitute not only de facto but also legitimate bodies to take governmental decisions. As Simon James (1999: 84) has pointed out with regard to the late Thatcher era, this widely-shared perception had the bizarre effect that when a committee considered major issues affecting many departments, sometimes up to four-fifths of all cabinet members would attend. The cabinet's role as a decision-making body has declined even further under Blair. In contrast to most earlier administrations, Blair's strong reliance on 'task forces', 'stock takes', special advisers and bilateral relations with individual ministers has not only weakened the full cabinet but also the committees – though arguably not to the extent it seemed early in his premiership.

The second major structural development characterizing the post-war history of the British core executive has been the marked tendency towards centralizing decision-making in the Prime Minister's Office and the Cabinet Office. On the whole, British prime ministers are now much better equipped to oversee the whole government machinery than they were some decades ago, even though the Treasury has remained an immensely powerful, and partly independent, actor in the British core executive arena. Moreover, the growing fragmentation of the cabinet system may also be seen as having strengthened rather than weakened the strategic position of the prime minister, who forms the centre of a tightly woven web of interrelationships.

There has been a lengthy scholarly debate about how these changes should properly be interpreted. Most of the relevant arguments were exchanged within the framework of the prime ministerial versus cabinet government debate that was brought up in the early 1960s.[26] The advocates of the prime ministerial government thesis, suggesting a steady increase of prime ministerial power at the expense of the cabinet, seemed to win a sweeping victory during Thatcher's incumbency. But as the Thatcher era came to an end, and the leadership style of her successor began to dominate perceptions of the British premiership, the prime-ministerial thesis suddenly appeared as a bloodless academic construct, far from being able to capture the real state of executive leadership in Britain. Although Tony Blair sidelined the cabinet to an even greater extent than Thatcher had done, there was no simple revival of the 'prime ministerial government' paradigm. There are two different possible explanations for this phenomenon. Firstly, many observers were heavily influenced by Michael Foley's important work on 'the rise of the British presidency' (Foley, 1993). In fact, in many interim assessments of the Blair premiership, observers preferred to speak of 'presidentialism' rather than prime ministerial government. Second, a new generation of scholars drawing on the governance paradigm and the network approach, has come to dominate the debate over the changing features of the British core executive. From this perspective, the analytical differentiation between 'prime ministerial government' and 'cabinet government' is not seen as a useful one at all, as neither the cabinet nor the prime minister are considered to be able to provide effective leadership in an ever more fragmented political system (Smith, 1998: 68). As the protagonists of both schools would admit, though, a full assessment of prime ministerial power may not be made without paying due attention to the prime minister's role in the parliamentary arena and the wider political process, which is at the centre of Chapter 6.

4

Germany: Chancellor Dominance and Coalition Rule

The Political Profile of German Post-war Chancellors

From a British perspective, the conditions necessary to become German chancellor may appear to be exceptionally rigid and inflexible. However, while there is in fact a strong element of formality in the official nomination process leading up to the appointment of a candidate by the federal president, both the wider selection process of candidates and the constitutional qualifications of the office are more rather than less flexible than in Britain. Article 63 of the Basic Law stipulates that a candidate must secure an absolute majority in the first ballot before being appointed by the federal president,[1] but to be eligible, candidates are neither required constitutionally to hold a seat in the Bundestag nor to be the formal leader of the strongest party in parliament. Unlike in most other West European systems, neither the chairs of the parties nor those of the parliamentary party groups (*Fraktionen*) in the Bundestag represent natural candidates for the office of chancellor. Both leadership positions are to be distinguished from the position of 'chancellor candidate', for which each party specifically nominates a candidate in the run-up to a Bundestag election. Until 1993, when the SPD introduced a set of formal rules for electing its chancellor candidate, neither of the two major parties had established any specific nomination procedure, and even the Social Democrats did not follow the formal procedure when nominating Gerhard Schröder as the party's chancellor candidate in 1998.[2]

In stark contrast to the Weimar Republic, which experienced no fewer than fourteen chancellors in as many years, the overall number of chancellors in the Federal Republic has been remarkably small: there have been only seven chancellors in more than fifty years. All post-war chancellors belonged either to the CDU (Konrad Adenauer, Ludwig Erhard, Kurt Georg Kiesinger, Helmut Kohl) or the SPD (Willy Brandt, Helmut Schmidt, Gerhard Schröder). However, because of the virtually permanent existence of a coalition government, not all chancellors were drawn from the strongest party in parliament. In 1969, Kiesinger lost the chancellorship, even though the Christian Democrats remained the strongest party in the Bundestag, as Brandt managed to forge a new governing coalition between the SPD and FDP, which together controlled an absolute majority of seats. Also, in 1976 and 1980 the chancellor – Brandt's successor Helmut Schmidt – was drawn from the second largest party in the Bundestag.

The party experience of German chancellors has been significantly more expansive than that of American presidents but less impressive than that of British prime ministers. While eligible candidates for the German chancellorship do not have to be the chairman of their respective parties,[3] most of them in fact combined the two positions of party chair and chancellor. Helmut Schmidt stands out as the only incumbent who was never the chairman of his party. While all other German chancellors were, at least for parts of their respective incumbencies, the chairmen of their parties, only Brandt and Kohl held the party chair well before gaining the chancellorship. Erhard, Kiesinger and Schröder all became party chairman only between six months and two-and-a-half years after winning the chancellorship.[4] The early Schröder chancellorship provides the only example of a split between the positions of chancellor and party chair (Oskar Lafontaine) with the latter having a seat in the cabinet. Early in 2004, Schröder set another precedent by becoming the first post-war chancellor ever to renounce the chair of his party while in office.

As a somewhat closer look reveals, all incumbents had a considerable body of political experience in different areas. Adenauer had held diverse political positions at the regional level during the Empire and served as mayor of Cologne throughout the Weimar Republic. He was also one of the Federal Republic's founding fathers and the first party chairman of the CDU at federal level. His successor, Erhard, became famous as the 'father of the German economic miracle', serving as minister of economics under Adenauer for fourteen years before eventually securing the chancellorship. Unlike Adenauer and Erhard, Kiesinger had former experience as a member of the Bundestag but had not been a federal minister before being appointed chancellor. He re-entered the federal stage in 1966 from the post of minister-president of Baden-Württemberg. When Brandt became chancellor in 1969 he had the combined experience of a former member of the Bundestag, mayor of Berlin and foreign minister under Chancellor Kiesinger. Moreover, he was also SPD party chairman before assuming the office of chancellor – a position he retained for more than a decade after leaving the chancellery. Schmidt had by far the most impressive parliamentary career before advancing to the chancellorship. Not only had he spent seventeen years in the Bundestag, but he had also been the chairman of the Social Democratic parliamentary party group between 1966 and 1969. He had, furthermore, considerable experience as a government minister at both state and federal levels. Kohl started his professional political career in the state of Rhineland-Palatinate where he held the position of minister-president between 1969 and 1976. Although he had rather modest experience as a member of the Bundestag before becoming chancellor (six years),[5] he has been the only incumbent to gain the chancellorship from the position of parliamentary opposition leader in the Bundestag.[6] His successor, Gerhard Schröder, who spent six years in the Bundestag between 1980 and 1986, gave up his position as minister-president of Lower Saxony to become chancellor in 1998.

In a three-country sample focusing on the average parliamentary experience of the chief executive at the national level, Germany (8.6 years) takes the middle position ahead of the United States (7.4 years) but well behind Britain (23 years).[7] One obvious reason for this must be seen in the interruption of the history of parliamentary government in Germany, which favoured structurally a modest pre-war parliamentary experience of the early holders of the post-war chancellorship. History is not the only variable to be considered, though. The rather moderate parliamentary experience of German chancellors also, and in particular, reflects the specific conditions of political recruitment in a federal system, which widens the opportunity structure for professional politicians to a significant extent. No less than four out of seven chancellors served as minister-presidents in one of the German states (*Länder*) before gaining the chancellorship, and each of them held on to this position for more than five years. The central role of the state level as a recruitment pool for German chancellors is also helpful in explaining the rather modest proportion of incumbents with former cabinet experience at the federal level. What marks a rare exception to the rule in Britain – with Tony Blair being the only post-war prime minister with no previous cabinet experience at all – constitutes a rather common characteristic of German chancellors. Indeed, only three incumbents had former experience as cabinet minister at the federal level (Erhard, Brandt and Schmidt).

The strong representation of former minister-presidents among German chancellors is reminiscent of the important role that former governors have played in the recent history of staffing the office of the US president. It is, however, important to note that the relationship between the state governments and the national legislative arena is much closer in Germany than it is in the United States. The prominent role of the minister-presidents at the federal level, and their extremely strong representation among the parties' official chancellor candidates,[8] is facilitated by the privilege of members of the Bundesrat (who are invariably members of the state governments) to speak in the Bundestag whenever they wish (Article 43 (2) of the Basic Law).

No less diverse than the role of the regional factor at the level of political recruitment is the role of vice-presidents, 'vice-chancellors', and 'deputy prime ministers' in the three countries concerned. Whereas there is a position of 'deputy' or 'vice-chancellor' in Germany – the Basic Law avoids the latter term – it shares more with the office of the British 'deputy prime minister' than with the office of the American vice-president. Neither the position of German 'vice-chancellor' nor that of British 'deputy prime minister' produce 'heirs apparent' to the incumbents in the chancellery and 10 Downing Street, which constitutes, however, a key characteristic of the vice-presidency in the American system. The reasons for this are even more obvious in Germany than in Britain. In Germany, the position of 'vice-chancellor' is not held by the 'crown prince' within the chancellor's party but usually offered to the party chairman or most senior cabinet member of the junior governing party. Ludwig Erhard represents the only candidate to advance to the chancellorship directly from the position of 'vice-chancellor' (and minister of economics) under Adenauer, though it was clearly the party's explicit decision to nominate Erhard as Adenauer's successor rather than the position of 'vice-chancellor' that secured Erhard the chancellorship. Willy Brandt, serving as a Social Democratic deputy of a Christian Democratic chancellor, marks the only other example of a German chancellor having been 'vice-chancellor' in a previous administration.

Another key feature of the political profiles of German chancellors is their considerable length of term in office. With an average of 7.8 years, the average score is significantly higher than for Britain (4.9 years) but also higher than for the United States with its fixed terms for the chief executive (5.9 years).[9] Even more impressive is the political longevity of some chancellors, including Helmut Kohl (16.1 years) and Konrad

Adenauer (14.1 years) in particular. While there is still a notable inclination among German political scientists to explain government stability with constitutional provisions, it is clearly the parties (or more specifically the structure of the party system) rather than the stabilizing effects of the 'constructive' vote of no-confidence[10] that are chiefly responsible for the high average terms in the office of chancellor and the even higher amount of government stability (in terms of party complexion of the government).[11] However, the overall stability of the German post-war party system, which has always centred on the two major parties CDU/CSU and SPD, alone cannot explain the extremely long average terms of some German chancellors. Whereas it undeniably created a favourable playground, neither Adenauer nor Kohl would have been able to stay in power for more than a decade had it not been for the unwavering support of their party, favourable circumstances, good health and a fair share of luck. The relevance of these important intervening variables is underscored by a direct German/British comparison: between 1951 and 1964 – a period being slightly shorter than Adenauer's hold on the German chancellorship (1949–63) – the Conservative Party 'used up' no less than four different prime ministers.

A comparative perspective is also helpful when it comes to spotting the peculiarities of how German chancellors came to and fell from power. Whereas in the United States and Britain the large majority of chief executives have been elected into office, there were only two clear-cut cases of German chancellors gaining office for the first time as a direct result of an electoral victory. These relate to Adenauer (1949) and Schröder (1998). Brandt's case was ambigious, as the SPD in fact failed to become the strongest party in the 1969 Bundestag election. There was also no clear-cut coalition statement of the later governing parties, SPD and FDP, in favour of a Social–Liberal coalition government during the run-up to the election.

In each of the three countries, there has been a significant proportion of successors filling suddenly emerging vacancies in the office of president, prime minister or chancellor. What makes Germany a special case in this regard is the fact that even major changes of government – that is, significant alterations in the party composition of the government including a change in the office of chancellor – occurred between two elections (such as in 1966 and 1982).

What, finally, is remarkable about German chancellors is the large proportion of cases of politically forced resignations without the direct involvement of the electorate. Adenauer and Erhard had to go after losing the support of the CDU/CSU parliamentary party; Kiesinger became a victim of the FDP's altered coalition preferences; and Schmidt was ousted by a parliamentary vote of no-confidence. By contrast, both more or less voluntary resignations (Brandt) and resignations following electoral defeat (Kohl) remained an exception. The change of government in 1998 in fact marked the first occasion in the Federal Republic's history that the voters succeeded in producing a 'wholesale alternation' (Mair, 2002: 94) of the parties in government.

Staffing the Cabinet and the Chancellery

From a historical perspective, the constitutional provisions regarding the chancellor's authority to organize his government have been judged as the single most important step towards strengthening the position of the head of government under the Basic Law (Niclauss, 1999: 31). The constitution grants the chancellor the unconditional right to choose his ministers and decide upon the number, distribution and area of responsibility of government departments. While constitutional lawyers have identified a number of legal limits of the chancellor's organizational power, most formal restrictions (such as the Bundestag's prerogative to decide upon the budget) have not played a major role in constitutional practice. The key restrictions of a chancellor's room for manoeuvre have all been of a genuinely political character. In contrast to Britain and the United States, cabinet formation in Germany takes place after a lengthy bargaining process among potential coalition partners. It was in 1961 that the results of these negotiations were for the first time fixed in a written contract. Whereas no single contract-like documents were needed between 1966 and 1976, any coalition since 1980 has produced a formal coalition contract covering both personnel matters and the key areas of public policy (Saalfeld, 2000: 51–60).

Generally speaking, coalition government in Germany has tended to give unproportional power to the smaller coalition parties, even though the office of chancellor has firmly remained in the hands of the two major parties. The whole exercise of negotiating the key aspects of the future government's programme and drawing up a coalition contract before the government is formally inaugurated, clearly strengthens the junior coalition partner's rather than the chancellor's party.

Several more specific indicators of this trend can be identified. The first looks at the sheer period of time during which the smaller parties have been in office: in 2004, the party with the most extensive record as a governing party at the federal level since 1949 was neither the CDU/CSU nor the SPD, but the FDP. Second, the smaller parties have tended to gain a larger share of seats on the cabinet than would have been justified in strictly statistical terms.[12] On this dimension, the smaller parties were particularly successful between 1949 and 1957, between 1983 and 1984, and between 1991 and 1994.[13] Third, the smaller parties have often managed to secure some of the most prestigious and important cabinet portfolios: for example, since 1969, the Foreign Office has always been in the hands of the smaller coalition partner. Also, the important Ministry of Justice has more often been headed by a minister from the junior coalition partner than by a member of the chancellor's party. Finally, it is important to note that, virtually from the start, the junior coalition parties have secured the right to decide on their personnel on the cabinet more or less autonomously, and even the chancellor's constitutional right to dismiss any minister at his discretion has rarely been used against ministers representing the junior coalition party.

A closer look at the historical dynamics of cabinet-building in Germany confirms that there are few, if any, fixed patterns. Even the formation of the very first German post-war government in 1949 was special, for a number of reasons. Highlighted in Adenauer's memoirs as one of the biggest successes in his whole political career, the creation of a CDU-led 'bourgeois' coalition set the course for more than fifteen crucial years in German post-war history. A core feature of Adenauer's first cabinet related to the rather modest number of politically strong personalities. There were in particular virtually no ministers with former cabinet experience gathered during the Weimar Republic (with Minister of Finance Fritz Schäffer, who had held a cabinet office at state level, marking the only exception). Moreover, those enjoying a high public reputation, such as Ludwig Erhard, lacked any independent political power base within their party. After the 1953 Bundestag election, Adenauer enjoyed much more favourable conditions of coalition-building than in 1949. The number of parties in the Bundestag was reduced from eleven to six, and with winning 244 out of 487 seats the Christian Democrats secured a wafer-thin absolute majority which made any coalition against the CDU/CSU impossible. The inclusion of a fourth party, the GB/BHE, alongside the CDU/CSU, FDP and DP – which Adenauer was keen on with a view to securing a reasonable amount of parliamentary support for his foreign policy – proved the most difficult aspect of the 1953 coalition-building process.

From the perspective of coalition theory, Adenauer's third cabinet to be formed in the aftermath of the 1957 Bundestag election was certainly the most interesting one. Even though the Christian Democrats commanded a rather comfortable absolute majority in the Bundestag, the new government included the small DP. Adenauer's decision to do so may be explained primarily with the requirement of a two-thirds majority for passing constitutional amendments, and the large proportion of bills during the first legislative periods falling into this category. Moreover, the Christian Democrats' coalition strategy towards the DP, which also pervaded the electoral arena, was designed to strengthen the CDU's electoral support in regions with low proportions of Catholic voters. Finally, the coalition also helped Adenauer in checking the critics within his own party (Saalfeld, 2000: 45). However, if the birth of this government was exceptional, so was its dissolution: after about half the legislative period, the CDU/CSU–DP government was quietly transformed into a Christian Democratic single-party government, as the ministers from the DP joined the CDU.

The aftermath of the 1961 Bundestag election witnessed major changes at cabinet level, part of which can be explained by the transformation of a single-party government into a CDU/CSU–FDP coalition government. Among the more noteworthy changes was the appointment of Franz Josef Strauss as minister of defence, and the appointment of the first female federal minister in German post-war history, Elisabeth Schwarzhaupt. Another widely noticed appointment was that of former CDU/CSU *Fraktion* chairman, Heinrich Krone, as minister without portfolio, as it seemed to place Krone in the position of a chief contender for Adenauer's succession in the office of chancellor. Adenauer's 1961 cabinet proved to be one of the least stable cabinets in the Federal Republic's history. Following the '*Spiegel* affair'[14] in November 1962, about half of the ministers appointed in 1961 resigned (most of whom, however, returned to the cabinet shortly afterwards).

The change in the chancellery from Adenauer to Erhard had remarkably few immediate repercussions on the composition of the cabinet. While there had been ambitious plans to use the change in the office of chancellor to bring about a reduction in the number of cabinet departments, structural changes remained limited, as did personnel changes. The large amount of continuity, which Erhard tolerated rather than pursued actively, was justified publicly by considerations among the CDU/CSU not to squander any political energy for major changes to the governing machine with the next federal election being less than two years away. Among the most notable features of Erhard's first cabinet was the exclusion of some influential personalities from both the CDU and the CSU, such as Rainer Barzel and Franz Josef Strauss in particular, who had been prominent members of the last Adenauer cabinet.

Erhard's second cabinet, formed in the aftermath of the 1965 Bundestag election, emerged from a lengthy intra-coalition bargaining process. Most observers found that Erhard's position within the new cabinet was weaker than before. Of the five heavyweights among CDU/CSU ministers, only two (Gerhard Schröder and Hermann Höcherl) shared Erhard's main policy positions. A major cabinet reshuffle, demanded by many in the party as the government slid into a lethal crisis in 1966, was not undertaken. Four weeks before Erhard left the chancellery on 30 November 1966, the four FDP ministers in the cabinet resigned, leaving Erhard as the head of a CDU/CSU single-party minority government.

No other post-war chancellor has been faced with a similar amount of pressure to distribute cabinet portfolios as neatly as possible among the two coalition partners as was Kurt Georg Kiesinger, head of a CDU/CSU–SPD government. Leaving aside the position of chancellor, which remained in the hands of the Christian Democrats, the CDU/CSU held ten portfolios, just one more than the Social Democrats. The Kiesinger cabinet was a gathering of the most senior heavyweights from both parties, with Rainer Barzel and Helmut Schmidt, who served as the *Fraktion* chairmen of their respective parties, marking the only exceptions. Remarkably, the rather unusual coalition formula did not lead to a further increase in the number of cabinet portfolios. In fact, at nineteen, their number was even slightly lower than under the previous government.

Brandt managed to cut down the cabinet's size from nineteen to fourteen members. The FDP gained three seats, including the Foreign Office and the Ministry of the Interior. Most SPD ministers who had already served under Kiesinger kept their seats. The most important 'newcomer' in the cabinet was Helmut Schmidt who, albeit rather reluctantly, accepted the offer to serve as minister of defence. Also Alex Möller, who became minister of finance, had to be persuaded in lengthy talks with Brandt and Wehner to join the cabinet. There were some mid-term developments worth mentioning, most importantly the resignations of Möller in May 1971, leading to the creation of a 'super ministry' of finance and economics headed by Karl Schiller, and of Schiller himself in July 1972. After Schiller's resignation, the 'super ministry' was headed by Schmidt until the end of Brandt's first term.

The cabinet-building process following the 1972 Bundestag election, which provided the SPD for the first time with a lead in votes and seats over the Christian Democrats, foreshadowed Brandt's waning authority during the last two years of his chancellorship. The chancellor's weak position in the cabinet-building process may be attributed chiefly to Brandt's poor health at this time. Many key aspects, including the number of portfolios and the distribution of these among the parties, were negotiated between Schmidt and Wehner from the SPD, and Scheel and Genscher from the FDP, and only later authorized by the chancellor. Securing no fewer than five cabinet positions (two more than between 1969 and 1972), the FDP clearly emerged as the winner of the coalition bargaining process.

When Schmidt succeeded Brandt in the office of chancellor in May 1974, he introduced a number of major changes at cabinet level. The cabinet seats held up to that point by some leading Social Democratic intellectuals (such as Horst Ehmke or Klaus von Dohnanyi), were given to representatives from the centre of the party to which Schmidt himself felt closest. There were also some changes with regard to the Liberal ministers, most of which, however, concerned just the allocation of cabinet portfolios among the former. On balance, Schmidt's cabinet appointments underlined his determination to avoid spectacular per-formances of competing stars at the cabinet table (Jäger, 1987: 10–11). This overarching aim also governed Schmidt's appointment policy after the 1976 Bundestag election, which reduced the majority of the Social–Liberal coalition. The cabinet-building process in the aftermath of the 1980 Bundestag election was by far the least exciting of Schmidt's chancellorship: there were no changes at all among the four FDP ministers, and only a minor one among the Social Democratic cabinet personnel.

Kohl's first cabinet (1982–3) included twelve ministers from the CDU/CSU, three of whom had experience under previous Christian Democratic chancellors, and four FDP ministers. There was a remarkable amount of continuity among the latter, as three of the four portfolios secured by the Liberals were given to those individuals who had held the post in the last Schmidt cabinet. There were few changes at cabinet level after Kohl's first Bundestag election victory in 1983. The largest amount of public attention in 1983 focused on the much-debated question of taking the then CSU party chief Franz Josef Strauss into the cabinet. All speculations of this kind were, however, ended by Strauss's decision to stay on as minister-president of Bavaria. The most important changes within Kohl's third cabinet (1987–90) – including the appointment of Wolfgang Schäuble as minister of the interior, Theodor Waigel as minister of finance, and the rather ill-fated choices of Rupert Scholz as minister of defence and Ursula Lehr as minister for youth, family, women and health (neither of whom held a seat in the

Bundestag) – occurred in the middle of the legislative term. Kohl's fourth cabinet, the first one to be formed after German unification, included nineteen ministers, three of whom came from the territory of the former GDR. Again, with the resignations of Wolfgang Schäuble as minister of the interior in late 1991 and Hans-Dietrich Genscher as foreign minister in May 1992 – by far the most important changes occurred in the middle of the legislative term. The changes at the start of Kohl's last cabinet (1994–8) were influenced heavily by the FDP's rather weak performance in the 1994 Bundestag election, whose share of the total vote fell from 11 per cent in 1990 to below 7 per cent in 1994. In consequence, the representation of the Liberals at the cabinet table was reduced from five to three, and for a time it even seemed possible that the FDP might lose the 'vice chancellorship'.

The first Schröder government, formed in late 1998, was exceptional in several ways. To begin with, there was an unusually large proportion of ministers holding no seat in the Bundestag (five out of fourteen). When Oskar Lafontaine and Franz Müntefering left the cabinet in 1999, they were replaced by two recently defeated SPD minister-presidents (Hans Eichel and Reinhard Klimmt), neither of whom had a seat in the Bundestag. There were several other reshuffles, which reduced the number of ministers from outside the Bundestag from five to three. The large number of female cabinet ministers (increasing from four in 1998 to five towards the end of Schröder's first term) and ex-minister-presidents in the cabinet, as well as the appointment of a non-party technocrat as minister of economics, were other key characteristics of the 1998–2002 Schröder government.

After his re-election in the autumn of 2002, Schröder reduced the overall number of cabinet departments by one, to thirteen, which made the newly formed cabinet the smallest since 1949. This reduction was brought about by abolishing the Ministry of Labour, whose responsibilities were distributed between the significantly upgraded and enlarged Ministry of Economics (now Ministry of Economics and Labour) and the Ministry of Health (now Ministry of Health and Social Security). The creation of a Ministry of Economics and Labour marked a real innovation in the history of German post-war governments, though the idea was clearly adopted from the Christian Democratic reform programme put forward during the 2002 election campaign. Despite the improved electoral result of the Greens and the considerable losses of the Social Democrats, there were no changes with regard to the distribution of cabinet portfolios between the two coalition partners (as the fourteenth cabinet minister in the first Schröder government, resigning after the

2002 election, had been a non-party minister). The new cabinet was widely perceived as a 'Red–Green all-star team', and a manifestation of Schröder's remarkable self-confidence (*Süddeutsche Zeitung*, 17 October 2002). Each of the four newly appointed cabinet members belonged to the SPD. While at least three of them could be described as Social Democratic party heavyweights (Wolfgang Clement, Manfred Stolpe and Renate Schmidt), none of them held a seat in the Bundestag, whereas two of them had former experience as minister-presidents. Even the proportion of female cabinet ministers further increased, to slightly more than 46 per cent (six out of thirteen).

The 'second layer' of political appointments in the German core executive includes the various positions to be filled in the Federal Chancellor's Office (*Bundeskanzleramt*), which, although with certain qualifications, may be considered the equivalent to the White House Office and the British Prime Minister's Office. The Federal Chancellor's Office, which is not mentioned specifically in the Basic Law, was established in 1949. Historical roots of the contemporary chancellery may be traced back well into the nineteenth century (Schöne, 1968).[15] The Chancellor's Office is headed by a chief of office who may either be appointed as a civil servant or as a federal minister with special responsibilities. Its functions within the core executive include the provision of information and inter-ministerial co-ordination as well as the formulation and supervision of selective areas of government policy. Although the chancellor's staff also help to improve the efficiency of the cabinet, the Office is not a cabinet secretariat. There is in fact no such institution in the German core executive.

The general developmental tendency of the Chancellor's Office has been towards growth and functional specialization. Before 1958, the Office had just a single division, and it remained of modest organizational shape throughout the Adenauer years. There was also a rather limited amount of organizational innovation under Adenauer's two Christian Democratic successors, though with hindsight the creation of a small policy planning bureau and review unit (made up of three civil servants, three external academics and two other staff members) marked an important change. It was, however, the first term of Willy Brandt's chancellorship that became the 'birth moment' of the modern Chancellor's Office (Müller-Rommel, 1994: 119). Within just one year the overall number of staff working in the chancellery more than tripled. The number of main divisions rose to five, including a generously staffed planning division (of about thirty-five people). However, the Brandt experience has not set the course for the functional development of the Chancellor's

Office.[16] Whereas there was a major policy planning directorate in the chancellery during Gerhard Schröder's first term, which displayed all the usual characteristics of a policy unit, it was abolished shortly after the Red–Green coalition's re-election in September 2002.

In the middle of Schröder's second term, the Office was organized into six main divisions: the first, usually referred to as the 'central division', was responsible for the Office's overall organization (including personnel and the budget) as well as for the areas of interior and judicial policy. Most other divisions focused on different policy fields: foreign affairs and security, and global questions (division 2); social policy, education and research policy, environmental policy, traffic, agriculture and consumer protection (division 3); economic, finance and labour market policy (division 4); and European policy (division 5). Division 6, finally, was concerned with the supervision of the Federal Intelligence Service (*Bundesnachrichtendienst*).

Under Schröder, the overall number of staff in the chancellery rose to about 500. However, the proportion of genuinely political appointments remained very small, including just a dozen or so senior figures. Most of them belonged to the group of 'political civil servants', career civil servants who can be retired temporarily for political reasons: the head of office, the heads of the main divisions, and the state secretaries.[17] The small number of parliamentary state secretaries – a position created in 1967 designed to establish an equivalent to British ministers of state – marked the only other positions in the Office to be filled at the chancellor's discretion.

There has been a considerable variation in appointment policies since the early days of the Chancellor's Office. Under Adenauer, appointments to senior positions in the chancellery were still expected to adhere to a complex system including various criteria, such as a reasonable religious balance and a regional proportion (Müller-Rommel, 1997: 10). There were few noteworthy changes in terms of appointment policy under Chancellor Erhard. At the top, Erhard relied heavily on some figures he had previously worked with in the Ministry of Economics. By the start of the Kiesinger chancellorship the focus on regional and confessional balance in recruiting senior staff in the chancellery had lost much of its former clout. Instead, more emphasis was placed on recruiting staff with professional experience in the field of public administration.

Under Brandt, many SPD party members were brought in as civil servants and placed in key positions within the Chancellor's Office (Berry, 1989: 342). The strongly partisan approach of the Federal Republic's first Social Democratic chancellor contrasted sharply with the practice under his successor, Helmut Schmidt. Of the 'Big Three' in Schmidt's chancellery (famously referred to as the 'clover leaf' – *Kleeblatt*) – chief of the Office Manfred Schüler, governmental spokesman Klaus Bölling, and minister of state Hans-Jürgen Wischnewski – only the latter was a member of the SPD. Helmut Kohl revived the strongly party-driven recruitment pattern, which was combined with a notable emphasis on including close personal confidants of the chancellor.

Following the example of Chancellor Erhard, Gerhard Schröder assigned some of the most senior positions in the Chancellor's Office to individuals with whom he had already worked during his term as minister-president of Lower Saxony. Since 1999, both the positions of chief of the Office and that of chief of the chancellor's bureau have been held by long-term members of Schröder's 'Hanover clan'. Under Schröder, there have been for the first time three parliamentary state secretaries in the Federal Chancellor's Office, including a 'representative of the federal government for cultural affairs and the media' (*Beauftragter der Bundesregierung für Angelegenheiten der Kultur und der Medien*). More spectacular than the actions of the latter was the decision-making process leading to the creation of the post. To the dismay of many MPs, Schröder insisted on selecting another personality from outside the Bundestag, even though the position was formally classified as 'parliamentary state secretary'. It soon became clear that Schröder's appointment of Michael Naumann to that post early in 1999 had set an important precedent, as both of Naumann's two successors (Julian Nida-Rümelin and Christa Weiss) were also recruited from outside the Bundestag.

Core Executive Leadership in Germany

In contrast to both the situation in the United States, where the constitution is silent about the cabinet and most other crucial parts of the modern presidency, and Britain, where the whole executive branch has remained an area governed by constitutional conventions, there are quite a few constitutional provisions in the Basic Law relating to the core executive.[18] There is a broad consensus that the 'chancellor principle', as anchored in Article 65 (1) of the Basic Law, constitutes the dominant constitutional provision in the core executive territory (Stern, 1980: 299; Böckenförde, 1998: 147–73). However, more recently, even the bulk of constitutional lawyers, hardly renowned for pragmatic thinking, have come to acknowledge that the dynamics within the core executive are, in fact, determined by political factors rather than the Basic Law.

Konrad Adenauer has held a unique position among German post-war chancellors that can only be compared with the role of Charles de Gaulle in the politics and government of the French Fifth Republic. Adenauer's central role in recent German history is owed to a specific combination of historical, political and other factors. These included the foundation of a completely new political order built on the ashes of the imploded and defeated Nazi regime, his unusually long stay in office, a series of spectacular successes, particularly in the area of foreign policy, as well as the mostly unimpressive historical predecessors of Adenauer in the inter-war period. The latter aspect may also explain why most historical assessments of the Adenauer chancellorship have centred on a comparison between Adenauer and Bismarck rather than between Adenauer and the Weimar chancellors, while most major works focusing on the post-war period have readily accepted Adenauer's leadership record as the natural yardstick of comparison.

Adenauer's dominance of the executive branch is legendary. Some observers considered the position of cabinet ministers under Adenauer to have more in common with the role of the state secretaries under Bismarck than with that of cabinet ministers in other contemporary parliamentary democracies (Allemann, 1956: 350). Among those having a more extended stay in the cabinet, Ludwig Erhard, Fritz Schäffer, Franz Josef Strauss, and Gerhard Schröder came closest to enjoying a reasonable amount of independence, although even they remained far from being serious potential challengers or 'veto players'. Somewhat ironically, Adenauer's position was stabilized considerably by his advanced age, which virtually from the outset fuelled speculations about a potential successor and produced a remarkable amount of 'obedience' among those aspiring to the chancellorship. Far more important was, however, his virtually unchallenged position within his own party (Dedring, 1989: 191–4).

Despite the much-debated 'autocratic' facets of Adenauer's leadership style,[19] the cabinet and individual cabinet ministers did not lack political influence. Ministers enjoyed a considerable leeway within their own port-folios, as long as activities did not challenge publicly the government's overall policy, or endanger its position in the parliamentary arena and with the public at large. Whereas there was no such thing as an 'inner cabinet' (Schwarz, 1989: 19), Adenauer established several informal bodies designed to facilitate core executive decision-making. Members included selected ministers and senior staff from the chancellery as well as external policy advisers, such as Robert Pferdmenges and Hermann Josef Abs, who enjoyed a close personal relationship with the chancellor.

Three different levels of informal co-ordination may be distinguished: regularly held 'coalition talks' (*Koalitionsgespräche*), including the chancellor, individual cabinet ministers and members of the majority parliamentary parties; regular meetings of the 'coalition committee' (*Koalitionsausschuss*) at the level of the parliamentary party groups; and the occasional attendance of members of the majority parliamentary party groups at cabinet meetings. Until the late 1950s, the closest circle around Adenauer included only representatives from the CDU/CSU and a handful of personal confidants. Later, reflecting Adenauer's considerably weakened position after the 1961 Bundestag election, the FDP was co-opted into the core of the executive decision-making system (Küpper, 1985; Rudzio, 1991).

The considerable variety of informal bodies in place did not, however, limit the central role of the Chancellor's Office within the early post-war governing machine. Throughout the Adenauer years, the Office remained what Kenneth Dyson (1974: 365) has called an 'instrument of personal power'. In using the chancellery as a powerful resource within the governing process, Adenauer relied heavily on his (third) chief of the Office, Hans Globke (1953–63), who provided the chancellor with important strategic information gathered through a net of former staff members of the chancellery who had moved on to senior positions in the departments. Globke even attended most 'bilateral meetings' between Adenauer and individual ministers or other guests in the chancellery. Such was the extent of Globke's influence in the Adenauer administration that observers did not hesitate to speak of an 'Adenauer/Globke era' (Hennis, 1974: 222).

Adenauer's overall impact as policy leader was certainly strongest in the area of foreign policy, especially during the very early days of the Federal Republic, when there was not even a Foreign Office (Baring, 1969a). Even the change in the office of minister of foreign affairs from Adenauer to Brentano in 1955 did not abolish the well-established pattern of 'chancellor rule' in foreign policy. It was only the appointment of Gerhard Schröder as the Federal Republic's third foreign minister in late 1961 that came to mark the end of Adenauer's superior position in foreign affairs. The chancellor's personal involvement in domestic policy was patchier, but there was still virtually no major area of domestic policy that remained completely beyond Adenauer's focus of attention. The pensions reform of 1957 arguably marked Adenauer's greatest personal policy success in the domestic arena (Hockerts, 1980: 320–425).

Whereas the first change in the office of chancellor from Adenauer to Erhard did not alter the party composition of the government and entailed few immediate changes at cabinet level, it marked a major watershed in terms of political style. If Adenauer was the prototype of a 'power politician', it has been doubted whether Erhard could reasonably be classified as a genuine politician at all (Hildebrand, 1984: 233–4). Erhard seemed to be bored with much of what political leadership in a parliamentary democracy is all about. Broad theoretical conceptions of political and social reform fascinated him more than the usual wheeling and dealing over ideas and programmes in the competitive arena. Only rarely was the excessively pursued abstract analysis of issues followed by any kind of political initiative. Erhard's strong reservations about 'party government' led him to proclaim a 'people's chancellorship' (*Volkskanzlertum*) – a vision which from the beginning appeared rather ill-fated and unconvincing, as it obviously did not fit well with his staunch commitment to a Christian–Liberal coalition.

Cabinet meetings under Erhard were marked by an unprecedented amount of collegiality, with departmental ministers being positively encouraged to present their views on a given issue. The more relaxed atmosphere in the cabinet room reflected, to some extent, the significantly improved intra-coalition climate between the CDU/CSU and the FDP. Meetings also lasted slightly longer than under Adenauer. Such favourable judgements of Erhard's cabinet and coalition management, dominating the perception of many observers of the time, have been been challenged fundamentally in more recent works on the Erhard chancellorship. As Volker Hentschel (1996: 534) has argued, the fact that cabinet meetings under Erhard lasted longer than under Adenauer indicated a serious lack of leadership and a poor working discipline, rather than a generally improved working atmosphere within the core executive. Moreover, Erhard's inclination to allow room for debate in the cabinet has been considered to be largely determined by his extremely limited knowledge of the bulk of more sophisticated policy issues.

Whereas the cabinet's overall role within the executive decision-making process increased, the informal decision-making bodies established under Adenauer, such as the 'coalition talks' in particular, were not abolished altogether. Erhard's key vision, a rather utopian model of a corporatist society free from egoistic and particularistic interests called *Formierte Gesellschaft* (disciplined society), emerged neither from deliberations with individual ministers nor from 'coalition talks'. It was the brainchild of a group of advisers (the so-called *Sonderkreis*) which held weekly meetings from October 1964 onwards (Laitenberger, 1986: 193–4).

Although Erhard struggled to establish an efficient governing machine in the chancellery, like the one that had served his predecessor so well, he did not really succeed. A new division within the Office was created, designed to provide longer-term planning and to serve as a liaison unit developing contacts with external research institutes and individual scientists. As under Adenauer, Erhard's chief of the Office, Ludger Westrick, was also Erhard's closest adviser. What appeared to be problematic with this construction, however, was Erhard's role in the chancellery rather than Westrick's. The most senior members of staff enjoyed virtually unlimited access to the chancellor, whereas all important business was dealt with by Westrick.

In stark contrast to Adenauer, Erhard's key policy ambitions clearly related to the area of domestic policy. Part of his disappointing record of achievements may be explained by the fact that he was a 'domestic chancellor' doomed to face major challenges in the international arena. Erhard's performance during the Middle East crisis in early 1965 was perceived widely to be an example of 'leadership failure', yet there were many other similar incidents in the area of domestic policy (Hildebrand, 1984: 128). Erhard's notably distant relationship with his party has rightly been highlighted as perhaps the single most important structural weakness of his leadership approach. It has even been suggested that the relationship between Erhard and the CDU was to be described more properly as a 'non-relationship' (Dedring, 1989: 264). The lengthy intra-party battle between 'Gaullists' (favouring an intensification of German–French relations) and 'Atlanticists' (who, including Erhard, continued to consider the United States as the Federal Republic's single most important ally) had its most visible and damaging effect on Erhard's room for manoeuvre in the international arena, though it created negative spillover effects in domestic politics. In the end, 'the father of the German economic miracle' stumbled over a comparatively minor economic crisis. It may well be argued, though, that Erhard's inability to get a grip on the 1966 recession was just another manifestation of his more general problem of providing vigorous leadership, which was mainly a result of his personality and a chronic lack of support from his party.

The Kiesinger chancellorship introduced yet another style of core executive leadership. Doomed to chair a grand coalition cabinet brimming with political heavyweights from both major parties, Kiesinger had to come to terms with an unusually restricted space for manoeuvre. In the public memory of the late 1960s, perceptions of Kiesinger as a 'walking mediation committee' still prevail over less populist judgements of his leadership qualities that mark the bulk of more recent works on the nature of executive leadership between 1966 and 1969. To what extent the Adenauer experience continued to shape the normative standards of executive leadership in the Federal Republic can be seen from the blunt assessments of Kiesinger's performance by observers usually known for their balanced historical judgements. In a paper published towards the end of the Kiesinger chancellorship, Arnulf Baring asked provocatively, 'Is there Kiesinger?', and suggested 'the disappearance of the chancellor in German constitutional practice' (Baring, 1969b: 21–2).

It was the cabinet rather than any informal gathering of influential party figures that functioned as the true decision-making centre for the new administration's first six months or so. The large number of heavy-weight ministers, the increased number of cabinet committees, and not least the near balance of strength of both parties at the cabinet table added up to a set of structural conditions that favoured the emergence of a cabinet-centred decision-making system (Rudzio, 1991: 130). The chancellor's role within the cabinet remained largely confined to that of a moderator. Whereas the area of economic and finance policy was dominated by the respective departmental ministers Karl Schiller and Franz Josef Strauss, the major initiatives in the area of foreign policy were launched by the then foreign minister, Willy Brandt. If it is correct that foreign policy was Kiesinger's 'secret passion', as has widely been suggested, Brandt's prominent role in this field must have worried Kiesinger even more than the exposed position of the minister of economics, Schiller, who soon became the chancellor's chief competitor in terms of public popularity. The recurrent irritations marking the relationship between Kiesinger and Brandt, especially from 1968 onwards, however also reflected the considerable programmatic differences between the CDU/CSU and the SPD, which were (even) more substantial in foreign policy than in most areas of domestic policy. Despite the multitude of divergent views on many issues, the overall atmosphere in the cabinet remained rather collegial, with few formal votes being taken (Hildebrand, 1984: 295).

Nevertheless, as early as mid-1967 – after the bulk of urgent legislative measures outlined in the coalition treaty had been passed by parliament – the cabinet effectively ceased to be the real decision-making centre of the Kiesinger administration. Regular meetings were arranged, to include the party chairs, the general-secretaries and the chairs of the CDU/CSU and SPD parliamentary party groups. Other members of the cabinet and policy specialists from the parliamentary parties were invited to participate in the meetings on an *ad hoc* basis. This so-called 'Kressbronn circle' (*Kressbronner Kreis*), named after Kiesinger's summer retreat near Lake Constance where the first meetings were held, initially met once a week on Tuesdays, with intervals between meetings becoming greater later in the government's term (Knorr, 1975: 223–9).[20]

During the final year of the Kiesinger government the influence of the two *Fraktion* chairmen of the CDU and SPD, Rainer Barzel and Helmut Schmidt, increased to an extent that made them appear to be the key actors keeping the grand coalition project running (Schneider, 1999: 18). Kiesinger's rather weak position within his own party was even more noticeable in the 'Kressbronn circle' than it was in the cabinet. If his cabinet leadership relied on the effects of publicly rebuking ministers who had violated the 'cabinet discipline', this approach could not produce equivalent results in a purely informal decision-making arena. Whereas the grand coalition scored extremely low in terms of 'chancellor government', its policy achievements were all the more remarkable. In fact, no other German post-war government passed a similarly large number of constitutional amendments as did the Kiesinger government, including several genuinely ground-breaking bills (Schmoeckel and Kaiser, 1991).

Assuming office in late 1969, Willy Brandt soon acquired a public standing based on a combination of respect for his specific policy achievements in the area of East–West relations, and much deeper dimensions of personal charisma. At least for much of his first term, Brandt managed to transform his exceptional public popularity into a high degree of political authority. As Brandt's first cabinet included most of the top rank of political leaders from both coalition parties, there seemed to be little need to establish an additional informal decision-making network alongside the cabinet. In contrast to the second Brandt administration, there were no regularly held 'coalition talks' sidelining the cabinet in the core executive decision-making process. Still, the full cabinet remained far from being the true decision-making centre. A considerable proportion of major governmental bills emerged from cabinet committees[21] and inter-ministerial committees that were merely formally approved by the full cabinet. The total number of cabinet committees in operation during the mid-1970s has been estimated at sixty to seventy. Many of them were established by an act of self-organization at the level of senior staff in the individual departments; others were initiated directly by members of the cabinet (Brauswetter, 1976: 110, 152, 186–7).

During the first half of Brandt's tenure, the Chancellor's Office played a central role as a co-ordinating force within the core executive. At the same time, Brandt evinced a remarkable inclination to avoid tough decisions in the cabinet. Issues belonging to the area of domestic policy, and economic policy in particular, were rarely debated and decided in the cabinet, which reflected Brandt's rather limited interests in this area. None of the major domestic policy issues were decided by the chancellor. When there were more complex issues of economic policy on the cabinet's agenda, Brandt would even leave the chair to his minister of economics. By contrast, crucial decisions in foreign policy were clearly made by the chancellor and his close confidant, Egon Bahr, state secretary in the chancellery, rather than by the full cabinet or Foreign Minister Walter Scheel.

Although many components of Brandt's leadership style were present for the whole of his incumbency, there were also marked differences between his first and second terms. In both political and policy leadership, Brandt scored significantly lower during his last two years in office. The cabinet lost much of the clout it had enjoyed up to the Bundestag election of 1972; cabinet meetings became much less effective, and 'coalition talks', which included the leading figures from both governing parties, were installed, to be summoned once a week. Brandt's position in the core executive was further weakened by major changes of personnel in the Chancellor's Office. While the style of Brandt's first chief of the Office, Horst Ehmke, had been criticized severely by many for his hyperactivity, it had at least had the effect of forcing Brandt to face issues and make decisions. The new team in the chancellery, by contrast, seemed to enhance Brandt's growing remoteness and indecisiveness, rather than to compensate for the increasing number of 'leadership gaps'.

Brandt's overall record as policy leader remained rather mixed. His personal achievements in the area of East–West relations soon came to be regarded as an equal counterpart to Adenauer's policy of *Westintegration*. In domestic policy, Brandt's record remained much less impressive – for all his ambitious declarations at the beginning of his first term and his retrospective reassurances that he spent the bulk of his time in the chancellery on issues of domestic policy (Jäger, 1986: 127). Even if the latter statement was wrong, no decent assessment could be made without taking into account the crucial role of various 'veto players'. In fact, the Brand administration became the first German post-war government to experience the tremendous power of the Federal Constitutional Court and the Bundesrat, who were both less than enthusiastic about the ambitious reform programme of the Social–Liberal government (Schmidt, 1978: 217–21).

Brandt's replacement by Schmidt in May 1974 was as significant in terms of political personality and style as that from Adenauer to Erhard (even though the direction of change was reversed). If Brandt was a political 'visionary', Schmidt had more in common with an effective manager considering 'politics', especially lengthy conflicts with his own party, as something to put up with rather than to be enjoyed. This is at least what his style of government looked like to most outsiders, although Schmidt himself is reported to have felt hurt by his dominant public image as a 'man of action' or 'crisis manager' (Ellwein, 1989: 129). Perhaps a characterization as 'action-intellectual' (Stephan, 1988: 184) does more justice to Schmidt's political personality and his performance as political leader.

Schmidt could draw on a broader body of experience as a federal minister than any other holder of the German chancellorship after 1945. Together with an iron discipline and a notable inclination not to appoint potential rivals to high political office, Schmidt's impressive policy expertise provided the basis for his firm grip on the cabinet. Whereas the chancellor probably felt most at home in economic policy, he also considered foreign affairs to be very much his own domain. It is even possible to identify a close relationship between Schmidt's activities at the international level and in domestic policy. As Karlheinz Niclauss (1988: 177, 217) has argued, Schmidt's prominent role in the international arena had a similar function to that during the incumbencies of Adenauer and Brandt: like his two predecessors, Schmidt exploited the admirable reputation he acquired in the field of foreign (economic) policy to strengthen his position in the domestic arena.

Given his rather weak position within his own party, Schmidt had a strong interest in making the Chancellor's Office a key resource for policy analysis and political advice. While, compared to the Brandt years, the hierarchical-bureaucratic element in the chancellery was strengthened significantly, there was still a notable *esprit de corps* among Schmidt's staff, and a fairly extensive involvement of senior staff in virtually all major aspects of core executive management. Regular meetings on a daily basis between the top-level administrative and political officers in the chancellery, the so-called *Lage*, were established early on. At the height of the domestic crisis triggered by a string of major terrorist attacks in the second half of the 1970s, other organizational innovations were created, such as the *großer politischer Beratungskreis*, including party and *Fraktion* chairmen as well as the minister-presidents and interior ministers of the states. In addition, a centre of crisis management, the *Lagezentrum*, was established. Until the late 1970s, the *Kleeblatt* remained at the centre of decision-making in the chancellery, though former members of the body have dismissed its wide-spread perception as a policy think tank, describing its main role rather as a body designed to sort out options to increase administrative efficiency (Merz, 2001: 73). In 1979, the *Kleeblatt* model was abandoned. Later attempts to revive it failed, and towards the end of Schmidt's term the Chancellor's Office largely ceased to function as a powerful institutional resource for the chancellor to draw upon.

For at least the first five years of Schmidt's chancellorship, there were no informal decision-making bodies within the core executive. When they eventually emerged in 1979 they signalled Schmidt's gradual loss of authority, which was a combined result of waning support from his party, the growing dissatisfaction of the German public with the general state of public affairs, and Schmidt's deteriorating state of health.

From 1974 until 1979 virtually all major decisions were made either by the cabinet or within the SPD parliamentary party (Jäger, 1987: 11), although the chancellery represented a key player in its own right, which significantly strengthened Schmidt's position in the core executive. The logic behind Schmidt's style of organizing the core executive decision-making process was fundamentally different from that of his predecessor. Whereas Brandt brought most issues to the cabinet as it gathered together most of the political heavyweights of the two coalition parties, Schmidt concentrated most business in the cabinet exactly because he considered its weakness in terms of political seniority to be a major structural advantage from his own point of view. Nevertheless, the cabinet remained a collegial decision-making institution. As former ministers have revealed, there were even some occasions on which the cabinet voted formally on an issue. Moreover, as Hans-Dietrich Genscher, foreign minister under both Schmidt and Kohl, has maintained, Schmidt generally granted ministers from the junior coalition partner more independence and discretion than did Chancellor Kohl (Merz, 2001: 68, 71).

When a more informal decision-making structure emerged in 1979, it was centred on a body whose members included the chancellor and selected cabinet ministers alongside members of the parliamentary party groups and party leadership circles of both coalition partners. The key actors involved were largely identical with the group of party figures who negotiated the coalition agreement in 1980. The central position of this body in the core decision-making process was underscored by the regularity with which it was summoned just before meetings of the cabinet. Its character as a party-dominated body was reflected by the fact that SPD chairman Brandt enjoyed a much stronger position in it than did Chancellor Schmidt (Rudzio, 1991: 132–3).

Schmidt's term as chancellor ended on 1 October 1982, when the Christian Democrats joined forces with the FDP to topple him by a vote of no-confidence in the Bundestag. The underlying cause of the government's demise was the bitter split between the Social Democrats and the FDP over the government's economic policy programme. The decision of the FDP ministers to leave the cabinet on 17 September 1982 also reflected the growing fears among the Liberals of losing their status as Germany's natural governing party if they continued to participate in what had become a highly unpopular government. The party's rather unfavourable performance at various state elections in the very early 1980s clearly signalled the challenges, and dangers, that lay ahead (Helms, 1994: 238).

An assessment of Schmidt's record of policy achievements has to acknowledge the difficult circumstances of his chancellorship, especially in terms of the overall state of the economy. Schmidt had to concentrate much of his political energy on the domestic front to defend the financial basis of the sweeping reforms launched during the Brandt years. Most of the administration's programmes for domestic policy are best described as consolidation measures. It is not surprising, then, that Schmidt's most notable successes were in the international arena, more specifically in the field of international economic policy. His single most spectacular achievement became the creation of the European Monetary System (EMS) in 1978.

With slightly more than sixteen years in office, Kohl's tenure in the chancellery was not only the most extended in German post-war history; there was also a remarkable variation in the public perception of Kohl's performance as political leader reaching beyond the usual ups and downs that tend to characterize any single incumbency (Smith, 1994: 185–8). Interestingly enough, there was remarkably little change in terms of Kohl's leadership style in the core executive. In fact, much of what came to characterize Kohl's core executive leadership style as chancellor was already present during his term as minister-president of Rhineland-Palatinate between 1969 and 1976. This is true especially for the exceptionally high degree to which Kohl relied on close personal relationships and effective party management as key resources of leadership and control (Clemens, 1994). Both factors contributed significantly to what may be described as a gradual 'de-formalization' of core executive decision-making. On the other hand, it is true that Kohl went out of his way to formalize the initially informal decision-making bodies, such as the 'coalition talks' and 'coalition rounds' (Jäger, 1994: 41, 57). During the Kohl chancellorship the media became accustomed to paying far more attention to the announcements of the regularly held coalition meetings than to the formal 'rubber-stamp' decisions of the cabinet.

The dominant pattern of governing through the 'coalition round' may not be viewed as separate from Kohl's approach to leading the cabinet, though. Rather, it would seem that the prominent role of the coalition bodies gradually developed out of Kohl's style of cabinet leadership. While the overall climate at the cabinet table appears to have been decently pleasant, cabinet meetings were not always marked by a developed culture of debate. Kohl would not hesitate to ask ministers with strongly divergent views to leave the room and talk things over until they reached an agreement. Even this could appear as a rather modest manifestation of Kohl's penchant for applying schoolmasterly measures against ministers. During his term as minister-president of Rhineland-Palatinate, Kohl reportedly once interrupted a cabinet meeting because he disliked the haircut of a minister, and did not resume the meeting before the rebuked colleague returned from the hairdresser (Dreher, 1998: 122). Much more important for the gradual transformation of core executive decision-making than such peculiarities of personal style was Kohl's decision to break with the long-standing tradition of holding cabinet meetings on a fixed day every week. Summoning the cabinet irregularly and spontaneously, Kohl significantly strengthened his position in the cabinet towards his ministers, who often found themselves ill-prepared to counter the chancellor's initiatives (Maser, 1990: 211–12).

Increasing internal opposition to this practice became a key motive for setting up the system of 'coalition rounds' (Dreher, 1998: 327). As in previous bodies of its kind, Kohl's 'coalition round' was primarily a gathering of influential representatives of the governing parties, with the chancellor acting as the leader of the largest governing party rather than the head of government. However, whereas the party and *Fraktion* chairs and secretary-generals were always included, the presence of cabinet ministers was much more open to variation. In fact, as early as the second half of the 1980s the attendance of cabinet ministers at meetings of the 'coalition round' became an exception rather than the rule (Schreckenberger, 1994). Even after the 'coalition round' had replaced the cabinet as the centre of decision-making, Kohl tried to further strengthen his own position within the system by keeping the composition of the 'coalition round' and other *ad hoc* meetings flexible. This system was combined with, and supported by, a host of bilateral contacts between the chancellor and individual ministers, which played a crucial role in the early stages of policy formulation (Rudzio, 1991: 135–6).

The prominent role of the CDU party organization and the party-dominated coalition bodies also had an effect on the internal organization and strategic position of the Chancellor's Office within Kohl's overall leadership conception. The hierarchical-bureaucratic structures that had characterized the Office under Schmidt were weakened significantly under Kohl. Relying heavily on his party organization, Kohl did not consider the chancellery to be a primary source of political and policy advice. Even the dynamics within the chancellery reflected the strong influence of party politics. While there was a general scarcity of personal interaction between the chancellor and his staff, those enjoying the closest contacts with him were long-standing party fellows and Kohl confidants rather than those holding the most formal senior positions (Berry, 1989: 351). The chancellery was upgraded politically in 1984 by the appointment of former CDU/CSU *Fraktion* chairman Wolfgang Schäuble as chief of the Chancellor's Office. However, like both of his successors in this position (Rudolf Seiters and Friedrich Bohl), Schäuble acted very much as Kohl's agent, and power was given to him personally rather than to the chancellery as a whole.

The opening chapters of German unification witnessed a new variant of Kohl's leadership style. None other than Wolfgang Jäger, who had put forward the most substantial critique of the traditional 'chancellor democracy' paradigm in the late 1980s (Jäger, 1988), described the role Kohl and the chancellery played between the fall of the Berlin Wall and the early stages of the unification process as a manifestation of 'chancellor democracy' (Jäger, 1998: 19). Key decisions were made neither by the 'coalition round' nor by any gathering of senior party or cabinet figures, but largely by the chancellor alone. Kohl's famous unification speech in the Bundestag on 28 November 1989 came as a surprise even to his closest supporters and confidants.

Whereas Kohl's overall self-presentation and public standing, at home and abroad, changed in the aftermath of German unification, it could be difficult to prove that unification was an independent factor shaping his leadership style in the core executive. Some observers, such as Clay Clemens (1998: 108), have suggested that Kohl became more 'presidential' after unification. While it is true that there were no conspicuous manifestations of weakness after 1990 as there were during the early years of the Kohl administration, the notable absence of awkward and powerful intra-party 'veto actors', such as Franz Josef Strauss (who died in 1988) or Heiner Geissler (the CDU's secretary-general ousted by Kohl in 1989), was probably a more 'liberating' factor than Kohl's increased public standing. Without a doubt, the sheer length of Kohl's term as CDU party leader, which started as early as 1976, played a major role in making him considerably less vulnerable to possible intra-party challenges than most other German chancellors. The full extent of Kohl's power over his party was only to be revealed in the wake of the CDU party funding scandal in late 1999 and 2000, which was very much a 'Kohl crisis' (Helms, 2000b). It showed a party whose leader had managed to set aside even the most basic forms of intra-party 'checks and balances' and replace them with a system of 'noncharismatic personalism' (Ansell and Fish, 1999). Even though the crisis broke only a year after Kohl had resigned from the office of chancellor, it threatened to leave a major stain on the historical record of his chancellorship – a rather mixed one in any case in terms of policy achievements, with the notable exception of European integration (Wewer, 1998).

The holder of the German chancellorship at the time of writing, Gerhard Schröder, early acquired the reputation of a politician who enjoyed the prestige of the office more than the possible chance to change the country's course of public policy. One of the most remarkable aspects of the election campaign of 1998, which brought the Red–Green government to power, was the keenness of the SPD to persuade voters that, if elected to office, it would do many things better (than had the Kohl government), but change few things fundamentally. This strategy surely owed a lot to the widespread, and deep-rooted, reservations about large-scale reform of the German welfare state among the electorate. More specifically, it reflected the characteristic programmatic/ideological patterns of the German party system. Even though Schröder and other important figures in the SPD party leadership very much liked the idea of being part of the international 'third way' coalition, there was no credible way of letting the other major party in the system, the CDU/CSU, appear to be extreme – which marked one of the key strategies of Clinton and Blair in the United States and Britain, respectively (Campbell and Rockman, 2001).

In contrast to the notable emphasis on continuity at the policy level – which did not exactly fit the interim assessments of the administration's policy record after its first term in office, which highlighted various areas of change (Egle *et al.*, 2003) – the government was keen to break away from the 'Kohl system' of core executive decision-making. The first Red–Green coalition treaty, signed on 20 October 1998, mentioned a 'coalition committee' consisting of eight representatives from each governing party. However, it also made clear that the committee was not designed as a standing body, but was to be convened only at the explicit request of one of the two parties. Nevertheless, after less than two months in office, intra-coalition conflicts reached their first peak, which could only be overcome by calling a committee meeting in the chancellery. So anxious to avoid the impression of a 'crisis meeting' was the government, that it felt compelled to emphasize that the group of key figures from both sides gathering on 2 December 1998 was not the official coalition committee mentioned in the coalition treaty (*Handelsblatt*, 2 December 1998).

Still, this meeting proved to be a stepping stone towards creating a whole system of informal co-ordination bodies. And while some decisions were made by smaller circles, including just the chancellor, the chairman of the SPD parliamentary party and the responsible minister (*Frankfurter Allgemeine Zeitung*, 21 September 2001), many major issues were in fact debated and decided by the 'coalition round'.[22] By the time the Schröder government entered its second term, coalition meetings had become sufficiently institutionalized for the new coalition treaty, signed on 16 October 2002, to stipulate explicitly that regular meetings of the coalition parties were to be held at least once a month. In contrast to these institutional remedies to a looming coalition gridlock, several other ideas put forward by the junior coalition partner during the early days of the Red–Green coalition, such as appointing a representative from the Greens to a senior position in the chancellery, failed to secure Schröder's support.

The rather limited success of the Greens in expanding their position within the governing machine appeared to be symptomatic of the rather moderate overall influence of the junior coalition partner in the Schröder government. Whereas it was the Greens who eventually secured a second term for the government in 2002,[23] the period of 1998–2002 witnessed a stunning series of ignominious defeats of the party at state elections. After only a few years in federal government, the Greens appeared to have become the prototype of a genuine opposition party that was deeply unfit to govern (Raschke, 2001). On the other hand – while not being significantly more successful in the bulk of state elections after 1998 than their junior coalition partner – the Social Democrats remained the player in the German party system that enjoyed by far the largest number of feasible coalition options, which strengthened their position towards the Greens as much as towards the various opposition parties.

As at the level of coalition management, it took some time to set the new parameters of decision-making in the chancellery. While the overall number of staff in the chancellery increased to about 500, the chancellor's personal advisory staff became even smaller than under Kohl. Schröder's first chief of the Office, Bodo Hombach, specifically chosen to keep in check the power of Finance Minister Oskar Lafontaine (Walter and Müller, 2002: 497), lacked any specific experience in the field of core executive management. This notwithstanding, he apparently liked to see himself as the chancellor's chief adviser and the government's chief planner. After Lafontaine had resigned from office in the spring of 1999, Hombach also became increasingly dispensable. His successor, Frank Walter Steinmeier, was very much a 'chief administrator' in the narrower meaning of the term. He introduced a more coherent and straightforward organization of the chancellery, with virtually all contacts between the chancellor and his senior staff being channelled through his office. Steinmeier also became heavily involved in handling issues of coalition management. Some observers considered Steinmeier to be more influential within the administration than any individual cabinet minister (*Süddeutsche Zeitung*, 19 July 2000), and his influence within the core executive appeared to be increasing rather than decreasing.

However, even Steinmeier's impressive performance at the very centre of the administrative core executive could not save the government from harsh criticism. To some observers, the aftermath of the 2002 election witnessed the strange dissappearence of any real strategic centre at the heart of the governing machine. The policy planning directorate in the chancellery, in operation throughout Schröder's first term, was abolished, and the innermost circle of Schröder confidant(e)s in the chancellery appeared to have shrunk to less than a handful of people, including Steinmeier, Sigrid Krampitz, the chief of the chancellor's bureau (a member, as was Steinmeier, of Schröder's 'Hanover clan'), and the chancellor's wife, Doris Schröder-Köpf (Kister, 2002).

The considerable dynamic in the administrative core executive was to be accompanied by changing patterns of power at the level of cabinet ministers. The most influential ministers during the government's first term included Lafontaine (Schröder's first finance minister and SPD party chairman who resigned from both offices only a few months into the administration), his successor as finance minister (Hans Eichel), the foreign minister (Joschka Fischer), the interior minister (Otto Schily) and, though more patchily, the defence minister (Rudolf Scharping), and the non-party minister of economics (Walter Müller). Whereas both the working and personal relationships between Schröder and Lafontaine were troublesome from the very beginning until their early end,[24] the relationship between the chancellor and most other heavyweight ministers was based on a combination of personal rapport and professional respect.

There has been much speculation about the informal geometry of power in the post-2002 election cabinet. Early in 2003 it seemed as though the new cabinet was built on a new axis between the chancellor and his 'super-minister' Wolfgang Clement, former Social Democratic minister-president of North Rhine–Westphalia and the first German federal minister ever to be responsible for both economic and labour policy. Even though the history of personal relations between Schröder and Clement included similarly irritating areas as those between Schröder and Lafontaine, most fellow cabinet members described relations between the chancellor and his 'super minister' as being cordial and above average (*Der Spiegel*, 21 December 2002: 21, 24). Many considered Eichel to be the main loser of Schröder's second term, and even Fischer and Schily seemed to have lost some ground to Clement.

The informal hierarchy within the cabinet remained, however, a persistent issue – for outside observers as much as for the protagonists themselves. For one of the most seasoned and high-profile observers of the German chancellorship, Foreign Minister and 'vice–chancellor' Fischer – rather than anyone else – remained the true number one minister in Schröder's squad. Even Schily and Eichel were considered to be more powerful players than Clement, who was believed to have become a victim of Schröder's ambition to reserve the position of key decision-maker in economic policy for himself (Hofmann, 2003: 3). Whereas in most other fields individual ministers enjoyed a reasonable, even remarkable, amount of discretion over their respective departmental policies, Schröder's approach seemed to be influenced by a strong element of strategic calculation – including the maxim of letting individual ministers 'take the heat' for tough and highly unpopular decisions.

A closer look at Schröder's record of policy leadership reveals that his involvement in the more detailed aspects of policy-making remained rather modest. Like Kohl, Schröder did not shy away from 'pragmatic' solutions, and appeared to be more interested in political than in policy results (Sturm, 2003: 106). Even in most areas of domestic policy, manifestations of policy leadership remained rather thin on the ground. There have been several occasions, such as the 'Green Card' initiative of 2000 (to allow a limited number of highly skilled, foreign IT specialists to immigrate on special conditions), or the government's decision at the height of the BSE crisis to ban some forms of animal stockbreeding, in which Schröder in fact made ample use of his 'policy guideline competence'. But cases such as these were clearly outnumbered by others in which the chancellor appeared to be a 'consensus-seeker' rather than a 'chief executive'. Schröder's most important domestic policy accomplishment in his first five years or so in office became the enforcement of the government's major welfare reform programme (*Agenda 2010*), which brought the relationship between the chancellor and his party – never an easy one (Padgett, 2003: 52–5) – to its breaking point. Whereas Schröder's political capital proved just enough to get his way, he had used all his available resources of party support by early 2004. His announcement early in February 2004 that he was to step down as SPD party chairman, to be succeeded by Franz Müntefering, came as a surprise, though in fact it appeared as no less than a logical consequence of the previous months.

At least at the beginning, Schröder's involvement in foreign policy remained even more low-key than in domestic policy. This seemed to reflect a combination of his rather modest experience and a limited interest in foreign policy. During the Kosovo crisis, it was clearly Foreign Minister Fischer and Minister of Defence Scharping, rather than the chancellor, who called the shots. The first signs of Schröder acting as the government's true key decision-maker and chief diplomat abroad did not emerge before his extended visit to the Middle East in late October 2000. Schröder's 'EU initiative' in May 2001, a proposal focusing on the institutional and constitutional future of the European Union, was widely considered to signal the chancellor's growing ambitions in the international arena (*Neue Zürcher Zeitung*, 3 May 2001: 1–3). Still, even after that date, the bulk of the key decisions in German foreign policy were made at least as much in the Foreign Ministry as in the chancellery. With the notable exception of Schröder's involvement in the raging debate about Germany's participation or non-participation in the looming US-led military attack on Iraq, and its possible implications for German–American relations – an argument, many felt, to be triggered for obvious domestic reasons[25] – there were few major foreign policy iniatives by the chancellor. The two meetings between Schröder, Blair, and the French President Jacques Chirac in Berlin, in September 2003 and January 2004 – summoned to sort out the different positions in the three countries' Iraq policies, and to work out a common strategy of EU reform – remained isolated highlights of Schröder's foreign policy record during the first half of his second term.

Conclusion

In a classic article on the German post-war chancellorship, the office of chancellor was described as a position fitting an incumbent with all the constitutional and administrative devices of leadership he may possibly desire (Hennis, 1964: 27–8). While the powers of office of a German chancellor, and the administrative support structures that have been added, are in fact considerable, any serious attempt at understanding executive leadership in the Federal Republic has to reach beyond the realm of constitutional stipulations and administrative resources. This holds true for any of the different aspects of core executive leadership which, for analytical reasons, have been examined separately in the previous sections.

A historical perspective on leadership styles of German chancellors, including appointment policies and approaches to organizing the core executive, reveals both similarities and major differences among individual incumbents. As in Britain and the United States, the party affiliation of different office-holders may hardly be considered as an independent key variable determining the overall performance of different German post-war chancellors. In fact, just as in the two Anglo-Saxon countries, many of the most striking similarities at the level of core executive leadership styles relate to chancellors from different parties. While Adenauer and Schmidt evinced a notable inclination to keep the number of 'big guns' in their cabinets to a minimum, the cabinets of Kiesinger and Brandt were remarkable for the large number of heavyweights among cabinet ministers. The latter phenomenon has, admittedly, to be seen primarily as a reflection of the specific historical circumstances (the creation of a grand coalition cabinet in 1966, and the formation of the first post-war government headed by a Social Democrat in 1969, respectively), rather than the personal preferences of Kiesinger and Brandt. Schröder's appointment policies at cabinet level have been exceptional, both in terms of the political and social background of ministers and the rather high turnover rate among members of the cabinet. Moreover, like Erhard, Schröder showed a strong inclination to recruit the top layer of personnel in the chancellery from a pool of people with whom he had developed a close working relationship at an earlier stage of his political career.

The full cabinet has rarely been the true decision-making centre of German post-war administrations. In this regard, the Erhard government, the early years of the Kiesinger administration, Brandt's first term, and large parts of the Schmidt chancellorship – adding up in total to just about twelve years – mark the only major exceptions. In contrast to the historical developments in Britain, the limited role of the full cabinet has not been compensated by the rise of 'cabinet committee government'. Unlike their powerful British counterparts, cabinet committees in Germany do not enjoy any constitutional authority to make final decisions in lieu of the full cabinet. Moreover, their number has decreased, rather than increased, since the 1970s (Rudzio, 2003: 291). In functional terms, 'cabinet committee governance' in Germany had its heyday during the early years of the Brandt government, when many key legislative proposals emerged from the committees, yet this did not give rise to any kind of more persistent pattern of core executive decision-making.

The Chancellor's Office and, even more importantly, the informal, and essentially party-governed, decision-making bodies, such as 'coalition rounds' and 'coalition talks', are easily identified as the most important 'competitors' of the full cabinet as the decision-making centre within the German core executive. The chancellery played a significant role in virtually all administrations. The Kiesinger years, significant parts of the Erhard chancellorship and Brandt's second term mark the major exceptions to the rule. The chancellery's role in the core executive decision-making process was particularly powerful under Adenauer and Schmidt, during the first years of Brandt and, though to a lesser extent, under Schröder. Under Kohl, who generally relied on alternative resources, such as the CDU party organization in particular, the chancellery rose to rare prominence in 1989–90.

'Coalition rounds' and related informal decision-making bodies have played a part in each of the seven post-war administrations, with their overall impact being greatest under Kiesinger and Kohl. A historical perspective suggests that the emergence of informal decision-making becomes more likely as the years of an administration pass. Whereas there have been examples of German post-war administrations operating without feeling the need to establish informal 'sub-governments' for several years, all of them sooner or later found it necessary to modify and complement the existent structures of core executive decision-making. The effects of 'informalizing' core executive decision-making on the chancellor's leverage have varied greatly between different administrations. Whereas Kohl clearly profited from the prominent role of the 'coalition rounds', Schmidt's position in the core executive became weaker once 'coalitions talks' were adopted – though it may be argued that the gradual decline of Schmidt's political authority in fact *preceded* the emergence of a more informal, and party-driven, pattern of core executive decision-making.

Most other features of core executive leadership in post-war Germany have been shaped even more obviously by the complex mixture of different leadership styles and preferences, opportunities and restraints. As to coalition management – undoubtedly a key dimension of executive leadership in Germany's coalition democracy – Adenauer and Schröder are easily identified as the two office-holders of the post-war period who enjoyed the firmest grip on their party's junior coalition partner.

Whereas Adenauer profited significantly from the CDU/CSU's strong representation in the Bundestag, Schröder could long rely on his party's 'blackmail potential' towards the junior coalition partner flowing from the SPD's favourable strategic position in the party system. With the exception of Kiesinger, who faced by far the most unfavourable conditions of all the German chancellors – at least in terms of practising textbook 'chancellor government' – Erhard, Brandt and Schmidt all had a rather restricted room for manoeuvre within their coalition.

As to their policy expertise, Adenauer and Schmidt stand out as 'the great professionals' among German chancellors of the post-war period. Most of their fellows in the office of chancellor had a considerably more limited knowledge of policy details, though all office-holders since 1949 had extended experience in professional politics. Whereas most German chancellors enjoyed the different climate in the field of foreign policy more than the daily wheeling and dealing in domestic policy, only about half of them (including Adenauer, Brandt, Schmidt and Kohl) had their most important achievements in the international arena.

Part III

Executive Leadership in the Wider Political Process

5
The United States: Providing Leadership in an 'Anti-Leadership Environment'

Presidential Leadership in the Congressional Arena

While it is now common to refer to the president as the 'chief legislator' within the American system, this role of the president did not emerge before the 1930s, and became an established feature of American government only after the Second World War. It was clearly not intended by the framers and has to date never been codified in the constitution. For nineteenth-century presidents it was highly unusual even to formally address Congress. Woodrow Wilson, having in mind a model of prime ministerial government for the American presidency, was the first president since the days of Thomas Jefferson to address Congress in person in his 1913 State of the Union message. The idea of a more activist government took shape during the presidency of Theodore Roosevelt and his 'stewardship theory' of presidential leadership. The real historical turning point in presidential–congressional relations, though, came with Franklin D. Roosevelt's famous first '100 Days'. Since then, there has been a firm expectation among both the political elite and the wider public that presidents consider it one of their foremost duties to provide strong leadership in the legislative arena. However, it took until the late 1960s before it became the norm to expect presidents to expand their policy-making role from the economic sphere to more specific areas of domestic policy, such as social welfare and civil rights measures.

While the Roosevelt presidency marked a sea-change in the history of presidential–congressional relations, it did not establish anything like a permanent structural predominance of the presidency over Congress. Rather, the institutionalization of the modern presidency created the basis for a more balanced relationship between the two branches of government, which has come to be reflected in the major currents of scholarly debate. The bulk of more recent work on the subject shares a general perspective – the so-called 'tandem institutions' approach[1] – which emphasizes the dynamic and variable character of presidential–congressional relations. In compliance with the overall focus of this study, this chapter looks at presidential–congressional relations from a presidential perspective.

Apart from plenty of *ad hoc* public announcements, presidents outline their policy agenda on a number of formal occasions, by far the most important of which is the president's annual State of the Union Address.[2] As the constitution does not give the president the right to initiate any legislation by introducing a bill in Congress, proposals have to be initiated formally by members of Congress (who normally belong to the president's party). Whereas most congressional work on a bill is done in the committees, much of the wider legislative decision-making process takes place in issue networks in which the president usually does not play a prominent role. This only increases an administration's need for legislative liasion.

Legislative liaison was first put on a permanent institutional basis under Eisenhower, who created the Office of Congressional Relations, which later became the Office of Legislative Affairs. The Office of Legislative Affairs is headed by an assistant to the president and has a staff of up to thirty-five people. It has historically been divided into those working with the House and those working with the Senate, but there have been special units working in accordance with either the congressional committees being covered or particular issues pending. As the White House has no office of its own at the Capitol, its Office staff regularly use the offices of their party's leadership at the House, or the vice-president's suite at the Senate, as temporary command centres (Patterson, 2000: 119–28).[3]

There have been a number of more recent changes regarding the structural parameters of presidential leadership in Congress. To begin with, despite the marked increase in internal cohesion within both congressional parties and the significant strengthening of the congressional party leadership, political power in Congress has become much more dispersed since the early 1970s. The most important aspects of congressional reform included the weakening of the seniority rule, the considerable increase in the number of sub-committees, and the strengthening of sub-committee chairs and the rank-and-file. As a consequence, the number of possible negotiation partners who are to be persuaded by the president and his staff has increased enormously since the 1970s, making the whole coalition-building process between the two branches of government much more complex. 'Strategic coalitions', broad-based and comparably stable, were largely replaced by the alternative pattern of '*ad hoc* coalitions', which dissolve after an issue has been resolved (Sinclair, 1995). There has, however, been a reverse trend more recently. Given the growing party politicization of the legislative process, there has been an increase in more stable patterns of congressional voting on legislative measures. Before taking a closer look at this, it is important to consider the basic constitutional parameters of the legislative decision-making process.

A major constitutional resource that presidents have at their disposal for dealing with the legislative branch is the presidential veto against bills passed by Congress. Most constitutional lawyers stick to the view that the president's real strength in the legislative process stems from his veto power. According to Article 1, section 7 of the Constitution, every bill – with the exception of proposed constitutional amendments – must be presented to the president for approval or veto. For over a century it has been recognized that the president may veto a bill, for any reason. The president has ten days from the presentation of a bill to veto or approve a measure. A presidential veto may be overridden by a two-thirds majority (of members being present) in both the Senate and the House. No amendments are allowed to a vetoed bill, and all congressional votes on vetoed bills have to be recorded. A different procedure applies to the so-called 'pocket veto', which allows the president to prevent a bill passed within ten days of the adjournment of a session from becoming law simply by not signing it. In contrast to such cases involving the 'normal' presidential veto, Congress cannot override a 'pocket veto'. The bill must be reintroduced when Congress comes back into session and passed anew for it to be reconsidered.[4]

Individual post-war presidents used their veto power to a very different extent. By contemporary standards, Truman and Eisenhower used it excessively. This made them reminiscent of Franklin D. Roosevelt who, during the twelve years of his incumbency, vetoed no less than 49 per cent of all bills, which marked a record for the twentieth century. The average rate from Kennedy to Clinton was just 9.3 per cent. George W. Bush stands out among recent presidents, as, after more than three years in power, he had not used his veto once. Early in 2004 it seemed in fact conceivable that he would become the first president since John Quincy Adams (1825–9) not to use his veto pen in an entire term.

Sophisticated empirical inquiries into the conditions leading to the use of the presidential veto revealed that both institutional factors (especially congressional 'provocations') and the personal inclinations of individual presidents governing under similar historical conditions, are responsible for the frequency with which the veto is applied (Gilmour, 2002). However, in contrast to very early holders of the presidency, all modern presidents have considered the veto – if only the threat to make use of it[5] – a legitimate weapon in the political confrontation with Congress. Another important difference between the veto power of contemporary presidents and their historical predecessors relates to the reactions of Congress. In contrast to the late nineteenth century, it now marks a rare occurrence that Congress overturns a presidential veto. This holds true even for periods of 'divided government'. Of the thirty-seven vetoes President Clinton launched between 1995 and 2000, only two were overturned (Allred, 2001: 177).

Many more recent works on the presidential veto focus specifically on the conditions under which presidents *threaten* to use their veto, which has been considered a powerful resource in its own right. According to a recent statistical survey, presidents are most likely to launch a veto threat if a decision is considered highly relevant by the public, or is part of a chain of decisions that has been vetoed. Moreover, decisions in the area of foreign policy face a larger risk of being vetoed than domestic policy bills (Deen and Arnold, 2002). The overall effects of veto threats in terms of congressional concessions to the president have long been considered to be rather modest, especially during periods of 'divided government'. More recent empiricial research suggests, however, that even during 'divided government' veto threats can often be remarkably effective in wresting concessions from Congress (Cameron, 2000: 178–98). The Clinton years are a prime example of the president's ability to advance his own legislative agenda by threatening Congress with vetoing its decisions.

There is at least one other major instrument or strategy that presidents may use in order to strengthen their position towards Congress: presidents may turn directly to the public at large to mobilize support for their legislative agenda (an activity commonly referred to as 'going public'). As one of the leading scholars in this field has defined the character of this facet of presidential leadership: 'Going public is a class of activities that presidents engage in as they promote themselves and their policies before the American public... but in going public, the ultimate object of the president's designs is not the American voter, but fellow politicians in Washington (Kernell, 1997: ix). The logic behind this activity is that high public approval ratings for the president with regard to any specific matter make it much more difficult for Congress to withhold support for the president than under circumstances marked by public indifference towards a given issue. Whereas some observers have wondered if 'going public' has ever been more than a construction of political scientists extrapolating from the experience of the Reagan presidency, it is certainly true that, despite earlier ground-breaking manifestations of public leadership such as Roosevelt's 'fireside chats', 'going public' as a systematic leadership strategy did not emerge much before the 1970s. In Stephen Skowronek's model of different structures of presidential power, the 'plebiscitary' mode of governmental operations (to be observed since 1972) marks the fourth stage in a historical transition process (Skowronek, 1993: 53).[6] As Samuel Kernell has argued, the emergence of 'going public' as a central leadership resource and strategy cannot be explained by the revolution in communication technology alone (Kernell, 1997: 12–38). Another important development relates to the overall structure of the political process, which has experienced a transformation from 'institutionalized pluralism' into 'individualized pluralism', marked by looser coalitions and more individualistic politicians, a growing number of decision-makers and political interest groups, and significantly increased public pressure on decision-makers. Others have pointed to the possible connection between the rather limited congressional experience of more recent presidents and an increased likelihood of 'going public' being adopted as a key strategy for dealing with Congress (Mans, 1995: 850).[7] To 'outsiders' lacking any Washington experience, 'going public' may seem a more natural strategy to be applied than seeking compromise with Congress through the traditional channels of legislative bargaining.

An important way of assessing presidential performance in the legislative decision-making process is to measure presidential success rates in Congress statistically. The object of historical comparisons between different presidents is the proportion of legislative measures that have been supported explicitly by the president and met with the approval of Congress.

Legislative success rates have varied greatly among individual post-war presidents. The highest ever score of 93.9 per cent was achieved by Johnson in 1965; the historical low relates to Clinton, who was successful with only 36.2 per cent of supported measures in 1995. The highest average scores were measured for the presidencies of Kennedy, Johnson and Carter, who produced average success rates of 84.4, 83.0 and 76.4 per cent, respectively. At the other extreme are Reagan, Clinton and Ford, whose average success rates in Congress were 61.8, 57.6 and 57.7 per cent, respectively. Another noteworthy aspect relates to the variations in presidential success rates in the legislative arena that occur during the tenure of a single administration. The largest variation was measured for the presidencies of Clinton, Reagan and Eisenhower (with a range of 50.2, 38.9 and 37.0 percentage points, respectively). It is hardly surprising that short incumbencies tend to produce lower variations of presidential success in Congress, with Carter, Kennedy and Ford – none of whom stayed in office for more than four years – marking the three most notable cases (3.2, 6.1 and 7.2 percentage points, respectively). George W. Bush managed to win 87 per cent of all roll-call votes in Congress on which he took a clear position during 2001, and even a slightly higher score (87.8 per cent) in 2002. In 2003, his score dropped to 78.7 per cent, which for the first three years of his presidency combined was still the highest success rate of any president since Lyndon B. Johnson.[8]

There are, however, several methodological problems with this purely statistical approach to assessing presidential performance in the legislative arena. First, the scores presented above measure only the proportion of bills that the president supported publicly; they do not account specifically for the proportion of legislative measures actually being initiated by the president. Some presidents, including George W. Bush, deliberately keep a rather low profile in order to avoid a public showdown with Congress and the danger of suffering a major public defeat.

Another key problem of assessing presidential performances simply on the basis of statistical data must be seen in the inability of this approach to account for qualitative aspects, such as, in particular, the importance of presidential measures passed by Congress.[9] Sweeping policy changes may be brought about by a few major bills, whereas the effect of a very large number of bills may be comparatively small. The importance of taking into account the qualitative dimension of the presidential success rate in the legislative arena may be demonstrated by a comparison of the first two years of the presidencies of Ronald Reagan and Bill Clinton. Although Clinton achieved one of the highest scores of any post-war president during his first two years in office, probably no serious observer would contend that Clinton's legislative performance between 1992 and 1994 was more impressive than Reagan's back in 1981. While most authors would judge the legislative record of the early Reagan presidency as one of the most convincing examples of presidential leadership in the legislative arena – to be compared only with the historical records of Roosevelt in 1933 and Johnson in 1965 – Clinton's legislative achievements during the first two years of his presidency received rather modest grades from the majority of qualified observers (Campbell and Rockman, 1996; Herrnson and Hill, 1999).

How may the core features of presidential–congressional relations in the post-war period be explained? Despite due reservations about determinist, party-centred theories of the American legislative process, many authors consider political parties – that is, the actual pattern of party control of the two branches ('unified government' versus 'divided government') – as the single most important variable in explaining presidential–congressional relations (Davidson, 1997: 339). Other things being equal, the president's efforts to a build a legislative coalition stand a considerably better chance if his party controls Congress. This can be explained by the structure of policy preferences, which tend to be more similar among members of the same party, as well as strategic considerations among members of Congress in terms of possible presidential 'coat-tail effects' (Sinclair, 1999: 294–9).

After 1945, 'divided government' has been the dominant pattern of party control of the two branches of government. This marks a stark contrast to earlier periods of American history.[10] Between 1945 and early 2004, 'divided government' had existed for thirty-eight years – that is, almost two-thirds of the whole period. The usual configuration of 'divided government' after 1945 has been a Republican president facing a Congress controlled by the Democratic Party. When President Eisenhower was re-elected in 1956, he was the first Republican post-war incumbent to face a Democratic Congress from the beginning of his (second) term. Until the start of George W. Bush's term in the Oval Office, all other post-war Republican presidents had to work with at least one of the two Houses controlled by the opposition party. The constellation Clinton encountered after 1994 (a Democratic president facing a Republican Congress) marked an exception. Only one other post-war president – Truman in the period 1947–8 – experienced similar party constellations to Clinton after 1994.

The impact of the government's status as either 'unified' or 'divided' on the opportunity-structure for presidential leadership in Congress has increased considerably since the end of the 1980s. This has been because of the notable intensification of 'party government' in Congress. Both congressional parties have become much more homogeneous ideologically since the 1980s, as both have lost their respective anomalous wings (that is, the conservative southern faction within the Democratic Party, and the liberal/moderate group among congressional Republicans). Figures for 2003 indicate that Congress has become more polarized than it had been since the measurement of annual 'party unity votes' began several decades ago (*Congressional Quarterly Weekly Report*, 3 January 2004: 49). The recent changes have been particulary evident in the

Senate, which (at least statistically) has traditionally been the less party-governed chamber. Yet not all dimensions of the recent changes can be captured in statistical scores. The whole congressional atmosphere has become much more agresssive in recent years. As Eric Schickler (2002: 108) has remarked, 'the two parties' leaders, and many of their members, view the opposing party as an enemy in a protracted "war" for majority status'. This dynamic has been reinforced by very tight margins in both chambers, especially in the Senate, and the fact that the majority of members serving in the 107th and 108th Congress have never ever experienced a less combative and aggressive congressional atmosphere.

As the party leaderships' grip on individual members of Congress has tightened, even the congressional committees have largely lost their long-standing pre-eminence as the centre of legislative ideas and decision-making. Both the number of committees in the House and Senate and the number of committee meetings have significantly decreased since the mid-1980s. Moreover, there is now a much larger likelihood than in previous decades that the majority will rubber-stamp a pending piece of legislation, with any major changes, on a party-line vote. The specific impact of 'unified' or 'split party government' on the legislative decision-making process is especially obvious at the level of congressional conference committees, where it leads to a sharp reduction in the proportion of representatives from the minority party on the committees (Cohen *et al.*, 2004).

As a comparative assessment of American post-war presidents as actors in the legislative arena suggests, leadership styles and the relationship between presidents and powerful players in Congress have been important factors in shaping presidential–congressional relations after 1945, even though the overall record of presidential achievements has more often than not been strongly influenced by the general political circumstances in which administrations found themselves.

Truman was not too impressive a performer in the legislative arena, especially in terms of concrete legislative achievements. This was to a large extent the result of the persistent strength of the same conservative coalition of Republicans and southern Democrats that had already constrained Roosevelt's room for manoeuvre in the legislative arena. There were regular meetings between the president and Democratic legislative leaders, supplemented by various *ad hoc* meetings arranged at short notice. Truman's bargaining efforts in the legislative arena remained, however, rather modest – a phenomenon that has been explained by 'his belief in the importance of congressional independence' (Lammers and Genovese, 2000: 148). While a considerable proportion of the president's senior staff dealt in some way or another with Congress or specific policy issues, the administration's activities in the legislative arena were largely confined to the area of legislative agenda-setting. In contrast to many later presidents, Truman considered it his duty to introduce expansive legislative agendas, even if most issues stood a rather modest chance of finding the support of Congress. One of the administration's few seminal achievements in domestic policy was the Employment Act of 1946. By contrast, Truman's foreign policy record – including the implementation of the Marshall Plan, the Truman Doctrine and the creation of NATO – was more impressive, though perhaps his most lasting contributions to the modern presidency related to the administrative reconstruction of the office.

The Eisenhower administration, being exceptional among post-war administrations for its initial reluctance to promote its own legislative agenda, chose a different approach to dealing with Congress. According to an assessment by Ken Collier (1994), Eisenhower's approach included three major features. First, he had a strong desire to decentralize legislative responsibility within the executive branch. While Eisenhower created the first office in the White House designed solely for dealing with Congress (a move that may look like an attempt at centralizing rather than decentralizing legislative affairs), individual cabinet departments were encouraged to maintain their own liaison operations. Second, Eisenhower relied heavily on relations with congressional leaders. There were weekly meetings between the president, the vice-president and the White House liaision staff with Republican congressional leaders, which irritated lesser members of Congress as they felt they were being ignored. The president's reliance on congressional leaders made him heavily dependent on those holding the respective leadership positions. Whereas Eisenhower had an excellent relationship with the Senate's Republican majority leader, Robert Taft (who died in 1953, just six months into the Eisenhower presidency), his relations with Taft's successor remained wholly unpleasant from the president's point of view. By contrast, the relationship between Eisenhower and Republican Majority Leader Charles Halleck was exceptionally close: Halleck was included in the administration's congressional leadership meetings even after having given up his leadership position in the House.[11] A third important hallmark of executive–legislative relations during the Eisenhower years was the White House's notable avoidance of partisanship – even though the president was personally conservative in his policy views. On balance, the last two years of the Eisenhower presidency would appear to have been the most enjoyable period of presidential–congressional relations from the president's point of view, though Eisenhower's role in decision-making was not always dominant. The Civil Rights Act (1957) marked a landmark legislative enactment, but was a legislative compromise rather than a result of vigorous presidential leadership. A genuinely presidential achievement, by contrast, was the decision to launch the start of the Interstate Highway System in 1956 (Lammers and Genovese, 2000: 178–80). In retrospect, one of the key features of the Eisenhower administration's policy record was the notable lack of attention to several major issues, perhaps most obviously in the field of civil rights.

Kennedy's political capital was limited, because he had neither fought an election campaign focusing on a few major issues (which might have created a specific public mandate) nor won a particularly impressive election victory in the presidential election of 1960. Moreover, as the president's campaign had not saved the Democrats from bitter losses in the 1960 House elections, Kennedy's party support in Congress was also fairly limited. Generally, Kennedy proved to be effective in working with individual members of Congress, including the Republican Senate minority leader, Everett Dirksen. Yet he faced considerable problems in gaining the support of most congressional leaders (including the many influential Democratic figures), especially among those committee chairmen who had been his seniors during his term in the Senate. On the whole, persuasion through policy arguments was a more crucial element of Kennedy's leadership style in the legislative arena than traditional bargaining. Nevertheless, it was the Kennedy administration that established the practice of using interest group lobbyists to reach members who could not be persuaded by other means. Patronage and grants were used aggressively. Kennedy's overall legislative achievements were less than spectacular, though. There was some new legislation the president supported, but no presidential landmark bills were passed between 1961 and 1963. The rather moderate legislative record in domestic policy corresponded with a somewhat problematic record of the administration in foreign policy, including the 'Bay of Pigs' disaster, and Vietnam. This having been said, it is more obvious in Kennedy's case than in most of the others that the president's overall contribution to the state of American policy and politics cannot reasonably be measured exclusively in terms of concrete policy achievements and failures, but has also to include less tangible aspects of political inspiration.

Nelson Polsby's authoritative judgment that 'Johnson was at home in the congressional arena as any president in American history' (Polsby, 1983: 11) remains true in the early twenty-first century. Johnson's spectacular legislative successes in the aftermath of the 1964 presidential election have become a historical yardstick for gauging the legislative achievements of American presidents. The stunning successes during the first years of the Johnson presidency – including the Civil Rights Act, the Economic Opportunity Act, Medicare and Medicaid, the Voting Rights Act, and a major tax cut – were facilitated by a mix of favourable conditions. They included an unusually strong economy, a high level of trust in the government, and large congressional majorities (in 1965 and 1966). However, with hindsight, Johnson's commitment and his leadership skills appear to be even more important factors than the favourable political circumstances. Not only had Johnson had an impressive body of experience in the legislative arena, which provided him with invaluable insights into the world of Congress, he also spent most of his time and energy during the first three years of his presidency on managing the legislative process. He ensured that all members of Congress felt that he was generally accessible, though in practice meetings with committee chairs were granted considerably more time than contacts with rank-and-file members. Generally, Johnson preferred an 'intimate' bargaining atmosphere with Congress, which excluded the public, and considered the idea of putting Congress under public pressure as no more than an option of last resort. From early on, Johnson practised the art of dispensing special favours to gain members' support on a particular bill. Another hallmark of Johnson's approach to dealing with Congress was his close working relationship with party leaders. The intense involvement of the Democratic House and Senate party leadership in the White House decision-making process has prompted observers to argue that the whole system of executive–legislative relations during the Johnson years had more in common with a parliamentary system of government than with the traditional presidential one (Manley, 1978: 266). The later parts of the Johnson presidency witnessed a deep transformation in presidential–congressional relations, which manifested itself in a significantly reduced leverage of the White House in the legislative arena, and a sharp decline in presidential support. The last two years of Johnson's presidency, and much of his legacy in the public mind, was dominated by the administration's responsibility for the escalation of the Vietnam War.

Nixon was the first new president in more than 100 years to face a Congress whose two houses were controlled by the opposition party. Moreover, with just a 43 per cent share of the public vote, his personal political support basis was exceptionally weak. These circumstances alone would appear sufficient to explain the huge difference between Nixon's and Johnson's records of legislative achievements. Yet major differences at the level of political circumstances were accompanied by radically different leadership approaches. Nixon had a basic distrust of Congress (and even more so of its individual members) and was generally more interested in administrative and diplomatic issues than in legislative ones. He based his relationship with Congress on the principles of limited accessibility, minimal personal involvement in lobbying members of Congress, and a decidedly partisan approach to coalition building in terms of largely restricting his administration's bargaining efforts to the Republican camp.[12] Nixon's overall legislative accomplishments remained rather meagre, even if one takes into account his less than favourable opportunity structure. After 1970, presidential–congressional relations further deteriorated, as Nixon focused increasingly on circumventing Congress by adopting administrative and aggressive public leadership strategies. Most observers at the time tended to blame the notable rift between the president and Congress on Nixon's senior staff rather than on the president himself. In the bulk of more recent works on the subject there is a clear tendency to consider the president personally, rather than his staff, as chiefly responsible for the poor state of executive–legislative relations during the Nixon years (Collier, 1997: 124). In broader historical assessments of the Nixon years, admittedly, even the worst aspects of presidential leadership in the legislative arena contrast favourably with the administration's failures in the Watergate scandal, which eventually led to Nixon's forced resignation.

During the less than two-and-a-half years of Ford's term in the Oval Office, the 'post-imperial presidency' faced a 'post-reform Congress'.[13] Not only had the public mood turned against an all too powerful (and complacent) presidency, but Congress had also used the Watergate experience as a catalyst to expand its resources for dealing with the presidency. The Ford presidency was the first to encounter a Congress that had given itself a much more decentralized structure of decision-making. This largely limited the usefulness of approaches, banking on close relationships between the White House and a small number of party leaders and committee chairs. Moreover, Ford suffered from his status as an unelected 'minority president'. Even the historical coalition between Republicans and conservative southern Democrats, on which most earlier Republican 'minority presidents' were able to draw, was starting to show serious signs of dissolution. It has been rightly stressed that Ford did not only command a comparably impressive body of legislative experience and skill, as did Johnson, but that both also relied on rather similar leadership techniques in the legislative arena

(Jones, 1983: 117). Like Johnson, Ford enjoyed dealing with members of Congress, was accessible, and worked closely with congressional leaders. Still, as similar as Ford's and Johnson's basic legislative leadership techniques might have been – with the notable exception of Ford's frequent use of the presidential veto power –, their legislative accomplishments were very diverse, which reflected the rather different political settings of the Ford and Johnson presidencies.

The Carter presidency became a lasting testimony to the fact that, while 'divided government' usually increases the demand for skilful presidential leadership in the legislative arena, 'unified government' by no means automatically results in a harmonious relationship between the president and Congress, and significant legislative achievements by the president. Tensions between Carter and power-holders at Capitol Hill started even before Carter won the presidency, as he managed to defeat candidates with a congressional background in the race for the Democratic nomination. His campaign focused heavily on fighting Washington politics and pork-barrel spending. Coming to the White House without any Washington experience, Carter seemed significantly to underestimate the strong role of Congress in policy-making. This initial misjudgement proved fatal, as it blended with the president's general dislike of bargaining and patronage, and came to guide his general strategy for dealing with the legislative branch. Some formal meetings, such as the traditional breakfasts with congressional leaders, were continued, but there was hardly any serious attempt by the White House to win congressional support by bargaining and persuasion. Most members of Congress also found Carter's moralistic tone irritating, and unhelpful in achieving legislative compromise. Overall, Carter's legislative record remained rather unspectacular, lacking both the stunning successes (the Camp David Accords) and glaring failures (the handling of the Iranian hostage crisis) that defined his leadership performance in foreign affairs.

The Reagan administration's relationship with Congress continues to be remembered especially for the president's excessive use of 'going public', a strategy apparently foreshadowed by the Nixon White House. It is important to note, though, that despite superficial parallels, Reagan's strategy of appealing to the public as part of his legislative strategy was markedly different from Nixon's earlier attempts. In contrast to Nixon's 'public prestige approach', Reagan developed a 'merchandizing approach' designed to link public appeals to specific legislative battles (Collier, 1997: 208–9). Instead of trying to create a general pool of public support for the president that would generally strengthen the administration's role in the legislative arena at any given point in time, Reagan used appeals to the public as a device for winning a particular vote in Congress (which was believed in turn to translate into increased presidential popularity). Moreover, again very much unlike the Nixon administration, the Reagan White House did invest heavily in traditional forms of legislative lobbying. Also, Reagan's political opportunity structure, which was rather favourable, clearly displayed more parallels with the Johnson rather than the Nixon years. This came to be reflected in the rather different legislative accomplishments of the Reagan and Nixon administrations. Reagan's early successes – especially his tax-cut policies – were based on a highly concentrated legislative strategy by the White House, directed by his first chief of staff, James Baker, who acted as the head of a so-called Legislative Strategy Group. Even though he seems not to have enjoyed it much, Reagan showed a remarkable involvment in winning the votes of members from both sides of Congress. But as his presidency wore on, he became both less involved and less successful in persuading members of Congress to support the administration's legislative programme. This was, at least in part, a result of his waning image as an electorally powerful 'coat-tail' president. To many, the Tax Reform Act of 1986 represented the last major achievement of the rather unimpressive domestic legislative record of Reagan's second term, which did not rival his primary accomplishment in the international arena – the signing of the INF Treaty in October 1986 to reduce intermediate-range nuclear forces.

While George H. W. Bush may have underestimated the role of the bully pulpit aspect of the modern presidency, his different leadership style in the legislative arena was influenced chiefly by his long-standing legislative experience. Very much like Johnson and Ford, Bush felt at home in the legislative arena and considered members of Congress his friends. His personal involvement in congressional bargaining was exceptionally intense, and as within the executive branch, Bush liked dealing with individuals directly. When it came to 'going public', Bush's reservations against it grew primarily out of his respect for members of Congress. In that sense, ironically, Bush's many friendships in Congress became a hindrance rather than a help to his legislative agenda. But there were other problems with Bush's agenda too. Although the military victory in the Gulf War in early 1991 – which became one of the very few largely uncontested achievements of his presidency – gave Bush fabulous approval ratings, he was unable to exploit this public support to pass any major legislation. Many on the Hill felt that the administration simply had no serious domestic agenda at all. In the end, the Bush administration was most successful at stopping legislation by the frequent use of the presidential veto, which became a hallmark of executive–legislative relations between 1989 and 1993.

Clinton developed a partisan approach towards Congress during his first two years in office, which was to be combined with an excessive use of 'going public'. Contrary to a widespread perception, Clinton's strong inclination to appeal to the public did not, however, result in neglecting traditional legislative lobbying and bargaining. Both the president himself and the White House staff devoted a significant proportion of their time and energy to the field of executive–legislative relations. Still, even during the early stages of the Clinton presidency, White House control of the legislative branch was rather limited – a fact to be reflected in the overall record of legislative achievements. Most observers blamed Clinton's oversized and rather unspecific legislative agenda, stirring memories of the Carter years, for the modest results. The switch in party control of Congress in 1994 (from 'unified government' to 'divided government') had a major impact on the administration's performance in the legislative arena. This became particularly obvious at the level of statistically measured presidential success rates in Congress.[14] However, many observers, looking beyond statistical scores, found the immediate implications of the return to 'divided government' in 1994 not at all detrimental to Clinton's overall performance in the legislative arena. As Gillian Peele *et al.* (1998: 5) have argued:

> The advent of a Republican congressional majority with its own agenda forced Clinton to retreat to a style of politics which emphasized incremental policy achievements and bargaining around the center of the political spectrum while lowering expectations of presidential achievement. The strategy of 'triangulation', governing from a position to the right of the Democrats but to the left of the GOP, turned out to suit Clinton's style of presidential leadership. It played to his particular political strengths, enabling him to exploit opportunities for agreements that crossed party lines.

Clinton's overall policy record – including a very strong economy with low inflation and low unemployment, as well as welfare reform – was respectable. It appeared to be even more impressive, as it contrasted starkly with the scandals that engulfed the Clinton presidency.

On assuming office, George W. Bush encountered rather unusual conditions in the legislative arena. While being the first Republican president in over forty years to face a Congress controlled by his own party, the margins in both houses were wafer-thin. In the House,

Republicans held a majority of nine. The Senate was evenly split, with 50 Democrats and 50 Republicans, and a Republican voting majority was dependent on the speaker's vote. Moreover, Bush had not only no 'coat-tails' at all, but had to live with the burden of not having achieved a majority of the popular vote in the 2000 presidential election. In May 2001, the Republicans lost their majority in the Senate because of the defection of James Jeffords, a Republican from Vermont who opted to become an independent. This constellation – a Republican-controlled House and a Democratic-controlled Senate – remained the administration's legislative playing field until the November 2002 congressional election, which swept majority control of both chambers to the Republicans.

Before the terrorist attacks of 11 September 2001 – which increased pressure on all parties to engage in developing a genuinely bipartisan approach and at the same time strengthened the president's position towards Congress significantly – neither Bush's relationship with the Republican House majority leader, Dick Armey, nor that with the Democratic leadership in Congress, was particularly warm. The honey-moon of bipartisan policy-making that resulted from 11 September 2001 was short-lived and remained superficial. The second half of the 107th Congress became more noteworthy for the frequent clashes between the president and the Democratic majority leader in the Senate, Tom Daschle, than for serious bipartisan initiatives. Bush's rather limited ability to garner the support of the Democrats may, how-ever, hardly be explained in terms of personal relationships or presidential leadership skills alone. The president's failed attempt to revitalize the bipartisan approach of governing he had practised so successfully as governor of Texas, had more to do with the difference between the conservative Texan Democrats and their more liberal congressional counterparts than with the quality of Bush's bargaining skills as governor and president.

Signs of bipartisan legislative decision-making disappeared almost completely in the Republican-controlled 108th Congress. This became obvious at different levels of congressional activity. In the House, Speaker J. Dennis Hastert and Majority Leader Tom DeLay wasted no time in exploiting the newly gained generous majority. Defying well-established conventions of staffing congressional bodies, the established seniority system was circumvented to reward the GOP leadership's most loyal allies with important committee chairs. This move was accompa-nied by fiercely conservative proposals from the White House – from huge tax cuts to the nomination of judges with controversial records on racial issues – which found the approval of the president's most loyal backers within the GOP, but chipped away support from more moderate forces, both within and outside the Republican Party. By early 2004 there was a widespread feeling among members from both congressional parties that Bush's prominent inauguration pledge to 'change the tone in Washington' and 'move beyond the bitterness and partisanship of the recent past' had not materialized (Milbank and Broder, 2004).[15]

As to the concrete legislative achievements during Bush's first two years, there were more successes than failures from the president's point of view. From the major tax cut bill (2001), which had marked one of Bush's key campaign promises, to the creation of the Department of Homeland Security during the lame duck session in late 2002, it was the White House rather than Congress that set most of the legislative agenda. While wartime patriotism helped the president's cause, most observers found that Bush's accomplishments – or at least the public perception thereof – were also the result of his specific leadership style. As Jill Barshay (2002: 111) has remarked:

> Bush's signature strategy on Capitol Hill was to begin by outlining his desires in broad terms, rather than detailed legislative language. Then, after concluding that he had achieved the best outcome possible given the will of Congress, Bush often chose to declare the final compromise a victory – even when some of the principles he set out were scrapped or some of his desires were ignored.

Bush essentially stuck to this well-established strategy during the 108th Congress (2003–4), whose successes became more limited, however. This was mainly because of the increased partisan polarization of Congress, which became particularly obvious in the Senate, where the proportion of presidential defeats was considerably larger than in the House (Nather, 2004). The showcase of party confrontation, and the GOP's domination of the legislative process, in 2003 became the highly contentious Medicare Bill.

Another hallmark of the George W. Bush style of governing was the notably assertive use of executive orders as an important tool of leadership – a leadership device that enables the president to bypass Congress, on certain issues, altogether.[16] Arguably the most important executive order was the one allowing the government to use military tribunals to try non-citizens charged with terrorism, and to monitor communications between some detainees and their lawyers. Also widely noticed, particularly among presidential scholars, was another executive order that allowed sitting presidents to keep secret the papers of a previous president for longer than twelve years after the end of an administration (Aberbach, 2004: 63–4).

Presidential Leadership and the Influence of other Political Players in the American System

For all its power, Congress is far from being the only political player with a significant potential to restrict the scope of presidential leadership in the American political system. There are other institutions and actors that have to be taken into account when it comes to painting a realistic picture of presidential leadership in the wider political process.

The Supreme Court, having acquired its right to decide on the constitutionality of legislation in 1803 (*Marbury* v. *Madison*), would seem to be a particularly powerful player with the potential to influence the parameters of executive leadership in the United States. Interestingly, major Court rulings regarding the presidency have in fact long been rather thin on the ground, for at least two reasons (Biskupic and Witt, 1997: 169): first, the constitutional language describing the powers of the president provides a rather uncertain basis for constitutional challenges to presidential action. Second, the prestige of the office of president and its occupant in the public mind has made it more difficult to curb presidential powers in comparison to those of the other branches of government. Recent empirical research suggests that there even is a correlation between presidential popularity with the public and Court judgments, to the effect that popular presidents tend to face even less opposition from the Court than those commanding less popular support (Yates and Whitford, 1998).

Looked at from a broader historical perspective, the overall amount of legal constraint on presidential power has been fairly modest. On the basis of an overall assessment of important Supreme Court rulings concerning the constitutional powers of the president, Cronin and Genovese (1998: 228) concluded that the Court generally behaved as 'a friend of the presidency', especially (but not only) in the field of foreign policy. Many of those rare Court decisions that handed the president a defeat were softened by important qualifications, which in the long run proved to be clearly 'pro-presidential'. For example, *Youngstown Sheet & Tube Co.* v. *Sawyer* (1952) not only declared Truman's seizure of the steel mills invalid but also granted future presidents 'implied powers' allowing them to act outside the legal framework set out in the Constitution. In a similar vein, *United States* v. *Nixon* (1974), while defeating Nixon, acknowledged the existence of a limited 'executive privilege'. It is, however, obvious that Cronin and Genovese's (1998) assessment is less true for the more recent past than it was for earlier decades. Since the 1970s the Court has gradually become much less deferential to the president. According to Richard Neustadt (2001: 3–5), the Court's altered stance can even be seen as a major driving force behind the gradual loss of presidential power in the political system. For many, Richard Nixon's election as president in 1968 marked the start to a new era in presidential–judicial relations, as it triggered a long-term change in the recruitment process for Supreme Court appointments. While all presidents, before as much as after Nixon, have shown a keen interest in nominating candidates sharing their own political core beliefs, the Nixon administration was the first to recruit candidates who were sitting jurists rather than political insiders. As David Yalof (1999) has argued, other things being equal, justices without extensive political ties to an administration are significantly less likely to defer to the presidency than justices who have been recruited from the ranks of sitting jurists. The key factor explaining this important sea-change in the recruitment patterns of Supreme Court justices, according to the same author, has been the rise of 'divided government' – Nixon's was the first incoming administration in many decades to face a Congress entirely controlled by the opposition party – that has restrained significantly the room for manoeuvre of presidents in the recruitment process.

In indices of 'institutional pluralism' (Colomer, 1996: 9), independent central banks have been considered as important institutional features of political systems as are constitutional courts or second chambers. The US central bank, the Federal Reserve Board (Fed), has traditionally been ranked as one of the most independent central banks in the world. In a recent work, the Fed has been described as 'arguably the most influential policy organ in the United States' (Rockman, 2000: 249). Detailed assessments of the Fed's degree of political independence suggest that the presidential checks on the Fed – namely the president's power to appoint the chairman and other members of the Board of Governors – have been overestimated. As Irwin Morris (2000: 71–86) has emphasized, there are obvious limits to influencing monetary policy-making via appointment power. Not only are appointment opportunities infrequent in a president's term, but nominees also need the support of the Senate and, if confirmed, are not always the reliable supporters of the president's views that he may want them to be. Notably harmonious and close working relationships between the president and the Fed's chairman, as during the terms of President Gerald Ford and Chairman Arthur Burns, have remained an exception rather than the rule. Whereas explicit bargaining between the president and the Fed, as was observed during the Johnson presidency, does not present the normal pattern of White House–Fed relations, various case studies suggest that there has been overall a considerable degree of presidential influence on the decision-making process of the Fed's Board of Governors (Beck, 1982; Krause, 1994). Typically, open conflicts between the White House and the Fed are most likely to occur in presidential election years. George W. H. Bush famously blamed the Fed for his defeat by Bill Clinton in 1992, claiming that it had delayed economic recovery by being too slow to cut interest rates. The relationship between the Fed's long-serving chairman, Alan Greenspan (first appointed by Ronald Reagan in the late 1980s) and the administration of George W. Bush has been marked by a surprising amount of, if not always unconditional, support from the Fed for the president's tax-cut policies.

The federal system marks another important component or dimension of the institutional parameters of executive leadership in the wider political process. Compared with the room for manoeuvre of the national political executive in unitary states, any federal order inevitably limits the power of the national executive to some extent. However, not only does the distribution of power and competencies of different levels (national, state or regional) vary significantly between different federal systems; there is usually also a significant amount of change over time within individual federal systems. The general historical development of the US federal system has been towards centralization of power at the national level. As early as 1950, the doctrine of 'dual federalism', having been established by the framers, was declared dead. However, later decades were to bring even more rather than less nationalization, and most observers agree that a change of course did not emerge before the early 1980s (Walker, 1995).

What is important for understanding the relationship between presidents and the federal system is to acknowledge the fact that the latter is not simply a set of rules within whose boundaries administrations have to work. Rather, presidents are an important – though hardly the only – driving force behind the changing face of American federalism.[17] Moreover, few political iniatives by the White House are concerned specifically with changing the procedural rules of decision-making in the federation, though public pledges to changing the distribution of power between the national and sub-national levels of government have loomed large under recent administrations. In fact, as John Francis (2003: 91) has pointedly remarked, 'policy commitment [of an administration] drives where policy decision-making is to be placed' – rather than the other way round. For this reason, it would also be misleading to assume that presidents invariably strive to secure the largest possible leadership scope in regional terms; attaining this is hardly a goal in itself. An administration committed primarily to slashing federal taxes will rather welcome the possibility of expensive public services being provided by the states, rather than at federal level.

Most commentators on the state of American federalism contend that the Reagan and Clinton years marked a new era driven by the wish of the White House to 'devolve' federal power to the sub-national level. However, it is obvious that even Reagan and Clinton kept the option to revise their programmatic position towards devolution of governmental power whenever it was deemed necessary or expedient. For example, responding to growing public concern about problems such as crime and education, Clinton did not hesitate to launch several programmes that clearly expanded rather than cut back the role of the national government within the political system (Bailey, 1998: 125–7). The popularity of Reagan and Clinton, and their common theme of 'taking power back from the corrupt political elite in Washington' was itself a major factor in establishing what John Kincaid (2001: 147) has called a 'disjunction between devolution rhetoric and devolution reality in the United States'. Since the mid-1980s it has become difficult for presidential candidates and presidents not to deliver a public pledge to 'devolution'. Unsurprisingly, then, it was also an issue in George W. Bush's presidential campaign, during which he described himself as 'a faithful friend of federalism'. There has, however, been a reasonable amount of scepticism among observers whether Bush was really able, or willing, to defend or even increase the autonomous decision-making power of the states (Peele, 2002). From the beginning, the administration faced the pressure of powerful pro-business lobbies favouring uniform market laws to be enforced by the federal government rather than a territorial variation of rules. Perhaps more importantly, several major issues on the Bush agenda itself, education reform in particular, appeared difficult to reconcile with a reduced role of the federal government. In January 2002 Bush signed into law an education bill that greatly expanded the federal government's involvement in the American educational system. However, the single most important driving force behind a resurgent federal government became the terrorist attacks of 11 September 2001 – a forceful reminder that major crises tend to result in a reinvigorated role for the national government. This became most obvious in the field of domestic security, though it had important spillover effects in several other areas of public policy, from public subsidies for the farming industry to relief for the unemployed.

As in any liberal democracy, interest groups have long been considered important and highly influential actors that have the potential to constrain the president's power in the American political system. The explosive increase in the number of American interest groups characterizing the 1960s and 1970s, and the functional diversification of groups that has followed this stage of interest group development since the 1980s (Reilly, 1998: 162–3), have considerably intensified the challenge to presidential leadership from this corner of the political system. Traditionally, the natural target for interest groups' activities has been Congress, and even in the early twenty-first century, lobbying members of Congress remains essential for any interest group serious about seeking influence in Washington. However, as the White House has increased its influence over agenda-setting and other aspects of public policy-making, many interest groups have been keen to complement their primarily Congress-focused strategies for influencing policy by seeking direct access to the White House.

Interest groups can either foil presidential ambitions at the policy level (if not always at the stage of policy formulation, certainly at the implementation stage) or help to achieve them against the opponents of a given policy. As Daniel Tichenor (2003: 331) has argued, 'collaboration with the president is frequently less rewarding (and opposition more beneficial) for interest groups than is commonly presumed'. The price an interest group may possibly have to pay for its engagement in decision-making processes – especially if it faces a high-opportunity president – is co-optation, which may effectively lead to the frustration of its policy goals, as happened to the Christian Right during the Reagan presidency (ibid.: 338–41).

Relations between interest groups and the presidency are obviously not a one-way street. There has always been some sort of 'reverse lobbying' (Shaiko, 1998), that is, interest group mobilization from the White House. In recent decades, the efforts the White House has directed to managing contacts with interest groups have been expanded and intensified significantly. All administrations since Ford have maintained an outreach capability for interest groups, and few, if any, of the more recent administrations have shown an inclination to avoid explicit contact with certain groups (Pika, 1999: 59, 71).

Needless to say, administrations may well pursue more than one strategy at the same time; moreover, there can also be a significant amount of change during a president's term. This notwithstanding, there have been notable variations in the concrete approaches to dealing with interest groups, which may be classified theoretically. In an influential article, Mark Peterson (1992) distinguished four ideal-typical patterns of interaction between the White House and interest groups resulting from a combination of two dimensions: the breadth of group interactions can be either exclusive or inclusive; and the focus of these contacts can be either programmatic or representational in character. Ford provided an important example of an administration with an inclusive/representational approach to interest groups that was focused functionally on strengthening the president's image and prestige among the general public. Also inclusive in its character, but with a programmatic focus, was the 'consensus-building'-orientated strategy of the Johnson administration. With its exclusive/representational character of interest group policies, the Carter administration tried to provide representation to segments of the president's political coalition that otherwise lacked close ties to the government. Finally, there is the possible combination of exclusive and programmatic elements in a president's approach to dealing with interest groups, which focuses on partisan coalition building for the purpose of achieving programmatic goals: this was typical of most of the Reagan years.

The White House's dominant approach to dealing with interest groups pursued under George W. Bush was clearly one to be classified in the categories above as 'interest group liaison as governing party'. As Peterson (2004: 244) has argued, '[t]he current White House has not used interest group relations primarily, or significantly, or even moderately to elevate Bush's political, representational standing in the country as a whole'. Rather, Bush acted as 'a president who for the most part actively pursued a distinctly partisan programmatic agenda cultivated through close, often intimate, links to interests deeply embedded in the Republican electoral coalition. Where Bill Clinton succeeded primarily in "splitting friends" and "unifying enemies", George W. Bush has offered a government of chums' (ibid.: 228). This approach governed the White House's activities in the areas of energy policy and environmental protection as much as in the fields of trade policy and health care policy. The only major exception to this rule during the first three years of Bush's presidency was education policy, where the White House pursued a bipartisan, compromise-orientated strategy.

The Public Presidency

The history of the American presidency has been marked by a persistent trend towards publicity and personalization. To an ever-larger extent, the president personally rather than the presidency as a whole has become the centre of public focus in government, and much of what is being perceived as presidential leadership is in fact public leadership. Consequently, all post-war presidents have tried to increase their control over the relationship with the media and the public. Recent decades have seen the emergence of a pattern of public leadership and presidential government that has been referred to prominently as the 'permanent campaign', an ever-closer relationship between campaigning and governing (Ornstein and Mann, 2000a).

According to Hugh Heclo (2000: 19–29) there have been six main trends that have led to the emergence of the 'permanent campaign': to begin with, the role of the political parties has changed considerably over time. American parties are now significantly weaker in organization, candidate recruitment and mobilization, but stronger in ideology, social distinctiveness and attack politics than they were five decades ago. Second, the system of interest-group politics has become much more open and expansive. This has fostered the emergence of a new style of governing by including more people who consider campaigning with and against special-interest groups to be at the very heart of governing. A third key feature fostering the 'permanent campaign' relates to the rise of the new communications technology of modern politics, including television, talk radio, cable TV and the Internet. These new technologies have not only provided politicians with new devices of public leadership, they also have created a completely new dynamic of mass communication in which the reporting of politics and government increasingly takes the shape of dramatic entertainment. Fourth, new political technologies, in particular public relations and polling, have been created and used with ever more sophisticated professional skill. A fifth feature has been the growing need for political money, which was at least in part a direct result of the dramatically increased need to engage in a permanent campaign effort. Finally, as Heclo argues, the emergence of the 'permanent campaign' simply reflected the higher stakes for all actors in the political system in activist government: 'Campaigning has become big and permanent because government has become big and permanent' (ibid.: 27).

A thorough discussion of this sweeping assessment has been provided elsewhere (Ornstein and Mann, 2000b). Our focus here is confined to addressing the structural and behavioural changes in the area of public leadership that may be observed at the level of individual presidents and the presidency. There are, to begin with, several structural developments worth noting: since the late 1960s, public leadership has not only come to account for a considerable proportion of time in the president's schedule; there has also been a gradual institutional transformation of the presidency by the addition of so-called 'outreach' offices designed to buttress the president's popular support (Tenpas, 2000). The White House Press Office and the White House Office of Communications are the two most important sections of the institutional presidency dealing with the media.[18] Although there is much co-operation between the two offices, they do have different roles to play. While the former sees itself as something like an 'honest broker' between the president and the press, the Office of Communications – created by Nixon and consolidated as a key institutional resource of presidential leadership under Reagan – is responsible for the strategic aspects of presidential media management. Under more recent presidents, the Office of Communications has become a co-ordination centre regarding all aspects of public presidential leadership including questions of both presentation and public policy. As Timothy Cook (1998: 138) has pointed out,

> [t]he 'line of the day', which originated as a means largely to control the mass-mediated image of the president for electoral purposes, has become a way to specify what the presidency is to *be* and to *do*, setting out goals and missions, and coordinating the pursuit thereof throughout the executive branch.

While more recent research on presidential leadership of the public and agenda-setting in the American political system has questioned the conventional wisdom that sees the president as the country's 'chief agenda setter',[19] there can be no doubt that the aforementioned institutional adjustments to increasing challenges have strengthened significantly the president's structural capacity to provide public leadership. This having been said, a closer look suggests that much room is left for different leadership styles to generate a highly specific profile of the public presidency during different periods of time.

White House public relations exercises remained rather unsophisticated throughout the Truman years. Most of the activities of the press office were confined to issuing news releases and providing the necessary logistical support for reporters covering the White House. Thus, much depended on Truman's personal performance at press conferences, which revealed his limitations as a public speaker, especially when compared directly with his exceptionally gifted predecessor. These limitations came to the fore in particular when Truman talked off the cuff, occasions that often became 'an invitation to political embarrassment' (Greenstein, 2000: 39).

Although he 'invented' televised press conferences in 1955 (which were taped and broadcast with some delay), Eisenhower was the last president of the pre-television age. From a historical perspective, Eisenhower stands out as one of the most popular post-war presidents, though much of his public popularity as president was gained in his previous life as a military leader. His overall leadership approach as president relied to a rather limited extent on public persuasion. Nevertheless, Eisenhower not only devoted considerable energy to his public speeches, he even sought strategic advice from a Hollywood actor.

While many organizational features of the modern public presidency were created during the Nixon years, the Kennedy presidency is usually seen as the watershed in the history of relations between post-war presidents and the public. In retrospect, Kennedy has been described as 'a definite trailblazer in his use of the news media and in his overall communication strategy' (Han, 2001: 43). This assessment is based primarily on Kennedy's decision to hold live televised press conferences, which ever since have formed part of the White House's wider task of public relations. But there were other changes too. These included a better access for reporters to members of the White House staff than during the Eisenhower years, television specials centring on extended interviews with the president, off-the-record background briefings for key White House reporters, and various social events at the White House for journalists and publishers. Moreover, Kennedy recognized the importance of public opinion polls and started the practice of poll-testing several decisions and messages,[20] though some sources contend that he was so uneasy about this that he kept the polling data locked in a safe in his brother's office (Green, 2002: 13). The sophisticated efforts of selling the president to the public paid off well. Kennedy's public approval ratings remained marvellous throughout his term, though his largely unmatched public appeal seems to have had other underpinnings that lay beyond his performance as a public speaker.

Neither Johnson nor Nixon ever managed to step out fully from Kennedy's shadow. Both came over as rather stiff and uneasy on the bulk of formal occasions. Johnson could be persuasive in small groups and more informal settings, but lost his natural way when talking on television. Some observers felt that his long legislative career had somehow diminished his capacity for public leadership. Yet the rather negative relationship between the White House and the press during the Johnson years cannot be explained by the president's limited rhetorical skills alone. The growing disconnection between Johnson's public pledges about Vietnam and his administration's actions developed into what many scholars have described as a serious and unprecedented 'credibility gap' between the presidency on the one side and the press and the public on the other (Stuckey, 1991: 78).

Nixon was convinced that public relations mattered significantly, and directed a reasonable proportion of organizational and personal resources into this field. The overall level of his public activities decreased, however, with each year of his term (Han, 2001: 88–9). Much of his public strategy focused on certain televised events, whereas press conferences played a rather modest role in his concept of public leadership. The administration's overall success in mobilizing public support for specific policy measures remained limited. Although Nixon became the first post-war president to be associated with the notion of a more systematic effort of 'going public' as a substitute for legislative bargaining, re-election politics figured larger among his administration's strategic aims than building support for specific legislative measures (Lammers and Genovese, 2000: 233). The Nixon years left an important legacy regarding the relationship between the president and the press. While much of the distrust between the two sides had been sown and started to grow under his predecessor, it was Nixon who institutionalized the divide by providing the press corps with new official office space that was more comfortable but was located outside the West Wing reception area.

The rather unfavourable political circumstances that influenced the performance of the Ford and Carter presidencies in the area of executive – legislative relations had a similar effect at the level of public leadership. Despite their different approaches to public leadership, both Ford and Carter experienced serious limitations in (re)gaining the trust of the mass media and garnering the necessary amount of public support for their administrations' policies. This was also reflected in their rather low average ratings of public support, which remained consistently well below 50 per cent.

The record of the Ford administration is somewhat paradoxical in itself. On the one hand, Ford obviously lacked the qualities of an impressive public speaker and prompted comparisons with Truman rather than with Kennedy. On the other hand, he engaged desperately in various forms of public relations, developing a more intense schedule of public activities than any of his predecessors. Carter was not much better qualified and equipped as a public speaker than Ford and, in addition, showed little willingness to work to improve his performance. While his often moralistic (yet sometimes seemingly 'passionless') style helped to restore the integrity of the office of president, it did little to provide him with the necessary amount of support to achieve his policy goals. A key lesson for later incumbents in the Oval Office from Carter's performance as public leader was that overexposure in the media may weaken, rather than strengthen, the president's public standing.

Ronald Reagan seemed perfectly fitted to the age of television politics, and to the specific needs of appearing convincing on television. His rhetorical skills on television have remained unmatched, and for many represented Reagan's strongest point. Alongside his remarkable rhetorical gift, 'likeability' was Reagan's most important political resource in winning the public over (despite widespread and sometimes serious reservations about his staunchly conservative policies). While 'likeability' may to a large extent be considered a natural gift, Reagan's public profile was to be shaped significantly by an event that happened early in 1981. Only two months into his presidency Reagan was shot, but instead of withdrawing from public view, he smilingly addressed the nation from his hospital bed just hours after the incident. What has been highlighted as 'the defining moment of his presidency' (Gergen, 2000: 176) changed Reagan's perception among the public for ever, making him appear as 'someone who had guts'. There was a highly efficient support structure in the White House designed to exploit Reagan's public appeal to the full. Exceptionally effective use was made of the 'line-of-the-day' approach to presidential messages, with even minor public events being skilfully arranged to generate a very special atmosphere. However, as Richard Neustadt (1990: 275) has contended, 'the senior officer in government who helped the most was Reagan himself'. It was the president rather than anyone else who insisted that media relations were consistently treated as being more important than all other issues in his appointment schedule – an order of priorities that distinguished his presidency from previous administrations, and even more sharply so from his immediate successor in the Oval Office.

George H. W. Bush's rather modest performance as public leader has been widely acknowledged as one of the key weaknesses of his leadership style. His shortcomings as a public speaker contrasted unfavourably with Reagan's mastery, and made them appear even more serious than would have been the case had Bush been the direct successor to, for example, Ford or Carter. Whereas, in policy terms, Bush regarded himself very much as a guardian of the public order created under Reagan, he tried hard to break free from Reagan's public leadership style. In an attempt to distance himself from the Reagan approach, Bush largely replaced prime-time press conferences and addresses with frequent informal press conferences in which questions could be asked in a setting

designed to avoid the typically adversarial nature of evening press conferences. Moreover, serious efforts were made to establish a culture of
having substantive discussions on specific policy issues, on which Bush
was at his best. However, this approach found little favour with the
White House press corps, whose members agreed almost unanimously
that Bush was anything but an effective communicator.

The Clinton administration has widely come to be seen as the ultimate
example of the modern public presidency, one in which governing
became virtually synonymous to campaigning (Jones, 1996). An excessive
travel schedule, an enormous spending record, and the frequent use of
unconventional and innovative communication strategies, including
the Internet, talk shows and town hall meetings, merged into a largely
unprecedented public leadership exercise. The campaign mode of
governing may have fitted Clinton's personal operating style nicely, as
much as the use of unconventional communication channels was
favoured by the highly tensioned relationship between the press and
the White House. However, the key motive behind the administration's
excessive commitment to 'going public' was the fact that it served as
a compensation for the very modest share of the vote with which Clinton
won office both in 1992 and 1996. After the dramatic mid-term losses
of the Democrats in the 1994 congressional elections, and as a result of
these, Clinton fashioned a new communications strategy which was
much more defensive than his initial approach, designed mainly to
defend the status quo against changes supported by the Republican
majority in Congress. While this paid off in terms of public support for
the president, it forced the administration to co-opt many items from
the Republican agenda, such as balancing the budget in particular.
Measured against the extraordinary amount of time and money spent on
public relations, Clinton's public approval ratings remained surprisingly
modest for the whole of his first, and large parts of his second, term.
Remarkably, public approval ratings for Clinton (as president, not as
a private person) were highest in 1998 and 1999, during the period of
the impeachment trial (Norris, 2001: 9).

During the early stages of his presidency, George W. Bush stuck to
a rather low-profile approach to public leadership. Bush's public presentations lacked a sophisticated style of public speaking, and attempts were
made to keep meetings with the press to a minimum. Many of his early
speeches lasted for less than fifteen minutes, and if he agreed to televised
interviews, it was made sure in advance that these remained far from
any sort of hard talk. As Frank Bruni (2002: 241) has observed, Bush's
first extended national television interview as president was to a sports

commentator on the subject of baseball. Yet there was not only a lack of interest on the president's side to engage in public relations. The administration also had remarkable difficulty in obtaining time on television for presidential speeches and, perhaps even more importantly, in gaining an audience when coverage of public activities was provided (Edwards, 2002: 43).

As in other fields, the key focus of many early assessments has been a comparison between George W. Bush and his immediate predecessor, Bill Clinton. In his early announcements, partly dating back to his election campaign, Bush went out of his way to highlight the differences between his own and Clinton's style. There were in fact notable differences, especially at the level of public self-presentation and with regard to the policy content of public speeches. Another key difference between the Bush and the Clinton White House related to the degree of accessibility by the media, which was remarkably low from the beginning of the Bush presidency, with a tendency towards a further decline.[21] Moreover, unlike previous administrations, the Bush White House generally did not provide briefings for reporters on policy initiatives from the White House podium. Information was shared only with a small group of trusted journalists, while more general presentations and explanations of policy were left to cabinet secretaries (Kumar, 2003: 392).

On many other dimensions there were, however, considerable similarities, which became more evident as the Bush presidency went on. To begin with, the press and communications operations under Bush and Clinton involved notably similar numbers of people, though the proportion of people assigned to the Press Office under Bush was considerably smaller than under Clinton (Kumar, 2002: 40). This was seen largely to reflect a somewhat lesser emphasis of the Bush White House on day-to-day press operations. Parallels between Bush and Clinton also emerged at the level of their respective domestic travel schedules and the partisan nature of their campaign efforts (Cook, 2002: 757–62). Furthermore, most observers identified increasing similarities between him and his predecessor in terms of polling. While Bush prominently denounced any decision-making by polls and promised an end to the 'permanent campaign' during the presidential race, there was a broad consensus among those covering the White House that Bush's leadership style was not significantly less political or fundamentally different from Clinton's (Harris, 2001; Green, 2002).

The effect of 11 September 2001 on the development of the public presidency can hardly be exaggerated. Several post-9/11 changes related to the internal workings of the communication section of the

White House and the public presentation of the president. Before the terrorist attacks, Bush had hardly ever attended the 'message meetings' at which the administration's communications strategy was planned. After 11 September 2001 he participated regularly at daily meetings designed specifically to set the right tone to meet altered public expectations (Bruni, 2002: 246–7). While still not being a naturally gifted public speaker, Bush became significantly more assertive and articulate. What mattered perhaps more than (limited) rhetorical sophistication was the fact that Bush managed to create a rare degree of 'authenticity' while addressing the nation – at least as long as the focus remained firmly on the subject of war on terrorism.

Even more visible were the effects of 11 September at the level of poll data. In a historically comparative overview, focusing specifically on the amount of increase in different presidents' public approval in the aftermath of major events, Bush stood out uniquely, with an increase of no less than 35 percentage points – going from 51 per cent to 86 per cent (*The Economist*, 2 February 2002: 27).[22] However, even Bush's unprecedented second honeymoon with the American public could not last. The president's approval ratings fell more or less steadily from a peak in September 2001 until the eve of the war against Iraq, which provided a major boost to his approval score. A similar, though less dramatic, surge marked the immediate aftermath of the capture of Saddam Hussein in mid-December 2003. But by March 2004, Bush's approval ratings had, for the first time, fallen to less than 50 per cent. According to Gallup poll data, just 49 per cent of Americans approved, while 48 per cent disapproved, of the job Bush was doing as president. This not only prompted inevitable comparisons with his father's presidency, but also led many to consider Bush's decision to go to war in Iraq as the ultimate, and defining, issue of his presidency (Schneider, 2004).

Conclusion

The differences in leadership skills and strategies among post-war presidents in the wider political process have been no less significant than within the core executive territory. Other things being equal, however, the impact of individual leadership styles at the level of the wider political system is considerably more limited than within the core executive. As the president's position in the wider political system is so much weaker than within the executive branch, the specific style of an individual president marks just one factor among many others that shape the national decision-making process and its outcomes. Cases of similar leadership styles, developed by presidents having to act under rather different historical circumstances, are even more illuminating than examples including obvious differences in style. Lyndon Johnson's and George H. W. Bush's strong emphasis on traditional legislative bargaining clearly reflected their common nature as 'legislative creatures'. But, however similar their approaches to dealing with the legislative branch may have been, their legislative achievements could hardly have been more different (though this holds true only if the focus is confined to Johnson's early years).

While, presidential leadership styles may change over time, both in the core executive and in the wider political process, there is a higher probability that changes in style at the wider political system level are the direct result of changes in the political environment, such as changing patterns of party control in Congress. There is also no 'natural' path of change – comparable to the common tendency of presidents to abandon 'cabinet government' later in their terms – which presidents follow in the wider political process as their incumbency goes on. Whereas the basic policy convictions of presidents may be persistent, choosing appropriate leadership styles for achieving specific policy goals in the wider political process remains to a large extent a reactive action. Moreover, as the Clinton experience suggests, sometimes a change in style, initiated by changing circumstances, may well be followed by notable changes at policy level.

The party affiliations of different presidents – when considered as a factor in their own right – seem to have had virtually no measurable effect on the overall performance of individual presidents in the wider political process. Some of the most obvious parallels in style and performance relate to representatives of different parties. Whereas Kennedy (D) and Reagan (R) have been the only truly 'great communicators' after 1945, it is Reagan and Johnson (D) who stand out as the masters of the post-war legislative presidency. It may, however, be said that, at least in some respects, post-war presidents from the same party encountered similar political circumstances. Whereas most Republican presidents of the post-war period were 'minority presidents' (in terms of patterns of party control between the executive and the legislative branch), most of their Democratic counterparts could govern with a Congress controlled by their own party. This familiar pattern has, however, started to show signs of change more recently: whereas Clinton was the first Democratic president who faced a Congress controlled by the opposition party for two-thirds of his term in office, George W. Bush was the first Republican incumbent since 1953 to start his presidency under the conditions of 'unified government', and the only Republican president after the Second World War who succeeded in overcoming the state of 'divided government' later in his presidency.

As in the field of core executive decision-making, there have been major historical changes both with regard to the structural conditions and the actual manifestations of executive leadership in the American political system. The emergence of 'divided government' arguably marks the single most important, though certainly not the only, major element of change characterizing the post-war period. While the 1970s witnessed important structural reforms in Congress, resulting in a greater amount of decentralization and fragmentation of the legislative arena, the period since the early 1990s has been marked by an increasing amount of 'party politicization' of congressional politics. Moreover, there has been an explosion in the number of interest groups keeping the presidency (and Congress) under siege, while public expectations towards the presidency and towards public leadership by the president have risen dramatically.

The consequences of these complex transformations remain very much open to debate. While it may seem reasonable to argue that, given the recent structural changes, the leverage of the 'postmodern presidency' within the political system has decreased considerably (Schier, 2000), not all features may be accepted at face value. In particular, the effects of 'divided government' remain rather ambiguous. As the findings of more recent works suggest, split party control – especially since the emergence of increased 'party discipline' and 'party warfare' in Congress – makes it more difficult for presidents to get their way, or at least more likely that presidents oppose significant legislation (Edwards *et al.*, 1997). Other effects of 'divided government' seem to have been more positive from the president's point of view. As Michael Bailey has revealed, presidents since Truman have been able to maintain or even to improve their popularity when facing a Congress controlled by the opposition party, and statistically have enjoyed better re-election chances during periods of 'divided government' than under 'unified government'. The same author describes 'divided government' as 'an escape hatch for presidents, allowing them to maintain the appearance of heroism without needing to deliver the goods' (Bailey, 2002: 44). At the same time, 'divided government' can work as a major additional catalyst of the 'permanent campaign', helping to overcome possible personal reservations of individual presidents about more aggressive forms of public leadership. George W. Bush's early transformation from a deliberately low-profile public performer into a prime example of 'permanent campaigner' during his first years in office provides the most recent case in point.

What the current chapter of the development of the American presidency also suggests is that there remains a large amount of unpredictability as to future challenges and parameters of presidential leadership. In a carefully drafted argument published in the late 1990s, Richard Rose (1998) argued that future presidents would find it more important than ever since the end of the Second World War to put domestic politics and policy first. This could have hardly been wider of the mark for the presidency of George W. Bush. However – given the completely unforeseeable challenges of 11 September 2001 and its aftermath – neither the erring presidential scholar nor in fact even the president himself should be blamed for that.

6
Britain: Executive Leadership from the Top

Executive Leadership in the Parliamentary Arena

The most basic rule governing the constitutional and political relationship between the executive and parliament in Britain, as in any parliamentary democracy, is to be seen in the government's obligation to step down if it loses the support of the parliamentary majority. As in the bulk of other major West European parliamentary democracies (with the notable exception of Italy, where governments can be forced to resign by a vote of either house of parliament), the right to dismiss the government rests with the first chamber, the House of Commons.[1] However, as with so many other arrangements of the British constitution, this key principle of British parliamentary government has experienced remarkable transformations over time. In traditional constitutional theory, the view prevailed that governments had to resign, and call a general election, after losing a major bill at the second reading stage. In the early 1970s, the convention emerged that a government was to step down only after suffering a defeat in an explicit vote of censure. Even though there was no firmly established practice of governments resigning on a single lost second reading vote in the House of Commons before 1970, the premiership of Edward Heath (1970–4) is widely seen as a crucial watershed regarding the agreed terms of when governments are to resign (Norton, 1981). Whereas the number of occasions on which governments lost a division in the Commons has increased since the 1970s, only one administration of the post-war period – the Callaghan minority government in March 1979 – has in fact been brought down by a vote in the Commons.

The genuinely parliamentary character of the British governmental system would appear to make any conception of 'executive–legislative relations' an ill-suited device for studying executive leadership in the parliamentary arena. Still, as Anthony King (1976: 14) has shown, it is both possible and analytically useful to distinguish different patterns of interaction characterizing the legislative decision-making processes in parliamentary democracies.[2] In Britain, the 'intra-party mode' (which refers to the relationship between the government and the backbenchers of the governing party) and the 'opposition mode' (concerning the relationship between government and opposition) are of particular relevance.

The 'intra-party mode' is of crucial importance in any parliamentary system, which makes it largely useless for distinguishing different types of parliamentary democracies. What is noteworthy about the British model is its specific organizational devices designed to facilitate the intra-party dimension of executive leadership in the parliamentary arena. The British system is special for its sophisticated system of party whips (usually between nine and eleven for each of the two major parties, plus several assistant whips), whose main task it is to act as a channel between the executive and parliament and help to produce the necessary amount of 'party discipline' in parliamentary voting. The government whips work not only from parliament but also use a special office in Downing Street. The duties of the governmental chief whip extend far beyond securing parliamentary support for the government's policies. The Chief Whip's Office acts as an important link between the government and the opposition. Moreover, it is very much involved in organizing the government's legislative programme, including the difficult task of balancing competing demands of individual departments. As Lee *et al.* (1998: 223) have pointed out, the chief whip is rarely made a member of the cabinet in order to maintain his or her freedom to sort out disputes between ministers, which, however, hardly diminishes his or her role as the prime minister's agent in parliament. As any other member of the government, the chief whip is bound by collective ministerial responsibility which obliges him or her to refrain from criticizing the government's policies in public; but, unlike ministers, he or she has no right at all to speak in the chamber (Searing, 1994: 280–1).

While both the 'intra-party mode' and the 'cross-party mode' of executive–legislative relations play a certain role in the British context,[3] it is clearly the 'opposition mode' that represents the dominant pattern of interaction in the parliamentary arena, and distinguishes the British case from other, more consensus-orientated, West European parliamentary democracies (King, 1976: 17–18; Norton, 1998: 21–4).

There are several reasons to explain the dominance of the 'opposition mode'. Most important of all, there are crucial institutional parameters. Among the major West European countries only the French variant of *parlementarisme rationalisé* comes close to, or in fact even exceeds, the degree of governmental domination of parliament to be observed in Britain. The minority parties in the House of Commons are effectively deprived of virtually any potential co-governing devices that mark the opposition's institutional opportunity structure in most other parliamentary democracies. There is neither a minority veto for bills with particularly far-reaching implications or constitutional amendments,[4] nor any recent tradition of co-governing by the opposition in the standing committees (for which, again, most structural preconditions are missing in the British House of Commons). Moreover, there are various legal devices, such as the 'guillotine' (allowing timetabling of debate) and the 'closure' (allowing debate to be ended), designed to guarantee that the government gets its way. In line with the constitutional doctrine of 'parliamentary sovereignty' (see page 175 in this volume), there is also no extra-parliamentary institution, such as a constitutional court, that opposition parties could turn to in order to challenge the legislative actions and policies of the government. One of the very few decision-making powers of the minority parties in the House of Commons may be found in the area of parliamentary agenda-setting. Standing Order 14 stipulates that the opposition has the right to determine the subject of parliamentary debate on twenty days of each session, with seventeen days being reserved for the largest opposition party.

As a consequence, practically all parliamentary activities of the opposition concentrate on scrutinizing and challenging the government through parliamentary debates and question hours.[5] Among the different devices of parliamentary questioning, Prime Minister's Question Time marks by far the most prominent and important device for scrutinizing the government in parliament, which has largely managed to defend its special status even in the age of 'mediated politics', as both the press and television pay particular attention to it. In operation for a very long time, Prime Minister's Question Time was placed on a regular basis for the first time in 1961 when the questions to the prime minister were given a guaranteed slot in the House of Commons agenda, at 3.15 pm on Tuesdays and Thursdays. In 1997, Blair introduced a 30-minute long Prime Minister's Question Time, to be held from 3.00 to 3.30 pm on Wednesdays – a change that has been greeted with reasonable scepticism by many observers. There are now fewer members who get the opportunity to ask supplementary questions, and issues arising in the second half of the week stand a much smaller chance of becoming the subject of Prime Minister's Question Time than before (Seaton and Winetrobe, 1999: 153). Since January 2003, Prime Minister's Question Time has been held on Wednesdays from 1.00 to 1.30 pm. Compared with the important effects of the 1997 reform, the latest changes have had a rather modest impact on parliamentary procedure. Other things being equal, it gives the opposition a little less time to prepare topical questions carefully.

The institutional parameters shaping the political processes in the parliamentary arena include other devices, some of which constrain not only the opposition parties. In notable contrast to the situation in many other West European parliamentary democracies, backbenchers of the majority party in the House of Commons face virtually the same serious restrictions regarding the initiation of bills as do their fellows on the other side of the House. There is a strict separation between 'government bills' (which may only be initiated by a government minister), and 'private members' bills', for which there is a sophisticated procedure laid down in the House of Commons' Standing Order 14. Another serious restriction relates to the financial dimension of legislative initiatives. As Standing Order 48 specifies, the House of Commons 'will receive no petition for any sum relating to public service or proceed upon any motion for a grant or charge upon the public revenue...unless recommended from the Crown' – that is, the government. Moreover, the government possesses the authority to dissolve parliament and call an election at any time.[6] Once a matter to require the consent of the full cabinet, the decision to dissolve the House of Commons has long become part of the prime minister's prerogative. While the prime minister's ability to use the power of dissolution as a means to 'discipline' backbenchers of the governing party may have been overestimated at times, it undoubtedly remains an important instrument of control in the hands of the chief executive for which there is no equivalent in many other parliamentary democracies.[7]

The institutional features structurally favouring the dominance of the 'opposition mode' also include the British two-party system – 'two-party' in so far as only two parties stand a reasonable chance of forming a single-party (majority) government, rather than in terms of the overall number of parties holding seats in parliament.[8] A historical perspective on government/opposition relations in Britain suggests that it was in fact the party system that shaped parliamentary rules and the actors' behaviour rather than the reverse. Before the 1867 electoral reform – which triggered the evolution of a two-party system with coherent party organizations and a dramatically increased degree of 'party discipline' in parliament – strategies for parliamentary co-governing were rather common even in the British House of Commons (Harrison, 1996: 278–9). Finally, the dominance of the 'opposition mode' in the parliamentary arena, and its extensions beyond Westminster (Johnson, 1997), must also be seen as a reflection of the British political culture which values transparency and a clear separation of responsibilities more than any kind of pooling of government and opposition expertise behind closed doors.

Institutional and cultural parameters of executive leadership in the parliamentary arena have been mixed with genuinely political factors, the most important of which has been the size of the government's parliamentary majority in the House of Commons. The overwhelming majority of British post-war governments have been majority governments.[9] While some of those were riding on the edge (such as the last Attlee government, 1950–1, and the Churchill government, 1951–5), others enjoyed parliamentary majorities sufficient almost to demoralize the opposition (such as the Thatcher government in the 1983–7 parliament, and the Blair government since 1997). However, there have been several occasions on which governments lacked proper majority support in the House of Commons. Whereas Wilson in February 1974 started his administration on the basis of an electoral result that had produced a 'hung parliament', Callaghan inherited a majority government from Wilson in March 1976 that soon lost its majority status through a string of by-election defeats. Callaghan's minority government tried to secure a reasonable capacity to act by forging an agreement with the Liberal Party, the so-called 'Lib–Lab pact', which was in force from March 1977 until July 1978 (Maor, 1998: 71–81). In late February 1997, about ten weeks away from the general election, the Conservative Party, under John Major, finally lost its absolute majority through a long series of crushing defeats at by-elections. However, the Tories stayed in power until the May 1997 general election, as the government was able to draw on the support of the small Ulster Unionist Party.

As already mentioned, strong 'party discipline' at parliamentary divisions (and beyond) marks a key feature of the British model of parliamentary government. This notwithstanding, it is possible to identify a slight fall in the voting cohesion of British parliamentary parties since the 1970s. Significant votes, offering serious threats to the government's majority status, were virtually non-existent until 1970. They became more frequent between 1970 and 1979, however, and again in the period 1992–7 (see the figures in Norton, 1997: 162–3). During its first term

(1997–2001), the Blair government became the first administration since the 1960s not to lose a single division in the House of Commons. Detailed analysis reveals, however, that this was largely because of the government's huge parliamentary majority. As Philip Cowley (2001: 820–1) has calculated, no less than a third of all Labour MPs voted against the government at least once. During Blair's second term, 'party discipline' among Labour MPs further decreased, on several occasions to an extent that brought the government to the verge of parliamentary humiliation.

A number of different explanations for the notable increase in parliamentary dissent have been put forward. Rather poor empirical evidence exists to support the thesis that the change of voting behaviour in the House of Commons has much to do with the changing constitutional convention of bringing down a government as a result of a significant lost vote; that is, the end of the so-called '100 per cent rule' (Baxter *et al.*, 1986). Two other explanations are more convincing. The first focuses on long-term changes in the membership of the House of Commons. Since the 1970s, members have on average been better educated, more 'professional', and much less deferential than previous generations of MPs – a change that is assumed to have generated a much more critical stance towards 'discipline-focused' approaches to parliamentary decision-making. The second explanation emphasizes the strong impact of poor executive leadership in the House of Commons on the voting behaviour of MPs. According to Philip Norton (1995), Heath's 'Olympic style' marks the most important single variable in explaining the dramatically decreasing 'party discipline' among the Conservatives in the 1970–4 parliament, and many contemporary Labour MPs would appear likely to give similar reasons for their opposition to the Blair government. The latter explanation's emphasis on the leadership styles of prime ministers brings us to an assessment of the parliamentary performance of post-war governments, focusing especially on the role of the prime minister in the parliamentary arena.

Compared to many other British post-war prime ministers, Clement Attlee was not a particularly impressive parliamentary performer, not least because of his rather modest rhetorical skills and his legendary terseness in speech. Nevertheless, he enjoyed a reasonable authority over the House. The prime minister's performance in the House of Commons corresponded to an overall strong position of the government in the parliamentary arena, resulting from a number of different factors (Dowse, 1978: 45–8). Among them, the extensive formal consultative network between the government and the Parliamentary Labour Party (PLP), established by Herbert Morrison, was of particular importance.

It consisted mainly of a liaison committee (including Morrison, the chief whip, the secretary of the PLP, a Labour peer, and two other members), a large number of MPs organized into functionally specialized groups, and bi-weekly meetings of the parliamentary party. The latter were frequently attended by the prime minister and other members of the cabinet. The size of Labour's majority allowed a relaxation of the standing orders on discipline to be introduced in 1946. As the 1945–50 parliament progressed, dissent grew stronger, with five members being expelled from the PLP (though mainly for alleged communist sympathies and activities outside parliament). It also played into the hands of the government that the far left, as the most likely intra-party veto power, was rather weak and moreover lacked a parliamentary leadership free from the reins of collective responsibility. After the 1950 general election, which brought Labour's majority down to only five seats, the government's room for manoeuvre became rather limited, although it suffered no major defeat. Another factor that made managing the Commons considerably more difficult during the last months of the Attlee government was the much greater cohesion among Labour backbench dissidents who rallied behind Aneurin Bevan after his resignation from government in April 1951.

Churchill profited significantly from the deference of many MPs to his historical record as Britain's war leader. Still, leading the Conservatives and governing the Commons during the first half of the 1950s was anything but easy. Partly responsible for this was the Tories' rather slim parliamentary majority, which reportedly led Churchill to instruct his minister of transport to ensure that at no time should more than five Conservative MPs be aboard the same areoplane in order not to have 'too many eggs in one basket' (Ramsden, 1995: 239). Garnering backbench support for the government's priorities became more difficult as ministers lost their right to hold formal membership of the 1922 Committee. In an attempt to facilitate communication between both sides, whips were eventually given the right to attend (but not to vote at) meetings of the 1922 Committee. On the whole, serious backbench revolts remained extremely rare during Churchill's post-war premiership. There were only ten divisions during the 1951–5 parliament on which any Conservative MPs voted against the whip, and only two of them involved more than three MPs (ibid.: 238, 265). Churchill's last two years as prime minister were overshadowed by the dramatically declining state of his health. In particular, his growing deafness proved an even more serious handicap in dealing with the Commons than it did in the cabinet room.

Eden's performance in parliament was a rather mixed one. This had much to do with his persistent ill-health and his rather restricted policy experience in areas other than foreign affairs. Still, it has rightly been pointed out that the diminishing respect that the House of Commons showed towards the end of Eden's term was mainly the result of serious policy misjudgements on the government's side (Borthwick, 1995: 98). During and after the Suez crisis, the prime minister's position in parliament became virtually untenable. Despite the blistering attacks the prime minister faced in the Commons, the government's grip on parliament would almost certainly have been even worse had it not been for Heath's highly skilful dealing with the Conservative parliamentary party's and R. A. Butler's refusal to give the dissenters a clear lead during the Suez crisis (Ramsden, 1995: 306–11).

Macmillan started his incumbency as an unusually dominant figure in the parliamentary arena. His hold over the House tightened even further after the impressive 1959 election victory of the Conservatives, which increased their majority to a hundred. To a considerable extent, Macmillan's powerful position in the Commons reflected his strong position within the Conservative Party, which became particularly evident in the aftermath of the Suez crisis. The Liaison Committee – having been established as early as 1952, but without being a particularly efficient body during the Churchill and Eden years – became a very useful channel for government–backbench relations, in particular regarding questions of policy presentation. In 1957, it was complemented by a new Steering Committee, to be chaired by the prime minister, whose task was to develop medium-term strategies of Conservative policy. Macmillan also had a strong personal interest in developing good relations with Conservative backbenchers. His efforts were supported efficiently by the remarkable skills of his two successive parliamentary private secretaries, Robert Allan and, from 1958, Anthony Barber, who both had former experience in the Whips' Office (Ramsden, 1996: 26). The negative repercussions of the spectacular cabinet reshuffle of July 1962 did not leave the prime minister's standing in parliament untouched, however. A number of major policy failures, including Britain's unsuccessful attempt to join the European Community – a project Macmillan had set his heart upon – did their part to undermine the prime minister's position in parliament and among the public at large. From February 1963 onwards, any convincing parliamentary performance by the prime minister was made even more difficult by a change in the office of Labour opposition leader, in which Hugh Gaitskell was replaced by the energetic Harold Wilson.

Douglas-Home remained a rather pale figure in the House of Commons. His total number of parliamentary days in office did not amount to more than 155, and his major parliamentary speeches were limited to less than half a dozen. As Ian Gilmour and Mark Garnett (1997: 210) have noted, 'In the House of Commons the prime minister was so modest, friendly and open with his backbenchers that he won over even those who thought he was the wrong man for his office.' However, this did not save Douglas-Home from becoming one of the least powerful leaders in parliament after 1945. Not only did he compare unfavourably with most of his recent predecessors at 10 Downing Street; he also, and more importantly, appeared as a helpless victim in the hands of his main opponent from the Labour Party, Harold Wilson, who remains for many Britain's most outstanding opposition leader of the twentieth century. Also, Douglas-Home's position in the Tory camp was utterly constrained. His personal popularity with some older and conservative fellows must not be confused with any kind of political command of the Conservative parliamentary party. The most spectacular parliamentary decision of Douglas-Home's premiership – the abolition of Resale Price Maintenance (RPM) in May 1964 – was initiated by the secretary for trade and industry, Edward Heath, rather than the prime minister. Heath's forcefully triggered initiative left Douglas-Home with few other options than to throw his support behind Heath's bill, even though he was not fully convinced it was the right thing to do. The bill produced the biggest backbench revolt since the fall of Chamberlain in May 1940 (Thorpe, 1996: 355–8). In retrospect, the abolition of RPM has been described as 'Sir Alec's Poll Tax' (Gilmour and Garnett, 1997: 207) – a measure that alienated the government from many within the party and had even more serious effects in the electoral arena.

In his early days as prime minister, Wilson fully lived up to the high expectations he had fuelled by his impressive record as opposition leader. At least during the first two or three years of his premiership he dominated the House in the same way that he dominated his cabinet. He was a brilliant parliamentary speaker, an impression enhanced by the rather poor performances of his main challengers from the opposition benches. Astonishingly, his triumphant election victory in 1966 marked a negative turning point with regard to his hold over the Commons. For whatever reason, Wilson somehow seemed better at managing a narrow parliamentary majority, marking the first years of his premiership, than a strongly Labour-dominated House. In 1968, when public support ratings for the prime minister became very low, there was even speculation among MPs about replacing him. This proved a passing danger, though.

Between March 1974 and early 1976 – Wilson's last term at No. 10 – the House witnessed a much less dominant prime minister. The reasons for Wilson's changed parliamentary performance were largely the same as those defining his altered position within the cabinet (see Chapter 3). In addition, his less dominant role in the parliamentary arena reflected the increased stature and self-confidence of his senior fellows in the PLP. However, as Dennis Kavanagh and Anthony Seldon (2000: 109) have maintained, parliamentary business remained high on Wilson's agenda until the end of his incumbency. He was arguably the last post-war prime minister to hold strongly to the belief that the prime minister should not be out of the country when the Commons was sitting. Also, Wilson's duties as party leader remained closely embedded in the parliamentary arena, with weekly meetings with the Labour Party being held in the parliament building.

Edward Heath, the first Conservative leader chosen by MPs in a con-tested election, was not a particularly good parliamentary performer, although his thorough preparation for parliamentary debates and his policy competence gained him a reasonable amount of respect among MPs on both sides of the House. Like Eden, Heath has been described as being 'notoriously poor at relaxing with backbenchers' (Barber, 1991: 61). More importantly, he did not think that parliamentary support for the government should have to be gained through painstaking persuasion exercises. Another reason for the rather reserved, even hostile, stance of many backbenchers towards the prime minister may be seen in Heath's reluctance to carry out frequent cabinet reshuffles, which deprived ambitious MPs of a chance to climb the ministerial ladder. The small number of other party heavyweights in the cabinet, who could have served as 'double agents' between the government and Conservative backbench MPs, marked another factor contributing to the poor and distant relationship between the government and its parliamentary majority. Finally, the radical nature of the government's legislation, the departure from manifesto policies and major U-turns in various fields all fostered serious discontent among Conservative MPs (Ball, 1996: 328–30, 342). Despite its initial majority of thirty seats the government suffered six major Commons defeats.

James Callaghan faced the most unfavourable majority conditions of any British prime minister of the post-war period. Nevertheless, Callaghan's style of dealing with a difficult parliament appeared 'relaxed and avuncular' (Borthwick, 1995: 99). Being an exceptionally experi-enced former cabinet minister, Callaghan was used to defending himself against blistering attacks from the opposition. The highly effective briefing by the prime minister's staff at No. 10 further helped to exploit this resource of influence. From a historical perspective on executive leadership in the parliamentary arena, Callaghan's record is, however, perhaps even more remarkable for the sharp decline in the prime minister's contributions to parliamentary business, especially in terms of impromptu and unscripted debating interventions. Callaghan's interventions at parliamentary debates were less than half as frequent as those of any previous prime minister – a historical record that was to be exceeded dramatically, however, by his immediate successor, Margaret Thatcher (Dunleavy *et al.*, 1990: 134–5).[10]

Although Thatcher certainly did not particularly enjoy the thrust of parliamentary politics – which might have had something to do with the fact that she was the first female prime minister ever to deal with an overwhelmingly male (at that time even more so than today) institution – most observers tend to rate highly her overall performance in parliament. As Peter Riddell (1989: 112) has maintained, the mastery Thatcher displayed in answering questions during Prime Minister's Question Time should be seen as a crucial dimension of her general political strength. Particularly during her early years, Thatcher devoted considerable time to developing a close relationship with Conservative backbenchers – a quality that gradually disappeared, however, during the later stages of her premiership. Her authority in the Commons was further strengthened by the swiftly changing composition of the Conservative parliamentary party in the 1980s.[11] At least until the mid-1980s, both Thatcher's personal standing and her government's strategic position in parliament also profited from the weakness of their political opponents. Whereas the overall performance of the Labour opposition in the House of Commons slightly improved after the leadership change from Michael Foot to Neil Kinnock in 1983, Labour remained far from representing a credible 'alternative government'. In terms of seats, the Labour opposition in the 1983–7 parliament was even weaker than it had been between 1979 and 1983. Towards the end of the 1980s, both the Labour opposition and Conservative backbenchers became more serious opponents to the Thatcher government, and even the House of Lords gained rare prominence as a committed 'veto player' against Conservative rule (Shell, 1992: 157–78). Among this group of unequal players, the Conservative parliamentary party was the single most important actor. There was a growing resentment among Conservative backbenchers, many of whom felt that they had not been properly rewarded by being offered ministerial offices or, even more often, had been dismissed from office in disgrace. The circumstances of Thatcher's fall from power, triggered by a bitter leadership challenge within the Conservative parliamentary party in late 1990,[12] came as a timely reminder to those about to forget that parliament remains the ultimate check on British prime ministers and their administrations. Those affected may temporarily have included Margaret Thatcher herself, who pointedly remarked towards the end of recounting the events of November 1990, that 'no one will ever understand British politics who does not understand the House of Commons' (Thatcher, 1993: 858).

John Major was forced to pay considerably more attention to both the House of Commons and the Lords than his predecessor. Though earlier assessments suggesting that intra-party opposition in the House of Commons reached unprecedented levels under Major have been dismissed in more recent works (Cowley, 1999), it is still true that the crucial opposition to the government came from the Tory backbenches rather than from the Labour frontbench. It was European integration that became the most prominent battleground between the party leadership and the parliamentary party. The government survived the Commons Maastricht vote in late 1992 only because of the support of the Liberal Democrats. It seems fair to argue that Major achieved much in not letting divisions become even more severe than they did. As Peter Riddell (1994: 47–8) has remarked, Major 'has, at heart, been a chief whip *manqué* ... extremely skilful in handling MPs, understanding their personal and constituency interests'. Major made more parliamentary statements and spoke more frequently in debates than did Thatcher; however, his greater parliamentary activity was largely dictated by his circumstances, including a series of particularly pressing issues such as the Gulf War, BSE and Northern Ireland. From the mid-1990s onwards, managing the Commons became an uphill struggle. Not only did the modest majority gained in the 1992 general election gradually evaporate, but the Labour opposition became an ever more serious political challenger. Whereas the Labour Party eagerly rallied behind its new leader, Tony Blair, who succeeded John Smith in 1994, Major felt he had no other option but to resign from the party leadership in a desperate attempt to restore his authority. Although he was confirmed as leader in the ensuing leadership contest held on 4 June 1995, he barely succeeded in enhancing his control over the defiant Conservative parliamentary party.

The Blair government has enjoyed at least one major advantage in dealing with parliament over most other administrations of the post-war period: both in 1997 and 2001, the Labour Party secured uniquely generous majorities in the House of Commons. The glaring weakness of the parliamentary opposition, to be compared only with stretches of the Thatcher period, became a key aspect shaping the Blair government's performance in the parliamentary arena. The aftermath of the 2001 election witnessed a notable revival of the public and scholarly debate on the possible emergence of a British 'one-party state' that had prospered during the last third of the extended spell of Tory rule (1979–97). After the election of Iain Duncan-Smith as Tory leader in mid-2001, even serious observers started to wonder whether the Conservatives would ever be able to regain office (Garnett and Lynch, 2002: 37).

Among the key characteristics of the Blair style of parliamentary government has been the exceptionally sparse involvement of the prime minister in the Commons voting procedures. Whereas even Thatcher – commanding a comparably sizeable Conservative parliamentary majority in the 1983–7 parliament to Blair after 1997 – participated in about a third of divisions in the 1983/4 session, Blair attended only 5 per cent of divisions during the first session of the 1997–2001 parliament (Riddell, 1998). Despite his patchy involvement in parliamentary business, and occasional suggestions that he lacked an understanding of the House of Commons (Norton, 2003: 550–1), Blair's skills at Prime Minister's Question Time appeared reasonably impressive, if sometimes only because of the shortcomings of his main contenders from the opposition benches. Whereas William Hague, Conservative leader between 1997 and 2001, had some of his fairly infrequent highlights as opposition leader at Prime Minister's Question Time, the parliamentary performances of his successor, Iain Duncan-Smith, became the object of widespread criticism, and even scorn. Duncan-Smith's successor, Michael Howard – elected in November 2003 as the fourth Tory leader in less than seven years – had a promising start at the despatch box. However, observers remained divided over the question as to whether this would become the basis for a more fundamental revitalization of the Conservative Party's electoral appeal.

Given the weakness of the Tory opposition, the key issues plaguing the Blair government's position in parliament were related to the intra-party dimension of legislative decision-making. As if it were anticipating problems in the parliamentary arena, the Labour leadership enforced a new Code of Conduct for Labour MPs as much as a year before being elected to office. Later measures designed to increase the control of the government over the PLP included the appointment of the chief whip to the cabinet. Although there were other devices that were more focused on generating consensus and compromise – such as the weekly meetings between the prime minister and the Labour parliamentary committee (including six backbenchers and the chairman of the PLP) – they did not disperse the overwhelming atmosphere of mutual suspicion and 'control'. Even Blair's reluctant agreement in April 2002 to give evidence before the House of Commons Liaison Committee – a major constitutional innovation in British parliamentary history that seemed sure to bind all future prime ministers – did not make him in the eyes of many a 'parliament man'.

Blair's second term in particular witnessed a series of very serious backbench revolts, including those over Iraq in March 2003, over the creation of foundation hospitals later the same year, and over the introduction of 'top-up tuition fees' at British universities early in 2004. On the Iraq issue, no fewer than 139 Labour MPs voted against their government (*The Times*, 19 March 2003). Divisions on the highly contentious Health and Social Care Bill and Higher Education Bill saw defections on a similar scale. The Higher Education Bill was passed by 316 votes to 311 on its second reading, the largest revolt at this stage for any bill in the previous sixty years (*The Times*, 28 January 2004). Many Labour MPs used these opportunities to voice their opposition to the government's style of legislative leadership and governance, which relied excessively on last-ditch arm-twisting without much previous consultation.

Backbench frustration over what has been dubbed 'legislation by nervous breakdown' can, however, explain only part of the government's persistent problems in the parliamentary arena. The reasons behind the government's considerable problems in the legislative arena have been more diverse. One key factor at work has been the growing dissatisfaction among MPs with the contents of several major bills that were perceived to violate some of the remaining core beliefs of 'old' Labour. This transformed some members of the government, such as Chancellor Gordon Brown and Deputy Prime Minister John Prescott, into leading protagonists of legislative liaison and management, and indispensable supporters of the prime minister. Another factor was related to the prevailing patterns of political recruitment. The spectacular pace of Blair's ministerial reshuffles created a growing pool of former ministers who discovered the joy of speaking out against a government that had thwarted their ministerial ambitions. About five years into the Blair premiership, the number of members of the PLP that had resigned or, more often, been sacked, was more than three dozen; they contrasted with just a handful of others who had been given a second chance to hold governmental office. Finally, there was no obvious cost to rebellion – either to the government or to the rebels themselves. By early 2004, it appeared, in fact, that voting against the government had become a mark of distinction rather than a stain of shame.

In Blair's second term, parliamentary rebellion against the government increasingly involved even the House of Lords. By November 2003, the government had suffered more defeats in the Lords that year than any other government since 1976, with much opposition focusing on the government's Criminal Justice Bill (*The Times*, 5 November 2003). In December of the same year, the Lords took the radical, and highly unusual, step of voting against part of the Queen's Speech (the Lords Reform Bill), which had appeared only once before since the Second World War. The government's most significant defeat of the first quarter of 2004 related to the Constitutional Reform Bill (including the abolition of the post of Lord Chancellor), which was defeated by a surprisingly large majority.

The Scarcity of Institutional Barriers against Majority Rule

The concentration of governmental power in the hands of the executive and the near absence of strong barriers against majority rule are at the very heart of definitions of the traditional Westminster model of democracy. Many of its more specific features are reflections of the overarching doctrine of parliamentary sovereignty. According to the classic definition by A. V. Dicey (1915: 37–8), 'parliamentary sovereignty' implies that parliament has 'the right to make or unmake any law whatever, and further that no person or body is recognised by the law of England as having a right to override or set aside the legislation of Parliament'. This definition has traditionally been interpreted by British constitutional lawyers as comprising four essential features of parliamentary sovereignty: there is no higher legislative authority; no court can declare acts of parliament to be invalid; there is no limit to parliament's sphere of legislation; and no parliament can legally bind its successor or be bound by its predecessor.

Although the doctrine of parliamentary sovereignty has been qualified in practice since the late nineteenth century, it has granted British governments, including the various administrations of the post-war period, a unique authority to rule the country. Among the many challenges to parliamentary sovereignty, the incorporation of the European Convention of Human Rights (ECHR) into British Law in 1998 stands out as the most powerful source of change. There is now a widespread agreement among scholars of the British constitution that the precedence accorded to European law can lead to legislation being suspended or declared to be unlawful and that, as a consequence, parliament has been experiencing an effective challenge to its traditional kind of sovereignty. As Gillian Peele (2000: 79) has specified, the Human Rights Act 1998 'provides a novel mechanism for dealing with cases where the Convention and legislation conflict. Where a judge finds legislation incompatible with the ECHR (and cannot remove the incompatibility by interpretation) she must make a declaration of incompatibility.' However, the provisioned procedures are based on the assumption that in such a case the government will be prepared to remedy the conflict, and so 'much depends on the willingness of a government to comply with judicial decisions'. Thus, despite these major qualifications regarding the doctrine of parliamentary sovereignty, which have prompted radical assessments suggesting that '[f]ear of judicial review ha[s] become a more stringent discipline on ministers than is either Parliament or the media' (Foster, 2000: 344), there is still no institutionalized system of national judicial review regarding acts of parliament,[13] as for example in the United States, that could strike down unconstitutional legislation and serve as an important institutional check on executive power in the political system.

Among the institutional arrangements facilitating, rather than qualifying, strong executive leadership in the British political system, the long absence of virtually any kind of central bank independence marks an often neglected component of the traditional Westminster system. The Bank of England was nationalized by the Attlee government in 1946 and its role was largely confined to serving as the Treasury's agent during the period of post-war construction. The Bank's impact on the major strategic decisions of the government, including the decision not to devalue the pound in 1964 and the applications for EEC membership, remained extremely limited well into the 1970s. Its influence in the area of economic and monetary policy even further declined under the Thatcher and Major governments (Elgie and Thompson, 1998: 61–95).

It has been the Blair government that (partly) abolished this component of unfettered majority rule in Britain by transferring some decision-making power in the field of monetary policy, such as the operational control of setting interest rates in particular, from the Treasury to a newly created nine-member Monetary Policy Committee. Although the Bank of England is still less independent from the government than are the central banks of some other Western countries, including the United States and Germany, the relevance of the 1997 reform can hardly be exaggerated. Some scholars, such as Anthony King, have not hesitated to refer to it as a major piece of 'constitutional change', that 'altered completely one of the most important rules governing the relations among the organs of the government in the UK' and 'simultaneously created . . . a new source of autonomous power in the British system' (King, 2001: 63).

The territorial dimension, which inevitably affects several other components of the political system, has also been among the key features of the traditional Westminster system. From a perspective on legislative institutions, perhaps the most remarkable feature of the British polity is the existence of a second chamber that is not in any way based on the idea of territorial representation. Peers owe their membership of the House of Lords to birth, or nomination by the prime minister as life-time or hereditary peers,[14] which has kept their democratic legitimacy, and because of that, their decision-making power in the legislative arena, to an absolute minimum. Reform of the Lords has been at the centre of the ongoing constitutional debate for most of Blair's second term, without, however, having come to fruition at the time of writing (mid-2004).[15] The odd character of the Lords is, however, by no means the only feature betraying the traditional weakness of the principle of vertical power-sharing in the British political system.

At least until the recent constitutional reforms of the Blair government that implemented an ambitious devolution programme bringing independently elected assemblies to Wales and Scotland, the United Kingdom was in fact the prototype of a unitary state (which it remains in purely constitutional terms even after these important changes). The concept of the British unitary state implies that sub-central government, including elected local councils, is subordinate to central government, and can, technically at least, even be abolished by the latter. The constitutional and political superiority of central government over local government has, however, led neither to a complete equalization of infra-structure and living standards at local level, nor to an absence of conflict between the two levels of government. In fact, the history of central–local government relations since 1945 has been marked by a series of minor and major confrontations, which reached their climax during the Thatcher years (Levy, 1997). The dominant trend in recent decades has been clearly towards centralization; that is, weakening elected local government and strengthening central control. In constitutional practice, the effects of legislative measures have tended to be reinforced by a decision-making culture among members of the central government that has internalized deeply the long-standing tradition of a strong centre in British politics. Many ministers feel it is their duty to protect the public from the worst consequences of bad council policies.

This notwithstanding, the policies of the central government are often 'subverted' at local level, and local authorities claim to have a mandate to do so. Thus, there can be no doubt that, in practice, there have long been very obvious limits to the dominant constitutional idea of governing from the centre, which have become more manifest after the enforcement of the devolution measures of the late 1990s.

While Britain's new, post-devolution territorial order is marked by some degree of political autonomy for the individual parts of the United Kingdom, the regional scope of national executive leadership in Britain is still larger than in any real federal system. And this is not only because England accounts for about 85 per cent of the United Kingdom's population. Even the degree of independence enjoyed by the government of Scotland, has obvious limits. Whereas the Scottish Parliament enjoys the right to vary slightly the rate of income tax north of the Scottish border up or down, it does not have any effective control over Scotland's revenue, which continues to be provided for by a huge block grant from the centre. Still, as Vernon Bogdanor (2003: 229) has argued, through devolution 'Westminster has become a quasi-federal parliament', which is 'no longer a Parliament for the domestic and non-domestic affairs of the whole of the United Kingdom.' Belying the true meaning of the term 'devolution', which would seem to imply a mere delegation of powers rather than a formal division of them, it is also rather unlikely that the Scottish Parliament and the Welsh Assembly could be abolished by a simple parliamentary vote at Westminster.

While most potential 'veto players' restricting the executive's scope of action elsewhere have been (largely) non-existent in Britain for the best part of the post-war period, all British governments have been faced with challenges from powerful interest groups. In comparison, though, the checks on executive power and leadership from this corner of the system have also been rather modest.

Prima facie, several of the parameters of decision-making at the political system's level would seem to favour a particularly powerful role of interest groups. For example, British interest groups have faced a civil service dominated by generalists rather than policy experts, which has been marked by a notable degree of dependence on external specialist advice. Moreover, interest groups in Britain should have been able to claim a special degree of legitimacy, as – reflecting the effects of the first-past-the-post electoral system – no British post-war government has been elected by an absolute majority of voters (Richardson, 1993: 86, 89). However, not all factors shaping the opportunity structure of interest groups in the political system have been favourable from the viewpoint of lobbyists. Even though governments usually listen to major interest groups, and were keen to establish networks of information exchange, there has been no general legal obligation for governments to consult. Furthermore, as A. G. Jordan and Jeremy Richardson (1987: 289) have noted, British pressure groups traditionally have suffered from being regarded with suspicion by large sections of the public. For much of the post-war period, trade unions in particular were perceived by a majority of Britons to be unreasonably powerful – a trend to be partially reversed only in the mid-1990s after years of highly restrictive Conservative trade union policy.

Even in Britain – traditionally ranked as one of the least corporatist countries in Western Europe – several developments during the first three post-war decades were discussed under the heading of 'tripartism' (Marsh and Grant, 1977). While the mere existence of tripartist structures generally does not say too much about the power and influence of the major interest groups, the overall impact of groups (especially the unions) on governmental decisions was undoubtedly stronger before 1979 than it has been since. For a number of reasons, including the character of the Tories themselves, most Conservative governments of the first three decades of the post-war period were considerably less hostile towards incorporating organized labour into national-level discussions and decision-making than was the Thatcher government (Dorey, 1995). Thatcher not only put an end to any sort of tripartist practices, but also revolutionized the basic conditions of trade union politics in Britain by enforcing radical changes in industrial relations law. Despite initial announcements to the contrary, there was little change in the field of trade union policies under Major – if there were any, they were in the direction of more anti-trade union legislation. Thatcher's distaste for 'vested interests' led to a gradual shift in lobbying strategies, which focused more than during previous decades on parliament rather than on the executive (Norton, 1991: 66). Other established patterns of interest group–government relations, however, remained largely in place. There was no such thing as a 'Thatcher revolution' at the level of consultation between groups and civil servants in government departments.

The most spectacular changes in government–interest group relations under Blair were related to the new 'bias' of close contacts. There has been an unprecedentedly close relationship between the Labour government and senior representatives from the business sector, with more than a quarter of the FTSE-100 companies offering either their chairman or their chief executive as a part-time adviser to the government. In comparison with this 'new corporatism' (Holliday, 2000a: 103), the historical 'entente' between Labour and the unions has declined significantly as a factor shaping public policy in Britain. There was an increase in the number of contacts between the TUC and the government after the change of power in 1997, though there is rather limited evidence that this revitalization of formal contacts had any significant impact in terms of public policy (Ludlam and Taylor, 2003). However, as in most other West European democracies, trade union power in Britain has diminished, not only in terms of 'union-friendly' government policies, but also with regard to the veto power of the trade unions (if calculated in terms of membership and financial resources). Looked at from the vantage point of the early twenty-first century, scenarios of the 1970s that considered the unions as actors contributing most to the state of 'ungovernability' in Britain, appear as reflections of the dim and distant past. Many of the more recent contributions to the field of interest group politics have highlighted a significantly increased influence of individual firms and corporations on the governmental decision-making process (Crouch, 2003: 201–3). This notwithstanding, it would seem to be no less true than in the past that British governments have larger capacities for 'freezing out' individual interests, and interest groups, than do governments in most other major liberal democracies.

British Governments, the Public and the Media

Whereas the policy-making role of the British House of Commons has been rather modest for virtually the whole post-war period, its role as a recruitment pool of candidates for ministerial offices and as a central stage for public leadership and opposition has been all the more significant by international standards (Norton, 1993). It is certainly the latter function of the House of Commons that has experienced the most fundamental changes over recent decades. As a result, the balance between the importance of executive leadership in the parliamentary arena and that of media management, in terms of the resources directed to either area, has gradually shifted in favour of the latter.

The normative foundations of the 'parliamentary state' (Judge, 1993) have remained very much alive, though. It is difficult to imagine any other country in which the speaker would officially rebuke a minister for disclosing important bits of political information to the media before having introduced it to parliament, as happened in Britain early in 2000 (Riddell, 2000: 162). Historically, the well-established position of parliament as a prime focus of public political debate has, however, not been the only factor limiting the direct impact of the media in the

British political process, as well as the visible efforts of politicians to manage relations with the media. At the level of political institutions, the persistence of the two-party system and the strength of the parties in the governmental system played important roles in 'shielding' the system against outside public opinion. There were also other factors working in the same direction. For much of the early post-war period, direct contact between members of the executive elite and journalists remained few and far between because of the glaring social class divide separating the two groups of actors from one other (Seymour-Ure, 1996: 209–10). Institutional and social factors have been accompanied, and reinforced, by the strong impact of political cultural traditions. As Jay Blumler *et al.* (1996: 62) have pointed out, 'British politicians are uneasy about it being known that they receive help with presentation. They fear that it may provide ammunition for charges that they lack principles and convictions.'[16]

For all these barriers against media-domination of politics, the role of the mass media in British politics has increased significantly in recent decades. As in other advanced democracies, the 'personalization' of the political process belongs to the most tangible elements of this development. While the parties inside and outside parliament remain key actors in the British political system, both political campaigning and media coverage of politics has come to focus more and more on the leaders of the two major parties.

There have been significant differences in popularity among individual political contenders as well as variations in the performance of individual candidates over time. According to Gallup poll data, no British post-war prime minister has ever been as unpopular as John Major, whereas few have gained similarly high approval ratings as has Blair. Major suffered from the double handicap of facing the competition of an effective opposition leader, and having to live in the shadow of Margaret Thatcher. For much of his term, the press (including traditional supporters of the Conservative Party) focused on faithfully reproducing the image of a weak personality lacking an overall strategy (Broughton, 1999: 204–5, 216–17). Blair started out with exceptionally high approval scores, which appeared even more impressive in comparison with the miserable ratings of the first two Conservative opposition leaders of his premiership. In a survey carried out by MORI in May 2004, Michael Howard became the first Conservative challenger to earn a higher job satisfaction score than Blair – though, ironically, the scores for both Blair and Howard at that occasion were rather low, at 29 and 30 per cent, respectively.

As these figures indicate, Blair's approval ratings have been marked by an exceptionally high degree of volatility reminiscent of the recorded figures for Macmillan, Wilson and Major (Rose, 2001: 122, fig. 6.1). According to MORI poll data, the difference between the highest and lowest scores measured between Blair's inauguration in May 1997 and June 2004 was no less than 46 percentage points (with the highest and lowest scores measured in September 1997 and September 2003/May 2004, respectively). January 2002 was the last month in which slightly more than an absolute majority of the public (51 per cent) was satisfied with Blair's performance as prime minister.

Needless to say, British governments have not passively followed the growing influence of the media and the ever-more prominent role of the prime minister in the public perception of politics. The current stage of affairs has emerged only slowly, though. In the immediate aftermath of the Second World War, paying systematic attention to the media, let alone investing much time and money in explicit media management, was still far from being considered a natural field of activity for British governments. This was reflected in the level of public perception of the involvement of governments in media management. As Colin Seymour-Ure (1996: 227) has noted, there was a widespread – albeit largely misguided – perception among the public that governments do not have media policies at all, or at the most something like 'a traditional policy of no policy'.

Contacts between the government and television in particular took considerable time to develop into a professionally managed relationship. Attlee and Churchill paid great attention to the press, but never became accustomed to the new visual medium. During most of his post-war premiership, Churchill 'reacted to the TV cameras in the manner of a seventeenth-century aristocrat who did not want the vulgar mob to stare at him' (Cockerell, 1988: 22). Both Churchill and Eden were convinced that the BBC was infiltrated by communists, but this did not hinder the latter in becoming the first British prime minister aspiring to use television as a tool of government. Eden was also the first to deliver a live address to the British nation at the height of the Suez crisis – an event, though, perhaps more memorable for the scathing reply it provoked from the leader of the opposition a few hours after Eden's speech, in which the prime minister's immediate resignation was demanded (ibid.: 49–50).

During the first two post-war decades, the power of television and, as a consequence, the crucial role of the prime minister's performance on television, could mainly be experienced *ex negativo*, as in the case of

Douglas-Home, who became the first British prime minister effectively to be destroyed by television. The modern age of media politics in Britain, giving rise to the thesis of a British presidency in the making, started with Wilson's first term at No. 10 (Foley, 1993: 105). Although Wilson's predecessor, Macmillan, had some very impressive performances on television, he did not rely to the same extent on the audio-visual media as did later prime ministers. Wilson, who was said to have had 'a little love affair with the TV screen', chose John F. Kennedy as his television role model. Especially during his early years as prime minister, Wilson offered himself much more often for televised interviews than the BBC would have prefered. As Michael Cockerell (1988: 95) has observed, Wilson 'was the first prime minister to see television as an impressionistic medium and to acquire some of the skills needed to create a favourable impression'.

Despite Wilson's trail-blazing example of public leadership, there was no steady development of the office of prime minister into the highly media-focused institution it has become under Tony Blair. Wilson's immediate successor at 10 Downing Street, Edward Heath, appeared willing to turn back the clock. In contrast to several other prime ministers, such as Margaret Thatcher or John Major during the first years of their respective premierships, Heath did not lack the necessary skills in dealing with the media. He had, in fact, fought an exceptionally sophisticated and successful television election campaign in 1970 before becoming prime minister. But Heath had fundamental reservations about the idea of buttressing his public image as prime minister with the advice of media specialists and frequent appearances on television. His press secretary, Donald Maitland, was a career diplomat who shared the prime minister's distaste for the Wilson style of public leadership, and during his first hundred days in office Heath did not once appear on television. But, the defensive Heath approach to public leadership was not able to halt the looming transformation of the 'public premiership'.

Until rather recently, the emergence of media management as a major category of political leadership has been reflected only modestly at the organizational level of the core executive. The traditional media-related structures of the British governing machine, in place until well into the 1990s, were characterized by a remarkable degree of functional fragmentation and compartmentalization. While no post-war prime minister has followed Churchill's (failed) attempt to work without a press secretary, most incumbents confined themselves to adjusting carefully and optimizing the existing structures (Franklin, 1994: 75–95). Downing Street's press secretary, a post created by Ramsay MacDonald in 1929, has played a central role in managing the media in most post-war administrations (Seymour-Ure, 2003: 122–68). It was, however, left to Blair's high-powered press secretary, Alastair Campbell, to introduce a set of completely new standards. In fact, Campbell's role was much more central than that of any of his predecessors had been. Not only did he enjoy total access to the prime minister, he also formed the very centre of a tight web of control (including the cabinet secretary, the chief of staff in the Prime Minister's Office and the head of the Policy Unit, as well as a senior figure from the Treasury). He even attended cabinet meetings and was often referred to as the 'real deputy prime minister'. After the 2001 general election, Campbell's role was altered in response to widespread feelings that he had become too much of a media celebrity in his own right. The post of chief press secretary to the prime minister was abolished and replaced by two senior civil servants (Godric Smith and Tom Kelly) acting as the prime minister's official spokespersons. Campbell was appointed head of a newly created Communications and Strategy Unit at 10 Downing Street – a position obviously modelled on the head of press in the US White House.

Campbell's departure in September 2003 – a move triggered by his prominent involvement in the battle between No. 10 and the BBC over allegations that Downing Street had 'sexed up' the dossier on Iraqi weapons of mass destruction[17] – was used to introduce important structural changes. Campbell's successor, David Hill (who worked as director of communications for the Labour Party between 1991 and 1997), was not granted the same rights as Campbell to give executive orders to civil servants. To underline the distinction between Hill's political role and the management of a communications empire, the government adopted the recommendations from a review of government communications chaired by Bob Phillis, chief executive of the Guardian Media Group, to install a new permanent secretary in the Cabinet Office to oversee the Downing Street communications team (*The Times*, 2 September 2003). The latter position was filled by Howell James, a former political secretary to John Major. Though he was chosen in open competition by a panel that did not include any member of the Blair administration, his appointment provoked widespread opposition as he appeared to many to be too deeply involved with friendships at No. 10.

The central motive behind these changes was Blair's determination to break away from suggestions that he was running a presidential regime. It also drove his decision to leave the task of delivering the government's message and answer questions of the day in the daily Westminster lobby briefings to ministers, rather than the prime minister's official spokesman (*The Times*, 20 January 2004). These adjustments to counter a changing public feeling about the government's public relations operations have, however, to be seen in the context of the wide-ranging earlier changes. By far the most important one involving the prime minister himself was the introduction of regularly-held general, and televised, prime minister's press conferences.[18] It marked a crucial departure from the well-established British tradition of public leadership based on the principle of reserving the right to question the prime minister for parliament, and taking the principle of collective ministerial responsibility seriously. The first prime ministerial press conference was held on 20 June 2002 in Downing Street, and was followed by others at intervals of several weeks.

Such organizational innovations by the Blair government were accompanied by several new strategies for dealing with both the British public and the media. Some components of its multi-faceted media strategy – such as the so-called 'Heineken approach' (that is, providing selected regional newspapers with 'exclusive' information from the government that is expected not to receive a similar amount of attention in the national media; *The Times*, 6 February 1999) – would hardly be considered noteworthy in many other countries. However, whereas the monopoly of public television was broken earlier in Britain than in most other West European countries, the British media system has been marked by strong centralism in the print media, with a few national newspapers dominating the market.

The obsession with opinion polls and focus groups marked another, arguably *the*, key feature of the Blair government's strategy of public leadership. Symptomatically, from early in his premiership Blair started each working week with a meeting with Philip Gould, the government's chief pollster and political strategist at No. 10 (*The Times*, 9 November 1999). Even more important were the exceptionally close contacts between the prime minister and other top advisers in the field of public relations, such as Alastair Campbell and Peter Mandelson. Both remained, even after their respective resignations, important informal sources of strategic advice for the prime minister.

If restricting the news media's autonomy was in fact at the core of the government's reactive/proactive approach to public relations and media management, as has been suggested (Heffernan, 1999: 64), it can only be judged a major failure. Indeed, the government's dominant strategy of self-presentation and political communication rather had the effect of increasing the media's self-confidence and their influence in the political process – to a degree that not only circumscribed Blair's room for manoeuvre but also threatened to degrade the office of prime minister. As Andrew Rawnsley (2002) has put it,

> They have conducted themselves not as a government, something detached from and grander than journalism, but as a rival media group, scrapping in the gutter of a ratings war...Just as newspapers try to build circulation with 'exclusives', so has this government attempted to boost popularity with 'initiatives'...In his treatings with media owners, Mr Blair has presented himself not as their superior, but as an equal, as if he were just another press baron himself.

The increasing prominence of the prime minister in the public arena has been accompanied by significant changes in the relationship between prime ministers and their parties. The traditional differences in the organizational features of the two major British parties (Kelly, 1994) and different leadership styles of individual prime ministers/party leaders (Shell, 1995b) have been overshadowed by more general trends at the level of public perceptions of parties and their leaders, and in the area of intra-party democracy. The traditionally strong focus of the public and the media on party leaders has gradually been transformed into a widespread public perception of leaders *being* their parties. To a growing extent, leaders are perceived as the embodiment of their parties rather than merely the chief advocates and representatives of the parties' manifestos and policies. In spite of recent organizational party reforms that increased the formal decision-making powers of the rank-and-file in both major parties (Seyd, 1998; Peele, 1998), the position of the leader has been (further) strengthened in a way that looks very much like an empirical manifestation of the influential 'cartel party' model introduced by Richard Katz and Peter Mair (1995).

Party leadership – as much as executive leadership, of which party management, at least in parliamentary democracies, is part and parcel – remains based as much as ever on a combination of different factors. Blair's ups and downs as Labour leader and prime minister reflect the whole magnitude of the challenges involved. If there was one overriding lesson to be learnt it was that, at least in British politics, party leadership cannot be replaced successfully by direct public leadership. At the height of the 'New Labour' euphoria, stretching from late 1994 until about mid-2000, Blair dominated his party like no other Labour leader had done before him.[19] Even before Labour gained power in May 1997, the party's statutes had been overhauled fundamentally to make it a convenient leadership device and campaign resource in the hands of the party leader. In a way unthinkable for earlier Labour leaders, Blair and his administration publicly defied resolutions of the party conference that challenged the government's policies. The bold remark attributed to a Conservative prime minister of the early twentieth century, that he would rather consult his butler than his party, appeared to have become an unlikely reality under Blair.

However, this period of domination neither could nor would last very long. There was a mounting dissatisfaction among Labour MPs with the government's policies and strategies of leadership, which manifested itself in a series of spectacular parliamentary rebellions. There was also a growing number of those in the PLP and beyond who considered Gordon Brown, rather than Blair, the chief representative of their cause. Even before Labour's second landslide victory of June 2001, Blair felt compelled to divert some of his resources to the field of traditional party leadership. In mid-2001, a Labour party chairman (Charles Clarke, later to be replaced by John Reid, and Ian McCartney) was appointed and given a seat at the cabinet table. In Downing Street the number of office-holders responsible for handling relations with the Labour Party was increased from one to three. Moreover, not only the political secretary but also the Cabinet Office minister in the Lords and the head of the government relations division were entrusted to tackle matters of government–party relations. The prime minister's increased personal involvement in party affairs included unpublicized question-and-answer sessions with Labour Party members, held at irregular intervals. Finally, in late 2003, a new initiative – 'The Big Conversation' – was launched, designed to improve the Labour Party's relationship with its rank-and-file and ordinary citizens (*The Times*, 29 November 2003).

The combined effects of this offensive remained in large part speculative. However, as Blair approached his tenth anniversary as Labour leader, and his party's seventh year at No. 10, it seemed undeniable that the parties had reconquered some of the ground of the British premiership.

Conclusion

For much of the post-war period, the British political system has been considered in international comparisons to represent an exemplary case of a highly power-concentrating polity. The scope of action enjoyed by British governments was virtually unmatched by other governments of the Western world. The Blair government's major constitutional reform programme, including the implementation of devolution in Scotland

and Wales as well as the reform of the House of Lords, alongside many other important changes, has altered the British polity significantly. Many core features of the traditional Westminster system have been transformed, weakened or abandoned in less than a decade. Still, it is obvious that the very strong position of the government in the political system, at least in relative terms, marks one of the crucial constitutional principles that have survived Labour's constitutional reform largely unscathed. Such an empirical assessment marks an area of common ground in the works of authors applying very different theoretical perspectives on contemporary British democracy, from traditional constitutional theory to the 'democratic audit' paradigm, with parts of the network paradigm literature marking the single most important exception.[20]

Whereas the task of providing effective executive leadership in the wider political process has become significantly more demanding over the post-war period, the traditionally strong role of the government in the parliamentary arena has remained a keystone of the British system. The existence of single-party governments, a rather powerless parliamentary opposition, a high degree of 'party cohesion' to be secured by a sophisticated system of whips, and a large 'payroll vote' (the proportion of MPs holding governmental office) have all worked to secure the executive's tight grip on parliament. Even though parliamentary reform has climbed the political agenda in recent years, tangible results in the Commons have essentially remained confined to increasing the independence and powers of parliamentary watchdog committees.

As in any parliamentary democracy, the size of a government's parliamentary majority constitutes the single most important component among the political parameters of executive leadership in the legislative arena. As to the parliamentary basis of British post-war governments, several observations may be made. Very large majorities – understood here to include those with more than 60 per cent of the overall number of seats – have been concentrated in the period after 1983. Three out of a total of four parliaments with exceptionally large governing majorities fall into the period 1983–2003 (including the 1983–7, parliament as well as the two parliaments elected in 1997 and 2001). Only one other post-war government – the Attlee government during its first term (1945–50) – enjoyed an equally large majority in parliament.[21] Looked at from this angle, it could be argued that governing in the parliamentary arena has become easier in the more recent past. But a closer look reveals that there is no strict linear historical trend towards larger parliamentary majorities. Very small governing majorities, including less than 51 per cent of MPs (including spells of minority status of the government), occurred after the four general elections of 1950, 1964, and 1974 (both February and October). The 1992 general election provided the Major government with a 51.6 per cent share of total seats in the Commons, which eventually fell to below 50 per cent thanks to a series of defections and by-election defeats.

While very small majorities certainly do not ease the task of governing, large majorities have occasionally had a stunningly modest positive impact on the government's room for manoeuvre, as backbenchers of the governing party may feel less compelled to support the government. Since the Heath premiership, the parliamentary success of British post-war governments has been explained more specifically by the leadership style and parliamentary performance of the prime minister. As a historical assessment reveals, the efforts of individual prime ministers to secure or broaden their basis of political support in the Commons did not in any case correspond neatly with the size of the government's parliamentary majority. Whereas Labour's minority status during much of the Callaghan years made some kind of formal parliamentary co-operation with another party almost inevitable, other examples of an inclusive governing style were not born out of immediate necessity. Both Churchill and Blair had a deeper-motivated interest in including various interests of the political spectrum beyond their own party and the creation of a broader coalition of social and political forces (even though Blair's early attempts at establishing a closer co-operation between Labour and the Liberal Democrats were clearly part of a rational power-securing strategy).[22] Such attempts at developing a more inclusive style of governing and leadership, especially in Blair's case, have, however, been faced with conflicting political cultural traditions and preferences. As Anthony King has put it, '[t]he present Prime Minister evidently finds the culture of contestation distasteful, but the apparent depth of his distaste is a good measure of the culture's continuing dominance' (King, 2001: 77).

There have been few examples of outstanding prime-ministerial leadership in the parliamentary arena. Perhaps, among post-war prime ministers, Labour leaders Wilson and Callaghan were the best parliamentary performers, especially with regard to their relationship with the party's backbenchers. Macmillan also had a more than respectable record in parliament, particularly in comparison with many other Conservative prime ministers. Some of the most embarrassing chapters of the relationship between No. 10 and the Commons related to the premierships of Anthony Eden and John Major. Still, the party affiliation of prime ministers can hardly be seen as a major independent variable in explaining the performances of different incumbents in the parliamentary arena.

The same largely holds true for the leadership qualities, and accomplishments, of different prime ministers in the field of media-management and public relations, though the two trail-blazers in this area, Wilson and Blair, were both Labour prime ministers. Both had a deeper interest in exploiting effective media management as a tool of government than had their immediate predecessors, and both raised the standards for their respective successors. The Blair government in particular has effectively set aside most of the system's inherent forces that have long served to prevent, or at least delay, the rise of 'media democracy' at the expense of parliamentary and party democracy in Britain.

For much of the post-war period, relations between the government and interest groups tended to be strongly affected by which party was in power. The early post-war Labour governments were the 'natural' allies of the trade union movement, whereas most Tory governments had their closest supporters clearly in the 'bourgeois' camp of organized interests. The Thatcher years not only witnessed an intensification of this class-determined pattern of government–interest group relationships; the administration also left its mark on the structural conditions of interest lobbying in the British political system, though established conventions of consultation between departments and groups were by no means completely abandoned. As the Thatcher government 'closed itself up' for many influence-seeking interest groups, parliament's role as a key target of interest group lobbying was enhanced, at least temporarily. Under Blair, some of the traditional features of government–interest group relations have changed, most visibly at the level of relations between Labour and the trade unions.

If one combines the individual assessments of the Blair style of governing at various levels (the cabinet system, the parliamentary arena, and the wider public arena) into a broader picture, Blair appears to be a leader breaking the mould of the British post-war premiership. The most substantial comparisons that can be made between the 'Blair effect' and the impact of other office-holders on the nature of the British prime ministership have to go back to well before the Second World War. Especially, but not only, in the area of core executive leadership, Tony Blair has inspired comparisons with David Lloyd George (Riddell, 2001). As Lloyd George did, but unlike many other post-war prime ministers who mounted an effective challenge to the established boundaries of prime ministerial leadership by their style (such as Margaret Thatcher in particular), Blair seemed certain to leave a heavy institutional legacy to shape the future of the British premiership (Kavanagh, 2001: 4–5).

7
Germany: Governing a 'Semi-sovereign State'

Executive Leadership in the Parliamentary Arena

The relationship between executives and legislative assemblies under parliamentary government has long been among the least understood subjects of German political science. At least two reasons for this weird phenomenon may be given. First, until recently parliamentary government had no deep roots in German political and constitutional history. Although the Weimar Republic may be classified as a 'parliamentary democracy with presidential dominance' (Steffani, 1995: 538), neither the constitution nor the constitutional practice in Weimar Germany did much to foster the idea of parliamentary government. Until the breakdown of the Weimar Republic it remained unclear what exactly 'parliamentary responsibility' (as stipulated in Article 54 of the Weimar Constitution) was meant to include (Gusy, 1997: 134). The second structural hindrance to a proper understanding of parliamentary government among a large quarter of the young discipline of German political science had much to do with the biographical background of some of the most influential figures in the field. Many early German 'political scientists' were trained public lawyers whose perspectives on the political process had an inevitably strong legal bias. The dominant interpretation of the German post-war parliamentary democracy was that of a 'balanced system', which implied notions of a reasonable independence of the executive and the legislative branch from each other. In fact, some early works on the Federal Republic's parliamentary system read very much like descriptions of a presidential system of government.[1] However, even when this approach came under attack from a new generation of scholars in the late 1960s and early 1970s, the problem of developing reasonable standards for evaluating the German post-war parliamentary system would not go away. Fervent admiration for the British Westminster type of parliamentary government, which united the younger breed of German parliamentary scholars, gave rise to a set of normative standards that challenged the legitimacy of the German model without acknowledging its specific strengths and accomplishments.

There are several institutional characteristics that distinguish the German model of parliamentary government from most other variants of parliamentary democracy. The formal parliamentary election of the head of government and the so-called 'constructive' vote of no-confidence (both having been mentioned previously) have remained its most famous characteristics. Symbolizing the unlikely success story of the German post-war model of parliamentary government, these devices have even come to inspire constitutional reforms in several other liberal democracies, such as in Belgium or Spain. Particularly from a British perspective, there are, however, quite a few other aspects worth noting.

Most importantly, even large absolute parliamentary majorities in the Bundestag do not enable German governments to force controversial bills through parliament. Perhaps the most obvious German/British difference on this count relates to the strength of the second chamber. Whereas the German Bundesrat[2] is, according to a judgment by the Federal Constitutional Court (BVerfGE 37/1974: 380), not a 'second chamber' at all, it performs most of the functions of 'genuine' second chambers elsewhere, and has even possessed a considerably stronger veto potential than many of them, including the House of Lords. The Bundesrat's veto power – or more precisely, the proportion of bills that the Bundesrat can effectively veto[3] – has increased significantly in recent decades. Since 1969, the proportion of 'approval bills' – which cannot be enforced against the Bundesrat's veto – has never accounted for less than 50 per cent of all federal bills.[4] As in many other countries operating bicameral systems, there has been a specific institutional device for conflict-solving in Germany, the *Vermittlungsausschuss* (mediation committee).[5] Its prominent position is underscored by the fact that the Bundesrat may only veto a bill after it has been dealt with by that committee. In recent decades, about 90 per cent of all cases reaching the mediation committee have been initiated by the Bundesrat. It has remained a contentious issue for many decades as to whether decision-making in the Bundesrat, and its inclination to veto measures passed by the Bundestag in particular, can be properly understood in terms of party politics. To many, the 'natural' assumption would be that if state governments, led by the same parties who represent the parliamentary opposition in the Bundestag, control the Bundesrat, then the latter is quite likely to behave like a political 'veto player' of the federal government of the day. As the assessments presented below suggest, though, the reality of legislative decision-making in the Federal Republic has been considerably more complex than the 'party politicization' thesis would have it.

Some of the less glaring features of the German model of parliamentary government relate to the internal organization and distribution of power within the Bundestag. The government's position in the Bundestag is weaker than that of its British counterpart in the Commons, both with regard to its agenda-setting capacity and to the availability of instruments for cutting debates and imposing deadlines for the consideration of bills. Even though the majority retains the final right to impose its agenda on the Bundestag, there is a special body (the *Ältestenrat*) including members of each *Fraktion* reflecting their respective strengths on the floor, designed to facilitate a peaceful agreement over the parliamentary agenda. Moreover, the standing committees of the Bundestag,[6] rather than the government, decides when to complete deliberations on a given bill. There is also no standing order, as in the British House of Commons, that would forbid non-members of the government from tabling certain kinds of bills (although most parliamentary rights in the Bundestag are reserved for the *Fraktionen*,[7] whereas the position of individual members in the legislative process is even more circumscribed than in the House of Commons). Another key German/British difference regarding the basic conditions of executive leadership flows from the constitutional requirement of a two-thirds majority (in both the Bundestag and the Bundesrat) for the passage of any constitutional amendment in Germany – a requirement that, given the significant proportion of bills falling into this category, marks a far more serious restriction for German governments than most British observers are likely to acknowledge.

The strong co-governing devices of the parliamentary opposition in the German Bundestag are part of a broader set of minority rights in the parliamentary arena, some of which can be classified more properly as instruments of parliamentary control. While several of the devices of parliamentary control to be established after 1945 have been inspired by the standing orders of the Commons, there is still no equivalent in the Bundestag to the British Prime Minister's Question Time. What comes closest to it is the questioning of the government, which takes place once a week directly after the weekly meetings of the cabinet. This usually starts with a brief report from a member of the government and lasts for about thirty minutes (Ismayr, 2000: 351). An even more visible departure from the British model must be seen in the non-existence of any official leader of the opposition in the Bundestag (even though the concept has remained a popular subject of debate among German political scientists). In stark contrast to the situation in the House of Commons, there is also no formal division within the parliamentary parties into a frontbench and a backbench, and no such thing as a formally appointed 'shadow cabinet' of the largest opposition party. Government ministers sit separately from the other members of their respective parliamentary party groups, and what usually passes as 'shadow cabinet' in media reporting on German politics is just a group of particularly well-known and popular figures from the opposition party which is presented to the public during the final stages of the election campaigning to boost the party's electoral chances.

Although there has been a high degree of 'party discipline' among members of both the governing and the opposition parties in the Bundestag (Saalfeld, 1995),[8] and a clear divide between government and opposition in terms of political rhetoric, most of the action in the German parliamentary arena falls somewhere between the 'opposition mode' and the 'cross-party mode'.[9] As long-term empirical assessments of the structure of legislative decision-making show, passing major bills with the support of both the government and (at least a significant proportion of) the opposition parties marks the dominant, if by no means the only, pattern of law-making in the Federal Republic (von Beyme, 1997). Explanations for the notable amount of power-sharing that has come to mark legislative decision-making in Germany cannot reasonably be confined to the institutional parameters of the legislative arena, though. Some of the key resources the parliamentary opposition can draw upon in their attempts at co-governing, and forcing the government to compromise, originate from outside the legislative arena. This is true for the valuable administrative support the parliamentary opposition receives from some of the state governments as much as it is for the important repercussions of the opposition's right to challenge a bill before the Federal Constitutional Court. No less importantly, the strong record of co-decision-making in the Bundestag, and between the Bundestag and Bundesrat, reflects the high appreciation of compromise and co-operation that marks the Federal Republic's political culture.[10]

Despite the prominent status of cross-party decision-making in the German parliamentary arena, the size of a government's parliamentary majority marks a key element of its opportunity structure in the legislative arena. Parliamentary majorities in the Bundestag have generally been sufficiently large to keep administrations in office and allow them to advance their respective legislative agendas. By far the most sizeable majorities existed between 1953 and 1957, and between 1966 and 1969, when the government controlled more than two-thirds of the total of seats in the Bundestag. Most other governments enjoyed considerably less generous parliamentary majority support. The past decade of German parliamentary government has been notable for the unusually narrow majorities of the coalition parties in the Bundestag. The federal elections of 1994 and 2002 produced the slimmest parliamentary majorities for any newly elected German government of the post-war period. Even minority governments have not been completely absent at the federal level. However, the political cultural reservations about minority government have been even stronger than in Britain, which explains why no minority administration has ever really *governed* post-war Germany. The three short-lived minority governments of 1962, 1966 and 1982 were all products of coalition crises, transforming majority coalition governments into lame duck minority single-party governments.

While the chancellor's position in the Bundestag is less exposed than that of the British prime minister in the House of Commons, he plays (or at least may play) a crucial role in exerting executive leadership in the parliamentary arena. A key event for any German chancellor is the major policy statement of the government delivered to the Bundestag shortly after an administration has assumed power. Since the early days of the Federal Republic, these events have been considered an opportunity to evaluate a chancellor's style of speaking and acting in parliament as much as an occasion to judge the government's policy programme (Korte, 2002a). Major programmatic speeches by the chancellor are not normally confined to the start of the legislative term, but occur at irregular intervals throughout a parliament. In constitutional practice, annual budget debates have also turned increasingly into general debates about the government's performance and planned policies, in which both the chancellor and the most senior figures from the opposition benches play a prominent part. Additionally, as in any other parliamentary democracy, there are numerous other occasions on which the chancellor, and other members of the government, can participate in the parliamentary process.

Speaking in 133 of a total of 763 plenary meetings held during his 14-year tenure, often more than once (Morsey, 1986: 16), Konrad Adenauer invested considerably more time and effort in parliamentary business than most accounts of his chancellorship would acknowledge.

Adenauer's strong position in the legislative arena was facilitated by the weakness of the early Bundestag as a political institution, and the uncompromising style of the first Social Democratic opposition leader, Kurt Schumacher. The latter phenomenon had the effect of closing the ranks among the governing parties and provided the chancellor with a welcome opportunity to criticize the opposition for its radicalism (Wengst 1984: 292–4). More importantly, the strongly adversarial style of the Social Democrats found little approval among the German electorate, who would have favoured a more constructive opposition. Unsurprisingly, then, the very different electoral performances of the two largest parties in the Bundestag became a hallmark of the Adenauer years. Whereas the CDU/CSU's share of the vote rose steadily in the first three federal elections (1949, 1953 and 1957), from 31 per cent to 50.2 per cent, the SPD stagnated, with even its best result in three elections remaining below 32 per cent of the total vote.

As the findings of an early case study on the nature of executive leadership in the parliamentary arena suggest, Adenauer maintained a rather distant relationship with the CDU/CSU parliamentary party during the first two legislative periods (Domes, 1964). There was little consideration of backbench opinion in particular, although relations between the chancellery and 'ordinary' Christian Democratic deputies slightly improved after the change at the *Fraktion* leadership from Heinrich von Brentano to Heinrich Krone in 1955. In managing the relationship with the CDU/CSU parliamentary party, Adenauer generally relied heavily on strong support from among the *Fraktion* leadership. Many major issues were negotiated informally between Adenauer and selected senior MPs before they reached the *Fraktion* for a broader debate (Küpper, 1985: 141). However, there were other structural devices designed to integrate the CDU/CSU parliamentary party into the government's work. They included the 'coalition committee' the participation of the *Fraktion* chairs in cabinet meetings, and the appointment of federal ministers without portfolio who were officially assigned the role of 'brokers' between the government and the parliamentary party groups (Rudzio, 1970: 210).[11]

While Adenauer remained a widely respected figure in the parliamentary arena, his grip on the CDU/CSU parliamentary party became weaker from the late 1950s onwards. After the so-called 'presidential crisis' in 1959 – when Adenauer first announced, and then shortly afterwards withdrew, his candidacy for the office of federal president in an ill-fated attempt to counteract the anticipated negative consequences of Ludwig Erhard in the office of chancellor – and the '*Spiegel* affair' of 1961, in particular, his position became rather vulnerable. The Bundestag election of 1961 reduced the number of CDU/CSU deputies from 289 to 251; at the level of votes, the 1961 election delivered the second heaviest losses for the Christian Democrats in any federal election between 1949 and 2002.[12] In retrospect, it seems consistent with these developments that it was the CDU/CSU parliamentary party rather than the CDU party organization, let alone the electorate, that eventually brought Adenauer's chancellorship to an end.

Erhard kept a rather low profile as legislative leader. His lack of interest in the bulk of policy matters that characterized his leadership performance in the core executive became even more visible in the parliamentary arena. Not even the most pressing issues in the field of foreign policy encouraged him to provide any guidance. Erhard's silence in the two major Bundestag debates on the limitation period for National Socialist war criminals in 1964/5, one of the single most spectacular issues of his whole tenure, irritated many observers and nurtured unfavourable speculations about his leadership capacities (Caro, 1965: 334). As a British scholar has observed, 'Erhard kept in regular contact with *Fraktion* leaders and attended its meetings, but his relations with it were not particularly warm' (Pridham, 1977: 149). It should, however, not be forgotten that Erhard had gained the chancellorship on the back of support from the CDU/CSU parliamentary party. It has even been argued that he did not come to realize the importance of the CDU party organization as a key leadership resource precisely because of his smooth relationship with the CDU/CSU parliamentary party (Laitenberger, 1986: 192). Erhard's position was weakened significantly by the election of the young and ambitious Rainer Barzel as CDU/CSU *Fraktion* chairman late in 1964. Barzel came to act as a powerful intermediary between the government and the CDU/CSU members of the Bundestag, without leaving anyone in doubt as to the strength of his loyalty to the CDU/CSU parliamentary party and the chancellery.

Not all of Erhard's problems were confined to the intra-party dimension of managing executive–legislative relations. His chancellorship witnessed the culmination of a development within the party system that paved the way for a change of government in 1966. Since the late 1950s, the SPD had gradually transformed itself into a moderate '*Volkspartei*' pursuing a strategy of rapprochement. While the late 1950s could be described as a period of 'co-operative opposition', the early 1960s witnessed the emergence of a 'silent opposition' (Heimann, 1984: 2030). The gentler strategy of the SPD was not to be confused with a less determined approach to gain office, though. On the contrary, the Social

Democrats' change of strategy was driven by, and focused on, this very aim. Their strong emphasis on compromise became a much more serious challenge to Erhard's own consensus-orientated leadership style than any aggressive adversarial style of opposition could possibly have been.

Although being a gifted public speaker and an experienced parliamentarian, Kiesinger can hardly be described as a political leader who dominated the parliamentary arena. Direct interventions by the chancellor in parliamentary debates remained largely confined to the area of foreign policy. Kiesinger profited considerably from the notable loyalty of CDU/CSU *Fraktion* chair, Barzel. Given the specific conditions of 'grand coalition government', however, precious little could be achieved on the basis of parliamentary support from the chancellor's party alone.

The changing relationship between the government and the Bundestag belongs undoubtedly among the most fascinating aspects of the historical record of the Kiesinger government. While most observers at the time feared that the dramatically oversized governing coalition would seriously weaken the Bundestag's capacity of parliamentary control, as the only opposition party held less than 10 per cent of the Bundestag seats, the three years between late 1966 and 1969 experienced a significant upgrading of the Bundestag as an institution of political control. Party cohesion among the CDU/CSU and SPD parliamentary parties fell below the levels recorded for earlier legislative periods (Saalfeld, 1995: 129); however, both intra-party control, especially by the SPD parliamentary party, and parliamentary control of the Bundestag as a whole intensified significantly. Both majority parliamentary party groups had a rather strong impact on the content of government bills through their work in the committees. They also made ample use of the traditional instruments of parliamentary control, such as parliamentary questions and debates (Schneider, 1999: 58–60). Neither before nor after 1966–9 has there been such a close working relationship between the chairs of the governing parliamentary party groups as there was during the grand coalition period.

Willy Brandt's first general policy statement as chancellor, delivered on 28 October 1969, was perceived widely as one of the most spectacular performances by a German chancellor in parliament. To a certain extent, his maiden speech as chancellor foreshadowed his parliamentary activities during the first years of his incumbency. Of the first hundred plenary debates of the 6th Bundestag (1969–72), Brandt contributed to almost a third.[13] His involvement in parliamentary debates centred on issues of foreign affairs, though he also made substantial contributions to parliamentary debates on questions of domestic policy if the issues tackled belonged to the government's reform programme, such as industrial co-determination or education (von Beyme, 1997: 258).

Some of the most remarkable features of the early Brandt years related to the behaviour of the parliamentary opposition, though. The 6th Bundestag (1969–72) was the first ever to host a Christian Democratic opposition. There was a notable bitterness among many senior figures of the party which came to be reflected in the Christian Democrats' rather weird, and incoherent, opposition strategy. On the one hand, members of the CDU/CSU parliamentary party went out of their way to prevent the government from introducing fundamental changes in the Federal Republic's relationship with the East European states, including the GDR. This competitive strategy – which was not in the event strictly adhered to, as most Christian Democrats abstained during the finalizing parliamentary divisions on the Moscow and Warshaw Treaties – dominated the CDU/CSU's perception as the opposition party among the wider public. On the other hand, the CDU/CSU behaved very much like a 'would-be governing party' (Veen, 1976). Both the overall number of bills initiated by the opposition between 1969 and 1972 and the proportion of opposition bills securing the Bundestag's approval have remained unmatched in German post-war history.

Until 1972, Brandt was able to draw on his charisma and high public approval ratings when it came to garnering the support of the SPD parliamentary party. Given the extremely slim parliamentary majority of his government, these qualities were badly needed. As the parliamentary going got really tough, especially, but not only, over the government's policies towards Eastern Europe, the Social-Liberal government's majority in the Bundestag gradually evaporated. On 27 April 1972 Brandt became the first German post-war chancellor to be challenged by a vote of no-confidence. He survived it by the narrowest possible margin, but the result clearly signalled that the coalition had lost any working parliamentary majority. After the government had failed to pass its budget bill, Brandt also became the first German post-war chancellor to launch a question of censure, on 20 September 1972. As had been anticipated, the division confirmed that there was no proper parliamentary majority to support the government. An early election was called, for the 19 November 1972, which returned the Social-Liberal government to office with a comfortable lead over the Christian-Democratic opposition. Strangely enough, Brandt's grip on the SPD parliamentary party notably weakened, despite – or perhaps because of – the considerably enlarged majority of the coalition parties in the 7th Bundestag (1972–6). Moreover, the personal relationship between Brandt and SPD *Fraktion* chairman

Herbert Wehner, never having been particularly warm (Jäger, 1986: 114), worsened dramatically after Brandt's re-election, which inevitably had unfavourable repercussions on the relationship between the SPD parliamentary party group and the government.

The overall record of executive leadership in the parliamentary arena during the Brandt years included a significantly upgraded position of the Bundesrat. There was, first of all, an increase in the proportion of bills considered to fall in the category of 'approval bills', which reflected the major constitutional reform of the federal system in 1969. More important was the 'discovery' of the Bundesrat as a potential instrument of political, and more specifically party-driven, opposition. For much of the 1950s and the first half of the 1960s the existence of a large variety of party coalitions at state level had prevented the governing and opposition parties from the successful employment of strategies of 'party rule'. Conflicts between the Bundestag and Bundesrat of that period had very much the character of institutional conflicts between the federation and the *Länder*, which focused on the legitimate role of the Bundesrat in federal legislation. The basis for a more 'political' role of the Bundesrat emerged when, from the early 1960s, coalition variants in the *Länder* started to become less numerous (Münch, 2001: 144–57). There can be no doubt, however, that the Bundesrat's staunch opposition to the Brandt government was more than an exercise in political muscle-flexing. There were genuine policy-related reservations among the conservative Bundesrat majority about the governing programme of the Brandt administration. Whereas the Bundesrat did not exactly 'sabotage' the legislative process, it effectively forced the government to water down most items on its proudly-announced reform agenda (Schmidt, 1978: 217–19).

Helmut Schmidt was not only a brilliant orator, he has also been described as a genuine 'parliament man' (Stephan, 1988: 185) having had a more extended experience in the Bundestag than any other post-war chancellor. His strong focus on the parliamentary arena has to be seen in relation to his appreciation of well-structured decision-making processes, and his general understanding of politics, which remained suspicious of most extra-parliamentary activities. Still, as his key interests were related clearly to the crafting of policy decisions within the executive branch, Schmidt often seemed to consider even parliamentary business a rather cumbersome activity. While the chancellor accepted that decisions had to secure the approval of the Bundestag (and Bundesrat), he showed a notably modest inclination to intervene in parliamentary debates (von Beyme, 1997: 258).

After 1976, mobilizing parliamentary majority support became more difficult. Not only did the common programmatic basis of the Social Democrats and the Liberals grow smaller, but the intra-party dimension of executive-legislative relations also became more demanding. There was a significant increase in younger MPs, especially among members of the SPD parliamentary party, who expected to be persuaded rather than 'forced' by the *Fraktion* leadership to lend their support to the government. While Schmidt initially profited from the division of leadership responsibilities between the chancellor, the SPD party chairman and the chairman of the SPD parliamentary party group, the so-called 'troika' (of Schmidt, Brandt and Wehner) gradually ceased to function in the late 1970s (Walter, 1997: 1308–9). This significantly weakened the chancellor's position in the parliamentary arena and beyond. Schmidt's question of censure in the Bundestag on 5 February 1982, even though it was answered by a unanimous vote of support from the coalition parties, fuelled rather than countered speculation about his drastically weakened position in the Bundestag and among the SPD. While the Schmidt administration faced a rather competitive CDU/CSU opposition in the Bundestag, a more distinct feature of the late 1970s and early 1980s was the strong impact of the extra-parliamentary opposition on the overall conditions of governance. This had a weird effect on government–opposition relations, as the extra-parliamentary opposition had closer affiliations with the leading governing party than with the parliamentary opposition (Jäger, 1987: 199).

Even though he was the only incumbent to advance to the office of chancellor from the position of opposition leader in the Bundestag, Helmut Kohl's relationship with the CDU/CSU parliamentary party remained rather distant throughout his chancellorship. As Peter Pulzer has observed, 'while his government could not survive without the support of the Bundestag majority, Kohl delegated the management of the parliamentary party to others. His parliamentary appearances were few. As far as possible he faced the Bundestag with *faits accomplis*' (Pulzer, 1999: 134). The quite smooth relationship between the government and the majority parliamentary parties in the Bundestag was helped greatly by the loyalty of the various chairs heading the CDU/CSU and FDP parliamentary party groups.[14] Moreover, the chancellor profited from the fact that some of his most senior cabinet ministers, such as Norbert Blüm in particular, took very seriously the task of explaining the government's policies to the majority parliamentary parties, and garnering their support. The appointment of personalities enjoying the trust of the CDU/CSU members of the Bundestag to the position of chief of the Chancellor's Office (starting with the recruitment of Wolfgang Schäuble in 1984) was another crucial device to bind the CDU/CSU parliamentary party to the government (Saalfeld, 1999: 166).

However, the single most important institutional device designed to integrate the majority parliamentary party groups into the governmental decision-making process and secure a reasonable amount of parliamentary support for the government's legislative agenda was the 'coalition rounds', which included the key representatives from the governing parties and the parliamentary party groups (Schreckenberger, 1994; see also Chapter 4). From 1983 onwards, the Kohl administration also benefited from the heterogeneity of the parliamentary opposition. The number of opposition parties in the Bundestag grew from one to two (in 1983), including the Social Democrats and the Greens, and later increased to three (in 1990), including also the PDS. Especially in the 1983–7 parliament, the policy distance between the coalition parties and the largest opposition party (SPD) was considerably smaller than between the two opposition parties. Whereas the SPD and Greens moved closer together in later legislative periods, there was no parliamentary co-operation between the SPD and the Greens on the one hand and the PDS on the other. Despite the adversarial political rhetoric that marked the Kohl era, the government could – well into the 1990s – draw on conditional *ad hoc* SPD support for the passage of many major bills, including a series of constitutional amendments. Only after the SPD leadership change from Rudolf Scharping to Oskar Lafontaine in 1995 did the Social Democrats become significantly less co-operative (Braunthal, 1998).

The last two years of the Kohl chancellorship were particularly remarkable for the existence of a powerful veto majority of the opposition parties in the Bundesrat and its strategic use (Lehmbruch, 1998: 165–75). Much of the public debate of the time focused on the SPD's uncompromising strategy in the Bundesrat. A closer look, however, reveals that, as the 1998 Bundestag election approached, both the government and the opposition parties had precious little interest in reaching a compromise over pending legislation. There seemed to be strategic speculations among the governing elite that publicly accusing the opposition of 'abusing' the Bundesrat as an 'opposition chamber' would discredit the SPD and boost electoral support for the government in the up-coming Bundestag election (Zohlnhöfer, 1999).

Whereas Gerhard Schröder has been described as a rather skilful performer in the media, his record in the parliamentary arena has been less impressive. Throughout the first year of the Schröder administration, then CDU party leader and CDU/CSU *Fraktion* chairman Schäuble was often judged the winner of parliamentary showdowns with the chancellor. During the major CDU crisis in late 1999 and early 2000, Schröder's strength appeared to be built on little more than his challengers' weaknesses. Also, in quantitative terms, Schröder can hardly be described as a parliament man, though his often-noted inclination to bypass the Bundestag has been reflected only moderately in his record of participation in parliamentary business. Of the first hundred plenary meetings after the chancellor's election in the Bundestag, Schröder contributed to every fifth meeting, an average score being higher than Erhard's and only slightly lower than those of Adenauer and Kiesinger.[15]

The government soon developed its own approach to managing its relations with the Bundestag. From early on, there have been weekly meetings between members of the *Fraktion* leadership of both coalition parties (initiated by the chairman of the SPD parliamentary party group). A strategic concept developed in the chancellery also included the idea of the governing *Fraktion* chairs attending cabinet meetings on a regular basis. The latter plan, however, did not work out in practice, as the chairs of both majority parliamentary party groups were fearful of becoming too much the agents of the government. On the whole, the government's management of the relationship with the majority parliamentary party groups has not been too impressive, though no major government bill failed because of withheld parliamentary support from the coalition parties. Whereas Kohl's 'coalition rounds' primarily sidelined the cabinet, Schröder's leadership approach weakened the Bundestag in particular, as the informal decision-making bodies created during his incumbency largely failed to include influential members of the leadership, and the policy specialists, of the parliamentary parties – a tendency likely to increase the effects of the notably modest proportion of senior parliamentarians in the cabinet.

Between 1998 and 2002, the Schröder government faced a fairly competitive opposition in the Bundestag, which, at least as far as the Christian Democrats were concerned, seemed to be determined by strategic imperatives and the changing structure of the party system, rather than fundamental differences between the two major parties on key areas of public policy.[16] During Schröder's first term, most examples of co-operative opposition in the area of domestic policy were confined to *ad hoc* support from the FDP. By contrast – with the notable exception of Schröder's stance on the Iraq issue – foreign policy remained a field in which the Christian Democrats, rather than the Green junior coalition partner, remained the most reliable ally of Schröder and his Social

Democrats. Nevertheless, the chancellor's decision to combine the Bundestag's vote on dispatching German troops to Afghanistan with a vote of censure was obviously designed to discipline the SPD parliamentary party as much as the rebellious Green members of the Bundestag (*Frankfurter Allgemeine Zeitung*, 17 November 2001).[17]

The Schröder government emerged from the 2002 federal election with the smallest parliamentary majority of any recently elected German government. Not only had the combined proportion of opposition seats increased dramatically since 1998, but the opposition 'camp' had also become more homogeneous.[18] Underlining the rougher climate in the early 16th Bundestag, only weeks after the election the CDU/CSU cancelled a long-standing 'pairing' agreement for parliamentary divisions, in which both government and opposition had declared their willingness not to exploit the temporary absence of individual members from either side by withdrawing the same number of parliamentarians in respect for the elected majority. The tense relationship between government and opposition was also reflected in Schröder's general policy statement, delivered early in November 2002, which included a host of disparaging remarks on the narrowly defeated Christian Democrats.

After a brief period of 'unified government' in the immediate aftermath of the 1998 Bundestag election, the Schröder administration had to govern without a majority in the Bundesrat, forcing the government to make significant concessions to the opposition parties on a number of issues (Zohlnhöfer, 2003: 410–13). The Bundesrat's approval of the government's major Taxation Reform Bill in the summer of 2000 could only be secured by offering generous financial support to those state governments prepared to defy the opposition party line. On other occasions, even the SPD-led state governments had to be persuaded in lengthy negotiations to support a government bill in the Bundesrat. The most spectacular showdown between government and opposition in many decades occurred, however, in March 2002, when the Bundesrat passed the highly contentious Immigration Bill with votes from the SPD–CDU coalition government of Brandenburg, despite the formal protest of a senior CDU member of that government during the Bundesrat meeting itself (Helms, 2002a: 60–2). The political fate of the Immigration Bill may serve as a case in point for the characteristic difficulty of getting a highly contentious piece of legislation passed and enforced. Whereas President Rau, after weeks of hesitation, eventually promulgated the law in June 2002, the Federal Constitutional Court declared it unconstitutional later in the same year.[19]

The government's – and especially the chancellor's – position in the legislative arena was weakened further by two crushing defeats of the SPD at state elections in Hesse and Lower Saxony early in 2003. In Schröder's home state of Lower Saxony, the SPD lost as many as 14.5 percentage points – one of the most bitter defeats in the party's history. The most important immediate effect of the heavy electoral losses was a further expansion of the opposition parties' majority in the Bundesrat, which made it seem highly unlikely that the government would succeed in breaking the Bundesrat's veto power by talking individual CDU-led governments round to defy the party line. Against this background, the government's ability to secure the Bundesrat's support for its (watered-down) *Agenda 2010* – the most ambitious reform bill in the field of German welfare state policies in many decades – marked a major accomplishment that few had considered possible. Many observers felt, however, that the true winner of this lengthy battle was the CDU/CSU opposition leader, Angela Merkel, who seemed to have gained in stature, rather than Chancellor Schröder (Niejahr and Ulrich, 2003). Unlike Merkel, Schröder could not even rely on the unconditional support of his own party, whose opposition against the reforms appeared to be at least as serious as that of the other parties. When the deep rift between the chancellor and the SPD eventually led to Schröder's resignation as party chairman, there was a widespread feeling, especially in conservative quarters, that the whole episode had not only damaged Schröder's position but had also disgraced the office of chancellor (Zastrow, 2004). The change in the party leadership opened up a new chapter in Social Democratic party history because, for the first time since the Second World War, the two positions of SPD party and *Fraktion* chairman were unified in the hands of a single incumbent, Franz Müntefering. Schröder and Müntefering did their best to 'sell' this new working arrangement between the chancellery, the party and the parliamentary party as the optimal response to the specific challenges facing a reform-committed government, but its immediate effects on the relationship between the government and the Bundestag remained rather patchy.

Executive Leadership in a 'Semi-sovereign State'

There are few contemporary parliamentary democracies in which the government faces a similarly large number of strong institutional barriers against majority rule, or potential 'veto players', as does the German federal government. While the existence of such *contre-gouvernements* (Wildenmann, 1969: 9) is widely acknowledged to represent a key feature of the German model of democracy, their actual role in checking the government's scope of action in the political system has rarely been assessed from a historical perspective.

Two of the most famous potential 'veto players' of the federal government, the Federal Constitutional Court and the Bundesbank, took up their work only a couple of years after the Federal Republic was established (in 1951 and 1957, respectively). In particular with regard to the Bundesbank, the lengthy struggles accompanying its creation suggest that the early post-war governing elite was very well aware of the seriously power-restricting effects of an independent central bank. As has been shown in a recent study, the political independence of the West German central bank, established about fifteen months before the founding of the Federal Republic, was decreed by the American occupying power despite serious opposition from German financial experts and leading politicians to such a plan. As the decentralized *Bank deutscher Länder* (*BdL*) soon acquired a high reputation among the German public, it proved politically unfeasible for those opposing a strong and independent central bank, including Konrad Adenauer, to replace the *BdL* by a central bank more open to governmental influence and control (Buchheim, 2001). Thus, the Bundesbank, established in 1957, was modelled very much after its predecessor.

Scholars have occasionally doubted the proverbially high degree of independence of the Bundesbank. For example, Roland Sturm (1995: 39) has highlighted Chancellor Kohl's largely successful efforts to increase influence on the Bundesbank through the back door of appointments that paid special attention to the party affiliation of candidates. The Kohl government also ignored the Bundesbank in the policy-making process, including issues involving highly important aspects of currency policy. Broader historical assessments tend, however, to confirm the strong and independent role of the Bundesbank towards the government that has been emphasized in comparative works on central bank independence in Western democracies. As Uwe Wagschal (2000: 163), drawing on a detailed empirical analysis of central bank decision-making and political control in the Federal Republic, has concluded, 'the Bundesbank won most of its conflicts with the government'. More specifically, the policies of the Bundesbank have even been considered to have had a direct influence on the termination of no fewer than three chancellorships – Erhard in 1966, Kiesinger in 1969 and Schmidt in 1982 (Marsh, 1992: 170).

Most of the traditional duties of the Bundesbank became obsolete after the D-Mark's replacement by the euro in 1999, when the Bank's well-established and powerful position within the German polity vanished overnight. In comparison to its original clout, its role within the newly created European Central Bank (ECB) appears rather modest (Geerlings, 2003). However, the supra-nationalization of monetary policy has barely increased the room for manoeuvre of German governments in this field. It could rather be argued that the ECB has turned out to be an even more relentless guardian of price stability, from the government's point of view, than the Bundesbank. Other things being equal, the ECB cannot reasonably be expected to pay any particular attention to the specific needs of the German economy. Schröder's scarcely disguised frustration over the ECB's decision early in March 2004 not to raise the interest rate, a step widely considered to be necessary to help in over-coming the German economic demise, was clearly reminiscent of earlier conflicts between the government and the Bundesbank.

In many works, by foreign scholars in particular, the Federal Consti-tutional Court is treated as the second key institutional hallmark of the German polity, alongside the Bundesbank. The creation of a powerful Constitutional Court marked a major innovative element in the wider process of post-war German constitutional engineering. Most observers would subscribe to Kommers' view that it is cases of 'abstract norm review' where 'the Constitutional Court is most politically exposed' (Kommers, 1997: 28). Cases of abstract norm review may be initiated by the federal government, a state government, or one third of the members of the Bundestag in case of doubts about the compatibility between a federal and a state law or, even more significant in our con-text, between these laws and the constitution. The procedure is 'abstract' in the sense that the question of the law's validity may be purely hypo-thetical and need not have arisen in the course of a legal dispute.

The possibility of invoking the Constitutional Court has long been considered to be one of the most effective components of the institu-tional opportunity structure of the opposition parties in the Bundestag. Recent empirical research into the use of different types of procedure has confirmed that the bulk of cases of 'abstract norm control', as well as disputes between institutions in the federation and those between the federation and the *Länder*, are usually initiated by the parliamentary opposition or actors (such as state governments) sharing the same party affiliation (Stüwe, 2001). The mere threat of invoking the Court may well strengthen the parliamentary opposition in conflicts with the government, as it forces governments to take into account the possible consequences of going ahead with the passage of a bill fundamentally opposed by strong minorities.

The important right to invoke the Court has, however, to be distinguished from the results of legal confrontations. After all, the decision on a given case lies in the hands of the Court, rather than in those of any player located in the competitive arena. This has focused the attention of observers on long-term patterns and trends of judicial decision-making. Although there have been cases in which the opposition managed to reverse the results of the parliamentary decision-making process by judicial means, empirical evidence supporting the thesis, which sees a powerful judicial counter-government operating at the very heart of the German polity, has remained rather patchy. According to a study by Göttrik Wewer (1991), rather the opposite thesis – which emphasizes the Court's inclination to support the general policy line set out by the ruling majority – seems to be true. The notable reservation of the Court about seizing the position of a counter-government has been explained with its limited institutional potential for doing so, and the need to maintain the largest possible amount of public acceptance by integrating itself smoothly into the larger social and political order.[20] Also, the more recent history of Court judgments does not provide much evidence in support of the counter-government thesis. In a carefully conducted interim assessment of the first four years of the Schröder government the notion of the Court as a committed 'veto player' to the government was dismissed explicitly (Zohlnhöfer, 2003: 413). In this respect, the previously mentioned Court judgment concerning the government's Immigration Bill in December 2002 marked an exception rather than the rule.

Taking into account the Court's far-reaching competencies and the general inclination rather to support the legislator's views it has shown virtually since its inception in 1951, it would appear more appropriate to describe the Constitutional Court as a 'parallel government' (Derlien, 1997: 160). There can be no doubt, though, that even the existence of a judicial 'parallel government' may significantly restrain an administration's ruling authority and room for manoeuvre in the wider political process. With about 40 per cent of the hundred most important legislative 'key decisions' between 1949 and 1994 having been dealt with by the Constitutional Court (von Beyme, 1997: 302), the existence of quite a high degree of 'judicialization' can hardly be denied. Its causes have, however, remained a contentious issue in their own right. It can, for obvious reasons, not be wholly convincing to consider the Court – which, after all, may neither initiate a case nor refuse to deal with a complaint by classifying it as a 'political question' – the only driving force behind the much-criticized 'judicialization' of German politics.

In more recent studies on the subject, assessments abound that highlight the notable inclination of administrations to shelve unpopular political decisions until such time as the Court eventually intervenes to decide a pending issue. This may also imply that judges, rather than the government, 'take the heat' for unpopular decisions – a scenario barely reconcilable with traditional notions of a political 'veto player'.[21]

The federal system marks another key component of the institutional parameters of executive leadership in the wider political process. In notable contrast to the internal distribution of power in many other federations, the Federal Republic represents a system in which few fields of legislation are completely beyond the federal government's reach. Whereas the federal government's scope was more limited in the very early post-war period, the dominant historical trend has been towards the gradual centralization of legislative competencies at the federal level. Education policy, several matters of internal security and cultural policy stand out as the only areas in which the states have preserved real legislative decision-making authority; the main task of the states under the German system, which lacks a full-scale federal administration to carry out federal legislation, centres on the implementation of legislative measures. Still, there are few areas in which federal governments are truly sovereign in terms of legislative decision-making. From a comparative perspective, perhaps the most stunning features of the German system are the exceptionally large number of areas in which (at least theoretically) legislative decisions can be made by either the federal government or the state governments, and the numerous 'joint tasks' that were created in 1969 – a system that has become famous as the prototype of 'interlocking federalism' (Scharpf *et al.*, 1976).[22] In practice, 'interlocking federalism' has meant 'executive federalism' – a system, in which the federal government and the state governments (rather than the states as a whole or the state legislatures) call the shots.

Conflicts between the federal government and the state governments are played out between the Bundestag and the Bundesrat. Given the specific character of the Bundesrat, changes in the party composition of a state government are reflected strongly at the federal level. However, as the observations presented in the previous section of this chapter suggest, the party factor alone cannot explain the structure of decision-making in the legislative arena convincingly. It may even be argued that, compared to the 1970s, there is now a considerably larger amount of unpredictability in the Bundesrat's voting behaviour. German unification has produced a glaring, and largely persistent, gap between the 'old' and the 'new' *Länder* (including stark inequalities in terms of financial resources), and triggered a dramatic increase in the variants of governing coalitions at state level (Sturm, 1999).[23] Still, as the more recent chapters of legislative decision-making at the federal level also suggest, patterns of party control have by no means become fully neutralized by the new regional/economical cleavages in post-unification German politics. Other things being equal, governments can be said to be significantly better off under the conditions of 'unified government'. Given the dominant pattern of party control in the Bundesrat over the post-war period – which has been marked by a heavy Christian-Democratic bias – SPD-led governments would appear to have more to gain from a further weakening of party-voting in the Bundesrat, or a formal trimming of its decision-making powers.

Still, as may be noted in our context, there has been no clear-cut correlation between the party complexion of federal governments and initiatives for the reform of the federal system. The most wide-ranging structural reform of the federal system to date was launched and seen through by the grand coalition government in the late 1960s. Both subsequent SPD-led and CDU-led governments, and most of their counterparts at state level, have largely defied the advice and proposals suggested by various reform commissions, focusing on the disentanglement of legislative competencies and a reduction of the Bundesrat's co-decision-making and veto powers.

As in any liberal democracy, interest groups of various kinds mark important players in German politics that any government has to take into account. From an American perspective in particular, the German 'landscape' of interest associations has been marked by an exceptionally high degree of centralization. Such an assessment largely holds true from a German historical perspective, too. Although there have been important elements of centralization and 'unitarization' of interest group politics in Germany reaching back to the late nineteenth century (Lehmbruch, 2003), the Federal Republic experienced a culmination of this broader historical trend. The single most important element of change related to the emergence of trade unions which, unlike their predecessors in Weimar Germany, had no formal ties to any specific political party.

The contemporary German model of interest group representation and lobbying comprises several other features. In the Federal Republic, interest groups are freer from government intervention than in many other countries, mainly because of the constitutionally warranted autonomy of the social partners in the area of wage-setting. On the other hand, unlike the situation in the other two German-speaking countries (Austria and Switzerland), there is no legal obligation upon the government to consult with the top interest groups over planned legislative bills. This is, however, compensated (some might say 'over-compensated') by the exceptionally strong presence of interest group representatives in the political institutions themselves, and the long-standing and close working relationships between individual interest groups and government departments.

Although both the Bundestag and the federal government have been well-established targets of interest group lobbyism, empirical surveys indicate that in the eyes of the professional lobbyists themselves, the executive marks the single most important addressee of interest group influence (Sebaldt, 2000: 200). The bulk of these contacts tend to focus on the individual departments, rather than the chancellery or the chancellor – a pattern in line with section 10 (2) of the standing orders of the federal government, which stipulates that direct contacts between interest groups and the chancellor are to be reserved for 'special occasions'. Whereas managing interest groups relations may be considered a central component of executive leadership in the wider political process, as Heidrun Abromeit (1994) has shown, direct contacts between the chancellor and interest groups have remained among the secondary features of interest group politics in post-war Germany. More important for the overall conditions of executive leadership at the political system level have been the major structural patterns of government–interest group relations.

Comparative assessments suggest that the Federal Republic may not be properly classified as a classic corporatist system (Wessels, 1999: 96–103), and there is a widespread consensus among scholars of interest groups that German unification weakened rather than strengthened the structural preconditions for corporatist arrangements (Simonis, 1998; Heinze, 1998). There have been periods during which the Federal Republic experienced forms of genuinely tripartist corporatism, however. The *Konzertierte Aktion* of the late 1960s and early 1970s, and its more recent successor *Bündnis für Arbeit* differed from each other in many ways (Schroeder and Esser, 1999) – not least in terms of efficiency and concrete achievements. In contrast to its fairly efficient counterpart in the field of health policy, the *Bündnis für Arbeit* hardly produced any concrete results whatsoever. With hindsight, its eventual scrapping by the Schröder government early in 2003 appears to have been on the cards since the summer of 1999 (Streeck, 2003).

It is important to note that – irrespective of the mixed record of tripartist decision-making in German politics – in particular, trade union power has always been considerable in the Federal Republic's history. To a significant extent, the notable strength of the trade unions has benefited from the fact that *both* major German parties, or at least powerful party factions within the SPD and the CDU/CSU, have felt a comparatively close affinity to some organizations among the trade union movement. Even in Germany, however, the co-governing potential and veto power of the unions has more recently grown weaker. The most important reasons for this ongoing process were largely the same as in many other West European countries: declining membership, an increase in intra-organizational conflicts over the distribution of scarce resources, growing competition among different groups from the same spectrum of political interests, and a political opportunity structure deteriorating because of the ever-scarcer financial resources of the state (von Winter, 2001). As in many other Western democracies, the entrenched position of the major associations from different parts of the political spectrum has additionally been challenged, if not completely undermined, by two parallel developments. The first relates to the increasing influence of major firms who focus their lobbying on highly specific and exclusive goals; the second and older one being the proliferation of social movements and minor interest groups (Leif and Speth, 2003). Both developments have further increased the already considerable intricacies of executive leadership in the wider political process.

Although the federal president has usually not been considered a major 'veto player' of German governments, this brief historical assessment of the conditions of executive leadership at the level of the wider political system would not be complete without a glance at the relationship between the president and the political executive. Two factors in particular may explain why most of the seven presidents serving between 1949 and early 2004 stuck to a rather low-key role for the president in the political system. First, the incumbency of the first office-holder, President Theodor Heuss (FDP, 1949–59), was early accepted as a role model for later presidents. Whereas Heuss enjoyed a considerable amount of public respect and political authority, which might have led others to seek a more activist role for the president in the decision-making arena, he emphasized the integrating and teaching functions of the office. Second, and even more importantly, the peaceful development and stability of German post-war democracy, and the party system in particular, have put a structural limit on the chances of the head of state becoming a major political player in his own right right.[24] The dominant pattern of presidential politics in the Federal Republic has therefore been marked by a reasonable amount of political self-restraint and the endeavour of office-holders to remain above the political fray. This notwithstanding, a closer look reveals that some presidencies have been more problematic than others, particularly from the government's point of view.

Arguably the most problematic presidency since 1949 was that of Christian Democrat Heinrich Lübke (1959–69) who faced three different chancellors, all belonging to the CDU (Morsey, 1996: 336–7, 345–6, 437–8). Lübke not only played a major role in establishing what has now widely come to be seen as the president's right to scrutinize the content of legislation. He was also self-confident enough to reflect publicly on his ideas regarding the most desirable party complexion of the federal government. His early enthusiasm for a grand coalition was well ahead of the developments in the party political arena, and inevitably clashed with the conservative parties' claim to power. In the area of personnel policy he tried, albeit in vain, to block a number of ministerial appointments in the course of the government-building processes in 1961, 1963 and 1965.

The presidency of Richard von Weizsäcker (CDU), particularly its second term (1989–94), also marked a period of recurrent tension between the president and senior members of the government. Many observers regarded von Weizsäcker as 'the most political of all the presidents of the Federal Republic' (Padgett, 1994: 16). His public statements on a wide range of political and social issues often attracted considerably more attention than the actions and public declarations of the federal government, and of Chancellor Kohl in particular. Despite the many occasions on which von Weizsäcker challenged, or even attacked, the federal government, it has been argued that his presidency may have been one of the factors stabilising Kohl's chancellorship. Whereas Kohl showed a strong inclination to 'sit problems out', von Weizsäcker was at his best when addressing public grievances and emotions, which many felt were largely ignored by the government (Leicht, 1993). His much-noted speech on the fifteeth anniversary of the end of the Second World War, early in May 1985, came to symbolize the power of the post-war German rhetorical presidency.

The presidency of Karl Carstens (CDU) supports the view that a different party affiliation of incumbents in the offices of president and chancellor by no means determines their relationship with each other. Carstens' behaviour during his first three years in office, which coincided with the chancellorship of Helmut Schmidt (SPD), was no less unobtrusive than after the change of government in 1982. He was the first incumbent who promulgated all bills passed by the Bundestag and Bundesrat and showed no intention of intervening in the sphere of day-to-day politics.

It has has even been maintained that the relationship between Carstens and Schmidt was altogether more congenial than that between the latter and President Scheel, Schmidt's former cabinet fellow under Chancellor Brandt (Jäger, 1994: 157).

While the brief period of President Herzog (CDU) facing Chancellor Schröder (SPD) in 1998–9 provides another example of a harmonious 'split party' pattern, Schröder's working relationship with President Rau (SPD) has been smoother than president–chancellor relations during most earlier periods of 'unified government'. The desirability or non-desirability of stem cell research in Germany remained the only major policy issue on which the president and the chancellor developed different positions, which were debated at length in public.

All this would seem to suggest that it is personalities, rather than the party affiliations of the actors involved, that must be considered as the key factor in shaping the relationship between federal presidents and chancellors (and their respective governments). In particular, what would still appear to be the most popular variant of the party affiliation thesis – suggesting a significantly more conflict-ridden relationship between chancellors and 'opposition presidents' – rests on rather feeble ground. Taking into account the Lübke and von Weizsäcker experience, it could even be argued that the constitutionally stipulated impartiality of the office has encouraged presidents to take a more critical stance towards the government if there is no risk of being blamed for supporting their own party.

In light of the performances of Herzog and Rau, it is also evident that scenarios of a higher-profile presidency, developed at the height of the 'von Weizsäcker era' (Padgett, 1994: 17–18), have not materialized. President Rau, in particular, showed a notable hesitation in assuming a more activist role, which many considered desirable as the Federal Republic faced a series of major domestic crises (including the rise of right-wing radical violence, the CDU party funding scandal and the BSE crisis). Also, his handling of the crisis over the Immigration Bill in 2002 underlined Rau's inclination to stick to a low-key role in the political decision-making process, even though his signature on the bill was accompanied by a rare formal rebuke of the government.

German Governments, the Public and the Media

Although both the public and the media have focused much of their attention on the chancellor since the very early post-war period, the chancellor's position in the public arena has continued to grow. In a process that has been described as a 'plebiscitarization' of chancellor democracy (Niclauss, 1987), chancellors soon emerged as the largely unchallenged focal point of the public political process. Even news media reporting on German election campaigns has been characterized by a so-called 'chancellor bonus' – an advantage of incumbent chancellors over challengers in terms of the amount of media reporting during the election campaign for which there seems to be no equivalent in the United States or in Britain (Schönbach and Semetko, 1995). The Bundestag election campaign of 1980, when Chancellor Schmidt was challenged by Franz Josef Strauss, marks the only example of an opposition candidate being mentioned significantly more often in the media than the chancellor. In 1983 there was a near balance between the recently elected chancellor (Kohl) and his challenger from the SPD (Hans-Jochen Vogel), whereas in 1998 the differences between Chancellor Kohl and Gerhard Schröder were minimal when compared with the usual pattern (Wilke and Reinemann, 2000: 101–7).

In German political science, the term 'chancellor bonus' has, however, traditionally been used to describe a different phenomenon, namely the (positive) difference between the amount of public support for the chancellor on the one hand and his party on the other. From the beginning of systematic empirical research into this field, in the late 1960s, until the early 1980s, chancellors enjoyed a larger amount of public support than did their respective parties. In 1983, Kohl became the first chancellor to enjoy less support than his party. Of the five Bundestag elections Kohl fought as chancellor, only one (in 1990) was marked by the existence of a modest 'chancellor bonus'. In 1998, public support for Kohl and the CDU/CSU was almost identical (36 per cent and 35.1 per cent, respectively). On the same occasion, Schröder became the first challenger to have a much stronger public support basis than his party (Rudzio, 2003: 228). In 2002, the 'chancellor bonus' re-emerged at an impressive level. At no time during the run-up to the federal election of 22 September 2002 was the SPD nearly as popular as Chancellor Schröder.

Virtually all chancellors enjoyed extended periods of public popularity, with Helmut Kohl marking the only major exception. Kohl had for most of his tenure a rather poor public standing, especially among journalists and intellectuals (Werz, 2000: 223–6), which increased only temporarily in the immediate aftermath of German unification. Adenauer, whose reputation and approval among the German public remain unique, profited considerably from the political culture of the early post-war period that had much appreciation for a vigorously acting paternalistic figure (Jäger, 1994: 19–20). Erhard has been the only candidate enjoying a solid amount of popularity well before assuming the position of chancellor. By contrast, in 1948–9 Adenauer was considerably less well-known among the German public than his Social Democratic challenger, Kurt Schumacher; Brandt and Schmidt also acquired charisma only as chancellor (Wildenmann, 1986: 99; Niclauss 1988: 90).

Schröder was judged much more favourable than Chancellor Kohl had been, virtually throughout the 1998 Bundestag election campaign, even though he did not enjoy the public prestige of being a national political leader. The 1999 European election campaign marked the first major occasion the SPD set out to 'promote' Schröder as a statesman-like political leader. However, while Schröder was for a long time significantly more popular than his party, few considered him to be among the most important chancellors in German post-war history. In a public opinion survey published few weeks before the end of Schröder's first term in 2002, only Kiesinger was ranked lower than Schröder, and both trailed far behind their counterparts.[25] For a chancellor whose key resource of leadership has been considered by many to lie in his talent for 'selling' himself to the public, Schröder's deep fall in public popularity in his second term marked an even more serious setback than it would have been for other chancellors. According to figures published in *Politbarometer*, a twice-monthly collection of survey data gathered by the Mannheim-based *Forschungsgruppe Wahlen*, Schröder ranked (on average) only eighth on the list of Germany's ten best-liked politicians during the first quarter of 2004. Whereas this marked an all-time low for Schröder, the considerably higher score for Joschka Fischer marked a much more persistent feature of the public approval ratings of individual members of the Red–Green coalition. There was hardly a single serious opinion poll published between 1998 and early 2004 in which Schröder secured a higher score in public popularity than his foreign minister from the junior coalition partner.

All German governments from the early 1950s onwards have acknowledged the need to develop some kind of media management. At least two structural features in the area of information gathering and media management are worth mentioning. There is, first of all, the Federal Intelligence Service (*Bundesnachrichtendienst*), which works for the chancellor but is of rather limited use as a device of leadership as information may only be gathered abroad. The Federal Press and Information Office (*Presse- und Informationsamt der Bundesregierung*), the government's principal information and publicity agency, provides a somewhat more powerful resource. Until 1958, when it was established as an independent agency headed by a state secretary, the Federal Press and Information Office existed as a unit within the chancellery. Today, it performs basically two functions – providing the chancellor with information about the state of public opinion in Germany and abroad, and providing the media with information about the government's policies. Its overall performance has prompted scholars to describe it as the chancellor's 'speaking-tube and ... ear-trumpet' (Niclauss, 2000: 69).

All governments have been forced to adapt their strategies of public leadership to the changing structure of the media system.[26] Nevertheless, it is possible to discern rather different styles of media management and public leadership, which reflect to a considerable degree the different personalities of individual post-war chancellors. Adenauer was obsessed with following news media reporting on his government, which led him to read seven to eight different newspapers each day. To some extent this exceptional amount of attention to the media seems to have been inspired by his deep suspicion of the bulk of news media journalists, whom he considered to have a strong SPD bias (Küster, 1988: 17, 27–8). Although he invested much time in speaking in public, Adenauer hated press conferences and had a strong preference for more informal ways of dealing with the media. The so-called *Teegespräche*, informal meetings between the chancellor and journalists, soon became the most important element in Adenauer's concept of media management and public leadership. The concrete strategic aims of individual meetings varied. Interviews with foreign journalists had the main function of preparing the ground for pending government decisions or influencing current decision-making processes. By contrast, meetings focusing on explanations of government policies were designed mainly to garner the support of the German public.

While Adenauer's skills in dealing with the media remained largely unmatched for several decades,[27] his marked reservations about news media journalists were shared by most of his successors. Neither Schmidt nor Kohl had a particularly warm relationship with the overwhelming majority of the members of the media community, despite their general approaches to public leadership, and their public approval ratings, being very different. Unlike Kohl, Schmidt was a gifted and highly persuasive communicator. However, unlike Brandt, who was literally adored by many left-wing journalists who considered him to be the first chancellor of a new age (Zons, 1984), Schmidt had to work hard to gain a high reputation among the media elite and the public at large.

To some extent, both Schröder's positive reception by the bulk of the news media journalists, and the fairly high public approval ratings for most of his first term, may have been helped by his predecessor's rather low scores in the public arena. However, Schröder's popularity with the media has also been remarkable from a broader historical perspective. Much of his success with the media and the public has been the result of a sophisticated and highly professional strategy of public leadership, including a host of carefully prepared public activities – such as his participation in live television talk and game shows – as well as several less noticed, yet equally important, organizational innovations. Whereas Kohl had experimented with a system in which the government's spokesperson faced competition from another based in the chancellery (who often seemed to be better-informed than the government's), Schröder has concentrated all responsibilities in the area of public relations in the hands of the government's spokesperson and chief of the Federal Government's Press Office (Uwe-Karsten Heye, to be replaced by Schröder's biographer, Bela Anda, at the start of the government's second term). Although Heye (and later Anda), was constantly involved in the overall task of 'selling' the government's policies to the media and the public, the presentation of major decisions to the public has usually been left to the chancellor himself.

The priority Schröder has given to the task of media management and public leadership has largely been at the expense of party leadership in the traditional sense. His specific mix of (non-)preferences – including a remarkable neglect of traditional party management and leadership, a strong focus on public relations and image management, and the occasional collusion of representatives from the opposition parties into a large number of 'special commissions'[28] – has prompted observers to speak of a 'presidential chancellorship' (Lütjen and Walter, 2000).[29] A more systematic historical perspective on the relationship between German chancellors and their parties from Adenauer to Schröder (Helms, 2002b) suggests that Schröder's performance as party leader has not been as exceptional as some have suggested. For example, Schröder can hardly be described as 'a new type of party leader, leading his party from the Chancellor's Office' (Korte, 2000: 9). This had already been a core feature of Adenauer's style of leading the CDU, though this comparison should not be carried too far. Whereas Adenauer used the chancellery as de facto CDU headquarters as there was virtually no such thing as a CDU party organization for much of the 1950s and early 1960s, Schröder repeatedly ignored, and violated, the well-established patterns and expectations of leadership in Germany's most tradition-conscious party.

Prima facie, Schröder's performance as party leader would appear to display similarities with that of Britain's Tony Blair – a comparison unlikely to be considered as an insult by Schröder and his supporters, who were more than willing to highlight any possible affinities between the two leaders. However, there are few substantial similarities between the Blair and Schröder approaches to party leadership, or even the idea of party leadership. In contrast to Blair, Schröder did not start out as a committed programmatic and organizational reformer of his party. Not only was there no remotely comparable programmatic reform within the SPD as in the Labour Party during both parties' extended periods in opposition; it has even been doubted whether the SPD – a party as fragmented and decentralized as the political system in which it has operated – could ever be reformed as the Labour Party was between the mid-1980s to mid-1990s. However, structural differences between the British and German party systems alone cannot explain the difference between Schröder and Blair. Even the specific German conditions do not make party leadership impossible. There was a glaring lack of interest by Schröder in assuming the role of party leader, which showed parallels with Ludwig Erhard rather than Tony Blair. Ultimately, the office of SPD party chairman came to Schröder rather than the other way round. After Lafontaine's surprise resignation as party chairman in March 1999, Schröder had few other options but to fill – at least formally – the leadership vacuum at the top of his party by accepting the much-despised party chairmanship. Although Lafontaine's early departure gave Schröder a freer hand, it also deprived him of the possibility of practising burden-sharing (in terms of garnering party support), that has characterized the Brown–Blair axis so much within the Labour Party. The later leadership tandem between Schröder and Müntefering, formally established in March 2004, appeared to have been born too much out of political crisis to mark a promising new beginning of the relationship between the chancellery and the largest governing party.

Future assessments of the Schröder chancellorship, and the chancellor's record as party leader, are likely to divide the Schröder years into periods marked by either the existence or non-existence of a personal union between the office of chancellor and the post of SPD party chairman. However, no closer inspection will be able to deny seriously that, even at the best of times, the relationship between Schröder and the SPD has been governed by a notable degree of mutual suspicion and distrust. In many interim comparisons of the Federal Republic's three Social

Democratic chancellors focusing on the respective patterns of party management and support, Schröder was assigned a position somewhere between Brandt and Schmidt. If the parties in parliament are subsumed under the wider notion of 'party',[30] then Schröder is identified easily as the Federal Republic's Social Democratic chancellor least inclined to define executive leadership in terms of party leadership.

Conclusion

Whereas German chancellors clearly have more in common with British prime ministers than with American presidents with regard to their room for manoeuvre in the executive branch, their scope for action in the wider political process is undoubtedly more reminiscent of the conditions of executive leadership in the American separation-of-powers system. Such comparisons – to be elaborated in Chapter 8 – should not be carried too far, however. Many of the limitations to strong executive leadership that German chancellors and their governments face are rather different from those encountered by American presidents and their administrations.

The type of parliamentary government introduced by the Basic Law puts a premium on stability. In constitutional practice, the founding fathers' strong emphasis on stability has been supported by a breed of political parties that took the task of governing seriously. Whereas both the high amount of government stability and the parties' strong focus on their office-seeking and governing functions distinguish the Federal Republic from its historical predecessors, it is primarily the generous opportunity structure of the opposition parties (both within and beyond the parliamentary arena) that makes the German post-war polity a special case among the family of contemporary parliamentary democracies. What is even more important than the specific brand of German political institutions itself is the fact that the basic institutional arrangements have had rather a strong impact on the overall structure of the political process in the Federal Republic (see also Schmidt, 1996).

Virtually the whole range of different dimensions of executive–legislative relations that may be distinguished theoretically has played a role in the German legislative arena. In particular, the 'inter-party' and 'cross-party modes' have figured more prominently than in many other countries. Still, as in any parliamentary democracy, the first responsibility of governments has been to secure the support of their own parties. Most German post-war governments have tried to improve the relationship with their respective parliamentary majorities by including influential figures from the parliamentary parties in informal decision-making bodies designed to make coalition government work more smoothly. While most chancellors have shown some degree of involvement in parliamentary business, few of them have been key actors in the process of mobilizing parliamentary support for their administrations' policies. The most unusual pattern of executive–legislative relations occurred in the late 1960s when the Bundestag as a whole, rather than the (tiny) opposition, performed much of the function of parliamentary control over governmental action. This experience was followed by the most unusual strategy of parliamentary opposition – a rather strange mix of over-ambitious co-governing and parliamentary obstruction – that marked the 6th Bundestag (1969–72).

None of the numerous powerful 'veto players' marking the German polity has functioned constantly as an institutional barrier against strong executive leadership and majority rule in the wider political process. If any meaningful comparisons between such different institutions and actors as second chambers, central banks and courts may be made, the Bundesbank is easily identified as the most uncompromising 'veto player' German governments were forced to put up with for much of the post-war period. The Constitutional Court, by contrast, not only showed a reasonable regard for the legislative decisions of governing majorities; it occasionally even eased the burden of German governments by 'taking the heat' for unpopular decisions and pointing the way for the legislator to follow. Interest groups, while being powerful, have not considered protest and opposition as their natural strategy towards the government. Whereas tripartist forms of governance always include a certain loss of autonomous decision-making power by the government, the predominantly peaceful integration of the most powerful interest groups served governments from Adenauer to Schröder fairly well. Finally, the founding fathers' vision of an extremely restricted position for the head of state has materialized fully. From a historical perspective, Lübke and von Weizsäcker stand out as the only incumbents who (temporarily) challenged the rather narrow parameters of 'presidential leadership' in the Federal Republic, albeit without ever seriously questioning the superiority of the political executive in the governmental system.

Even though chancellors from the very early post-war years have enjoyed a special position in the public arena, the much-noted 'chancellor bonus' at elections and in other public confrontations between the chancellor and other actors is not a natural attachment to the office; it has, to a large extent, to be earned. As in any other contemporary Western democracy, German governments have been virtually forced by important structural changes of the media system, and changing public expectations, to devote an increasing amount of time and energy to managing their relations with the media and the public at large. Although Schröder has by no means been the first post-war chancellor to emphasize his role as government leader at the expense of his role as party leader, the government's preoccupation with issues of media and image management reached unprecedented levels during his chancellorship. Whereas Erhard's aloofness from his party was very much a reflection of his *Weltanschauung*, Schröder's notably distant relationship with the SPD, at least in the beginning, was part of a well-calculated concept of leadership, designed to widen the government's electoral support base beyond the comparatively narrow pool of diehard supporters of Red–Green. Whereas it will remain fascinating to see how far such a strategy carries in a system that has become famous for the strength of its parties throughout the political system, there were unmistakable signs by mid-2004 that the Schröder way of governing had reached its limits.

Part IV
Conclusion

8
Making Sense of Complexity: Comparative Perspectives and Conclusions

For many decades, it seemed, the favourite writer and poet of most Anglo-Saxon political comparativists was Rudyard Kipling – if only for the legitimacy and dignity that his eagerly-quoted observation about the impossibility of understanding England from a purely English view added to their own work. Times have changed, though. There is no longer any need to buttress, or justify, comparative ambitions in political science by citing patron saints from outside the discipline. Today, it would seem, there is a greater burden on those who are unwilling to shed at least some comparative light on their subjects.

Nevertheless, neither have committed country specialists died out, nor has the discipline of comparative politics been relieved of their specific challenges and problems. Alongside the many methodological problems that comparative research sees itself confronted with, one of the more practical ones (especially in the sub-discipline of qualitative comparative politics) relates to the necessary knowledge required for drawing meaningful comparisons. On the face of it, it would seem unfair to expect comparativists to have the same knowledge about the individual cases of their sample that (country) specialists may have about their familiar object of study. Yet, unfair or not, there is no denying that no comparative assessment can be more substantial than the author's knowledge of any of the individual cases to be covered admits it to be. Worse still, comparing without a reasonable knowledge of the phenomena themselves, and the specific research paradigms in a given area, is likely to result in what Giovanni Sartori (1991) has called 'miscomparing'.

This study has responded to that problem by looking at the leadership performances of American presidents, British prime ministers and

German chancellors separately before engaging in comparative conclusions. In Chapters 2 to 7, the perspective was confined largely to the level of historical comparison. This concluding chapter's primary focus is on the international dimension of comparison, though this will not be allowed to eclipse the historical dimension for the sake of methodological 'purity'. Both are equally important for a deeper understanding of the phenomenon of executive leadership in Western democracies.

Most of what follows is devoted to a comparative discussion of the various manifestations of executive leadership within the core executive and in the wider political process in the United States, Britain and Germany. Then, a more specific perspective will be offered that focuses on the much-debated phenomenon of 'presidentialization' in Britain and Germany. The concluding section discusses the significance of, and interplay between, different variables shaping the performance of executive leaders against the background of the key findings of this study.

Executive Leadership within the Core Executive

Even executive leadership within the comparatively small territory of the core executive comprises a number of different aspects or dimensions. These include the appointment process, the organization of both the administrative and the political core executive, and a 'chief executive's' performance in the decision-making process in the narrower sense. As in the previous country chapters, these different dimensions will be addressed here individually in turn.

Staffing the Core Executive

From a West European perspective, the structural advantages that American presidents enjoy over their counterparts in parliamentary democracies when selecting their cabinet team appear to be enviable. With most of the constitutional stipulations and party constraints that tend to shape the government-building process in parliamentary democracies being absent, the most serious check on the president would clearly seem to be the requirement to have cabinet nominees approved by the Senate. Prima facie, even this has hardly proved to be a major restriction on presidential power in the cabinet-building process. Since 1789, only nine cabinet-level nominations have been rejected, six of them before 1900. However, as a closer empirical inspection suggests, the Senate's veto power has in fact worked very much as an 'anticipated check' on the president's appointment power. In recent decades, many cabinet-level nominees have been withdrawn before a Senate vote, when the president sensed that they would be defeated (Krutz *et al.*, 1998). Even if a president eventually gets his way, his victory usually comes at a fairly high price in terms of precious time resources that have to be invested to secure senatorial approval.[1]

There is at least one other factor flowing from the basic institutional features of the presidential system of government that has the potential to weaken the president's cabinet appointment power: the incompatibility rule, which forces members of Congress to give up their seat in the legislature before taking up a position in the executive branch. There has been a notable reluctance among selected candidates to accept a cabinet appointment – which contrasts starkly with the typical ambitions of career politicians in the parliamentary democracies. Several good reasons may explain this degree of reservation. First, incompatibility implies that candidates cannot simply return to Congress should their tenure in the cabinet terminate abruptly (which marks a contrast to the incompatibility rules established in several West European parliamentary democracies, such as Norway or Sweden). The choice of possible candidates holding a seat in Congress is made even harder by the high public standing that members of the American legislative branch, especially senators, usually enjoy. The public respect, and political influence, that congressional leaders and committee chairmen command equals that of the cabinet secretaries in Washington, and dwarfs the public reputation and influence of many, even senior, MPs in parliamentary democracies. No less importantly – at least in terms of the typical career patterns in parliamentary democracies – the considerable risk involved in switching between the two branches rarely pays off, as cabinet membership in the United States cannot be regarded as a springboard to the country's political top position – that is, the office of president. Herbert Hoover, cabinet secretary of trade under Presidents Harding and Coolidge, was the last candidate who managed to advance directly from a cabinet position to the office of president, and there has been just one other president in the twentieth century who had ever sat in the cabinet, Howard Taft.

Any British/German comparison of the cabinet-building process has to start with acknowledging the constraints that German chancellors face as leaders of coalition governments. While the coalition-related restrictions in Germany may seem modest when compared with the cabinet-building practice in countries in which governments typically include up to four or more different parties, such as Finland or Belgium, the coalition factor in the Federal Republic *is* indeed rather strong. From the early post-war period, chancellors have enjoyed very little discretionary power in appointing or dismissing candidates of the junior coalition partner. The historical trend towards making the distribution of cabinet posts among the coalition partners an issue to be settled in a written coalition treaty has tended to circumscribe further the chancellor's constitutional prerogative in the government-building process. This has long been reflected in the staunch opposition from constitutional lawyers against that practice.[2]

From a German perspective, the widely acknowledged leeway of British prime ministers in the cabinet-building process appears less impressive than it does through the eyes of most British observers. As the German cabinet included no fewer than ten different non-parliamentary cabinet ministers between late 1998 and early 2004, the constitutional requirement of British ministers to hold a seat in parliament may be considered a major check on the prime minister's discretionary powers in the cabinet-building process. However, it is easy to make too much of this. Many German observers, for their part, are likely to overlook how small the British political elite beyond Westminster is, compared with the much broader pool of professional politicians and would-be ministers in the German federal system. For most of the post-war period there have been very few professional politicians in the British political system outside Westminister that prime ministers might have wished to have in the cabinet (although their number may increase in the future because of the side-effects of devolution on political elite-breeding and recruitment). The British system of by-elections also provides better opportunities for bringing people whom the prime minister wishes to appoint to ministerial office into parliament between two general elections – a device of which there is no equivalent in Germany.[3]

Traditionally, many observers tended to consider the existence of a 'shadow cabinet' as the single most powerful check on an incoming prime minister's room for manoeuvre in the cabinet-building process. Historically, 'quasi-automatic' promotion for shadow cabinet ministers to the cabinet was considered to be more typical under an incoming Conservative prime minister than under a Labour counterpart (Mackintosh, 1977: 438). Since the early 1980s it has appeared that the respective restraints would be more serious for prospective Labour prime ministers, because in 1981 the Labour Party changed its statutes to oblige any incoming Labour prime minister to appoint the whole shadow cabinet to ministerial office (though the right of disposition of offices among ministers was left to his discretion). The real impact of these rules has, however, proved to be rather modest. There have been frequent 'violations' of the rules by leaders from both major parties, including Tony Blair.

As the findings of a recent empirical assessment suggest, there are not only major differences at the level of the constitutional and political parameters of the cabinet appointment process in the United States, Britain and Germany, but also notable differences with regard to the key characteristics of cabinet members in these three countries (Helms, 2002c).[4] During the period 1945/9–2000 German cabinet ministers had both the longest total average tenure (64.2 months) and the longest tenure in a single cabinet position (43.9 months). More than 9 per cent of all German federal ministers of the post-war period stayed in the cabinet for more than ten years, whereas scarcely more than 6 per cent of all British cabinet ministers and no American cabinet secretary after 1945 served for more than a decade. Slightly more than 4 per cent of all German cabinet ministers between 1949 and 2000 in fact held the same cabinet position for more than ten years – a record not matched by any British or American cabinet minister.[5] Whereas the total average term of British cabinet ministers was considerably longer than that of their American counterparts (53.4 months and 35.2 months, respectively), the average tenure of cabinet ministers in a single position was longer in the United States than it was in Britain (32.4 months and 26.2 months, respectively).

To be understood fully, these findings have to be viewed in relation to the rather different body of experience that cabinet ministers in the three countries had in different cabinet posts. More than 90 per cent of US cabinet officers, but less than half of their British counterparts, held only a single cabinet position. With little less than three-quarters of all federal ministers having held only a single cabinet position, German cabinet ministers occupy a medium position, somewhat closer to that of the United States. Particularly remarkable is the large proportion of British cabinet ministers who held four, five or even six different cabinet posts. Whereas only one German cabinet minister and one American cabinet secretary held four different cabinet posts (Franz Josef Strauss and Elliot L. Richardson), no fewer than thirty-five British cabinet ministers – more than a full quarter of all British cabinet ministers in the period 1945–2000 – held four or more different cabinet posts.

The picture painted so far may be refined by information relating to the political background of cabinet ministers in the three countries considered.[6] On being appointed to the cabinet, 81.8 per cent of German cabinet ministers and 99.6 per cent of their British counterparts during the period 1945/9–2000 held a seat in the Bundestag or the House of Commons, respectively. While the incompatibility rule in the United States precludes a strict comparison, it is still worth noting that only

15.8 per cent of all US cabinet officers serving from the first Truman cabinet until December 2000 were former members of Congress. There is a comparable divide between the United States and the two major West European parliamentary democracies with regard to the proportion of cabinet ministers with a formal party affiliation: all British cabinet ministers and the overwhelming majority of their German counterparts were members of the governing party/parties, and many belonged to the leadership circles of their parties or parliamentary party groups. There are no reliable figures for the United States, although the available empirical assessments of the political profile of cabinet secretaries draw a picture that is dominated by candidates who combine weak or absent party ties with a high degree of expertise in one or a few policy fields.[7] The latter marks the exact opposite to British cabinet ministers, who are almost invariably 'non-specialists', whereas the degree of policy specialization among German ministers, albeit being virtually always members of the governing party elite, is almost as high as among their US counterparts.[8]

The rather clear-cut profiles of cabinet personnel in the three countries concerned that emerge from a comparative assessment of aggregated data, have not prevented scholars from identifying trends of convergence for selected periods of time. For example, the selection of cabinet nominees under George H. W. Bush has been compared with the cabinet-building process in parliamentary democracies (Warshaw, 1996: 174), whereas occasional appointments of policy experts without a strong power base within the governing party, or from outside parliament, in the West European parliamentary democracies have been considered to be reminiscent of the typical cabinet-building process in the United States. Transatlantic similarities in this area are, however, easily overdone.

In particular, the suggestion to consider the very high turnover rate among cabinet ministers under Blair and Schröder as a 'presidential element' in their respective leadership styles (Korte, 2002b) is untenable for a number of reasons. To begin with, frequent personnel changes at the cabinet level seem no longer to be a key characteristic of the US cabinet, as the experience with the Clinton presidency and the first three years of the George W. Bush presidency suggest. There was in fact a smaller turnover rate in the Clinton cabinet than in the cabinets of Tony Blair and Gerhard Schröder. No fewer than four of Clinton's cabinet secretaries remained in office for a full eight years, and this trend continued under Bush. By April 2004, thirty-nine months into the George W. Bush presidency, only two of the fourteen cabinet ministers appointed in early 2001 had been replaced.[9] Second, if frequent dismissals of cabinet members are to be judged as manifestations of power in the hands of the chief executive, resignations may not simply be counted as dismissals in the narrower sense. While carefully considered dismissals may strengthen the chief executive's position, resignations may well hurt his or her standing, both in the core executive and among the public at large. As a closer look at the cabinet reshuffles under Gerhard Schröder reveals, of the eight ministers taking their leave during the government's first term, only two were in fact dismissed (Karl-Heinz Funke in 2000, and Rudolf Scharping in 2002). Third, as challenges to the chief executive's power within the core executive tend to originate from 'long-term ministers' serving in the same position for an extended period of time, the focus should be on this dimension, rather than on the overall turnover rate among cabinet members. However, if this criterion is considered as the relevant dimension of comparison, then the figures presented above would not let it seem reasonable to consider a brief term of a cabinet minister as the head of a specific department as a characteristic feature of presidential government at all. In fact, the average tenure of cabinet ministers in a single post has been longer, rather than shorter, in the United States than in Britain.

The different styles of individual presidents, prime ministers and chancellors at the level of cabinet appointments may be considered in relation to their respective approaches to the organizational structure of their cabinets. Interestingly, there seems to be no strong correlation between a chief executive's inclination to change the organizational structure of the cabinet and his or her willingness to change the cabinet personnel and/or move serving members from one department to another. While there are some chief executives scoring highly on both dimensions, such as Nixon in the United States or Wilson and Blair in Britain, there are examples to be found in each of the three countries which suggest that the frequency and intensity of reshuffles on the one hand and changes of the departmental structure on the other do not necessarily correspond closely, if at all, with each other. The administrations of Thatcher and Major, who both reshuffled their cabinet extensively, were marked by a rather low degree of 'machinery change'. By contrast, Heath, who was criticized harshly by Conservative backbenchers for his notable inclination to carry out very few reshuffles to bring in new personnel had a particularly impressive record as a forceful reorganizer of the executive branch (Davis *et al.*, 1999: 21–7).

While cabinet appointments may be seen as the politically most important area of recruitment from the chief executive's point of view – at least for Britain and Germany, if not to the same extent for the

United States[10] – a comparative discussion of the appointment powers of chief executives in the three countries has to reach further. The president's room for manoeuvre in staffing the 'presidential branch' is unmatched by any head of government of a West European parliamentary democracy. Even though the Office of Policy Development stands out as the only major EOP agency whose complete staff is made up of political appointees, presidents face few, if any, restraints in staffing their closest environment of political and policy advisers in the White House Office. Moreover, even these appointments represent only a small proportion of the overall number of positions to be filled by an incoming president.

The appointment power of British prime ministers displays a different pattern. Although the British prime minister may be described as enjoying the most generous appointment power of all heads of government in Western Europe, extending to members of the second chamber of parliament and dozens of (junior) ministers below the cabinet level, his or her power to appoint to positions in the Prime Minister's Office and the Cabinet Office has traditionally been very modest. In the late 1960s, an observer intimately familiar with both the American and British system of government went as far as to characterize the potential tensions between the prime minister and the senior civil servants in the Prime Minister's Office and the Cabinet Office as 'a second, reinforcing check-and-balance of the system', alongside the possible divisions between the prime minister and his cabinet (Neustadt, 1969: 146). While the proliferation of special advisers in the Prime Minister's Office since the 1970s, and their more recent dramatic increase under Blair, has modified the prime minister's appointment power in the administrative core executive, the latter remains to a greater extent immune from prime ministerial patronage than many other areas of the British polity.

By British standards, the German chancellor's appointment power beyond the cabinet level looks rather modest at best. There is no equivalent in Germany of the prime minister's role in appointing members of the second chamber; there is also no comparable involvement of the chancellor in selecting sub-cabinet political office-holders. Appointments both within the group of parliamentary state secretaries – the German equivalent to British junior ministers – and the top level of civil servants who may be retired temporarily for political reasons ('political civil servants') are decided formally by the full cabinet, or by individual cabinet ministers, rather than the chancellor. And the gradual informalization of the recruitment process – the trend towards making decisions about the overall number of parliamentary state secretaries, and the distribution of them among the coalition partners, an issue to be settled in the coalition treaty – has done little to strengthen the chancellor's hand in this area. The 'political civil servants' and parliamentary state secretaries in the chancellery are the only posts to be filled at the chancellor's discretion. Also, the chancellor's formal and informal roles in selecting candidates for top positions within the Bundesbank and the Federal Constitutional Court (areas that prompt comparisons with the American president rather than the British prime minister) have remained rather unimpressive.

Patterns of Core Executive Leadership

Staffing the core positions of the executive branch, and controlling the decision-making process in the executive branch are, however, clearly not the same thing. Most of the challenges that chief executives face start only after the transition period. As to the narrower manifestations of executive leadership, a framework put forward by Rudi Andeweg (1997) provides a useful reference concept. In contrast to some other authors who use the terms 'collegiality' and 'collectivity' of cabinets as synonyms, Andeweg distinguishes systematically between different levels of collegiality and collectivity, which leads to the three-by-three diagram reproduced in Figure 8.1.

In the United States, the combination of 'monocratic' government (at the collegiality level) and 'fragmented' government (at the collectivity level) represents the dominant pattern of core executive decision-making. The typical variant of cabinet government in Britain has been

Figure 8.1 Dimensions of cabinet government

	COLLECTIVITY		
COLLEGIALITY	Fragmented (individual minister)	Segmented (cabinet committee)	Collective (cabinet)
Monocratic (prime ministerial)			
Oligarchic (inner cabinet)			
Collegial (ministerial equality)			

Source: Andeweg (1997: 80).

'monocratic-oligarchic/segmented'. The country most difficult to classify is Germany, which has witnessed rather different combinations of dimensions of collegiality and collectivity over the past half-century, though on balance 'monocratic-oligarchic' elements (in terms of collegiality) and 'fragmented-collective' patterns (in terms of collectivity) figured more prominently than their possible alternatives.

Among more recent US administrations, the Clinton administration provides the clearest example of the 'monocratic/fragmented' type of core executive decision-making. From the beginning, the cabinet was in an extremely weak position. Cabinet meetings were substituted at an early stage by so-called 'cabinet briefings', chaired and managed by Clinton's White House chief of staff rather than the president himself. While most presidents granted the cabinet more leeway in the field of domestic policy than in foreign affairs, under Clinton even this rule of thumb was challenged by the president's notable obsession with even the most minor details of decisions, which became particularly evident in the area of domestic policy.

If the 'monocratic/fragmented' type has marked the dominant variant of American 'cabinet government' since 1945, the most far-reaching departures from this pattern occurred during the Eisenhower presidency, and (though more temporarily) under Nixon and Carter. They all shared an inclination to allow a more collective style of core executive decision-making. Even under Eisenhower, the cabinet did not become a genuine decision-making body, but his administration provides the last example of the cabinet enjoying a more powerful position in the policy-making process than the White House Office.

At the collectivity level, the creation of cabinet committees under Reagan introduced a new element of decision-making, which remained, however, deeply embedded in the dominant working logic of presidential government. Reagan's cabinet committees cannot properly be described as sub-divisions of the full cabinet. The individual committees included both members of the cabinet and senior representatives from the White House staff, with the latter often being the dominant participants. Moreover, the president himself attended meetings only during a very early stage of the experiment which lost much of its vigour as the administration entered its second term. All successive presidents from Bush I to Bush II have experimented with similar structures involving White House staff and cabinet members, which suggests the consideration of cabinet committees or cabinet councils as a 'thoroughly institutionalized' aspect of the contemporary presidency (Walcott and Hult, 2003: 151)

Irrespective of the different approaches of individual presidents to dealing with the cabinet, the White House staff has played a more prominent role in policy development than the cabinet in every administration since John F. Kennedy. A more prominent role of the cabinet, or several of its members, in some of the later administrations has rarely been the result of deliberate attempts at upgrading its position in the core executive decision-making process. It was often just a mere side-effect of serious frictions within the 'presidential branch', which drew the White House's attention away from watching the activities of cabinet secretaries. The lack of collectivity at the cabinet level has not been compensated by a strong sense of collegiality and collectivity in the 'presidential branch'. The dominant trend there has rather been towards ever-higher levels of functional specialization and fragmentation, fostering internal competition, empire building and divided loyalties among the staff rather than any kind of collegial spirit and collective decision-making.

In Britain, a system has evolved in which the prime minister has long been the single most powerful member of the cabinet – a 'first without equals' (Rose, 2001: 3), in fact, rather than a 'first among equals'. Although the cabinet as a whole matters, since the mid-1970s it is clearly the cabinet committees that have, at the expense of the full cabinet, emerged as the true centrepieces of core executive decision-making in Britain. Even though the constitutional norm of collective ministerial responsibility has survived into the early twenty-first century, there were few serious attempts at establishing early-twentieth-century 'textbook cabinet government' in post-war Britain. The last Churchill administration, during its first two years at least, stands out as a rare experiment of practising a truly collective form of cabinet government with no 'inner cabinet' and a sparse use of cabinet committees. More recent, and more temporary, examples of collective cabinet government were not to the same extent as under Churchill manifestations of a collectivity-focused leadership philosophy. As during the premierships of Douglas-Home, Major or Wilson (during his second term), the revived role of the full cabinet often signalled the inability of a beleaguered prime minister to install a more hierarchical regime, though the boundaries between inability and unwillingness remained rather flexible in most cases.

The historical assessments made in Chapter 3 suggest that weak policy expertise in a prime minister does not necessarily benefit the cabinet: it may boost the influence of individual ministers within the administration, or wreck the whole performance of the government. Under Douglas-Home, the prime minister's glaring lack of expertise in most areas of domestic policy gave rise to an extremely 'collegial-collective' form of cabinet government, yet under Eden, who displayed deficits in policy leadership as serious as Douglas-Home's, the full cabinet played a rather modest role.

Since the mid-1960s, all prime ministers have been able to draw on a specific support structure in the Prime Minister's Office, and in the Cabinet Office, to strengthen the policy-making role of No. 10 and its overall control of the core executive decision-making process. It remains doubtful, however, whether some of the weaker prime ministers of the earlier post-war period, such as Eden or Douglas-Home, would have in fact fared significantly better under the conditions of the post-1970 premiership. The enlarged administrative resources of the prime minister do not make other resources, such as party support in particular, less indispensable. Moreover, whereas the expanded resources at the prime minister's exclusive disposal in theory enable office-holders to pursue their goals with greater vigour (or at least with a greater chance of success), the hesitant or heavy-handed operation of these devices is all the more likely to expose a prime minister's leadership weakness.

The German post-war history of executive leadership in the core executive territory continues to be read by many as a story about different shades of 'chancellor rule'. Its starkest manifestations surely relate to the chancellorship of Konrad Adenauer. One observer even felt that the German model of the 1950s and early 1960s was 'very much closer to the American than to the British cabinet' (Ridley, 1966: 456), especially with regard to the notable weakness of most cabinet ministers. Among Adenauer's successors, Schmidt came closest to the first chancellor's record of dominating the cabinet. Erhard, Kiesinger, Brandt, Kohl and Schröder all evinced a stronger inclination to delegate responsibilities – though with different overall effects on their position within, and beyond, the core executive. The Chancellor's Office was crucial in making the constitutionally acknowledged 'chancellor principle' viable in the real world of political decision-making. With the exception of the Kiesinger years, significant parts of the Erhard chancellorship and Brandt's second term, the Office played a prominent role in all post-war administrations. In particular, Adenauer's and Schmidt's powerful roles within the core executive owed much to the smoothly operating support machinery in the chancellery.

Defying the cabinet-centred ideas of core executive decision-making among some constitutional lawyers, the constitutional practice since the early post-war years has seen the 'chancellor principle' being challenged far more often by manifestations of strong 'departmentalism' than by a cabinet unified in opposition to the chancellor. The political clout of individual cabinet ministers, or the cabinet team as a whole, has, however, varied enormously between different administrations. The extremes on this count are represented by Kiesinger and Brandt at one end, and Adenauer and Schmidt at the other.

The second, and even more important, challenge to 'chancellor rule' in the German core executive resulted from coalition government, and some of its most tangible institutional manifestations, such as 'coalition rounds' and 'coalition talks'. The art of governing by 'coalition talks' and 'coalition rounds' – at the expense of the cabinet – reached the point of perfection during the extended chancellorship of Helmut Kohl. Kohl's record as 'coalition chancellor' also marked a turning point in the history of the German chancellorship, in so far as his chancellorship seemed to prove that the party-driven informalization of core executive decision-making does not necessarily have to weaken the chancellor's position within the decision-making machinery.

What, then, are the major functional effects of the different structural conditions of core executive decision-making on the position of the chief executive? As the founder of modern studies of presidential leadership in the United States has argued, 'the British cabinet system tends to cover up the weaknesses and to show up the strengths of the top man; ours tends to do the opposite' (Neustadt, 1990: 162). To the extent that this statement is correct, one should be able to find similar qualities in Germany to those that Neustadt attributes to the British system.

What Neustadt seemed to have in mind was the idea of collective ministerial responsibility that continues to characterize the constitutional doctrines of parliamentary democracies. At least theoretically, the potential weaknesses of a prime minister may in fact be partly compensated by the strong performance of individual cabinet ministers without completely undermining the public reputation of the government; and public support for individual cabinet ministers or the cabinet as a whole may well transform into electoral support for the governing party or coalition of parties. Whereas the presence of strong ministers would, on the face of it, seem to involve the risk that a prime minister could be toppled from within his or her own government, this risk has in fact proved to be a rather modest one in practice. As Jock Bruce-Gardyne and Nigel Lawson (1976: 160) have observed, '[r]ivalry for the succession creates an uneasy balance which underpins the sitting tenant. The ambitious minister on the way up may be too busy carving out his departmental reputation to spare a thought for the wider scene, where ambition also incites caution.'

For some observers, the more recent trend towards personalization of politics in terms of media reporting has further increased the incentives for cabinets not to challenge the prime minister's position (Foley, 1993: 278). Even before the latest transformations of the conditions of executive leadership in the bulk of West European parliamentary democracies it was true that the American president was a lonelier figure in the executive branch than were the heads of government in parliamentary democracies, and who had little to gain politically from a strong performance of individual cabinet secretaries.

However, this would seem to represent only about half the truth. There are different expectations regarding the chief executive under presidential government and parliamentary government. These may expose the possible weaknesses of a prime minister at the level of core executive leadership even more clearly than those of an American president. The single most important aspect to be mentioned here is the required, or expected, policy expertise of the chief executive. Whereas Carter and Clinton enjoyed a – much-criticized – outsider status among American post-war presidents as 'policy wonks' (Henderson, 1997), the majority of British prime ministers and German chancellors commanded a reasonable amount of expertise in several fields of public policy. Those who did not – including Eden, Douglas-Home and Erhard, in particular – have widely been considered to top the list of disappointing leaders in their respective countries (though their problems were clearly not confined to their limited policy expertise). Compared with their counterparts in Britain or Germany, American presidents find it significantly easier to delegate decisions, and receive policy expertise from other sources, without risking being seen as 'out of control'. At least on this count, Neustadt's assertion that the American system tends to cover up the strengths and to show up the weaknesses of the 'top man' appears hardly to be tenable. In fact, even if one argues that policy expertise in the US context, after all, does not even qualify as a potentially important strength of the chief executive, it remains difficult to see what the American system does to cover up the strengths of a given president.

Administrative Resources

A closer look at the administrative resources at the disposal of American presidents, British prime ministers and German chancellors also reveals considerable differences. A first, major resource relates to the overall number of staff working in the White House Office, the Prime Minister's Office and the Chancellor's Office. For each of the three countries, figures vary significantly according to the concrete definitions of staff.[11] Still, all sources suggest that the overall number of staff in the White House Office and in the Chancellor's Office has been significantly higher – indeed, about four to five times higher – than in the Prime Minister's Office (the approximate figures for the mid-1990s were about 450 in the White House Office, 450 in the Chancellor's Office and about 100 in the Prime Minister's Office).[12]

Similar differences exist with regard to the historical dynamics of change to be observed in the American, British and German administrative core executive. The total figures for budgeted and actual personnel in the White House Office were considerably higher during the early 1970s than they were in the 1990s, and cutting down numbers of staff in the EOP has remained high on the agenda of presidents committed to 'reinventing government'. By contrast, the overall number of staff in the Prime Minister's Office has increased virtually continuously since the 1970s, although the overall increase rate was just about 20 percentage points from the late 1970s until the mid-1990s. The respective developments in the Chancellor's Office have been much less incrementalist. According to figures presented by Ferdinand Müller-Rommel (1997: 9), the overall number of staff doubled from 200 to 400 in just four years between 1966 and 1970. There has been a further increase in the overall number of staff from 400 to about 500 since the early 1980s.

Figures such as these, however, say very little about the actual staff support available to presidents, prime ministers and chancellors. The White House Office is part of a larger staff structure in the EOP which exists solely to provide the president with policy and political advice, and administrative support. Some of the most well-known units, such as the National Security Council, have been described as 'de facto parts of the White House' (Patterson, 2000: 5), and the whole structure of units and agencies referred to as the EOP is staffed by the president (though not all positions to be filled are political appointments in the narrower meaning of the term). The rather modest number of staff in the British Prime Minister's Office is equally misleading, as each balanced comparative assessment has to take into account the major role of the Cabinet Office as a potentially powerful administrative resource of the prime minister. The Cabinet Office's overall number of staff more than tripled from the mid-1970s to the mid-1990s and was well above 2,000 at the start of the twenty-first century – providing a potentially valuable administrative resource for the prime minister.

The proportion of political appointees in the German Chancellor's Office appears very small by American standards, but is still relatively generous in comparison with the permanent staff structure in the British core executive. Constitutional norms protecting the cabinet and individual ministers from being challenged, or even sidelined, by external special advisers working for the chancellor alone have been more resistant to change in Germany than in Britain. There is no comparable structure of special advisers in the chancellery to that marking the British core executive in the more recent past.

There are some other differences relating to the basic organizational structure of the Chancellor's Office, the Prime Minister's Office, and the White House Office. From a broader comparative perspective, the so-called 'mirror units' (*Spiegelreferate*), focusing specifically on the area of responsibility of an individual cabinet department, stand out as one of the organizational core features of the Chancellor's Office. Second, in contrast to the situation in the United States and Britain, the government's administrative resources for managing its relations with the media are not placed directly in the chancellery, although the Federal Press and Information Office works under the direct control of the chancellor. There is, finally, also no equivalent in the Chancellor's Office to the Office of Legislative Affairs in the White House Office. This could, prima facie, be considered as an institutional reflection of the fundamental difference between the parliamentary and presidential system, and the rather different roles of the president and the chancellor in the legislative arena. There is, however, also no equivalent in the Chancellor's Office of the British prime minister's parliamentary private secretary in the Political Office of the Prime Minister's Office, who is mainly responsible for liaising with the governing party's backbenchers (Finch, 1996).

Apart from such structural differences, the Chancellor's Office combines most functions that traditionally have been divided between the Prime Minister's Office and the Cabinet Office. It has been argued that the chancellor's staff exists mainly to improve the efficiency of the cabinet, but there is no such institution as a cabinet secretariat in Germany. From the earliest days of the Federal Republic, the Chancellor's Office has served as a powerful administrative resource of the chancellor rather than the cabinet.

One major feature of the staff structure in the American 'presidential branch' that has provoked much criticism from American and foreign observers alike relates to the professional background of many staff members in the president's closest environment. Many members of the 'presidential branch' have been judged to lack the necessary professional competence to advise the chief executive of a major advanced democracy. It is true that many positions, which in Britain and Germany (as well as most other West European systems) are filled with career civil servants, have long been occupied by members of the president's campaign team. However, it seems an open question to what extent this will continue to be considered a major structural disadvantage of the American model as the boundaries between governing and campaigning in the United States – but not only there – have become increasingly blurred. The more recent developments in Britain would seem rather to suggest that the reference model for providing chief executives with advice and support in the early twenty-first century may share significantly more with the American model than with the traditional British one.

Executive Leadership in the Wider Political Process

Equally fundamental differences between the three countries may be observed at the level of executive leadership in the wider political process, including the nature of executive–legislative relations and public leadership as well as the role of 'veto players' and counter-majoritarian institutions.

Executive–Legislative Relations

Whereas the most fundamental differences at the level of executive–legislative relations in our sample of countries clearly reflect the basic institutional divide between presidential and parliamentary government, the differences between Germany and Britain are more substantial than most American observers are likely to acknowledge. The structural advantages that British governments enjoy over their German counterparts in the parliamentary arena are manifold, including their unchallenged position in the process of parliamentary agenda-setting, the absence of powerful veto rights or any serious 'co-governing potential' of the opposition, and the structure of the committee system in particular. There are other crucial differences between the two countries relating to the structural devices governments have at their disposal to mobilize the support of the majority parties in parliament.

In Britain, the necessary support for government bills among MPs belonging to the majority party is organized by a sophisticated system of whips. The chief whip of the governing party usually attends cabinet meetings, though he or she has usually not been made a full member of the cabinet (as in the government of Tony Blair). There is no exact equivalent in Germany to the position of chief whip in Britain. If a member of the majority parliamentary parties attends cabinet meetings, it is the *Fraktion* chair rather than the *Erster Parlamentarischer Geschäftsführer*, who is otherwise the closest equivalent to the British chief whip in terms of generating 'party discipline' at parliamentary divisions. The two most important differences between the chief whip in the House of Commons and the chairman of the largest governing parliamentary party in the Bundestag concern the rules of recruitment and their roles as parliamentary speakers. Whereas the chief whip is appointed by the prime minister and has no right to speak in the chamber at all, the *Fraktion* chairman of the chancellor's party, as of any parliamentary party in the Bundestag, is elected by his or her fellow members and belongs to the most prominent and influential participants in parliamentary debates. With regard to the latter aspect, the *Fraktion* chairman of the chancellor's party seems to have much in common with the leader of the House in the British system, yet there are fundamental differences between the two positions in terms of appointment procedures, cabinet membership and other functions to be performed in the parliamentary arena.

Another major difference regarding the structural conditions of executive leadership in the parliamentary arena relates to the size of the so-called 'payroll vote' in the British House of Commons and the German Bundestag. The 'payroll vote' includes all MPs of the governing parties who hold a paid government post. The 'payroll vote' in the post-1945 House of Commons temporarily reached a level of more than 25 per cent (in the early 1980s, for example); that is, more than a quarter of MPs belonging to the majority party in the House of Commons held a paid government post.[13] In Germany, there has not only been a much smaller number of governing posts (in purely formal terms not even the parliamentary state secretaries are members of the federal government); there has also been a considerable number of cabinet ministers, and even, more recently, a handful of parliamentary state secretaries in the chancellery, with no seat in the Bundestag. As a consequence, the 'payroll vote' in the German Bundestag has never even come close to British levels. Often it has been below 10 per cent, and even in the immediate aftermath of German unification, which led to the creation of the largest government in German post-war history, it remained well below 15 per cent. Other things being equal, the significantly larger 'payroll vote' in Britain can be said to have made executive leadership in the House of Commons considerably easier than in the German Bundestag.

The comparative advantage of British governments in the parliamentary arena is further underscored by the very different power of the German and British second chambers – the Bundesrat and the House of Lords. In comparative works on the strength of bicameralism, Germany and Britain have been considered to be located at different ends of the spectrum. Also, the history of bicameralism in both countries has gone in opposite directions: whereas the Lords' veto powers were (further) capped in 1949, and have not been expanded since (despite much political rhetoric in favour of far-reaching reforms), the Bundesrat's effective veto power has gradually increased over the post-war period – to an extent that, since the sixth Bundestag (1969–72), has made at least 50 per cent of all bills subject to its explicit approval.

Still, the rather different structural parameters of executive leadership in the parliamentary arena have not determined the legislative process in Britain and Germany. As a historical perspective on the manifestations of executive leadership in the parliamentary arena reveals, there has been a wide variation in the overall performance of governments in the House of Commons and the Bundestag.

Virtually no British post-war government could afford to rely exclusively on the disciplinary effects of the sophisticated whip system. During the premierships of Attlee and Macmillan, specifically-designed consultative networks between the government and the parliamentary party played a particularly prominent role in managing the Commons. Blair, by contrast, has emphasized 'discipline' rather than 'co-operation' when imposing a new Code of Conduct on Labour MPs in 1996. As prime minister, like Thatcher before him, he profited considerably from his party's huge majority in the House. The Heath premiership became the first to provide hard evidence that a prime minister's style in managing relations with backbench MPs can make all the difference in terms of parliamentary support for the government.

Variations in style and success also mark the performances of German chancellors and their governments in the parliamentary arena. The final months of Brandt's first term came closest to the parliamentary experiences of the embattled Callaghan and Major governments. Most other German post-war administrations had an easier ride through the parliamentary arena. Whereas few German chancellors had an intimate working relationship with the backbenchers of the majority parliamentary party groups, most of them – with the notable exception of Erhard – could draw upon loyal supporters among the *Fraktion* leadership of their party in the Bundestag. Schröder has been less lucky in putting parliamentary support on a more permanent basis than some of his predecessors. However, judging by his notable inclination to recruit many key office-holders within his administration from outside the Bundestag, developing warm relations between the chancellery and the SPD parliamentary party has apparently not been particularly high on his agenda.

In both Germany and Britain, the professionalization of the parliamentary elite[14] has fundamentally altered the conditions of executive leadership in parliament, though the effects of professionalization in both countries have been rather ambivalent. On the one hand, the emergence of a class of career politicians has made the task of managing parliament more demanding, as better-educated and more professional MPs tend to be less willing than their historical predecessors to toe the party line on any major issue. At the very least, they expect to be persuaded, rather than forced, to support a given bill. On the other hand, the steady increase in career politicians has added structural strength to the position of the chief executive, as the concept of politics as a vocation includes the ambition of MPs to secure governmental office (King, 1991).

Other things being equal, the positive effects of professionalization from the executive's point of view have been much stronger in Britain than in Germany. This is primarily a result of the considerably larger patronage power of British prime ministers. The rather dissimilar career opportunities of professional politicians in the British Westminster system and Germany's federal system may be mentioned as an additional variable, though the departure of members of the Bundestag whose ministerial ambitions are disappointed, for an alternative career at state level has not formed a statistically relevant career pattern in German political history since 1949.[15]

Another, more recent, phenomenon that characterizes the constitutional practice in both countries may be seen in the growing tendency towards a silent 'de-parliamentarization' of the governing process (if not in the sense of a loss of parliament's formal power to legislate, certainly in terms of an decreasing involvement of the head of government in the parliamentary process). Tony Blair's degree of involvement in parliamentary business has marked an all-time low in British politics. In Germany, the somewhat moderate presence of Chancellor Schröder in the Bundestag was accompanied by other manifestations of 'post-parliamentary' government, including an exceptionally large proportion of non-parliamentary government ministers and a decision-making structure in which the majority parliamentary parties were often expected to lend their support to solutions that had been found in the chancellery or elsewhere outside the Bundestag.

Whereas American presidents do not depend on permanent and stable congressional support to 'survive' in office, managing executive–legislative relations holds a key position on any administration's agenda. From a somewhat more abstract perspective specifically focusing on the chief executive's involvement at different stages of the public policy-making process, presidential leadership in the congressional arena may be considered a functional equivalent to cabinet leadership of chief executives in parliamentary democracies (Rockman, 2003: 55). If the cabinet in a parliamentary system, enjoying the support of the parliamentary majority, has agreed formally on the content of a government bill, most of the chief executive's job is done. By contrast, in a presidential system, the formal initiation of a bill in the legislature usually marks the start of the battle from the president's perspective.

As the history of presidential–congressional relations suggests, the alternative patterns of party control – 'unified government' versus 'divided government' – provide limited guidance when it comes to assessing the dimension of a president's power in the legislative arena. Even the recent, largely unprecedented, levels of party polarization and party discipline among members of Congress appear to be fairly unspectacular when compared with the average figures in parliamentary democracies. Any further significant increase in terms of 'partyness' in the American legislative process would be conceivable only within a scenario of major constitutional reform aimed at replacing the existing presidential order by a parliamentary system of government – an idea that has stimulated some interesting intellectual thought-experiments (Manuel and Cammisa, 1998) without, however, having managed to find any support among relevant political decision-makers.

One aspect of the institutional features of executive–legislative relations in the United States that particularly invites comparison with Germany is the character and role of the second chambers, the Bundesrat and the Senate. However, even this comparison shows up more differences than similarities: differences start at the level of rules of recruitment for both chambers, which are reflected in the very different roles of individual members of the Bundesrat and the Senate in the legislative process. The Bundesrat basically represents the state governments, rather than a given state's population; its members are not elected, but are appointed as delegated members of the state governments. Therefore, very differently from US senators, individual members of the Bundesrat do not play any independent role in the legislative process at all – which requires completely different strategies by the executive when it comes to garnering the support of the Bundesrat or the Senate. The classification of both the Bundesrat and the Senate in many comparative works as very powerful second chambers would seem to suggest that there are close similarities at the level of competencies – which is, however, hardly the case. There is not only no equivalent in Germany of the Senate's far-reaching powers of scrutiny at the level of senior political and judicial appointments; the

Bundesrat also has considerably weaker veto powers in the legislative process than does the Senate, as – unlike the latter – it can on average block only about half of all bills passed by the other chamber. The most glaring differences in terms of executive leadership are, however, clear reflections of the institutional divide between the parliamentary and presidential form of government, which forms the political setting of the Bundesrat and the Senate, respectively. Until very recently, the Senate often proved (at least statistically) to be a more amenable body with which to deal for most presidents than was the House (Davidson and Campbell, 2000: 199) – a pattern that can be explained partly by the traditionally lower degree of party polarization in the Senate, which was of particular benefit to 'minority presidents' from either party. By contrast, no German chancellor could ever afford to have his strongest basis of parliamentary support in the Bundesrat, though Kohl in fact seemed to have more friends among CDU minister-presidents than among backbenchers of the coalition parties in the Bundestag.

One common feature of executive leadership in all three countries relates to the predominance of the executive over legislative assemblies in foreign policy. The executive's structural advantage in this area has received the largest amount of attention in the United States, where scholars went so far as to identify 'two presidencies' (Wildavsky, 1966) – a powerful one in foreign policy and a considerably weaker one in domestic policy.[16] The most-often cited example of the president's dominant role in foreign policy relates to the fact that the majority of more recent wars involving the United States were conducted without any formal declaration of war by Congress. In both Britain and Germany, the role of parliament in foreign policy has been confined strictly to that of a reactive player with limited veto powers. (In Germany, the Bundesrat's role in foreign policy has been the subject of much debate, with conflicts centring on the question as to whether a treaty under consideration does or does not require the Bundesrat's explicit approval. Whereas a large number of treaties have been considered to be 'approval matters', not a single major international treaty has been 'killed' by the Bundesrat). Despite the considerable differences that mark the German and British variants of parliamentary government, there has been a notable amount of convergence in terms of parliamentary involvement in national policy-making at the EU level in both countries (Weber-Panariello, 1995: 306–11).

Veto Players and Counter-majoritarian Institutions

There are other institutions that have a major impact on the scope of national executive leadership in a given polity. At the level of basic state structures, the difference between the federalism/unitarism divide merits first mention. In the United States and Germany, the federal system constitutes one of the most obvious institutional barriers against unlimited national executive leadership, at least in the area of domestic policy. Despite superficial similarities, both the basic institutional characteristics of the federal system and the cultural inclination towards the very idea of federalism have remained very different on either side of the Atlantic. While the American federal system has never fully lost the roots of its 'dual federalism', Germany has operated a system of 'interlocking federalism', in which the lion's share of legislation is mandated at the federal level, but its implementation is left to the states. In both countries, the first two or three decades after the Second World War were characterized by a dramatic shift towards strengthening the federal level at the expense of the states, and serious signs of a gradual recovery of state power did not emerge before the 1980s in either country. In both the United States and Germany, the courts marked a key driving force behind the process of strengthening the states towards the federal government. However, it would be wrong to interpret this development – which left the fundamental differences between the German and American type of federalism largely untouched – as a process restricting the federal government's decision-making power against its will. Particularly in the United States federal administrations have played an important role in reorganizing the distribution of power within the federation, driven mainly by the goal of reducing their overall financial burdens. On balance, both the financial responsibilities of the federal government and its decision-making capacity within the federal system have remained significantly larger in Germany than in the United States.

Even in Britain, the traditionally unlimited scope of nationwide executive leadership from the centre has been reduced slightly by the effects of the devolution measures of the late 1990s. As an American observer has rightly pointed out, however, 'being able to bring about this constitutional change so swiftly and decisively was itself a reflection of the power of the central authority in the United Kingdom' (Rockman, 2003: 53). It is clear, therefore, that the British central government's control over the country as a whole continues to be considerably more extensive than those of their American or German counterparts.

Constitutional courts are among those possible 'veto players' of governments that have received a particular amount of attention in the recent debate about governing and governance. In fact, the conditions of executive leadership in Germany and the United States cannot be understood without taking into account the powerful roles of the Federal Constitutional Court and the Supreme Court. While both courts have shown a reasonable reluctance to restrict the executive's authority or challenge their legislative programmes, the very existence of strong judicial review[17] has nevertheless had a potentially restraining effect on the executive's authority and scope of action.

There are obvious limits to comparing judicial review, and its systemic effects on the executive, in parliamentary and presidential systems, however. Given the basic institutional logic of parliamentary democracies, court judgements challenging the constitutionality of bills in Germany may in fact be considered as powerful checks against the executive in the legislative process. In the United States, such a perspective could only be applied with major qualifications. This is because by no means all bills enacted by Congress, including those to be passed during periods of 'unified government', can be properly classified as 'presidential bills'. In fact, the whole debate about 'judicial legislating' in the United States has centred on the relationship between the Supreme Court and Congress, rather than between the former and the presidency. 'Anticipatory effects' of judicial review have figured more prominently in Germany than in the United States, though they have not been completely absent in American politics (McCann, 1999: 67–76). Also, and partly as a result of the non-existence of any sort of 'political question doctrine' in Germany, the Constitutional Court's direct involvement in the legislative process – if invoked – has been more pronounced than that of the Supreme Court.

There is no British equivalent to the powerful constitutional courts in Germany and the United States. The recent strengthening of judicial review as a result of Britain's gradual adoption of European law may appear to be revolutionary from a British point of view, but it is hardly so from a broader comparative perspective. The public debate about the future of judicial review in Britain has remained firmly embedded in the traditional settings of a strongly majoritarian political culture. Even the Blair government's reform proposals to abolish the post of Lord Chancellor and to establish a constitutional court, have clearly not been inspired by the idea of abandoning the doctrine of parliamentary sovereignty. There have been no plans to give the court powers to strike down legislation.

A similar imbalance in terms of the institutional restrictions of executive decision-making power in the three countries may be observed in the area of monetary policy. In Britain, most of the post-war period has seen a central bank being strongly dependent on the government of the day. It was only shortly after the 1997 change of government that the Bank of England was granted greater autonomy, though even then the authority to set an inflation target was reserved to the government. By stark contrast, both the German Bundesbank and the Fed have long been among the most independent and powerful central banks in the world. Needless to say, what is more important than the structural degree of independence of a central bank is its actual behaviour. On the whole the Fed has not only 'tended to be somewhat more responsive to political demands than the Bundesbank', as Robert Elgie and Helen Thompson (1998: 32) have emphasized. A historical and international comparison also suggests, more specifically, that the Fed has responded much more readily to the political desires of American presidents than the Bundesbank has to the wishes of German chancellors. If the political victims of the Bundesbank's policies are counted, no fewer than three German chancellors – and as Richard Rose (2001: 6) has suggested, even one British prime minister (John Major) – may be identified.

In all three countries, governments have faced an ever-increasing number of interest groups from various areas, and of various kinds. But there are significant differences between the countries which, again, reflect – at least to some extent – the basic institutional differences between the presidential and parliamentary forms of government. Whereas interest groups in Britain and Germany have tended to focus their lobbying activities primarily on the executive, their American counterparts have concentrated their activities traditionally on Congress, though in all three countries both branches are being lobbied extensively. In Britain, the strong focus of the interest groups on the executive is not only a function of the executive's largely unchallenged dominance over parliament; it is also being favoured by the 'generalist profile' of the British civil service, which creates a strong need for specialist advice from groups possessing strategic information and 'know-how' in a given area. On balance, British governments have enjoyed a somewhat greater discretion than their German and American counterparts in determining which groups are included in executive/interest group networks. They also appear to have possessed a greater amount of discretion in defining the area of 'non-negotiable policies' (see also Page, 1992: 108–19). German governments have had the most far-reaching experiences with tripartist forms of decision-making (including the government and the social partners), whereas the United States has remained the prototype of a pluralist pattern of interest group politics. Its systemic effects have been intensified by the basic structures of the presidential system of government. As Martin Harrop (1992: 269) has noted, '[w]ell-organised groups confront a disorganised state'. Still, any comparative assessment must be careful not to overlook that the systemic role of powerful interest groups in the United States is not confined to circumscribing an administration's room for manoeuvre. Interest groups can also, and often do, serve as influential allies of presidents doomed to govern in a constitutionally highly fragmented system. In functional terms, interest groups under presidential government may thus fulfil some of the functions that in parliamentary democracies are normally performed by political parties.

Public Leadership

Public leadership represents another aspect of executive leadership in the wider political process, reflecting the basic institutional conditions of parliamentary and presidential government. While more recent research into the political agenda-setting process in the United States has questioned the conventional idea of considering the president as the system's 'chief agenda-setter', it is still true that presidents do not face any challenges from an 'alternative president' competing for limited resources of public attention, as do prime ministers and chancellors. The Gingrich experience of the mid-1990s suggests that, under the conditions of 'divided government', congressional majority leaders have the potential to become serious competitors of the president in the political fight for public attention. The first two years of the George W. Bush presidency seemed temporarily to provide a similar, though less high-profile, example, with Senate Majority Leader Tom Daschle taking the part of Newt Gingrich. Yet, as can also be learnt from these two recent episodes, any attempt at challenging the structurally exposed position of the president in the American political system cannot be sustained successfully for very long.

Other differences distinguishing the Unites States from the major West European systems – including the structure of the media system, the role of external media advisers in the core executive, and the cultural parameters of government–media relations – have been marked by a great amount of persistence. As Pippa Norris (2000: 174) has maintained, in contrast to the situation in the United States, experts in polling and political marketing are still 'not integral to the process of government' in Britain – and, as may be added, are even much less so in Germany.[18] In both Britain and Germany, campaigning, and especially governing, have essentially remained matters of party politics. This is not to say that there are no differences between Britain and Germany, though. Both the basic structural features of the media system and the cultural parameters of government–media relations have become more 'Americanized' in Britain than in Germany.

Whereas several features of the institutional presidency, and the structure of the political process in the United States, would seem to make the task of public leadership more manageable, in the end much comes down to the public leadership qualities of individual presidents. Perhaps surprisingly, it could not even be maintained that the specific nature of intra-party candidate selection, and the lengthy presidential election campaigns, in the United States ensure that only candidates who have a reasonable understanding of the requirements, and techniques, of public leadership are able to gain the presidency. There have, in fact, been astonishingly few outstanding public leaders among recent presidents, and only modest signs, if any, that more recent presidents have been on average more gifted public leaders than earlier office-holders. The first half of the 1990s saw a president (George H. W. Bush) who was clearly struggling to come to terms with the imperatives of his office in the field of public leadership – an even more notable feature in retrospective, as the Bush years marked an interregnum squeezed in between the reigns of two 'great communicators' among American post-war presidents. Also, George W. Bush's performance as a public speaker and leader have not exactly been out to set new standards of public leadership; his public appearances on television have clearly belonged to the least 'Reaganite' features of his presidency.

Similar differences among individual incumbents, as those observed in the United States, also characterize the history of public leadership in Britain and Germany. Some of the most charismatic personalities in the office of prime minister and chancellor, such as Macmillan, Thatcher or Schmidt, were succeeded by notably non-charismatic leaders (Douglas-Home, Major and Kohl, respectively). Both Blair and Schröder have proved much more effective in dealing with the media than their immediate predecessors, though it remains to be seen if their respective terms have really marked the beginning of a new era of more telegenic prime ministers and chancellors, as many have suggested.

An important difference concerning the nature of public leadership in the three countries relates to the systemic effects of 'going public' in presidential and parliamentary democracies. As has been argued above, presidential 'going public' in the United States is designed primarily to have an impact on members of Congress. They, rather than the public at large, are the real target group of an administration's efforts to mobilize public support for or against a bill. Given the structural independence of the executive branch from the legislature, 'going public' in the

United States fits in nicely with the constitutional parameters of executive leadership under presidential government (although the excessive use of 'going public' by several more recent presidents has been greeted with reasonable suspicion). Thus, it would seem absurd to accuse presidents applying this specific variant of public leadership of violating the underlying logic of democratic decision-making under the conditions of presidential government. Something different holds true for public leadership in parliamentary democracies, though. Here, public leadership – at least in normative terms – finds its natural place in the parliamentary arena, and observers holding serious reservations about 'de-parliamentarized' forms of public leadership cannot simply be written off as old-fashioned or sentimental about the very idea of parliamentary government.

It is important to see that not only public leadership but also public control of it takes place at different levels under presidential government and parliamentary government. While the government in parliamentary democracies is held to be politically responsible by parliament, it is the public at large in presidential systems that holds the president politically to account. It is against this background that some observers felt that the live coverage of presidential press conferences, introduced by President Kennedy in the early 1960s, might become the functional equivalent of the Prime Minister's Question Time in the British House of Commons (Morgan, 1995: 507–8).

In the constitutional practice of British and American government, both procedures have continued, however, to be very different in character. Presidential press conferences have remained a political exercise, the exact rules of the game of which (including their frequency) are to a considerable extent determined by the White House. It also makes a difference if a president or prime minister is faced with questions from journalists representing different aspects of the political spectrum (including close political supporters), or a direct contender for his or her office.[19]

Manifestations of 'Presidentialism' in Britain and Germany

In the earlier sections of this chapter, the focus has been on assessing the various manifestations of executive leadership in the United States, Britain and Germany from a broadly comparative perspective. This section offers a more specific assessment of the often-posed question as to whether – and if so, to what extent – the recent developments to be observed in Britain and Germany may be meaningfully described as 'presidentialization'. The assessments presented here are confined to the premiership and chancellorship of Tony Blair and Gerhard Schröder, respectively.

The debate about 'presidentialization' has suffered from much definitional confusion. This has not only hampered efforts in the field of international and comparative research on manifestations of 'presidentialism', but also undermined attempts at understanding the phenomenon within individual countries. However, rather than stifling research on the subject, the loose boundaries of the fashionable concept have had the opposite effect of triggering an inflation of works on different facets of 'presidentialization'. Since the early 1990s, traces of 'presidentialization' or 'presidentialism' at different levels – ranging from the electoral arena to aspects of administrative management in the core executive – have been detected in most major West European democracies.

The most sophisticated comparative studies to date have focused on electoral 'presidentialization' (Mughan, 2000; King, 2002a), which is remarkable in so far as the 'presidentialization' thesis emerged historically in the field of core executive leadership research. By far the most extensive research on a single country – including the electoral and decision-making arenas – has been carried out by Michael Foley in two major monographs on the 'presidentialization' phenomenon in Britain (Foley, 1993, 2000).[20]

The lowest common denominator of different conceptions of 'presidentialism' would appear to be the idea of a gradual transformation of key features of the political process in parliamentary democracies into political manifestations considered to be typical of the political process under presidential government. As there is no other role model of presidential government among the advanced democracies, 'presidentialization' could be, and has been, referred to alternatively as 'Americanization'.

As mentioned above, 'presidentialization' can be studied at different levels of the political system. In line with the focus of the other parts of this study, the sections to follow do not look specifically at the subject of electoral 'presidentialization'. We may, however, note in passing the findings of two recent case studies on Britain and Germany (Bartle and Crewe, 2002; Brettschneider and Gabriel, 2002), which both conclude that there is minimal empirical evidence in this field to support the 'presidentialization' thesis (according to which party leaders have become the key factor in determining their respective parties' electoral performances).

However, even if the focus is confined to the decision-making arena in the core executive and in the legislative arena, there is an obvious need for definitional clarification. As Anthony Mughan (2000: 8–9) has pointed out, 'presidentialization' can be the product of constitutional change, evolutionary change in the absence of constitutional change, or transient political circumstances. These three dimensions can be further divided into manifestations of 'presidentialization' based on constitutional change, and manifestations thereof relating to the behaviour of political actors (comprising Mughan's second and third categories).

In many recent contributions, these dimensions have been mixed, leading authors to deny the relevance of possible behavioural changes with reference to persisting constitutional differences between parliamentary and presidential democracies. There is no use in doing so; different dimensions of change have to be kept apart analytically, and the absence of change at one level does not say anything about stability or change at another.

It seems obvious that the behaviouralist perspective is the more rewarding one, if only because it is plain to see without much inquiry that there has been very little formal constitutional change in the major West European parliamentary democracies that would justify any talk of 'presidentialization'.[21] The concentration on the somewhat elusive behavioural dimension of politics and leadership in the parliamentary democracies makes it, however, all the more important to agree on a set of criteria of change that may reasonably be considered to indicate 'presidentialization'.

Despite some contestable indicators, the most valuable framework for analysing leadership-related manifestations of 'presidentialization' from a comparative perspective is that by Thomas Poguntke.[22] As to core executive decision-making, Poguntke (2000: 362–3) distinguishes four key indicators at the level of the core executive: a significant increase in personnel and financial resources for setting up an apparatus at the exclusive disposal of the head of government; a growing influence of external political and policy advisers working for the chief executive; a transfer of political and policy initiatives from the individual departments to the office of head of government or even bodies of external advisers; and an increase in the turnover rate of cabinet ministers.

As has been argued above (see page 230), Poguntke's fourth indicator – an increase in the turnover rate of cabinet ministers – may not be, or no longer is, considered a meaningful measure of 'presidentialism'. If it were to apply, the conclusion would have to be that the nature of executive leadership in the parliamentary democracies of Britain and

Germany has become more presidential than presidential government in the United States itself.

If one bases a comparative assessment of the more recent developments in the British and German core executive on Poguntke's remaining three criteria, a number of relevant observations may be made. First, there has been a dramatic increase in the overall number of special advisers in the British Prime Minister's Office and the Cabinet Office. Whereas there were just seven special advisers throughout Whitehall in 1979, by 2001 their number had increased to twenty-nine based in 10 Downing Street alone (Kavanagh and Seldon, 2000: 298–9; *The Times*, 28 April 2001) – a development for which there is no equivalent in the Federal Chancellor's Office. While the overall number of staff in the Chancellor's Office increased from about 450 in the early 1990s to around 500 after the 1998 change of government, Schröder's personal staff in the chancellery has been somewhat smaller than that of his immediate predecessor. Two new groups of staff at the disposal of the chief of the Chancellor's Office, appointed in the immediate aftermath of the 1998 Bundestag election, were scrapped after Schröder's first chief of the Office, Hombach, left the chancellery in mid-1999. A major policy planning directorate in the chancellery, which had also been created at the start of Schröder's first term, was abolished after the 2002 election, further reducing rather than enhancing the policy planning resources in the chancellor's immediate environment. However, even some of the more recent developments in the British core executive have been marked by a certain degree of ambiguity, challenging the popular view of a straightforward concentration of administrative resources at the exclusive disposal of the prime minister. Not only has the Treasury remained a very powerful player in the British core executive (in fact, there has been no recent chancellor enjoying such a strong position in Westminster and Whitehall as does Gordon Brown under Tony Blair). What also merits a mention in this context is the creation of a Deputy Prime Minister's Office in 2002, headed by the Labour heavyweight minister and Blair loyalist John Prescott, which dispersed (at least slightly) rather than further concentrated the structure of administrative resources within the core executive.

There can be no doubt that the overall influence of special advisers, located in the Prime Minister's Office and in the Cabinet Office, has increased significantly in recent years – though there have been signs during Blair's second term that, responding to soaring public criticism, their role has become somewhat more circumscribed. Again, no serious equivalents for these developments may be found in Germany. There has been a notable proliferation during the Schröder years of expert commissions focusing on different areas of public policy, such as BSE, immigration or unemployment.[23] However, the members of these expert bodies can hardly be considered to have served as the chancellor's personal political or policy advisers. Many commission chairs were offered to senior figures from the opposition party (including a former cabinet minister and speaker of the Bundestag, and a former federal president, who were both members of the CDU). Like any chancellor (or in fact any holder of senior political office) before him, Schröder has enjoyed contact with a handful of influential figures from different walks of life.[24] Most of these contacts remained, however, purely informal in character. Those combining membership of Schröder's circle of close confidants with a professional career in politics, such as Frank Walter Steinmeier or Otto Schily, held 'conventional' rather than newly created 'special' posts within the government.

With few exceptions, the development of policy initiatives has remained an area of responsibility of the individual departments in both Britain and Germany. Given the significant amount of resources that have been directed towards establishing a sophisticated system of 'joined-up government' in the British core executive, this finding is certainly more remarkable for Britain than for Germany. In both countries, the independent standing and influence of the chancellor of the Exchequer and the minister of finance in particular (as well as of some other senior cabinet ministers) seems to have increased rather than diminished in the more recent past. And rather than being overly in control regarding policy planning in the individual departments, both Blair and Schröder have been involved in the details of the policy-making process to a remarkably modest degree. Unlike his British counterpart, though, Schröder even seemed to find his natural role as a mediator between individual ministers who disagreed about the policy details of a government bill, such as during the lengthy quarrel between the economics minister and the minister of labour and social security over the reform of the co-determination law early in 2001.

As to the evaluation of possible manifestations of 'presidentialization' in the field of executive–legislative relations, Poguntke (2000: 364) proposes two indicators: an inclination of the majority parliamentary party group(s) to present themselves as independent actors; and the use of 'plebiscitary' techniques of leadership by the head of government, including the use of such devices as intra-party ballots on political issues.

As at the level of the core executive, empirical evidence suggesting the emergence of 'presidentialization' remains rather patchy in the parliamentary arena of both countries. There have been modest signs in

Germany of the majority parliamentary party groups attempting to maintain a certain amount of independence from the government. Early in Schröder's first term, the *Fraktion* chairs of the SPD and the Greens dismissed plans developed in the chancellery demanding their regular participation in cabinet meetings for fear of becoming too absorbed by, and identified with, the government. Also 'coalition rounds' – gatherings of senior figures of the executive and legislative branches, and the governing parties – have decreased rather than increased in importance since the end of the Kohl era. But these developments are not to be confused with any determined attempt of the majority parliamentary party groups to establish themselves as independent players in the political process. As the Red–Green coalition's tenure progressed, the *Fraktion* chairs did, in fact, start attending cabinet meetings, if only on an occasional basis. Even the increase in the number of major bills initiated by the SPD and Green parliamentary parties that marked the legislative process in the 14th Bundestag,[25] may not be accepted at face value to represent a valid indicator of a growing independence of the parliamentary majority from the government. A key motive for letting the governing parties in the Bundestag, rather than the government, initiate a bill is provided by Article 76 (1) of the Basic Law. It stipulates that any government bill (in contrast to bills initiated by the governing parties in the Bundestag) must first be submitted to the Bundesrat, which has up to nine weeks to produce a first response before the legislative process in the Bundestag can commence. Thus, there is a clear incentive in terms of time resources to have urgent bills initiated by the coalition parties in the Bundestag, rather than by the government. The incentives for doing so are even greater if the Bundesrat is controlled by the opposition parties (as has been the case for most of the time since the Red–Green coalition came to power in October 1998), which makes it more likely that government bills are delayed deliberately in the Bundesrat.

The overall picture remains similarly vague for Britain. Most of the first six years of the Blair government were marked by recurrent manifestations of dissatisfaction among Labour MPs, a trend that intensified during Blair's second term. However, this criticism clearly reflected the widespread desire among MPs to develop a closer working relationship between the government and the PLP rather than the ambition among the latter to take on the status of a more independent player – a scenario difficult to imagine in light of the standing orders of the House of Commons, which include hardly any provisions that could be used to establish a more independent role for the parliamentary party groups in relation to the government. Besides, whereas Blair has definitely not enjoyed a close relationship with Labour backbenchers, his government has gone further, in some respects, than most of its recent predecessors in binding the leadership of the PLP closer to the government. This has included a closer integration of the staff and offices of the government's business managers in the parliamentary arena into the Cabinet Office as well as the appointment of the government chief whip in the House of Commons to the cabinet.

As was highlighted earlier, in both Britain and Germany recent changes in the area of executive–legislative relations have been accompanied by changes at the level of party and public leadership. There is now a considerable degree of 'plebiscitary leadership' in both countries, which has developed at the expense of the political parties and traditional forms of party leadership. Both Blair and Schröder have striven constantly to widen their public support base beyond the members and voters of their parties. Intra-party changes have been more dramatic in Britain than in Germany, however, and have affected both the governing and the opposition parties. As one of the final stages of what may be described as arguably the most breathtaking example of party reform in recent British history, in 1997 Blair effectively scrapped the long-standing formal right of the Labour Party's leadership bodies to bind Labour governments to the party line. Also, both the Blair and the Schröder governments have used opinion polls, at least passively. However, there is scant evidence to suggest that the results of opinion polls have been used strategically to pressurize the governing parties in the House of Commons and the Bundestag. At the height of the Iraq crisis in 2003, Blair clearly acted against a majority within his party *and* the British public, and several of the government's more recent reform proposals in domestic policy did not enjoy particularly widespread public support either. In Germany, the recommendations of independent expert commissions, such as the Hartz commission – established in 2002 to produce proposals for wide-ranging labour market reforms –, rather than the results of opinion polls, provided the government with arguments and direction. Surveys of public opinion by *Forschungsgruppe Wahlen* measuring the support for the various items on the government's reform agenda revealed that many measures were in fact even more unpopular with the public at large than among reluctant coalition MPs in the Bundestag. Thus, rather than pursuing a plebiscitary, or populist, approach, both Blair and Schröder gradually developed the qualities of 'conviction leaders', ready to stick to a policy in the teeth of party and public opposition. Neither in Britain nor in Germany have intra-party plebiscites on concrete issues – highlighted specifically by Poguntke (2000: 364) as a potential means of a 'plebiscitary leadership style' – been used as a strategic device of the government and the party leadership to put pressure on the members of the governing parties in parliament to lend their support to possible 'solitary initiatives' of the prime minister or chancellor.

To sum up, there is rather limited evidence of 'presidentialization' – at least in Poguntke's terms – in both countries. This judgment holds true in particular for the various manifestations of executive leadership in Germany. However, even in Britain the significant increase in the number of special advisers and their increased influence within the executive branch stands out as the only piece of hard evidence of 'presidentialization' at the level of the core executive. In the area of executive–legislative relations, empirical evidence supporting popular notions of 'presidentialization' is even more limited for both countries.

Concluding Remarks

Many findings of the individual chapters of this book underline the importance of institutions. Even strong individual personalities do not neutralize the specific parameters of executive leadership to be found in presidential and parliamentary democracies – at least with regard to the countries considered in this study. Any broader comparative assessment will have to take into account, however, that there are major institutional differences even among the family of parliamentary democracies, which have a strong impact on the room for manoeuvre of chief executives. Prima facie, Richard Rose's famous verdict, that 'differences between national political institutions create more variation in the office of prime minister than do differences of personalities and circumstances within a country' (Rose, 1991b: 9) would seem to fall easy prey to any more detailed empirical assessment of executive leadership in different countries. Bold general propositions such as Rose's, which have remained a scarce and precious commodity in comparative leadership research, should, however, be judged in the broader context in which they have been developed. If one distinguishes different categories of countries, in which the chief executive is either a 'strong', 'medium-strong' or 'weak' player within the core executive (King, 1994a: 153; see also Table 1.2 on page 12 of this volume), there would almost certainly be very few, if any, examples of individual leaders having a proven impact that neutralizes the major institutional differences between countries belonging to different categories.[26] Among a group of countries showing more moderate institutional differences, though, it would appear that, to reverse Rose's statement, differences in personalities and circumstances within a country may very well create more variation in the office of prime minister than do differences between national political institutions.[27]

The historical evidence gathered in this book leaves no doubt that leaders, leadership skills and strategies all matter. The problem with leadership effects is that they can rarely be studied in isolation from other factors. Institutions and circumstances do not only have an impact on the range of possibilities that leaders have – that is why the achievements of individual leaders and their administrations must be studied with an eye on their respective opportunity structures –, but leaders' preferences and leadership strategies themselves may also change in response to changing circumstances.

While it is true that leaders 'move in concert with political trends' (Hargrove, 1989: 57), which makes it easier for them to achieve their goals if these correspond closely with those of a majority of other players and the public, it remains an open question whether the greatest performances of leadership in fact relate to periods marked by a close connection between the preferences among the leaders and society. Truly vigorous leadership – or 'transforming leadership' (Burns, 2003) – would rather seem to include the ability of leaders to shape and change public preferences, as well as the course of history. The inherent problem of democratic leadership is, admittedly, even enhanced in cases of transforming leadership, as this requires a particularly generous amount of what Giovanni Sartori (1987: 170) has called 'independent responsibility', in contrast to mere responsiveness of political leaders to public demands.

There can be little doubt that executive leadership research will remain an exceptionally demanding sub-discipline of comparative politics. This is not only because of the wealth of empirical variables that shape the overall performance of executives and executive leaders in contemporary liberal democracies. The executive territory of modern polities has remained an area more governed by secrecy than many other parts of the political system. Moreover, as the art of leadership includes a strong element of creating images that do not necessarily reflect the realities of the decision-making process, many things are not quite as they may seem at first glance. Besides, there are manifold normative aspects (and problems) of executive leadership in contemporary democracies that have not even been touched on in this study.

For all that, the obvious centrality of executive leadership as a key dimension of the democratic process in any liberal democracy does not allow us to turn away from it. As in other areas of political research, the genuinely comparative study of executive leadership would seem to hold the greatest rewards. If this study were to be considered to have shown the particular relevance of exploring executive leadership from a historically *and* internationally comparative perspective, it would have achieved one of its most ambitious aims.

Notes

1 Introduction: Studying Executive Leadership

1. Throughout this book, 'chief executive' is used as a collective term for the heads of government in Western democracies for reasons of style. The use of this term is not meant to dismiss the criticism of those who have argued that, given the strongly collegial character of executive leadership in parliamentary democracies, the heads of government in parliamentary democracies may not be described meaningfully as 'chief executives'. Rather, it is hoped that the comparative sections of this study will be seen as a useful contribution to this debate.

2. Among the latter, see in particular Burns (1977), Paige (1977), Blondel (1987), Rejai and Phillips (1997), Elcock (2001) and Lord (2003).

3. Whereas there have been virtually no such 'coat-tail' effects for a decade and a half after the end of the Reagan presidency, they re-emerged powerfully at the November 2002 congressional elections. The election, which gave control of the Senate to the Republicans and increased their majority in the House, was in fact a referendum on a popular president.

4. For a compilation of key texts in this area, see Lijphart (1992). It seems worth pointing out that the notions of a 'presidential system' (or 'presidential government') have remained fundamentally different among scholars of American politics on the one hand and scholars of comparative politics on the other. In the bulk of the works dealing with American politics, 'presidential government' is used to describe a temporary period of presidential dominance over Congress in one, or several, fields of public policy. While at this level 'congressional government' may be considered as the alternative to 'presidential government', the former represents neither a synonym of nor a functional equivalent to 'parliamentary government' in the parlance of scholars of comparative politics.

5. There are, however, some exceptions to this rule. In Israel, the constitutional reform of 1995 left the key principle of the parliamentary responsibility of the government untouched but introduced a direct election of the prime minister. Similar reforms have been discussed more recently in Italy and the Netherlands.

6. The term 'veto player', as well as the whole concept of thinking about political decision-making processes in terms of players and veto players, has been introduced and popularized by George Tsebelis (1995, 2002).

7. Recent constitutional reform in Britain has changed some of the parameters of the traditional Westminster model, as will be shown in Chapter 6. However, fundamental differences between the British and the German political system persist.

8. 'Interactionist' approaches to studying executive leadership can be, and have been, combined with power-resource-orientated approaches. Most authors working in this field tend to distinguish between 'leadership resources' (personal and positional) and 'environmental pressures' (constraints and opportunities) (Cole, 1994: 467).

9. The latter proposition does not include the assumption that all players have potentially equal resources, which would mean to deny the possible predominance of one actor over another. 'Power is relational between actors, but is also locational. It is dependent on where actors are to be found within the core executive, and whether they are at the centre or the periphery of core executive networks', as Heffernan (2003: 348) has rightly emphasized.

10. The comparative assessment of changing organizational patterns in the core executive to be offered in this study does not extend to the more specific effects of 'Europeanization' on the executive branches in Britain and Germany. For a detailed comparative analysis of these aspects, see Bulmer and Burch (2001) and Knill (2001).

11. In a comparative study on the United States, Britain, and Germany, one might take issue with the proposed focus on 'executive–legislative relations'. The use of this term is, however, neither meant to suggest that there are similar patterns of relationships in the three countries covered here, nor that these relationships may only be discussed in identical terms. Rather, highlighting the fundamental differences in this area forms part of our attempt at understanding the rather different conditions of executive leadership in the three countries. For a more thorough discussion of the terminological and practical problems of studying 'executive–legislative relations', see King (1976).

2 Patterns of Core Executive Leadership: The United States

1. George Wallace in 1968, who gained 13.5 per cent of the total vote, and H. Ross Perot, securing a share of 18.9 per cent in 1992, have been by far the most successful third-party candidates in the post-war period. The most serious third-party attempt in American history was made by Theodore Roosevelt in 1912, who ran on the Progressive 'Bull Moose' party ticket in 1912 and captured 27.4 per cent of the popular vote.

2. This put Bush in company with three nineteenth-century presidents – Rutherford B. Hayes, Benjamin Harrison and John Quincy Adams (alongside Bush, the only other president whose father had earlier occupied this office) – who also lost the popular vote but still won the presidency. Arguably the single most spectacular aspect of the 2000 presidential election related, however, to the prominent role played by the courts in interpreting and shaping the outcome, and the doubts that the result cast on the overall working of the electoral system (Norris, 2001).

3. The rules governing the succession in the office of president have been among the most debated aspects of the constitutional presidency. For more than one-and-a-half centuries questions in this field were answered by historical precedents which gradually added up to a set of specific constitutional conventions regarding the office of the vice-president. Only the Twenty-fifth Amendment (1967), proposed in the aftermath of the assassination of President Kennedy in 1963, stated more precisely the conditions and procedure of presidential succession.

4. As the number of positions to be filled by US presidents has grown steadily, this gap has widened rather than shrunk. When elected president in late 2000, George W. Bush had nearly 3,300 positions subject to his appointment.

5. Until well into the 1970s, Congress routinely granted various extensions of presidential reorganization authority, using the legislative veto as a means of keeping a grip on the decision-making process. As the Supreme Court declared legislative vetoes unconstitutional in 1983, Congress – unwilling to delegate authority without retaining some means of control – decided not to renew the president's grant of authority. Since then, the only way to bring about reorganizations of government has been through laws to be passed by both houses of Congress and signed by the president.

6. Of course, Nixon's record as a (rather unsuccessful) reformer of the cabinet structure is better remembered for his failed attempt in 1971 to create four new 'superdepartments' (Patterson, 2000: 26–7).

7. The departmental structure of the US cabinet has been the subject of various influential scholarly assessments of the core executive. The famous distinction between an 'inner cabinet' and an 'outer cabinet' was introduced by Cronin (1980: 276–86). Wyszomirski (1989: 49–51) has divided cabinet departments into 'national policy departments', 'constituency-oriented departments', and 'issue-area departments'. Drawing on a distinction introduced by Weisberg (1980), Cohen (1988: 122–45) has refined Cronin's typology further by distinguishing between an 'old outer-cabinet' and a 'new outer-cabinet'.

8. Giving a home to 170,000 employees from eight different cabinet departments and twenty-two government agencies, the creation of the Department of Homeland Security marked, in fact, the largest reorganization in government since that of the Defense Department in 1947. However, virtually all the basic ideas of the White House scheme had been at the centre of earlier bipartisan proposals and were not genuinely devised by the Bush administration (Broder, 2002).

9. The average score for Bush's five most recent predecessors within this category was 39.7 per cent, whereas the proportion of insiders among Bush's initial cabinet choices was 33.3 per cent. However, Bush's score was considerably higher than Clinton's. Figures calculated by the author on the basis of data provided by Borrelli (2002a: 47).

10. Since its inception, the EOP has included more than fifty different units, with most of them existing for a rather short time. This has led one observer to describe it as 'a holding company of many offices' (Pfiffner, 1998: 470), rather than a single control structure. Many units were created to symbolise institutionally more specific concerns of individual presidents.

11. Presidents have also tried to make top-level civil servants more responsive to the White House. The single most important innovation in this field was the creation of the Senior Executive Service (SES) by the Civil Service Reform Act 1978, which gave members a greater responsibility and introduced the principle of performance-based pay increases. The president may also appoint up to 10 per cent of the members of SES from outside the career civil service (Michaels, 1997: 16–17).

12. The White House's reluctant agreement in March 2004 to allow Bush's national security adviser, Condoleeza Rice, to be questioned under oath by a bipartisan congressional committee over the administration's security policy in the months before 11 September 2001, set an important precedent in this regard.

13. The responsibilities of one of the most senior members of the White House staff, Bill Moyers, included that of press secretary, speech writer, domestic

policy adviser, conduit to the bureaucracy, foreign policy gadfly and designer of the media campaign in the run-up to the 1964 election (Hess, 1976: 99).

14. Some scholars have judged this period to have lasted even less time. According to Michael Genovese (1990: 34), 'cabinet government' was the dominant idea only for a month or two, before it was replaced by 'staff government', which was eventually overcome by 'staff kingship', marked by a further narrowing of management within the White House.

15. A major self-inflicted burden became Ford's early pardon of Nixon, which met fierce public opposition and severely bruised the new president's public standing (Rozell, 1994).

16. Scholars remain, however, divided about Reagan's true intentions of establishing the cabinet committee system. To Thomas Cronin and Michael Genovese (1998: 290), 'Reagan was simply allergic to public policy discussions save when it came to his deeply held views on slashing taxes, increasing defence spending, or matters such as aid to the Contras and for the Strategic Defense Initiative. Cabinet councils, then, were a way of keeping the cabinet busy and giving them a sense of participation without having to involve the president directly.'

17. Any attempt at explaining Reagan's style by his comparatively advanced age – he was almost 70 when he won the presidency and approaching 78 when he left office – is being challenged by Reagan's historical record of leadership in public office. In fact, many features of Reagan's presidential leadership style had already marked his time as governor of California between 1967 and 1975 (Hamilton and Biggart, 1984: 183–200).

18. The constitutional profile of the vice-president has remained unchanged. However, the creation of a vice-presidential line item in the executive budget in 1969 allowing vice-presidents to hire talented staff, enhanced resources of information, greater physical proximity to the president and a significantly increased number of staff have equipped vice-presidents with the necessary capacities to act as a potentially effective senior adviser to the president. For an in-depth inquiry into the development of the office of vice-president, see Relyea and Arja (2002).

19. A certain moderating effect on the president's occasionally shirt-sleeved approach to addressing some issues in the post-9/11 international arena, largely carried out behind the scenes, has been the most that close observers of the Bush administration have been prepared to acknowledge as Laura Bush's role in her husband's administration. Her visibility, however, if not her involvement in the decision-making process, increased as the re-election campaign got under way.

20. Most observers gauged Rove's overall role within the administration as being considerably more influential than that of most chief advisers under former presidents. Caricatured as 'Bush's brain', Rove was located in Hillary Clinton's West Wing office, as if to symbolize that the president and his top adviser had had a long political marriage (Carney and Dickerson, 2002).

21. Two features – his routine of going to bed early, usually not later than 10 pm, and his passion for daily heavy exercising – came early to be seen as the defining characteristics of Bush's private life. A notable distaste for travelling and studying files, and a fair amount of self-irony, were other key features that figured large among public perceptions of the president as a private person.

22. There have been many more stunning parallels between Ronald Reagan and George W. Bush, including aspects of character and temperament, career paths, policies and leadership styles (Keller, 2003; Aberbach, 2004).
23. The party factor also seems to have been at work at the level of individual presidents' approaches to the idea of 'cabinet government'. The role of the cabinet (or individual members thereof) within the executive decision-making system was strongest during the presidencies of Eisenhower and, with some distance, Reagan and Bush – all of whom had a Republican background. By contrast, Carter stands out as the only Democratic president after 1945 who made a serious attempt to establish some kind of 'cabinet government' during the first years of his incumbency. However, it would seem unreasonable to try to explain these differences with the party affiliation of individual post-war presidents.
24. One author has even suggested the use of the term 'presidency' only when referring to the twentieth century (and beyond), and the term 'president' for all earlier periods of American government (Fabbrini, 1999: 105).
25. The position of any future first lady will primarily be dependent on the president's wish to consider her a key adviser, or not. There is, however, an important legacy from the Clinton years regarding the future of the first lady as a potential adviser to the president. In the case of *American Council for Health Care Reform* v. *Clinton*, the first lady was for the first time formally identified as a political actor in her own right (Borrelli, 2002b: 39–41).

3   Patterns of Core Executive Leadership: Britain

1. There is a list of constitutional disqualifications for membership of the House of Commons, from which a number of further qualifications for the office of prime minister may be deduced (Brazier, 1999: 206–9).
2. The last prime minister to be a member of the Lords was Lord Salisbury, who retired in 1902. The constitutional convention of a prime minister having to be a member of the Commons was firmly established in 1923, when King George V failed to appoint Lord Curzon as prime minister.
3. Even in March 1974, after the general election of the previous month had produced a 'hung parliament', the decision to form a Labour minority government was made by the party leaders with no recourse to the monarch. However, because of important changes at the level of the party system, any future occurrence of a 'hung parliament' is likely to see a significantly increased role for the monarch in the government-building process (Brazier, 1999: 35–44).
4. Wilson has been counted twice.
5. Douglas-Home was a peer when being selected but renounced his peerage before being appointed prime minister, and won a Commons seat in a by-election shortly afterwards.
6. The most recent historical example of a British prime minister lacking any ministerial experience also relates to a Labour leader. In 1924, Ramsay MacDonald became prime minister without having previously held any ministerial office. While Blair's inexperience was very much a result of the Labour Party's unusually extended period in opposition (1979–97), MacDonald's record must be considered against the background of the early-twentieth-century

party system, in which the Conservatives and the Liberals, rather than Labour, were the two big players.

7. In contrast to many other West European parliamentary democracies, not all members of the British government entitled to call themselves 'minister' are members of the cabinet. Junior ministers (ministers of state and parliamentary under-secretaries) hold no cabinet membership. The overall proportion of ministers remaining outside the cabinet has significantly increased since the early years of the twentieth century. As to the cabinet rank of individual departments, the period (starting from around the First World War) during which prime ministers had to decide which departments to exclude from the cabinet ended effectively in the early 1970s. The merger of ministries since the late 1960s has allowed a return to a virtually all-inclusive type of cabinet (Brazier, 1999: 64).

8. There is no equivalent legal provision limiting the number of members of the House of Lords who may be appointed to ministerial office, though since the 1920s it has become highly unusual for a prime minister to appoint more than twenty peers. In this regard, the Blair government marked a major exception to the rule.

9. According to a somewhat more provocative interpretation, Macmillan's aim was to promote effective television performers. One of the new ministers, William Deedes, was given the title of Minister without Portfolio but, as Cockerell (1988: 82) has argued, 'was in reality the Minister of Propaganda, charged with improving the image of the Prime Minister and his government'.

10. The JCC played a crucial role in hammering out a common constitutional reform programme. Originally, it had an additional purpose as a forerunner for any possible Lib–Lab coalition. After the Liberal Democrat leadership change from Paddy Ashdown to Charles Kennedy in August 1999, the frequency of JCC meetings fell to under one a year, signalling both the growing dissatisfaction of the Liberal Democrats with the pace of the government's constitutional reform policy and a less-than-cordial relationship between Blair and Kennedy.

11. Mandelson's first resignation was over charges of inappropriate business dealings, and the second over the charge that he lied to the prime minister over his role in the Hinduja passport affair (*The Times*, 24 January 2001). He was later cleared of the charges by an independent inquiry. Mandelson's departures, especially the first one, were considered a very heavy loss, as he was not only one of Blair's closest and most trusted advisers but also served as an internal 'counterweight' to Gordon Brown at the Treasury.

12. In particular, Blair's second term has seen a series of public anouncements specifying the government's plans to introduce ruthless private-sector tactics within government departments. Early in 2004, it emerged that Sir Andrew Turnbull, the cabinet secretary, according to a Cabinet Office internal consultation document, had decided that all 3,000 senior civil cervants should be put on four-year postings, to be reviewed after three years (*The Times*, 9 January 2004). Such more-or-less politically neutral measures were accompanied by others, that were designed more directly to tighten the government's grip on the civil service. There were, for example, regular meetings of a secret inner council (informally referred to as the 'Whitehall cabinet') consisting of traditionally neutral top Whitehall officials and political staff from Downing

Street 'to ensure Whitehall is fully attuned to Blair's thinking' (*Guardian*, 27 September 1999). For a detailed assessment of recent developments see Wilson and Barker (2003).

13. It may be noted that Blair's decision to appoint a chief of staff in the Prime Minister's Office was not unprecedented. In 1979, Margaret Thatcher appointed a chief of staff, mainly to ensure access for her personal political advisers.

14. See Burch and Holliday (1999). This issue has to be separated from the question as to whether or not there *should* be a Prime Minister's Department in Britain. For a discussion of this latter aspect, see James (1999: 244–5), and Lee *et al.* (1998: 258–60).

15. The two remaining ministers in the Cabinet Office would both report directly to the prime minister (*The Times*, 14 June 2002).

16. The French president, seen by many as the most powerful national chief executive in Western Europe, is not a head of government, but rather a head of state enjoying an unusually powerful position in the executive territory.

17. The bulk of customs and practice regarding the British executive branch is outlined in an official document prepared in the Cabinet Office – originally entitled *Questions of Procedure for Ministers*, but renamed *Minsterial Code* in 1997. For the most detailed assessment of the *Ministerial Code*, see Baker (2000).

18. The effects of this (largely misguided) perception remained by no means confined to aspects of core executive management. It clearly influenced Churchill's approach to cabinet building and, more importantly, also manifested itself in the administration's policies.

19. As Jacqueline Tratt (1996: 193), drawing on an in-depth inquiry into the internal decision-making process over Britain's position towards the European Union, has remarked, '[p]erhaps one of the most remarkable examples of the exploitation of informal power was the fact that there was no discussion of substance in the cabinet on the European issue between 13 July 1960 and 20 April 1961 – a time when British policy with regard to Europe underwent its most material modification'.

20. For an in-depth assessment, see Hennessy (2000: 306, 319–25).

21. See on this the transcription of a 'witness seminar' on the Heath government, edited by Michael David Kandiah (1995).

22. As a closer inspection of the developments leading to the ill-fated decision to postpone the general election to 1979 reveals, Callaghan did not fail to seek the advice of his cabinet. However, a majority (if not a very large one) of the cabinet was in favour of a 1978 election, as were the Labour Party's close allies, the trade unions. The final decision was clearly taken by Callaghan alone, and took even his closest personal staff by surprise (Donoughue, 1987: 160–5).

23. Kavanagh and Seldon (2000: appendix II) considered Geoffrey Howe, William Whitelaw, Norman Tebbit and Nicholas Ridley as the only ministers belonging to Thatcher's changing innermost circle. Among the cabinet committees, the so-called 'Star Chamber', set up to control public expenditure, and the 'E Committee', designed to tackle sensitive issues of monetary policy, were particularly important decision-making bodies of the Thatcher years.

24. The latter included the lengthy debate about Blair's role in the 'Kelly affair' and allegations that the government had knowingly inserted false claims into an intelligence dossier on Iraq's weapons programme, which was investigated

by an independent body, the Hutton commission. Although the Hutton commission cleared the government of any charges, Blair's public standing remained seriously damaged even after the commission published its report (*The Times*, 29 and 30 January 2004).

25. A dimension that shows some kind of correlation between the party affiliation of different prime ministers is the policy expertise of office-holders, and their degree of involvement in different policy areas. Churchill, Eden and Douglas-Home all felt considerably more attracted by, and at home in, foreign policy. However, besides that, all these examples related to the first quarter-century of the post-war period, explaining these preferences with the party affiliation of individual office-holders would seem to be a rather doubtful undertaking.

26. The most prominent contribution of that period was a study by Crossman (1964). The cabinet government thesis has been advocated most forcefully by Jones (1965, 1992).

4 Patterns of Core Executive Leadership: Germany

1. To date, this has always been the case. Overwhelming majorities for a chancellor candidate have, however, remained a rare occurrence throughout the post-war period. In 1998, Gerhard Schröder became the first candidate to secure not only the support of the two prospective governing parties, but also the votes of seven parliamentarians from the opposition benches.

2. The practice of intra-party selection of chancellor candidates in both major parties has been governed by highly integrative leadership circles, including key figures from both the party and the parliamentary party leadership bodies (Schüttemeyer, 1998: 113–247).

3. The position of chairman is the nearest equivalent to the position of party leader in Britain, where the post of chairman is an independent office further down the party leadership hierarchy.

4. Adenauer's case was different, as the CDU national party organization was only established in October 1950, about a year after the first chancellor election in the Bundestag.

5. The figures for previous office-holders, in years, are as follows: Adenauer, 0; Erhard, 14; Kiesinger, 9; Brandt, 8; Schmidt, 17.

6. However, even Kohl's decision to take up the position of opposition leader in the Bundestag after his failed attempt to win the chancellorship in 1976 did not result in establishing a British style of leadership recruitment in Germany. Although Kohl remained opposition leader in the Bundestag until winning the chancellorship in 1982, it was Bavarian Minister-President Franz Josef Strauss rather than Kohl who was chosen as the CDU/CSU's chancellor candidate for the federal election of 1980.

7. Figures for the United States do not include candidates' terms as vice-president.

8. About two thirds of all chancellor candidates since 1949 were serving minister-presidents. Their representation was particulary strong among more recent SPD chancellor candidates. Between 1983 and 1998, the party nominated no less than six incumbent minister-presidents as chancellor candidate (although only Schröder's bid in 1998 proved to be successful). Schröder's challenger in 2002, Edmund Stoiber (CSU), has also held the office of minister-president.

9. The figures given have been calculated for Truman to Bush II, Attlee to Blair, and Adenauer to Schröder, as of March 2004. In the British sample, Wilson has been counted twice.

10. This rule, laid down in Article 67 of the Basic Law, forces a parliamentary majority in revolt to agree immediately on a new candidate to replace the ousted chancellor. If the chancellor has been toppled, all other ministers lose their offices too.

11. This is also suggested by historical experience. Even during the Weimar Republic with its fourteen different chancellors, there were just three occasions on which governments were forced out of office by a formal parliamentary vote of no-confidence (Helms, 2002a: 45, note 24).

12. The positive effects of coalition government in Germany on the smaller parties even apply to the cabinet representation of the CSU, the CDU's smaller Bavarian 'sister party'. In all cabinets that included the CDU/CSU, the CSU received a considerably larger proportion of cabinet seats than did the CDU. This was particularly significant in the years 1949–53, 1983–4 and 1989–91.

13. Calculations by the author on the basis of figures provided by Schindler (1999: 1143–5). The cabinet representation of the Greens in the second Schröder government, formed in October 2002, continued to be notably weak, although the ratio between the proportion of Green coalition seats in the Bundestag (18 per cent) and the proportion of cabinet seats (23 per cent) remained positive.

14. After a lengthy campaign of the Hamburg news magazine *Der Spiegel* against Minister of Defence Franz Josef Strauss (CSU) and the publication of top-secret material on the state of the German armed forces, the conflict culminated when Strauss ordered on 26 October 1962 a search of the magazine's head-quarters and the arrest of two of its leading journalists. As these measures had not been agreed with the FDP-controlled Ministry of Justice, a deep rift between the CSU and the FDP became the most enduring legacy of the '*Spiegel*' affair'. The FDP's willingness to remain in the coalition had to be 'paid for' by the exclusion of Strauss from the cabinet, and Adenauer's promise to stand down by late 1963.

15. Its earliest historical predecessor, the Chancellor's Office (*Reichskanzleramt*), was originally designed to function as a central personal and administrative office for the chancellor. During the Weimar Republic the chancellery was gradually transformed from a personal office of the chancellor into an insti-tution with broad co-ordinating responsibilities. This included in particular the responsibility of preparing and organizing the cabinet's business. While the chancellery's organizational structure remained remarkably stable during the Third Reich, it lost much of its clout in the core executive decision-making process to the Nazi party chancellery (*Parteikanzlei*).

16. For a more detailed assessment of the organizational features of policy planning in the German core executive, see Thunert (2001).

17. In the early post-war period, the level of 'political civil servants' in the chan-cellery was defined slightly more broadly than in the other departments, and included a whole layer of senior civil servants (*höherer Dienst*).

18. By far the most important provisions regarding the constitutional powers of the German chancellor are to be found in Article 65 of the Basic Law. It sets out three basic – and potentially competing – organizational principles of

the core executive: the so-called *chancellor principle* assigns the chancellor the right to make ministerial appointments and organize the executive branch at his discretion; it also acknowledges the chancellor's prerogative to formulate the general guidelines of the government's policies (*Richtlinienkompetenz*). The *departmental principle* stipulates that every minister has the right to make policy decisions alone within his or her own department, and bears full personal responsibility for the activities of his or her department, whereas the *cabinet principle* acknowledges the idea that the cabinet functions as a collective decision-making body. All government bills and decrees require the formal approval of the cabinet. Disputes between individual cabinet ministers are to be decided by the full cabinet, rather than the chancellor.

19. Most early assessments of the Adenauer chancellorship highlighted the chancellor's infamous inclination to make even major decisions without consulting the cabinet or any of its members. More recent research on the core executive decision-making process during the Adenauer years has partly redrawn the older picture. As Jost Küpper (1985: 203–4, 258–60) has shown, Adenauer in fact made a number of 'solitary decisions', though few of them were of crucial political importance.

20. There is no consensus as to whether the 'Kressbronn circle' may properly be described as a 'subsidiary government'. Knorr (1975: 227) characterized the 'Kressbronn circle' as the 'collective holder of the policy guidelines competence', which the Basic Law assigns to the chancellor. By contrast, a recent case study on core executive decision-making under Kiesinger highlights the body's limited authority to produce final and politically binding decisions (Schneider, 1999: 95–6).

21. Cabinet committees are not mentioned in the Basic Law and, unlike their British counterparts, they do not possess the authority to make final decisions on behalf of the cabinet (Böckenförde, 1998: 246). However, as in Britain, (ministerial) cabinet committees are usually chaired by the head of government – that is, the chancellor – or by someone else to be chosen by the chancellor.

22. While the terrorist attacks of 11 September 2001 did not lead to the creation of a genuine war cabinet, as they did both in the United States and in Britain, there were some temporary repercussions of the international crisis on the German core executive. Regular 'crisis meetings' were called, sometimes as often as several times a day, to discuss the next steps. These gatherings included Schröder, Scharping, Schily, Fischer, and the chief of the Chancellor's Office, Steinmeier (*Frankfurter Allgemeine Zeitung*, 18 September 2001).

23. In the Bundestag election of 2002, the Greens' share of the total vote rose to 8.6 per cent (from 6.7 per cent in 1998), whereas the SPD's share dropped from 40.9 per cent to 38.5 per cent.

24. Schröder was the first chancellor to head a cabinet that included the chairman of the leading governing party (other than himself). The ideological gap separating the chancellor from his party chairman and cabinet fellow was at least as wide as between Schmidt and Brandt, and undoubtedly much wider than between Erhard and Adenauer. Perhaps even more important was the deep personal distrust Schröder had for Lafontaine. In 1995, Lafontaine had dismissed Schröder as the party's spokesman for economic affairs in a particularly ruthless way, and the lengthy intra-party race for the position of SPD

chancellor candidate between Schröder and Lafontaine in 1998 did little to heal the wounds.

25. The issue played a key role in the 2002 German electoral campaign. Schröder's categorical dismissal of any German participation gave a boost to the government's support among large quarters of the electorate and helped them towards a victory that only months before election day few would have considered possible (Helms, 2004).

5   Executive Leadership in the Wider Political Process: The United States

1. See, for example, Peterson (1990), Jones (1994), Thurber (1996) and Fabbrini (1999).
2. Other major occasions are the Budget Message (introduced by the Budget and Accounting Act of 1921) and the Economic Report (introduced by the Employment Act of 1946).
3. The lobbying team of George W. Bush, widely considered to be one of the most effective White House lobbying teams in several decades, also used a room of the Republican House majority whip and a Ways and Means Committee conference room – an expansion of the White House operation in Congress, which led to fierce protests from Democratic members who accused the administration of violating the doctrine of separation of powers (Ota, 2002: 3253).
4. In late 1996, Congress widened the choice of vetoes at the disposal of the president by passing a line-item veto permitting the president to veto parts of spending bills. Support for this reform was based on the expectation that the president would use this power to help reduce the public deficit by eliminating wasteful spending proposals – pork barrel proposals in particular. The line-item veto became effective on 1 January 1997; however, it was declared unconstitutional by the Supreme Court in *Clinton et al.* v. *City of New York et al.* on 25 June 1998. The overall legislative effect of the line-item veto remained much less spectacular than many had expected (Spitzer, 1998: 800–1).
5. While displaying an extreme reluctance to use the veto, even George W. Bush issued a whole series of veto threats, which usually helped him to get his way. Major issues included abortion funding, privatization of the federal workforce, sanctions against Cuba, media ownership, and the financial details of Iraq construction aid.
6. The other three are the 'patrician' mode (with the president acting as a national tribune above faction and interest, 1789–1832), the 'partisan' mode (in which the president grants much executive patronage to the party factions and serves himself as the broker for the national coalition, 1832–1900), and the 'pluralist' mode (marked by a complex bargaining process between the president, who serves as the steward of national policy-making, and leaders of very different political interest groups and institutions, 1900–72).
7. Of the past five presidents from Carter to George W. Bush, only George H. W. Bush had former experience in Congress.
8. All figures presented in this paragraph have been calculated by the author on the basis of data provided by *Congressional Quarterly Weekly Report*, various issues.

9. There are other problems with the statistical approach to studying presidential leadership with Congress, which are discussed in Bond and Fleisher (1990: 53–80).

10. In the nineteenth century 'divided government' occurred almost exclusively as a result of mid-term elections. It also clearly marked the exception rather than the rule during the first half of the twentieth century.

11. For a closer inspection of this important relationship, see Scheele (1993).

12. Despite the latter, there is some proof that many of Nixon's closest working relationships with members of Congress were with southern Democrats rather than with fellow Republicans (Ambrose, 1989: 406).

13. This characterization has been borrowed from Collier (1997: 151).

14. While Clinton achieved an outstanding score of 86.4 per cent support in roll calls in 1993 and 1994, his support rate dropped to just over 36 per cent the following year after Congress had been taken over by a huge and aggressively acting Republican majority. Although Clinton recovered temporarily with annual scores above 50 per cent, his overall legislative success rate remained rather modest by historical standards.

15. In scholarly assessments combining a more specific focus on the president with a broader historical perspective, Bush was characterized as 'the most radical president of the past fifty years' (Rockman, 2004: 352), who exacerbated significantly the problems stemming from intense partisanship.

16. Formally, an executive order is a presidential directive that draws on the president's authority to require or authorize some action within the executive branch. But, as recent research has shown, presidents have relied on executive orders to implement significant domestic and foreign policies. Other things being equal, executive orders are most likely to be used when presidents are unpopular, when they run for re-election, when they are faced with major crises that demand swift action, and after the White House switches party control (Mayer, 2001; Howell, 2003).

17. As in several West European countries, such as Germany or Spain, court judgments played a major role in changing the distribution of power within the federal system.

18. The two other units with core publicity responsibility to be mentioned are the Office of Media Affairs, and Speechwriting. In a specific response to the terrorist threat, George W. Bush added a Coalition Information Center and the Office of Global Communications. If the focus is not exclusively on the media but on the public arena more generally, the Office of Public Liaison and the Office of Political Affairs may be considered to represent two other key components of the 'outreach' section of the modern White House. Both had been foreshadowed in the Nixon administration but became fully established under later presidents. The Office of Public Liaison was established formally by President Ford in order 'to lobby the lobbies'. Its key task lies in the field of garnering the support of various constituents for the administration's key legislative proposals. The Office of Political Affairs was established formally during the Reagan presidency, with the aim of maintaining the president's electoral coalition by keeping in contact with party officials and key constituents across the country.

19. In most works, the president appears as a sort of 'issue entrepreneur', influencing the attention of other actors rather than dominating the public

agenda-setting process. See, for example, Edwards and Wood (1999) and Flemming *et al.* (1999).

20. The first opinion polls ever taken by a president date back to the early FDR era (1934). However, it was only during the Kennedy, Johnson and Nixon years that polling became an integral part of presidential leadership strategies. On the history of presidential polling, see Eisinger (2003).

21. This marked a major (and widely criticized) contrast, not only to the Clinton administration's approach to dealing with journalists but also to Bush's own approach during his time as governor of Texas (Cannon, 2002: 2090).

22. The second and third highest increases related to George H. W. Bush (+18 per cent) after the beginning of 'Desert Storm' in January 1991, and Richard Nixon (+16 per cent) after the Vietnam peace agreement in January 1973.

6 Executive Leadership in the Wider Political Process: Britain

1. This is not the only area in which the House of Commons is clearly superior to the second chamber, the House of Lords. The Lords' clout was seriously diminished in 1911, when it lost its right to veto any financial bills. In 1949 its suspensive veto against any other bill passed by the Commons was reduced from two years to one. Statute law has been supported, and refined, by constitutional conventions. There has been a long-standing self-imposed doctrine that no bill having secured approval by the Commons should be generally obstructed by the Lords, especially if the bill had been mentioned explicitly in the government party's electoral manifesto, or in the Queen's Speech.

2. As King himself acknowledges, most of the different modes to be observed in the parliamentary arena are not parliament-specific patterns of interrelationships, but rather more general modes of political conflict.

3. The 'cross-party mode' is traditionally of rather limited importance in Britain, though it has gained slightly in importance following the introduction of departmental select committees in the late 1970s (Norton, 1998: 21–4).

4. Because of the rather specific character of the British constitution, there is in fact no exact British equivalent to the constitutional amendments in most other Western democracies, which usually require specific procedural rules to be followed, and legislative 'super-majorities' to change the constitutional status quo.

5. Parliamentary question time – taking place on four days of the week during a parliamentary session and lasting about an hour – is a particularly well-established instrument of the opposition that puts parliamentary control on a permanent basis, though it has occasionally been derided as being 'more of an entertaining diversion than a method of parliamentary control of or influence over the government' (Brazier, 1999: 221).

6. There have been only two occasions during the whole post-war period (1964 and 1997) on which governments fully 'used up' their maximum five-year term (Charlot, 1997: 59). Both cases related to Conservative governments that saw their extended period in office brought to an end by the ensuing election.

7. For a comparative overview, see Kaltefleiter (1991).
8. The best comprehensive study of the British party system since 1945 is Webb (2000).
9. In contrast to several earlier governments, though, no administration of the post-war period could draw on an absolute majority of votes. Rather than being 'earned majorities', absolute majorities in the post-war House of Commons have been produced artificially by the first-past-the-post electoral system. With 49.7 per cent and 49.4 per cent, respectively, the Eden (1955) and Macmillan (1959) governments came closest to achieving an absolute majority of votes. Reflecting the growing representation of third parties, the electoral bases of majority governments have grown considerably smaller since the mid-1970s. In 2001, Labour gained 62.3 per cent of the seats for a mere 40.7 per cent of the total vote.
10. Interestingly, Dunleavy *et al.* even specifically considered the fact that Thatcher was socialized into party leadership under Callaghan, a possible factor shaping her own approach to dealing with parliament (ibid.).
11. In fact, almost three-quarters of Conservative MPs in the 1987–90 parliament were first elected in 1974 or later (Evans, 1997: 49).
12. In the first ballot for the Tory leadership on 20 November 1990, Thatcher led her challenger Michael Heseltine by 204 votes to 152, but was four short of the number required for an outright victory. She announced her resignation the same day.
13. However, acts of parliament must be distinguished from delegated legislation. The latter can be set aside by the courts. Moreover, since 1998 there has been a special constitutional court in the Judicial Committee of the Privy Council for devolution disputes.
14. All prime ministers have made ample use of their appointment power. However, as for conferring life peerages, Blair early secured a place in history as the most prolific dispenser of political patronage in the House of Lords since the enactment of the Life Peerages Act in 1958. Whereas Thatcher created 216 peers in eleven years – not a small number after all – Blair's count was at 248 after just four years in office (Dunleavy *et al.*, 2003: 11). As a major component of Labour's constitutional reform programme, the number of hereditary peers allowed to sit and vote in the Lords was restricted to ninety-two in 1999.
15. In its 2001 election manifesto, the Labour Party committed itself to a second stage of Lords reform, which would result in the creation of a more democratic and representative second chamber with a considerably greater say in the legislative process. However, in late January 2003, Blair surprised his party and the country by announcing that he wanted the Lords to remain a revising chamber, as an elected upper-house could lead to a serious gridlock in government. On a series of divisions being held on 4 February 2003, the earlier plans for an elected House of Lords were rejected by the Commons after serious pressure from government whips, whereas the Lords gave solid backing for the prime minister's favoured option.
16. Perhaps the most remarkable aspect of this assessment by three authorities in the field is that it was published just one year before the 'Blair/Campbell revolution' in British political communication.
17. See Chapter 3, note 24.

18. Emphasis must be laid on 'regularly-held, wide-ranging' press conferences, though. As Seymour-Ure (2003: 169) has pointed out, several British post-war prime ministers gave press conferences in some way or another, however without breaking the mould.

19. Hardly surprising, Blair's extremely exposed, and dominant, position has not produced only favourable assessments. Among the most striking – in fact, absurd – judgments made by British observers have been comparisons between Tony Blair and Benito Mussolini (Dibol, 1999), and even between Blair and Adolf Hitler (Beloff, 1999).

20. It should be noted, though, that the protagonists of the network paradigm have always devoted rather limited attention to the constitutional dimension of the policy-making process. Apart from that, the prominent 'hollowing out' thesis, according to which the state has largely lost its traditional steering capacity, is considerably older than the constitutional reforms of the Blair government. For a highly critical empirical assessment of the 'hollowing out' thesis, see Holliday (2000b).

21. Interestingly, whereas the Conservative Party's combined terms in office during the post-war period have been considerably longer than Labour's, it was Labour governments rather than Conservative ones, that held office on three of four of these occasions – an advantage that many would consider to have been neutralized by the greater problems Labour governments have tended to encounter in the field of government–party relations.

22. Whereas Churchill was viewed by many observers at the time as a 'dangerous maverick', placing himself and his administration outside the running game of party politics, more recent experience with the Blair government has prompted arguments about the possible rise of a 'partyless democracy' (Mair, 2000).

7 Executive Leadership in the Wider Political Process: Germany

1. Assessments such as these have had an unfortunate influence on the understanding of the parliamentary system among German MPs and the electorate. An empirical survey carried out in the 1990s revealed that 6 per cent of the members of the Bundestag, and no less than 18 per cent of German voters, were convinced that the Federal Republic was a presidential democracy (Patzelt, 1998: 739).

2. Members of the Bundesrat are not elected, but appointed as delegated members of the state governments. The number of seats a state may have in the Bundesrat varies according to demographics, but each state has to cast its vote as a bloc.

3. The Bundesrat may veto any bill that has been passed by the Bundestag, but only some bills, so-called 'approval bills' (*Zustimmungsgesetze*), require the explicit approval of the Bundesrat. Vetoes on other bills may be overruled by the Bundestag. However, if the Bundesrat has vetoed a bill with a two thirds majority, an equivalent majority in the Bundestag is needed to overturn a veto of the Bundesrat.

4. The increase of 'approval bills' reflected important changes in terms of federal and state legislative competencies. The state governments had a vested interest in compensating their gradual loss of legislative decision-making power by securing a greater say on federal bills via the Bundesrat. They could not have brought about this development, however, without the support of the Federal Constitutional Court, which issued a plethora of judgments that established notably generous co-determinative powers of the states (*Länder*) via the Bundesrat (Blair and Cullen, 1999).

5. Unlike the members of the American congressional conference committees, the now thirty-two members of the German mediation committee are not identical with the actors that were previously involved with the matter in question. Rather, they are chosen specifically in equal numbers by the Bundestag and the state governments, many of them serving for the whole legislative period. They are free to agree on any conceivable compromise.

6. The institutional features of the standing committees themselves may be seen as an important component of the opposition's institutional opportunity structure. The committees are staffed by the policy specialists of the government and opposition parties for the full length of the four-year legislative term, and a considerable proportion of committee chairs is held by members of the opposition parties.

7. More precisely, most parliamentary devices, such as the right to initiate legislation, are reserved for a *Fraktion* or a group of members including at least 5 per cent of the total of members of the Bundestag (which is also the required minimum size of a *Fraktion*).

8. Party discipline has been slightly decreasing since the early 1990s – a feature that has been explained by the more heterogeneous composition of the parliamentary parties in post-unification Germany and the greater complexity of issues to be tackled (von Beyme, 2000b: 41–2).

9. Needless to say, the 'intra-party mode' matters as much as in Britain, and in fact any other parliamentary democracy. However, there is no full equivalent in the Bundestag of the highly sophisticated British whip system and the position of chief whip in particular (see Chapter 8).

10. In notable contrast to what is considered the dominant direction of influence between political culture and constitutional/institutional arrangements, the Federal Republic is widely seen as an examplary case of a polity whose political values were shaped by the political institutions established after the Second World War, rather than the other way round. See Lepsius (1990: 63–84).

11. According to Küpper (1985: 238), the true motives for appointing no fewer than four '*Sonderminister*' (ministers without portfolio), in 1953 were related to coalition arithmetics.

12. The largest losses from one federal election to another occurred in 1998, when the party lost 5.3 percentage points since 1994.

13. Calculations by the author based on information provided by *Stenographische Protokolle über die Verhandlungen des Deutschen Bundestages*, various issues.

14. As Saalfeld (1999: 157) has argued, 'the homogeneity of the FDP's parliamentary organisation and its dominance *vis-à-vis* the extra-parliamentary organisation' had the additional effect of facilitating the management of the Christian–Liberal coalition throughout its existence.

15. The exact figures for Schröder's predecessors were as follows: Adenauer, 22 per cent; Erhard, 16 per cent; Kiesinger, 22 per cent; Brandt, 32 per cent; Schmidt, 25 per cent; and Kohl, 24 per cent. All figures calculated by the author based on information provided by *Stenographische Protokolle über die Verhandlungen des Deutschen Bundestages*, various issues.

16. For much of the 1960s, 1970s and 1980s changes of government had to be brought about effectively by the strategic attempts of the opposition at winning over one of the governing parties. This made a certain amount of rapprochement an indispensable element of any realistic opposition strategy. By contrast, the two-bloc structure of the post-unification German party system – a more balanced distribution of electoral support for the parties being to the right (CDU/CSU, FDP) and left of centre (SPD, Greens, PDS) – urges the opposition to concentrate their energy on mobilizing support among the electorate to vote the whole coalition out of office, even though there might be only moderate differences in the policy profiles of the competing parties.

17. Even though this division resulted in a rather narrow victory for the government (336 to 325 votes), both CDU/CSU and FDP had declared their respective support for the government's bill well in advance.

18. The total number of seats held by the highly isolated PDS fell from thirty-six to only two, leaving a 48.9 per cent share of the total of seats for the 'bourgeois' opposition parties CDU/CSU and FDP.

19. More precisely, the Court decided that the law had emerged from a procedure that violated the Basic Law.

20. In this sense, the Court's notable opposition to the Social–Liberal reform policies of the 1970s (Biehler, 1990) should be seen in relation to the government's extremely narrow majority in the Bundestag and the virtually permanent dominance of the conservative opposition in the Bundesrat, both reflecting the rather weak electoral mandate for sweeping Social–Liberal reform.

21. For a more detailed treatment of the aspects touched upon, and further references, see Helms (2000c).

22. The strong normative focus on equality in living conditions, and the exceptionally close co-ordination among the states, are other key features of the German model of federalism, which are of lesser importance in our context. The best English-language assessment of the German federal system from an internationally comparative perspective is Watts (1999); a finely balanced account of the historical developments is given by Benz (1999).

23. In January 2003 there were no fewer than eight different coalition patterns at the level of state government. Of the sixteen state governments, only two had exactly the same party composition as the federal government (SPD–Green), and just three others were pure CDU/CSU–FDP coalitions corresponding neatly to the composition of the 'bourgeois' opposition 'camp' in the Bundestag.

24. For a more detailed assessment of the constitutional and political factors shaping the office of president and the performance of its holders, see Helms (1998) and Rudzio (2000).

25. The respective scores of Germany's seven post-war chancellors, as measured by the *Institut für Demoskopie Allensbach*, were as follows: Adenauer, 73 per cent;

Brandt, 52 per cent; Kohl, 50 per cent; Schmidt, 43 per cent; Erhard, 24 per cent; Schröder, 8 per cent; and Kiesinger (3 per cent). See *Frankfurter Allgemeine Zeitung*, 21 August 2002.

26. Compared with the developments in the United States and (to a lesser extent) in Britain, the German media system was rather slow in adopting innovations such as cable TV and the Internet that have come to characterize the modern era of media development (Holtz-Bacha and Kaid, 1995: 12–14; Wilke, 1999).

27. In particular, Erhard's *Kanzlertees*, originally designed as a successor to Adenauer's version of informal meetings, proved a disaster, as Erhard seemed completely unable to structure the conversation in any way that might benefit the government (Hentschel, 1996: 476).

28. As Zohlnhöfer (2003: 416) has rightly observed, however, the government seemed to be more interested in a societal, rather than a cross-party, compromise. Both Rita Süssmuth and Richard von Weizsäcker, who were offered chairs of government commissions, were clearly not members of the current CDU party elite, and performed largely symbolic functions.

29. For an assessment of this interpretation, see Chapter 8.

30. Which makes it necessary to ignore the special status of the *Fraktionen* under German law, which considers the latter to be fully independent of their respective party organizations.

8 Conclusion: Making Sense of Complexity

1. There has been a growing consensus among observers that the formal scrutiny and appointment process of presidential nominations in the Senate has turned into a largely dysfunctional procedure. See on this the special issue of the *Brookings Review*, vol. 19 (2001), no. 2, ed. by G. Calvin Mackenzie.

2. There have been signs, however, that decades of informal constitutional practice might eventually have an effect on what is considered to be desirable in constitutional terms. More recently, even constitutional lawyers have suggested the formal acknowledgement of the parties' prominent position in the government-building process in the Basic Law, rather than to condemn it as a manifestation of 'illegitimate' party power (Zuck, 1998).

3. If a vacancy occurs, the seat is given to the person ranked next on the state party list used in the previous federal election.

4. The figures presented here have been calculated for the period 1945/9–2000. For reasons of style, *Bundesminister* (Germany), cabinet ministers (Britain), and cabinet secretaries (United States) are all referred to here as 'cabinet ministers'.

5. The only member of the British cabinet – not having been counted here as a 'normal' cabinet minister – who held a single position for more than ten years was Prime Minister Margaret Thatcher.

6. Unless other references are given, all figures presented in this paragraph are drawn from Helms (2002c).

7. See the figures presented by Riddlesberger and King (1986), Wyszomirski (1989) and Katz (1996).

8. See the respective assessments by King (1994b) and Kempf and Merz (2001).

9. This seems to reflect a more general historical trend. The average tenures of US cabinet secretaries have risen continuously since the Nixon presidency

(*National Journal*, 22 May 1999: 1387–8). The average term of Clinton's cabinet secretaries was only slightly less than four years.

10. However, even in the United States the composition of the cabinet is politically very important. Whereas many of the president's closest confidant(e)s are more likely to be placed in the White House rather than the cabinet, in terms of political representation the composition of the cabinet has long been seen as being far more important than the make-up of the president's team in the White House.

11. According to Lee *et al.* (1998: 31), the lowest number of staff in the Prime Minister's Office (excluding part-time and what is called 'support staff') since the late 1970s has been sixty-four, whereas Anthony King (1993: 435), writing in the early 1990s, estimated the overall number of staff in the Prime Minister's Office to be twenty-four to thirty (and 900 in the White House Office).

12. Figures according to Lee *et al.* (1998: 31), Müller-Rommel (1997: 9), and Relyea (1997: 27–8).

13. All figures presented in this paragraph have been calculated by the author on the basis of data drawn from Butler and Butler (1994) and Schindler (1999) as well as from various issues of *Dod's Parliamentary Companion* and *Keesing's Contemporary Archive*. Figures for Britain include whips, but not parliamentary private secretaries; for both countries, prime ministers and chancellors, if members of parliament, have been included.

14. For an empirical assessment of this aspect, see Borchert and Zeiss (2004).

15. Political careers at federal and state level have turned out to be rather independent pathways. As far as there are switches from one level to another, the typical direction runs from state to federal level, rather than the other way round.

16. It may be noted, however, that more recent research, focusing on the absolute levels of success on foreign policy votes in the House and Senate, has found little empirical evidence in support of the so-called 'two presidencies' thesis (Fleisher *et al.*, 2000).

17. In parts of the recent literature on constitutional courts, 'judicial review' has been strictly separated from 'constitutional review' (Stone Sweet, 2000: 32–3). According to this line of argument, constitutional review exists where constitutional courts have been assigned the exclusive and final constitutional jurisdiction (such as in Germany); by contrast, judicial review (such as in the United States) implies that any judge of any court has the power to declare a law unconstitutional. There is, however, still a broad consensus in the literature to consider judicial review as the overarching concept, which may separated empirically into centralized systems of judicial review (that is, constitutional review) and decentralized judicial review (Lijphart, 1999: 225). The term 'judicial review' is here being used in this more general sense.

18. Another British/American comparison focusing on the 1980s and 1990s has highlighted both converging and diverging trends in the area of campaign communication in both countries. According to the findings of Blumler and Gurevitch (2001), the American system has moved away from the British pattern with regard to the variation of media competition and the public service versus the commercial organization of the media.

19. Developments since 2002 have made it possible to compare not only presidential press conferences and Prime Minister's Question Time, but also the latter and prime ministerial press conferences. Whereas important similarities may be identified – such as the dominance of mostly hostile questions and questioners – the roles of the opposition and the existence of the speaker make Question Time different. As Colin Seymour-Ure (2003: 199–200) has noted, '[t]he performance of the opposition leader is under comparable scrutiny to that of the prime minister, while the Speaker's role as moderator has no press conference counterpart'.

20. Even though Foley's analysis is not limited to the electoral arena, and is full of astute observations regarding the transformation of political leadership in Britain, it remains unclear how exactly his concept of a 'British presidency' is related to any form of a 'presidentialization' thesis. On the one hand, most of Foley's work is concerned with highlighting different dimensions of political leadership on which Britain has moved in the direction of presidential leadership as observed in the United States. On the other hand, Foley concludes that 'the case advanced in this study for a presidential dimension in British politics is not the same as, and is not dependent upon, the case for the "presidentialization" of British government' (Foley, 2000: 352).

21. Admittedly, this assertion is more straightforward for Germany and the countries of continental Europe than for Britain with its different notions of a constitution.

22. Several other indicators of 'presidentialization' that have been put forward recently, such as the growing detachment of the government from the judiciary (Norton, 2003: 52), may seem reasonable for consideration in a study on Britain, but not for a comparative assessment that includes Germany.

23. The existence of such commissions has been considered as a key indicator of 'presidentialism' (Lütjen and Walter, 2000). However, as a historical assessment of the features of the German chancellorship suggests, there is little new about such expert commissions (Murswieck, 2003: 121–6).

24. For a tentative sketch of Schröder's network of informal advisers and supporters, see *Focus*, 6 May 2002: 64–5.

25. From the beginning of the 10th till the end of the 13th Bundestag (1983–98), the proportion of bills passed that were initiated by the governing parties in the Bundestag was 17 per cent. In the 14th Bundestag (1998–2002) this figure rose to 23.6 per cent. These calculations are by the author on the basis of data provided by the administration of the German Bundestag.

26. The scale of manifest differences is one thing, but the degree of institutionalization of rules circumscribing a leader's position is quite another. Other things being equal, the more limited the degree of institutionalization in a given area, the more likely are personalities and individual leadership styles to leave their mark on the basic structures in this field, and to become key factors determining an administration's overall performance. As to the three countries covered in this study, it would seem reasonable to argue that the overall degree of institutionalization of the core executive is higher in Britain and Germany than in the United States. See also Rockman (1996: 336), and Ragsdayle and Theis (1997).

27. Adenauer, for much of his incumbency, was not only significantly more powerful than most of his successors in Bonn and Berlin, but also at least as powerful a chief executive as Douglas-Home or even Eden. Interesting cases may also be found in the more recent past. Few observers, for example, would judge John Major to have been a considerably more powerful leader than Helmut Kohl during the early 1990s.

References

Aberbach, Joel D. (2004) 'The State of the Contemporary American Presidency: Or, Is Bush II Actually Ronald Reagan's Heir?', in Colin Campbell and Bert A. Rockman (eds), *The George W. Bush Presidency*, Washington, DC: Congressional Quarterly Press, pp. 46–72.

Abromeit, Heidrun (1994) 'The Chancellor and Organised Interests', in Stephen Padgett (ed.), *Adenauer to Kohl*, London: Hurst, pp. 157–77.

Alderman, R. K. (1992) 'Harold Macmillan's "Night of the Long Knives"', *Contemporary Record*, vol. 6, pp. 243–65.

Allemann, Fritz René (1956) *Bonn ist nicht Weimar*, Cologne: Kiepenheuer & Witsch.

Allen, Mike (2004) 'Cheney Is a Silent Partner No Longer', *Washington Post*, 26 January, p. A1.

Allred, Victoria (2001) 'Versatility with the Veto', *Congressional Quarterly Weekly Report*, vol. 59, pp. 175–7.

Ambrose, Stephen E. (1989) *Nixon: The Triumph of a Politician, 1962–1972*, New York: Simon & Schuster.

Andeweg, Rudy (1997) 'Collegiality and Collectivity: Cabinets, Cabinet Committees and Cabinet Ministers', in Patrick Weller, Herman Bakwis and R. A. W. Rhodes (eds), *The Hollow Crown*, London: Macmillan, pp. 58–83.

Andeweg, Rudy (2003) 'On Studying Governments', in Jack Hayward and Anand Menon (eds), *Governing Europe*, Oxford: Oxford University Press, pp. 39–60.

Ansell, Christopher K. and Fish, Steven M. (1999) 'The Art of Being Indispensable: Noncharismatic Personalism in Contemporary Political Parties', *Comparative Political Studies*, vol. 32, pp. 282–312.

Baggott, Rob and McGregor-Riley, Victoria (1999) 'Renewed Consultation or Continued Exclusion? Organised Interests and the Major Governments', in Peter Dorey (ed.), *The Major Premiership*, London: Macmillan, pp. 68–86.

Bailey, Christopher J. (1998) 'The Changing Federal System', in Gillian Peele, Christopher J. Bailey, Bruce Cain and B. Guy Peters (eds), *Developments in American Politics 3*, London: Macmillan, pp. 114–33.

Bailey, Michael E. (2002) 'The Heroic Presidency in the Era of Divided Government', *Perspectives on Political Science*, vol. 31, no. 1, pp. 35–45.

Baker, Amy (2000) *Prime Ministers and the Rule Book*, London: Politico's.

Ball, Stuart (1996) 'The Conservative Party and the Heath Government', in Stuart Ball and Anthony Seldon (eds), *The Heath Government 1970–1974*, London: Longman, pp. 315–50.

Ballinger, Chris and Seldon, Anthony (2004) 'Prime Ministers and Cabinet', in Anthony Seldon and Kevin Hickson (eds), *New Labour, Old Labour*, London: Routledge, pp. 173–89.

Barber, James (1991) *The Prime Minister since 1945*, Oxford: Basil Blackwell.

Baring, Arnulf (1969a) *Außenpolitik in Adenauers Kanzlerdemokratie*, Munich: Oldenbourg.

Baring, Arnulf (1969b) 'Über deutsche Kanzler', *Der Monat*, vol. 21, no. 252, pp. 12–22.

Barshay, Jill (2002) 'The Duel of Bush and Daschle', *Congressional Quarterly Weekly Report*, vol. 60, pp. 216–19.

Bartle, John and Crewe, Ivor (2002) 'The Impact of Party Leaders in Britain', in Anthony King (ed.), *Leaders' Personalities and the Outcomes of Democratic Elections*, Oxford: Oxford University Press, pp. 71–95.

Baston, Lewis and Seldon, Anthony (1996) 'Number 10 under Edward Heath', in Stuart Ball and Anthony Seldon (eds), *The Heath Government 1970–1974*, London: Longman, pp. 47–74.

Baxter, Alison, Franklin, Mark and Jordan, Margaret (1986) 'Who Were the Rebels? Dissent in the House of Commons 1970–1974', *Legislative Studies Quarterly*, vol. 11, pp. 143–59.

Beck, Nathaniel (1982) 'Presidential Influence of the Federal Reserve in the 1970s', *American Journal of Political Science*, vol. 26, pp. 415–45.

Beinart (2002) 'Personal Best', *The New Republic*, 9 and 16 September, p. 6.

Beloff, Max (1999) 'Third Way, or Reich?', *The Times*, 9 February, p. 16.

Bennett, Anthony, J. (1996) *The American President's Cabinet. From Kennedy to Bush*, London: Macmillan.

Benz, Arthur (1999) 'From Unitary to Asymmetric Federalism in Germany', *Publius*, vol. 29, no. 4, pp. 55–78.

Benze, G., James Jr (1987) *Presidential Power and Management Techniques*, New York: Greenwood Press.

Berke, Richard L. (2001) 'This Time, Dissent Stops At the White House Door', *New York Times*, 16 December, 'Week in Review', p. 3.

Berman, Larry (1988) 'Lyndon B. Johnson: Paths Chosen and Opportunities Lost', in Fred I. Greenstein (ed.), *Leadership in the Modern Presidency*, Cambridge, Mass.: Harvard University Press, pp. 134–63.

Berry, Phyllis (1989) 'The Organization and Influence of the Chancellery during the Schmidt and Kohl Chancellorships', *Governance*, vol. 2, pp. 339–55.

Beyme, Klaus von (1997) *Der Gesetzgeber*, Opladen: Westdeutscher Verlag.

Beyme, Klaus von (2000a) *Parliamentary Democracy*, London: Macmillan.

Beyme, Klaus von (2000b) 'The Bundestag – Still the Centre of Decision-Making?', in Ludger Helms (ed.), *Institutions and Institutional Change in the Federal Republic of Germany*, London: Macmillan, pp. 32–47.

Biehler, Gerhard (1990) *Sozialliberale Reformgesetzgebung und Bundesverfassungsgericht*, Baden-Baden: Nomos.

Biskupic, Joan and Witt, Elder (1997) *The Supreme Court and the Powers of the American Government*, Washington, DC: Congressional Quarterly Press.

Blair, Philip and Cullen, Peter (1999) 'Federalism, Legalism and Political Reality: The Record of the Federal Constitutional Court', in Charlie Jeffery (ed.), *Recasting German Federalism*, London: Pinter, pp. 119–54.

Blake, Robert (1985) *The Conservative Party from Peel to Thatcher*, London: Methuen.

Bledsoe, W. Craig and Rigby, Leslie (1996) 'The Cabinet and Executive Departments', in Michael Nelson (ed.), *Guide to the Presidency*, 2nd edn, Washington, DC: Congressional Quarterly Press, pp. 1145–212.

Blondel, Jean (1987) *Political Leadership*, London: Sage.

Blondel, Jean (1992) 'Executives', in Mary Hawkesworth and Maurice Kogan (eds), *Encyclopedia of Government and Politics, Vol. 1*, London: Routledge, pp. 267–78.

Blumler, Jay G. and Gurevitch, Michael (2001) '"Americanization" Reconsidered: U.K.–U.S. Campaign Communication Comparisons Across Time', in W. Lance

Bennett and Robert M. Entman (eds), *Mediated Politics*, Cambridge: Cambridge University Press, pp. 380–403.

Blumler, Jay G., Kavanagh, Dennis and Nossiter, T. J. (1996) 'Modern Communications versus Traditional Politics in Britain: Unstable Marriage of Convenience', in David L. Swanson and Paolo Mancini (eds), *Politics, Media, and Modern Democracy*, Westport, Conn.: Praeger, pp. 49–72.

Böckenförde, Ernst-Wolfgang (1998) *Die Organisationsgewalt im Bereich der Regierung*, 2nd edn, Berlin: Duncker & Humblot.

Bogdanor, Vernon (1994) 'The Selection of the Party Leader', in Anthony Seldon and Stuart Ball (eds), *Conservative Century*, Oxford: Oxford University Press, pp. 69–96.

Bogdanor, Vernon (2003) 'Asymmetric Devolution: Toward a Quasi-Federal Constitution?', in Patrick Dunleavy, Andrew Gamble, Richard Heffernan and Gillian Peele (eds), *Developments in British Politics, 7*, Basingstoke: Palgrave, pp. 222–41.

Bonafede, Dom (1997) 'The Men around Reagan', in Eric J. Schmertz, Natalie Datlof and Alexej Ugrinsky (eds), *Ronald Reagan's America. Vol. II*, Westport, Conn.: Greenwood Press, pp. 497–511.

Bond, Jon R. and Fleisher, Richard (1990) *The President in the Legislative Arena*, Chicago: University of Chicago Press.

Borchert, Jens and Zeiss, Jürgen (eds), (2004) *The Political Class in Advanced Democracies*, Oxford: Oxford University Press.

Borelli, MaryAnne (2002a) *The President's Cabinet: Gender, Power, and Representation*, Boulder, Col.: Lynne Rienner.

Borelli, MaryAnne (2002b) 'The First Lady as Formal Advisor to the President', *Women & Politics*, vol. 24, no. 1, pp. 25–45.

Borthwick, R. L. (1995) 'Prime Minister and Parliament', in Donald Shell and Richard Hodder-Williams (eds), *Churchill to Major*, London: Hurst, pp. 71–103.

Brace, Paul and Hinckley, Barbara (1992) *Follow the Leader: Opinion Polls and Modern Presidents*, New York: Basic Books.

Brady, Christopher (1997) 'The Cabinet System and Management of the Suez Crisis', *Contemporary British History*, vol. 11, no. 2, pp. 65–93.

Brady, Christopher (1999) 'Collective Responsibility: A Managerial Tool?', *Parliamentary Affairs*, vol. 52, pp. 214–29.

Braunthal, Gerard (1998) 'Opposition in the Kohl Era: The SPD and the Left', in Clay Clemens and William E. Paterson (eds), *The Kohl Chancellorship*, London: Frank Cass, pp. 143–62.

Brauswetter, Hartmut (1976) *Kanzlerprinzip, Ressortprinzip und Kabinettsprinzip in der ersten Regierung Brandt 1969–1972*, Bonn: Eichholz.

Brazier, Rodney (1999) *Constitutional Practice*, 3rd edn, Oxford: Oxford University Press.

Brettschneider, Frank and Gabriel, Oscar W. (2002) 'The Nonpersonalisation of Voting Behavior in Germany', in Anthony King (ed.), *Leaders' Personalities and the Outcomes of Democratic Elections*, Oxford: Oxford University Press, pp. 127–57.

Broder, David S. (2002) 'The Good and the Silly', *Washington Post*, 12 June, p. A31.

Broughton, David (1999) 'The Limitations of Likeability: The Major Premiership and Public Opinion', in Peter Dorey (ed.), *The Major Premiership*, London: Macmillan, pp. 199–217.

Bruce-Gardyne, Jock and Lawson, Nigel (1976) *The Power Game: An Examination of Decision-making in Government*, London: Macmillan.

Bruni, Frank (2002) *Ambling into History: The Unlikely Odyssey of George W. Bush*, New York: HarperCollins.

Buchheim, Christoph (2001) 'Die Unabhängigkeit der Bundesbank: Folge eines amerikanischen Oktrois?', *Vierteljahreshefte für Zeitgeschichte*, vol. 49, pp. 1–30.

Buchheim, Hans (1976) 'Die Richtlinienkompetenz unter der Kanzlerschaft Konrad Adenauers', in Dieter Blumenwitz, Klaus Gotto, Hans Maier, Konrad Repgen and Hans-Peter Schwarz (eds), *Konrad Adenauer und seine Zeit. Bd. 2: Beiträge aus der Wissenschaft*, Stuttgart: Deutsche Verlags-Anstalt, pp. 339–51.

Bulmer, Simon and Burch, Martin (2001) 'The "Europeanisation" of Central Government: The UK and Germany in Historical Institutionalist Perspective', in Gerald Schneider and Mark Aspinwall (eds), *The Rules of Integration*, Manchester: Manchester University Press, pp. 73–96.

Burch, Martin and Holliday, Ian (1996) *The British Cabinet System*, London: Prentice-Hall and Harvester Wheatsheaf.

Burch, Martin and Holliday, Ian (1999) 'The Prime Minister's and Cabinet Offices: An Executive Office in All But Name', *Parliamentary Affairs*, vol. 52, pp. 32–45.

Burke, John P. (2000) *The Institutional Presidency*, 2nd edn, Baltimore, Md: Johns Hopkins University Press.

Burns, James MacGregor (1977) *Leadership*, New York: Harper & Row.

Burns, James MacGregor (2003) *Transforming Leadership: The Pursuit of Happiness*, New York: Atlantic Monthly Press.

Burns, James MacGregor, Peltason, J. W., Cronin, Thomas E. and Magleby, David B. (1995) *Government by the People*, 16th edn, Englewood Cliffs, NJ: Prentice-Hall.

Butler, David and Butler, Gareth (1994) *British Political Facts, 1900–1994*, London: Macmillan.

Cameron, Charles M. (2000) *Presidents and the Politics of Negative Power*, Cambridge: Cambridge University Press.

Campbell, Colin (1996) 'Management in a Sandbox: Why the Clinton White House Failed to Cope with Gridlock', in Colin Campbell and Bert A. Rockman (eds), *The Clinton Presidency*, Chatham, NJ: Chatham House, pp. 51–87.

Campbell, Colin (1998) *The U.S. Presidency in Crisis: A Comparative Perspective*, New York: Oxford University Press.

Campbell, Colin and Rockman, Bert A. (eds) (1996) *The Clinton Presidency: First Appraisals*, Chatham, NJ: Chatham House.

Campbell, Colin and Rockman, Bert A. (2001) 'Third Way Leadership, Old Way Government: Blair, Clinton and the Power to Govern', *British Journal of Politics and International Relations*, vol. 3, pp. 36–48.

Cannon, Carl M. (2002) 'Goodbye to Goodwill', *National Journal*, vol. 34, pp. 2089–90.

Carey, John M. and Shugart, Matthew Sobert (eds) (1998) *Executive Decree Authority*, Cambridge: Cambridge University Press.

Carney, James and Dickerson, John F. (2002) 'W. and the "Boy Genius"', *Time*, 18 November, pp. 40–5.

Caro, Michael K. (1965) *Der Volkskanzler Ludwig Erhard*, Cologne: Kiepenheuer & Witsch.

Charlot, Monica (1997) 'Grande-Bretagne: une alternance annoncée', *Revue Politique et Parlementaire*, vol. 99, no. 988, pp. 59–67.

Clemens, Clay (1994) 'The Chancellor as Manager. Helmut Kohl, the CDU and Governance in Germany', *West European Politics*, vol. 17, no. 4, pp. 28–51.

Clemens, Clay (1998) 'Party Management as a Leadership Resource: Kohl and the CDU/CSU', in Clay Clemens and William E. Paterson (eds), *The Kohl Chancellorship*, London: Frank Cass, pp. 91–119.

Cockerell, Michael (1988) *Live from Number Ten*, London: Faber & Faber.

Cohen, Jeffrey E. (1988) *The Politics of the U.S. Cabinet*, Pittsburgh, Penn.: University of Pittsburgh Press.

Cohen, Richard E., Victor, Kirk and Bauman, David (2004) 'The State of Congress', *National Journal*, vol. 36, pp. 82–105.

Cole, Alistair (1994) 'Studying Political Leadership: The Case of François Mitterrand', *Political Studies*, vol. 42, pp. 453–68.

Collier, Ken (1994) 'Eisenhower and Congress: The Autopilot Presidency', *Presidential Studies Quarterly*, vol. 24, pp. 309–25.

Collier, Kenneth E. (1997) *Between the Branches: The White House Office of Legislative Affairs*, Pittsburgh, Penn.: University of Pittsburgh Press.

Colomer, Josep M. (1996) 'Introduction', in Colomer, Josep M. (ed.), *Political Institutions in Europe*, London: Routledge, pp. 1–17.

Cook, Corey (2002) 'The Permanence of the "Permanent Campaign": George W. Bush's Public Presidency', *Presidential Studies Quarterly*, vol. 32, pp. 753–64.

Cook, Timothy E. (1998) *Governing with the News*, Chicago: University of Chicago Press.

Corwin, Edward (1957) *The President: Office and Powers 1787–1957*, 4th edn, New York: New York University Press.

Cowley, Philip (1999) 'Chaos or Cohesion? Major and the Conservative Parliamentary Party', in Peter Dorey (ed.), *The Major Premiership*, London: Macmillan, pp. 1–25.

Cowley, Philip (2001) 'The Commons: Mr Blair's Lapdog?', *Parliamentary Affairs*, vol. 54, pp. 815–28.

Cronin, Thomas E. (1980) *The State of the Presidency*, 2nd edn, Boston, Mass.: Little, Brown.

Cronin, Thomas E. and Genovese, Michael A. (1998) *The Paradoxes of the American Presidency*, New York: Oxford University Press.

Crossman, Richard (1964) 'Introduction' to Walter Bagehot, *The English Constitution*, London: C. A. Watts & Co, pp. 1–57.

Crouch, Colin (2003) 'Comparing Economic Interest Organizations', in Jack Hayward and Anand Menon (eds), *Governing Europe*, Oxford: Oxford University Press, pp. 192–207.

Dahl, Robert (1999) 'The Shifting Boundaries of Democratic Governments', *Social Research*, vol. 66, pp. 915–31.

Davidson, Roger H. (1997) 'Presidential–Congressional Relations', in James Pfiffner and Roger H. Davidson (eds), *Understanding the Presidency*, New York: Longman, pp. 336–48.

Davidson, Roger H. and Campbell, Colton C. (2000) 'The Senate and the Executive', in Burdett A. Loomis (ed.), *Esteemed Colleagues: Civility and Deliberation in the U.S. Senate*, Washington, DC: Brookings Institution, pp. 194–219.

Davis, Glyn, Weller, Patrick, Craswell, Emma and Eggins, Susan (1999) 'What Drives Machinery of Government Change?', *Public Administration*, vol. 77, pp. 7–50.

de Winter, Lieven (1995) 'The Role of Parliament in Government Formation and Resignation' in Herbert Döring (ed.), *Parliaments and Majority Rule in Western Europe*, Frankfurt-am-Main: Campus and St. Martin's Press, pp. 115–51.

Dedring, Klaus-Heinrich (1989) *Adenauer – Erhard – Kiesinger*, Pfaffenweiler: Centaurus.

Deen, Rebecca E. and Arnold, Laura W. (2002) 'Veto Threats as a Policy Tool: When to Threaten?', *Presidential Studies Quarterly*, vol. 32, pp. 30–45.

Dell, Edmund (1991) *A Hard Pounding: Politics and Economic Crisis 1974–78*, Oxford: Oxford University Press.

Derlien, Hans-Ulrich (1997) 'Institutionalizing Democracy in Germany: From Weimar to Bonn and Berlin', in Heper Metin, Ali Kazancigil and Bert A. Rockman (eds), *Institutions and Democratic Statecraft*, Boulder, Col.: Westview Press, pp. 145–70.

Dibol, Mike (1999) 'The Duce of Downing Street', *The Times*, 6 August, p. 22.

Dicey, A. V. (1915) *Introduction to the Study of the Law of the Constitution*, 8th edn, London: Macmillan.

Domes, Jürgen (1964) *Mehrheitsfraktion und Bundesregierung*, Cologne: Westdeutscher Verlag.

Donoughue, Bernard (1987) *Prime Minister*, London: Jonathan Cape.

Dorey, Peter (1995) *The Conservative Party and the Trade Unions*, London: Routledge.

Dowse, Robert E. (1978) 'Clement Attlee', in John P. Mackintosh (ed.), *British Prime Ministers in the Twentieth Century. Vol. II: Churchill to Callaghan*, New York: St. Martin's Press, pp. 37–72.

Dreher, Klaus (1998) *Helmut Kohl*, Stuttgart: Deutsche Verlags-Anstalt.

Duffy, Michael (2002) 'Marching Alone', *Time*, 11 September, pp. 40–5.

Dunleavy, Patrick, Gamble, Andrew, Heffernan, Richard and Peele, Gillian (2003) 'Introduction: Transformations in British Politics', in Patrick Dunleavy, Andrew Gamble, Richard Heffernan and Gillian Peele (eds) *Developments in British Politics 7*, London: Palgrave, pp. 1–17.

Dunleavy, Patrick, Jones, G. W. and O'Leary, B. (1990) 'Prime Ministers and the Commons: Patterns of Behaviour, 1868–1987', *Public Administration*, vol. 68, pp. 123–39.

Dunleavy, Patrick and Rhodes, R. A. W. (1990) 'Core Executive Studies in Britain', *Public Administration*, vol. 68, pp. 3–28.

Duverger, Maurice (1980) 'A New Political System Model: Semi-Presidential Government', *European Journal of Political Research*, vol. 8, pp. 165–87.

Dyson, Kenneth (1974) 'The German Federal Chancellor's Office', *Political Quarterly*, vol. 45, pp. 364–71.

Edinger, Lewis J. (1990) 'Approaches to the Comparative Analysis of Political Leadership', *The Review of Politics*, vol. 52, pp. 509–23.

Edwards, George C., III (2002) 'Strategic Choices and the Early Bush Administrative Agenda', *PS: Political Science and Politics*, vol. 35, pp. 41–5.

Edwards, George C., III, Barrett, Andrew and Peake, Jeffrey (1997) 'The Legislative Impact of Divided Government', *American Journal of Political Science*, vol. 41, pp. 545–63.

Edwards, George C., III and Wayne, Stephen J. (1990) *Presidential Leadership*, New York: St. Martin's Press.

Edwards, George C., III and Wood, B. Dan (1999) 'Who Influences Whom? The President, Congress, and the Media', *American Political Science Review*, vol. 93, pp. 327–44.

Egle, Christoph, Ostheim, Tobias and Zohlnhöfer, Reimut (eds) (2003) *Das rot-grüne Projekt*, Wiesbaden: Westdeutscher Verlag.

Eisinger, Robert M. (2003) *The Evolution of Presidential Polling*, New York: Cambridge University Press.

Elcock, Howard (2001) *Political Leadership*, Cheltenham: Edward Elgar.

Elgie, Robert (1999) 'The Politics of Semi-Presidentialism', in Robert Elgie (ed.), *Semi-presidentialism in Europe*, Oxford: Oxford University Press, pp. 1–21.

Elgie, Robert and Thompson, Helen (1998) *The Politics of Central Banks*, London: Routledge.

Ellwein, Thomas (1989) *Krisen und Reformen*, Munich: dtv.

Evans, Eric J. (1997) *Thatcher and Thatcherism*, London: Routledge.

Fabbrini, Sergio (1999) 'The American System of Separated Government: An Historical-Institutional Interpretation', *International Political Science Review*, vol. 20, pp. 95–116.

Fenno, Richard (1966) *The President's Cabinet: An Analysis in the Period from Wilson to Eisenhower*, Cambridge, Mass.: Harvard University Press.

Finch, Tim (1996) 'Linchpin or Bag Carrier? A Study of the Importance of the Role of the Parliamentary Private Secretary to the Prime Minister', *Journal of Legislative Studies*, vol. 2, no. 2, pp. 110–23.

Fleisher, Richard, Bond, Jon R., Krutz, Glen S., and Hanna, Stephen (2000) 'The Demise of the Two Presidencies', *American Political Science Quarterly*, vol. 28, pp. 3–25.

Flemming, Roy B., Wood, B. Dan and Bohte, John (1999) 'Attention to Issues in a System of Separated Powers: Macrodynamics of American Policy Agendas', *Journal of Politics*, vol. 61, pp. 76–108.

Flinders, Matthew (2002) 'Governance in Whitehall', *Public Administration*, vol. 80, no. 1, pp. 51–75.

Foley, Michael (1993) *The Rise of the British Presidency*, Manchester: Manchester University Press.

Foley, Michael (2000) *The British Presidency*, Manchester: Manchester University Press.

Foster, Sir Christopher (2000) 'The Encroachment of the Law on Politics', *Parliamentary Affairs*, vol. 53, pp. 328–46.

Francis, John (2003) 'Federalism', in Robert Singh (ed.), *Governing America*, Oxford: Oxford University Press, pp. 75–93.

Franklin, Bob (1994) *Packaging Politics*, London: Edward Arnold.

Garnett, Mark and Lynch, Philip (2002) 'Bandwagon Blues: The Tory Fightback Fails', *Political Quarterly*, vol. 73, pp. 29–37.

Geerlings, Jörg (2003) 'Die neue Rolle der Bundesbank im Europäischen System der Zentralbanken', *Die Öffentliche Verwaltung*, vol. 56, pp. 322–8.

Genovese, Michael A. (1990) *The Nixon Presidency: Power and Politics in Turbulent Times*, New York: Greenwood Press.

Gergen, David (2000) *Eyewitness to Power*, New York: Touchstone.

Gilmour, Ian and Garnett, Mark (1997) *Whatever Happened to the Tories?*, London: Fourth Estate.

Gilmour, John B. (2002) 'Institutional and Individual Influences on the President's Veto', *Journal of Politics*, vol. 64, no. 1, pp. 198–218.

Goetz, Klaus H. (2003) 'Executives in Comparative Context', in Jack Hayward and Anand Menon (eds), *Governing Europe*, Oxford: Oxford Univesity Press, pp. 74–91.

Gould, Lewis L. (2003) *The Modern American Presidency*, Lawrence, Kan.: University Press of Kansas.

Green, Joshua (2002) 'The Other War Room', *Washington Monthly*, vol. 34, no. 4, pp. 11–16.

Greenstein, Fred I. (1982) *The Hidden-Hand Presidency: Eisenhower as Leader*, New York: Basic Books.

Greenstein, Fred I. (1990) 'Ronald Reagan – Another Hidden-Hand Ike?', *PS: Political Science and Politics*, vol. 23, pp. 7–13.

Greenstein, Fred I. (2000) *The Presidential Difference: Leadership Style from FDR to Clinton*, New York: Martin Kessler.

Gusy, Christoph (1997) *Die Weimarer Reichsverfassung*, Tübingen: Mohr Siebeck.

Hamby, Alonzo L. (1988) 'Harry S. Truman: Insecurity and Responsibility', in Fred I. Greenstein (ed.), *Leadership in the Modern Presidency*, Cambridge, Mass.: Harvard University Press, pp. 41–75.

Hamilton, Gary G. and Biggart, Nicole Woolsey (1984) *Governor Reagan, Governor Brown: A Sociology of Executive Power*, New York: Columbia University Press.

Han, Lori Cox (2001) *Governing From Center Stage: White House Communication Strategies During the Television Age of Politics*, Creskill, NJ: Hampton Press.

Hargrove, Erwin C. (1988) *Jimmy Carter as President*, Baton Rouge, La.: Louisiana State University Press.

Hargrove, Erwin C. (1989) 'Two Conceptions of Institutional Leadership', in Bryan D. Jones (ed.) *Leadership and Politics*, Lawrence, Kan.: University Press of Kansas, pp. 57–83.

Harris, John F. (2001) 'Clintonesque Balancing of Issues, Polls', *Washington Post*, 24 June, p. A1.

Harrison, Brian (1996) *The Transformation of British Politics 1860–1995*, Oxford: Oxford University Press.

Harrop, Martin (1992) 'Comparison', in Martin Harrop (ed.), *Power and Policy in Liberal Democracies*, Cambridge: Cambridge University Press, pp. 263–80.

Hart, John (1995) *The Presidential Branch from Washington to Clinton*, 2nd edn, Chatham, NJ: Chatham House.

Heclo, Hugh (2000) 'Campaigning and Governing: A Conspectus', in Norman J. Ornstein and Thomas E. Mann (eds), *The Permanent Campaign and its Future*, Washington, DC: American Enterprise Institute and the Brookings Institution, pp. 1–37.

Heffernan, Richard (1999) 'Media Management', in Gerald R. Taylor (ed.), *The Impact of New Labour*, London: Macmillan, pp. 50–67.

Heffernan, Richard (2003) 'Prime Ministerial Predominance?', *British Journal of Politics and International Relations*, vol. 5, pp. 347–72.

Heimann, Siegfried (1984) 'Sozialdemokratische Partei Deutschlands', in Richard Stöss (ed.), *Parteien-Handbuch. Bd. 2*, Opladen: Westdeutscher Verlag, pp. 2025–216.

Heinze, Rolf G. (1998) *Die blockierte Gesellschaft*, Opladen: Westdeutscher Verlag.

Helms, Ludger (1994) '"Machtwechsel" in der Bundesrepublik Deutschland', *Jahrbuch für Politik*, vol. 4, pp. 225–48.

Helms, Ludger (1998) 'Keeping Weimar at Bay: The German Federal Presidency since 1949', *German Politics and Society*, vol. 16, no. 3, pp. 50–68.

Helms, Ludger (2000a) '"Politische Führung" als politikwissenschaftliches Problem', *Politische Vierteljahresschrift*, vol. 41, pp. 411–34.

Helms, Ludger (2000b) 'Is There Life after Kohl? The CDU Crisis and the Future of Party Democracy in Germany', *Government and Opposition*, vol. 35, pp. 419–38.

Helms, Ludger (2000c) 'The Federal Constitutional Court: Institutionalising Judicial Review in a Semisovereign Democracy', in Ludger Helms (ed.), *Institutions and Institutional Change in the Federal Republic of Germany*, London: Macmillan, pp. 84–104.

Helms, Ludger (2002a) *Politische Opposition*, Opladen: Leske & Budrich.

Helms, Ludger (2002b) '"Chief Executives" and their Parties: The Case of Germany', *German Politics*, vol. 11, no. 3, pp. 146–64.

Helms, Ludger (2002c) 'Parlamentarismus, Präsidentialismus und Elitenstruktur – ein empirischer Drei-Länder-Vergleich', *Zeitschrift für Parlamentsfragen*, vol. 33, pp. 589–605.

Helms, Ludger (2004) 'The Federal Election in Germany, September 2002', *Electoral Studies*, vol. 23, pp. 143–9.

Henderson, Philip G. (1997) 'Clinton, Carter and the Policy Wonk Presidency', *Perspectives on Political Science*, vol. 26, pp. 149–56.

Henderson, Philip G. (1988) *Managing the Presidency: The Eisenhower Legacy – From Kennedy to Reagan*, Boulder, Col.: Westview Press.

Hennessy, Peter (1986) *Cabinet*, Oxford: Basil Blackwell.

Hennessy, Peter (2000) *The Prime Minister: The Office and Its Holders since 1945*, London: Allen Lane and Penguin.

Hennis, Wilhelm (1964) *Richtlinienkompetenz und Regierungstechnik*, Tübingen: Mohr.

Hennis, Wilhelm (1974) 'Die Rolle des Parlaments und die Parteiendemokratie', in Richard Löwenthal and Hans-Peter Schwarz (eds), *Die zweite Republik*, Stuttgart: Seewald Verlag, pp. 203–43.

Hentschel, Volker (1996) *Ludwig Erhard*, Lech: Olzog.

Herrnson, Paul and Hill, Dilys M. (eds) (1999) *The Clinton Presidency: The First Term, 1992–96*, London: Macmillan.

Hess, Stephen (1976) *Organizing the Presidency*, Washington, DC: Brookings Institution.

Heywood, Paul and Wright, Vincent (1997) 'Executives, Bureaucracies and Decision-Making', in Martin Rhodes, Paul Heywood and Vincent Wright (eds), *Developments in West European Politics*, London: Macmillan, pp. 75–94.

Hildebrand, Klaus (1984) *Von Erhard zur Großen Koalition 1963–1969*, Stuttgart: Deutsche Verlags-Anstalt.

Hill, Dilys M. (1990) 'Domestic Policy in an Era of "Negative" Government', in Dilys M. Hill and Phil Williams (eds), *The Reagan Presidency*, London: Macmillan, pp. 161–78.

Hill, Dilys M. and Williams, Phil (1994) 'Introduction: The Bush Administration – An Overview', in Dilys M. Hill and Phil Williams (eds), *The Bush Presidency*, London: Macmillan, pp. 1–16.

Hockerts, Hans Günter (1980) *Sozialpolitische Entscheidungen im Nachkriegsdeutschland*, Stuttgart: Klett-Cotta.

Hoff-Wilson, Joan (1988) 'Richard M. Nixon: The Corporate Presidency', in Fred I. Greenstein (ed.), *Leadership in the Modern Presidency*, Cambridge, Mass.: Harvard University Press, pp. 164–98.

Hofmann, Gunter (2003) 'Kabinett der Mittelstreckenläufer', *Die Zeit*, 14 August, p. 3.

Holliday, Ian (2000a) 'Executives and Administrations', in Patrick Dunleavy, Andrew Gamble, Richard Heffernan, Ian Holliday and Gillian Peele (eds), *Developments in British Politics 6*, London: Macmillan, pp. 88–107.

Holliday, Ian (2000b) 'Is the British State Hollowing Out?', *Political Quarterly*, vol. 71, pp. 167–76.

Holtz-Bacha, Christine and Kaid, Lynda Lee (1995) 'A Comparative Perspective on Political Advertising: Media and Political System Characteristics', in Lynda Lee Kaid and Christina Holtz-Bacha (eds), *Political Advertising in Western Democracies*, Thousand Oaks, Calif.: Sage, pp. 8–18.

Howell, William G. (2003) *Power without Persuasion: The Politics of Direct Presidential Action*, Princeton, NJ: Princeton University Press.

Hutton, Will (2002) 'War Looms between Blair and Brown', *The Observer*, 6 October, p. 30.

Ismayr, Wolfgang (2000) *Der Deutsche Bundestag im politischen System der Bundesrepublik Deutschland*, Opladen: Leske & Budrich.

Jäger, Wolfgang (1986) 'Die Innenpolitik der sozial-liberalen Koalition 1969–1974', in Karl Dietrich Bracher, Wolfgang Jäger and Werner Link, *Republik im Wandel 1969–1974*, Stuttgart: Deutsche Verlags-Anstalt, pp. 15–160.

Jäger, Wolfgang (1987) 'Die Innenpolitik der sozial-liberalen Koalition 1974–1982', in Wolfgang Jäger and Werner Link, *Republik im Wandel 1974–1982*, Stuttgart: Deutsche Verlags-Anstalt, pp. 7–272.

Jäger, Wolfgang (1988) 'Von der Kanzlerdemokratie zur Koordinationsdemokratie', *Zeitschrift für Politik*, vol. 35, pp. 15–32.

Jäger, Wolfgang (1994) *Wer regiert die Deutschen?*, Osnabrück: Fromm.

Jäger, Wolfgang (1998) *Die Überwindung der Teilung*, Stuttgart: Deutsche Verlags-Anstalt.

James, Simon (1994) 'Cabinet Government: A Commentary', *Contemporary Record*, vol. 8, pp. 495–505.

James, Simon (1999) *British Cabinet Government*, 2nd edn, London and New York: Routledge.

Jenkins, Roy (2001) *Churchill*, New York: Farrar, Straus & Giroux.

Johnson, Nevil (1997) 'Opposition in the British Political System', *Government and Opposition*, vol. 32, pp. 489–510.

Jones, Charles O. (1983) 'Presidential Negotiation with Congress', in Anthony King (eds), *Both Ends of the Avenue*, Washington, DC: American Enterprise Institute for Public Policy Research, pp. 96–130.

Jones, Charles O. (1994) *The Presidency in a Separated System*, Washington, DC: Brookings Institution.

Jones, Charles O. (1996) 'Campaigning to Govern: The Clinton Style', in Colin Campbell and Bert A. Rockman (eds), *The Clinton Presidency*, Chatham, NJ: Chatham House, pp. 15–50.

Jones, George W. (1965) 'The Prime Minister's Power', *Parliamentary Affairs*, vol. 18, pp. 167–85.

Jones, George W. (1987) 'The United Kingdom', in William Plowden (ed.), *Advising the Rulers*, Oxford: Basil Blackwell, pp. 36–70.

Jones, George W. (1992) 'Cabinet Government since Bagehot', in Robert Blackburn (ed.), *Constitutional Studies*, London: Mansell, pp. 14–31.

Jordan, A. G. and Richardson, J. J. (1987) *Government and Pressure Groups in Britain*, Oxford: Clarendon Press.

Jordan, Grant (1994) *The British Administrative System*, London: Routledge.

Judge, David (1993) *The Parliamentary State*, London: Sage.

Kaltefleiter, Werner (1991) 'Parlamentsauflösung in parlamentarischen Demokratien', *Jahrbuch für Politik*, vol. 1, pp. 247–68.

Kandiah, Michael David (ed.) (1995) 'The Heath Government', *Contemporary Record*, vol. 9, pp. 188–219.

Katz, Richard S. (1996) 'The United States: Divided Government and Divided Parties', in Jean Blondel and Maurizio Cotta (eds), *Party and Government*, London: Macmillan, pp. 202–24.

Katz, Richard S. and Mair, Peter (1995) 'Changing Models of Party Organization and Party Democracy: The Emergence of the Cartel Party', *Party Politics*, vol. 1, pp. 5–28.

Katzenstein, Peter J. (1987) *Policy and Politics in West Germany: The Growth of a Semi-sovereign State*, Philadelphia, Penn.: Temple University Press.

Kavanagh, Dennis (1972) *Political Culture*, London: Macmillan.

Kavanagh, Dennis (1987) 'The Heath Government, 1970–1974', in Peter Hennessy and Anthony Seldon (eds), *Ruling Performance*, Oxford: Basil Blackwell, pp. 216–40.

Kavanagh, Dennis (2001) 'New Labour, New Millenium, New Premiership', in Anthony Seldon (ed.), *The Blair Effect*, London: Little, Brown, pp. 3–18.

Kavanagh, Dennis and Richards, David (2001) 'Departmentalism and Joined-Up Government: Back to the Future?', *Parliamentary Affairs*, vol. 54, pp. 1–18.

Kavanagh, Dennis and Seldon, Anthony (2000) *The Powers Behind the Prime Minister*, 2nd edn, London: HarperCollins.

Keller, Bill (2003) 'Reagan's Son', *New York Times Magazine*, 26 January, pp. 26–31, 42–3, 61.

Kellerman, Barbara (ed.) (1986) *Political Leadership: A Source Book*, Pittsburgh, Penn.: University of Pittsburgh Press.

Kelly, Richard (1994) 'Power and Leadership in the Major Parties', in Lynton Robins, Hilary Blackmore and Robert Pyper (eds), *Britain's Changing Party System*, London: Leicester University Press, pp. 26–56.

Kempf, Udo and Merz, Hans-Georg (eds) (2001) *Kanzler und Minister 1949–1998*, Wiesbaden: Westdeutscher Verlag.

Kernell, Samuel (1997) *Going Public: New Strategies of Presidential Leadership*, 3rd edn, Washington, DC: Congressional Quarterly Press.

Kessler, Glenn and Slevin, Peter (2003) 'Rice Fails to Repair Rifts, Officials Say', *Washington Post*, 12 October, p. A1.

Kincaid, John (2001) 'Devolution in the United States: Rhetoric and Reality', in Kalypso Nicolaidis and Robert Howse (eds), *The Federal Vision*, Oxford: Oxford University Press, pp. 144–60.

King, Anthony (1976) 'Modes of Executive–Legislative Relations: Great Britain, France, and West Germany', *Legislative Studies Quarterly*, vol. 1, pp. 11–36.

King, Anthony (1991) 'The British Prime Minister in the Age of the Career Politician', in G. W. Jones (ed.), *West European Prime Ministers*, London: Frank Cass, pp. 25–47.

King, Anthony (1993) 'Foundations of Power', in George C. Edwards III, John H. Kessel and Bert A. Rockman (eds) *Researching the Presidency*, Pittsburgh Penn.: University of Pittsburgh Press, pp. 415–51.

King, Anthony (1994a) '"Chief Executives" in Western Europe', in Ian Budge and David McKay (eds), *Developing Democracy*, London: Sage, pp. 150–63.

King, Anthony (1994b) 'Ministerial Autonomy in Britain', in Michael Laver and Kenneth A. Shepsle (eds), *Cabinet Ministers and Parliamentary Government*, Cambridge: Cambridge University Press, pp. 203–25.

King, Anthony (2001) *Does the United Kingdom Still Have a Constitution?*, London: Sweet & Maxwell.

King, Anthony (ed.) (2002a) *Leaders' Personalities and the Outcomes of Democratic Elections*, Oxford: Oxford University Press.

King, Anthony (2002b) 'The Outsider as Political Leader: The Case of Margaret Thatcher', *British Journal of Political Science*, vol. 32, pp. 435–54.

King, James D. and Riddlesberger, James W. (1996) 'Presidential Management and Staffing', *Presidential Studies Quarterly*, vol. 26, pp. 496–510.

Kister, Kurt (2002) 'Abgeschottet in der Wagenburg', *Süddeutsche Zeitung*, 11 December, p. 2.

Knill, Christoph (2001) *The Europeanisation of National Administrations*, Cambridge: Cambridge University Press.

Knorr, Heribert (1975) *Der parlamentarische Entscheidungsprozeß während der Großen Koalition 1966 bis 1969*, Meisenheim am Glan: Anton Hain.

Koenig, Louis W. (1972) 'Kennedy's Personal Management', in Earl Latham (ed.), *J. F. Kennedy and Presidential Power*, Lexington Mass.: D.C. Heath, pp. 5–10.

Koerfer, Daniel (1987) *Kampf ums Kanzleramt*, Stuttgart: Deutsche Verlags-Anstalt.

Kommers, Donald P. (1997) *The Constitutional Jurisprudence of the Federal Republic of Germany*, 2nd edn, Durham, NC: Duke University Press.

Korte, Karl-Rudolf (2000) 'Solutions for the Decision Dilemma', *German Politics*, vol. 9, no. 1, pp. 1–22.

Korte, Karl-Rudolf (ed.) (2002a) *Das Wort hat der Herr Bundeskanzler*, Wiesbaden: Westdeutscher Verlag.

Korte, Karl-Rudolf (2002b) 'In der Präsentationsdemokratie', *Frankfurter Allgemeine Zeitung*, 26 July, p. 6.

Krause, George A. (1994) 'Federal Reserve Policy Decision Making', *American Journal of Political Science*, vol. 38, pp. 124–44.

Krutz, Glen S., Fleisher, Richard and Bond, Jon R. (1998) 'From Abe Fortas to Zoë Baird: Why Some Presidential Nominations Fail in the Senate', *American Political Science Review*, vol. 92, pp. 871–81.

Kumar, Martha Joynt (2002) 'Recruiting and Organizing the White House Staff', *PS: Political Science and Politics*, vol. 35, no. 1, pp. 35–40.

Kumar, Martha Joynt (2003) 'Communications Operations in the White House of President George W. Bush', *Presidential Studies Quarterly*, vol. 33, pp. 366–93.

Küpper, Jost (1985) *Die Kanzlerdemokratie*, Frankfurt-am-Main: Lang.

Küster, Hanns Jürgen (1988) 'Konrad Adenauer, die Presse, der Rundfunk und das Fernsehen', in Karl-Günther von Hase (ed.), *Konrad Adenauer und die Presse (Rhöndorfer Gespräche, Bd. 9)*, Bonn: Bouvier Verlag, pp. 13–31.

Laitenberger, Volkhard (1986) *Ludwig Erhard*, Göttingen: Muster-Schmidt Verlag.

Lammers, William and Genovese, Michael (2000) *The Presidency and Domestic Policy*, Washington, DC: Congressional Quarterly Press.

Lane, Jan-Erik (1996) *Constitutions and Political Theory*, Manchester: Manchester University Press.

Laski, Harold (1925) *A Grammar of Politics*, London: Allen & Unwin.

Lee, J. M., Jones, G. W. and Burnham, J. (1998) *At the Centre of Whitehall*, London: Macmillan.

Lehmbruch, Gerhard (1998) *Parteienwettbewerb im Bundesstaat*, 2nd edn, Opladen: Westdeutscher Verlag.

Lehmbruch, Gerhard (2003) 'Das deutsche Verbändesystem zwischen Unitarismus und Föderalismus', in Renate Mayntz and Wolfgang Streeck (eds), *Die Reformierbarkeit der Demokratie*, Frankfurt-am-Main: Campus, pp. 259–88.

Leicht, Robert (1993) 'Wenn der Beton sich lockert', *Die Zeit*, 18 June, p. 1.

Leif, Thomas and Speth, Rudolf (eds) (2003) *Die stille Macht: Lobbyismus in Deutschland*, Wiesbaden: Westdeutscher Verlag.

Lepsius, M. Rainer (1990) *Interessen, Ideen und Institutionen*, Opladen: Westdeutscher Verlag.

Levy, Roger (1997) 'The Disunited Kingdom: The Territorial Dimension of British Politics', in Lynton Robins and Bill Jones (eds), *Half a Century of British Politics*, Manchester: Manchester University Press, pp. 199–226.

Lijphart, Arend (ed.) (1992) *Parliamentary versus Presidential Government*, Oxford: Oxford University Press.

Lijphart, Arend (1999) *Patterns of Democracy*, New Haven, Conn.: Yale University Press.

Lord, Carnes (2003) *The Modern Prince*, New Haven, Conn.: Yale University Press.

Ludlam, Steve and Taylor, Andrew (2003) 'The Political Representation of the Labour Interest in Britain', *British Journal of Industrial Relations*, vol. 41, pp. 727–49.

Lütjen, Torben and Walter, Franz (2000) 'Die präsidiale Kanzlerschaft', *Blätter für deutsche und internationale Politik*, vol. 45, pp. 1308–13.

Mackenzie, G. Calvin (ed.) (2001) *Brookings Review*, vol. 19, no. 2.

Mackintosh, John P. (1977) *The British Cabinet*, 3rd edn, London: Steven & Sons.

Mackintosh, John P. (1978) 'Harold Wilson', in John P. Mackintosh (ed.), *British Prime Ministers in the Twentieth Century. Vol. II: Churchill to Callaghan*, New York: St. Martin's Press, pp. 171–215.

Maggs, John (2002) '41, Reconsidered', *National Journal*, 20 July, pp. 2156–64.

Mair, Peter (2000) 'Partyless Democracy: Solving the Paradox of New Labour?', *New Left Review* (Second Series), no. 2, pp. 21–35.

Mair, Peter (2002) 'Comparing Party Systems', in Lawrence LeDuc, Richard G. Niemi and Pippa Norris (eds), *Comparing Democracies 2. New Challenges in the Study of Elections and Voting*, London: Sage, pp. 88–107.

Major, John (1999) *The Autobiography*, London: HarperCollins.

Manley, John F. (1978) 'Presidential Power and White House Lobbying', *Political Science Quarterly*, vol. 93, pp. 255–75.

Mans, Thomas C. (1995) 'Leadership: The Presidency and Congress', in Philip John Davies (ed.), *An American Quarter Century*, Manchester: Manchester University Press, pp. 245–70.

Manuel, Christopher and Cammisa, Anne Marie (1998) *Checks and Balances? How a Parliamentary System Could Change American Politics*, Boulder, Col.: Westview Press.

Maor, Moshe (1998) *Parties, Conflicts and Coalitions in Western Europe*, London: Routledge.

Marsh, David (1992) *The Bundesbank: The Bank that Rules Europe*, London: Mandarin.

Marsh, David and Grant, Wyn (1977) 'Tripartism: Reality or Myth?', *Government and Opposition*, vol. 12, pp. 194–211.

Maser, Werner (1990) *Helmut Kohl*, Berlin: Ullstein.

Mayer, Kenneth R. (2001) *With the Stroke of a Pen: Executive Orders and Presidential Power*, Princeton, NJ: Princeton University Press.

Mayer, Kenneth R. and Price, Kevin (2002) 'Unilateral Presidential Powers: Significant Executive Orders, 1949–99', *Presidential Studies Quarterly*, vol. 32, pp. 367–86.

Mayntz, Renate (2003) 'New Challenges to Governance Theory', in Henrik P. Bang (ed.), *Governance as Social and Political Communication*, Manchester: Manchester University Press, pp. 27–40.

McAnulla, Stuart (1999) 'The Post-Thatcher Era', in David Marsh, Jim Butler, Colin Hay, Jim Johnston, Peter Kerr, Stuart McAnulla and Mathew Watson, *Postwar British Politics in Perspective*, Cambridge: Polity Press, pp. 189–208.

McCann, Michael (1999) 'How the Supreme Court Matters in American Politics: New Institutionalist Perspectives', in Howard Gillman and Cornell Clayton (eds), *The Supreme Court in American Politics*, Lawrence, Kan.: University Press of Kansas, pp. 63–97.

McCoy, Donald R. (1984) *The Presidency of Harry S. Truman*, Lawrence, Kan.: University Press of Kansas.

Merz, Hans-Georg (2001) 'Regierungshandeln im Lichte einer Befragung deutscher Bundesminister', in Udo Kempf and Hans-Georg Merz (eds), *Kanzler und Minister 1949–1998*, Wiesbaden: Westdeutscher Verlag, pp. 36–81.

Michaels, Judith E. (1997) *The President's Call: Executive Leadership from FDR to George Bush*, Pittsburgh, Penn.: University of Pittsburgh Press.

Milbank, Dana and Broder, David S. (2004) 'Hopes for Civility in Washington Are Dashed', *Washington Post*, 18 January, p. A1.

Milkis, Sidney M. (1993) *The President and the Parties*, New York: Oxford University Press.

Moe, Terry (1985) 'The Politicized Presidency', in John E. Chubb and Paul E. Peterson (eds), *The New Direction in American Politics*, Washington, DC: Brookings Institution, pp. 235–71.

Moravcsik, Andrew (1997) 'Warum die Europäische Union die Exekutive stärkt', in Klaus Dieter Wolf (ed.), *Projekt Europa im Übergang*, Baden-Baden: Nomos, pp. 211–69.

Morgan, David (1995) 'US Presidents and the Mass Media', *Parliamentary Affairs*, vol. 48, pp. 503–14.

Morris, Irwin L. (2000) *Congress, the President, and the Federal Reserve*, Ann Arbor, Mich.: University of Michigan Press.

Morsey, Rudolf (1986) 'Konrad Adenauer und der Deutsche Bundestag', in Hans Buchheim (ed.), *Konrad Adenauer und der Deutsche Bundestag (Rhöndorfer Gespräche, Bd. 8)*, Bonn: Bouvier, pp. 14–40.

Morsey, Rudolf (1996) *Heinrich Lübke*, Paderborn: Schöningh.

Mughan, Anthony (2000) *Media and the Presidentialization of Parliamentary Elections*, London: Palgrave/Macmillan.

Müller, Wolfgang C. and Strøm, Kaare (2000a) 'Coalition Governance in Western Europe: An Introduction', in Wolfgang C. Müller and Kaare Strøm (eds), *Coalition Governments in Western Europe*, Oxford: Oxford University Press, pp. 1–31.

Müller, Wolfgang C. and Strøm, Kaare (2000b) 'Conclusion: Coalition Governance in Western Europe', in Wolfgang C. Müller and Kaare Strøm (eds), *Coalition Governments in Western Europe*, Oxford: Oxford University Press, pp. 559–92.

Müller-Rommel, Ferdinand (1994) 'The Chancellor and his Staff', in Stephen Padgett (ed.), *Adenauer to Kohl*, London: Hurst, pp. 106–26.

Müller-Rommel, Ferdinand (1997) 'Management of Politics in the German Chancellor's Office', Paper presented at the ESCR conference on 'Administering the Summit', Nuffield College, University of Oxford, 20–21 June.

Münch, Ursula (2001) 'Der Bundesrat im Kontext neuer Regierungsprogramme', in Hans-Ulrich Derlien and Axel Murswieck (eds), *Regieren nach Wahlen*, Opladen: Leske & Budrich, pp. 133–66.

Murswieck, Axel (2003) '"Des Kanzlers Macht": Zum Regierungsstil Gerhard Schröders', in Christoph Egle, Tobias Ostheim and Reimut Zohlnhöfer (eds), *Das rot-grüne Projekt*, Wiesbaden: Westdeutscher Verlag, pp. 117–35.

Nakashima, Ellen and Milbank, Dana (2001) 'Bush Cabinet Takes Back Seat in Driving Policy', *Washington Post*, 5 September: pp. A1, A12.

Nather, David (2001) 'Clinton's Floor Vote Victories Yielded Few Accomplishments', *Congressional Quarterly Weekly Report*, vol. 59, pp. 52–4.

Nather, David (2004) 'Presidential Support Vote Study: Score Belies Bush's Success', *Congressional Quarterly Weekly Report*, vol. 62, pp. 18–22.

Neustadt, Richard (1960) *Presidential Power*, New York: John Wiley.

Neustadt, Richard (1969) 'White House and Whitehall', in Anthony King (ed.), *The British Prime Minister*, London: Macmillan, pp. 131–47.

Neustadt, Richard (1990) *Presidential Power and the Modern Presidents: The Politics of Leadership from Roosevelt to Reagan*, New York: Free Press.

Neustadt, Richard (2001) 'The Weakening White House', *British Journal of Political Science*, vol. 31, pp. 1–11.

Niclauss, Karlheinz (1987) 'Repräsentative und plebiszitäre Elemente der Kanzlerdemokratie', *Vierteljahreshefte für Zeitgeschichte*, vol. 35, pp. 217–45.

Niclauss, Karlheinz (1988) *Kanzlerdemokratie: Bonner Regierungspraxis von Konrad Adenauer bis Helmut Kohl*, Stuttgart: Kohlhammer.

Niclauss, Karlheinz (1999) 'Bestätigung der Kanzlerdemokratie?', *Aus Politik und Zeitgeschichte*, no. 20, pp. 27–38.

Niclauss, Karlheinz (2000) 'The Federal Government: Variations of Chancellor Democracy', in Ludger Helms (ed.), *Institutions and Institutional Change in the Federal Republic of Germany*, London: Macmillan, pp. 65–83.

Niejahr, Elisabeth and Ulrich, Bernd (2003) 'Sieger unter sich', *Die Zeit*, 17 December, p. 3.

Norris, Pippa (2000) *A Virtuous Circle: Political Communications in Postindustrial Societies*, Cambridge: Cambridge University Press.

Norris, Pippa (2001) 'US Campaign 2000: Of Pregnant Chads, Butterfly Ballots and Partisan Vitriol', *Government and Opposition*, vol. 36, pp. 3–26.

Norton, Philip (1981) *The Commons in Perspective*, Oxford: Basic Blackwell.

Norton, Philip (1991) 'The Changing Face of Parliament', in Philip Norton (ed.), *New Directions in British Politics*, Cheltenham: Edward Elgar, pp. 58–82.

Norton, Philip (1993) *Does Parliament Matter?*, New York: Harvester Weatsheaf.

Norton, Philip (1995) 'Parliamentary Behaviour Since 1945', *Talking Politics*, vol. 8, pp. 107–14.

Norton, Philip (1997) 'Parliamentary Oversight', in Patrick Dunleavy, Andrew Gamble, Ian Holliday and Gillian Peele (eds), *Developments in British Politics 5*, London: Macmillan, pp. 155–76.

Norton, Philip (1998) 'Old Institution, New Institutionalism? Parliament and Government in the UK', in Philip Norton (ed.), *Parliaments and Governments in Western Europe*, London: Frank Cass, pp. 16–43.

Norton, Philip (Lord Norton of Luth) (2003) 'Governing Alone', *Parliamentary Affairs*, vol. 56, pp. 543–59.

Ornstein, Norman J. and Mann, Thomas E. (eds) (2000a) *The Permanent Campaign and its Future*, Washington, DC: American Enterprise Institute and the Brookings Institution.

Ornstein, Norman J. and Mann, Thomas E. (2000b) 'Conclusion: The Permanent Campaign and the Future of American Democracy', in Norman J. Ornstein and Thomas E. Mann (eds), *The Permanent Campaign and its Future*, Washington, DC: American Enterprise Institute and the Brookings Institution, pp. 219–34.

Ota, Alan K. (2002) 'Calio's Assertive Style Moves Legislation, but Hill Republicans Have Paid a Price', *Congressional Quarterly Weekly Report*, vol. 60, pp. 3251–4.

Padgett, Stephen (1994) 'Introduction: Chancellors and the Chancellorship', in Stephen Padgett (ed.), *Adenauer to Kohl*, London: Hurst, pp. 1–19.

Padgett, Stephen (2003) 'Germany: Modernising the Left by Stealth', *Parliamentary Affairs*, vol. 56, pp. 38–57.

Page, Edward C. (1992) *Political Authority and Bureaucratic Power*, 2nd edn, New York: Harvester Wheatsheaf.

Paige, Glenn D. (1977) *The Scientific Study of Political Leadership*, New York: Free Press.

Paper, Lewis J. (1975) *John F. Kennedy: The Promise and the Performance*, New York: DaCapo.

Patterson, Bradley H., Jr, (1994) 'Teams and Staff', *Presidential Studies Quarterly*, vol. 24, pp. 277–98.

Patterson, Bradley H., Jr, (2000) *The White House Staff*, Washington, DC: Brookings Institution.

Patzelt, Werner J. (1998) 'Ein latenter Verfassungskonflikt?', *Politische Vierteljahresschrift*, vol. 39, pp. 725–57.

Pearce, Robert (1997) *Attlee*, London: Longman.

Peele, Gillian (1998) 'Towards "New Conservatives"?', *Political Quarterly*, vol. 69, pp. 141–7.

Peele, Gillian (2000) 'The Law and the Constitution', in Patrick Dunleavy, Andrew Gamble, Richard Hefferman, Ian Holliday and Gillian Peele (eds), *Developments in British Politics 6*, London: Macmillan, pp. 69–87.

Peele, Gillian (2002) 'Federalism and Intergovernmental Relations', in Gillian Peele, Christopher J. Bailey, Bruce Cain and B. Guy Peters (eds), *Developments in American Politics 4*, London: Macmillan, pp. 147–62.

Peele, Gillian, Bailey, Christopher J., Cain, Bruce and Peters, B. Guy (1998) 'Introduction: The United States in the 1990s', in Gillian Peele, Christopher J. Bailey, Bruce Cain and B. Guy Peters (eds), *Developments in American Politics 3*, London: Macmillan, pp. 1–14.

Peters, B. Guy, Rhodes, R. A. W. and Wright, Vincent (2000) 'Staffing the Summit – the Administration of the Core Executive', in B. Guy Peters, R. A. W. Rhodes and Vincent Wright (eds), *Administering the Summit*, London: Macmillan, pp. 3–22.

Peterson, Mark A. (1990) *Legislating Together*, Cambridge, Mass.: Harvard University Press.

Peterson, Mark A. (1992) 'The Presidency and Organized Interests: White House Patterns of Interest Group Liaison', *American Political Science Review*, vol. 86, pp. 612–25.

Peterson, Mark A. (2004) 'Bush and Interest Groups: A Government of Chums', in Colin Campbell and Bert A. Rockman (eds), *The George W. Bush Presidency*, Washington, DC: Congressional Quarterly Press, pp. 226–64.

Pfiffner, James P. (1986) 'White House Staff versus Cabinet', *Presidential Studies Quarterly*, vol. 16, pp. 327–39.

Pfiffner, James P. (1998) 'President, Executive Office of the', in George Thomas Kurian (ed.), *A Historical Guide to the U.S. Government*, New York: Oxford University Press, pp. 470–2.

Pika, Joseph A. (1999) 'Interest Groups: A Doubly Dynamic Relationship', in Steven A. Shull (ed.), *Presidential Policymaking*, New York: Sharpe, pp. 59–78.

Pious, Richard M. (1998) 'President as Chief Executive', in George Thomas Kurian (ed.), *A Historical Guide to the U.S. Government*, Oxford: Oxford University Press, pp. 472–8.

Poguntke, Thomas (2000) 'Präsidiale Regierungschefs: Wie verändern sich die parlamentarischen Demokratien?', in Oskar Niedermayer (ed.), *Demokratie und Partizipation*, Wiesbaden: Westdeutscher Verlag, pp. 356–71.

Polsby, Nelson (1983) 'Some Landmarks in Modern Presidential–Congressional Relations', in Anthony King (ed.), *Both Ends of the Avenue*, Washington, DC: American Enterprise Institute for Public Policy Research, pp. 1–25.

Porter, Roger B. (1988) 'Gerald R. Ford: A Healing Presidency', in Fred I. Greenstein (ed.), *Leadership in the Modern Presidency*, Cambridge, Mass.: Harvard University Press, pp. 199–227.

Pridham, Geoffrey (1977) *Christian Democracy in Western Germany: The CDU/CSU in Government and Opposition, 1945–1976*, London: Croom Helm.

Pryce, Sue (1997) *Presidentializing the Premiership*, London: Macmillan.

Przeworski, Adam and Teune, Henry (1970) *The Logic of Comparative Social Inquiry*, New York: John Wiley.

Pulzer, Peter (1999) 'Luck and Good Management: Helmut Kohl as Parliamentary and Electoral Strategist', in Stephen Padgett and Thomas Saalfeld (eds), *Bundestagswahl '98: The End of an Era?*, London: Frank Cass, pp. 126–40.

Ragsdayle, Lyn and Theis, John J. (1997) 'The Institutionalization of the American Presidency, 1924–1992', *American Journal of Political Science*, vol. 41, pp. 1280–318.

Ramsden, John (1995) *The Age of Churchill and Eden, 1940–1957*, London: Longman.

Ramsden, John (1996) 'The Prime Minister and the Making of Policy', in Stuart Ball and Anthony Seldon (eds), *The Heath Government 1970–1974*, London: Longman, pp. 21–46.

Raschke, Joachim (2001) *Die Zukunft der Grünen*, Franfurt-am-Main: Campus.

Rawnsley, Andrew (2002) 'Mr Blair versus the Barons', *The Observer*, 16 June, p. 25.

Redhead, Brian (1978) 'Clement Attlee', in John P. Mackintosh (ed.), *British Prime Ministers in the Twentieth Century. Vol. II: Churchill to Callaghan*, New York: St. Martin's Press, pp. 216–39.

Redlich, Norman, Schwartz, Bernard and Attanasio, John (1995) *Understanding Constitutional Law* (without publisher and place of publication).

Reilly, Steve (1998) 'Organized Interests in National Politics', in Gillian Peele, Christopher J. Bailey, Bruce Cain and B. Guy Peters (eds), *Developments in American Politics 3*, London: Macmillan, pp. 162–82.

Rejai, Mostafa and Phillips, Kay (1997) *Leaders and Leadership*, New York: Praeger.

Relyea, Harold C. (1997) 'The Executive Office Concept', in Harold C. Relyea (ed.), *The Executive Office of the President*, Westport, Conn.: Greenwood Press, pp. 1–37.

Relyea, Harold C. and Arja, Charles V. (2002) *The Vice Presidency of the United States*, New York: Nova Science Publishers.

Rhodes, R. A. W. (1997) *Understanding Governance*, Buckingham: Open University Press.

Rhodes, R. A. W. (ed.) (2000) *Transforming British Government*, 2 vols, London: Macmillan.

Rhodes, R. A. W. (2003) 'What is New about Governance and Why does it Matter?', in Jack Hayward and Anand Menon (eds), *Governing Europe*, Oxford: Oxford University Press, pp. 61–73.

Richardson, Jeremy J. (1993) 'Interest Group Behaviour in Britain', in Jeremy J. Richardson (ed.), *Pressure Groups*, Oxford: Oxford University Press, pp. 86–99.

Riddell, Peter (1989) 'Cabinet and Parliament', in Dennis Kavanagh and Anthony Seldon (eds), *The Thatcher Effect*, Oxford: Clarendon Press, pp. 101–13.

Riddell, Peter (1994) 'Major and Parliament', in Dennis Kavanagh and Anthony Seldon (eds), *The Major Effect*, London: Macmillan, pp. 46–63.

Riddell, Peter (1998) 'Does Anybody Listen to MPs?', *The Times*, 23 March, p. 22.

Riddell, Peter (2000) *Parliament under Blair*, London: Politico's.

Riddell, Peter (2001) 'Wasn't That Lloyd George I Just Spotted at No. 10?', *The Times*, 17 December, p. 14.

Riddell, Peter (2002) 'No. 10's Remote Control Focuses Vision for a Short Time Only', *The Times*, 26 July, p. 12.

Riddlesberger, James W. and King, James D. (1986) 'Presidential Appointments to the Cabinet, Executive Office, and White House Staff', *Presidential Studies Quarterly*, vol. 16, no. 4, pp. 690–9.

Ridley, F. F. (1966) 'Chancellor Government as a Political System and the German Constitution', *Parliamentary Affairs*, vol. 19, pp. 446–61.

Rockman, Bert A. (1992) 'Entrepreneur in the Constitutional Marketplace: The Development of the Presidency', in Peter F. Nardulli (ed.), *The Constitution and American Development*, Urbana, Ill.: University of Illinois Press, pp. 97–120.

Rockman, Bert A. (1996) 'Leadership Style and the Clinton Presidency', in Colin Campbell and Bert A. Rockman (eds), *The Clinton Presidency*, Chatham, NJ: Chatham House, pp. 325–62.

Rockman, Bert A. (1997) 'The Performance of Presidents and Prime Ministers and of Presidential and Parliamentary Systems', in Kurt von Mettenheim (ed.), *Presidential Institutions and Democratic Politics*, Baltimore, Md.: Johns Hopkins University Press, pp. 45–64.

Rockman, Bert A. (2000) 'Administering the Summit in the United States', in B. Guy Peters, R. A. W. Rhodes and Vincent Wright (eds), *Administering the Summit*, London: Macmillan, pp. 245–62.

Rockman, Bert A. (2003) 'The American Presidency in Comparative Perspective: Systems, Situations, and Leaders', in Michael Nelson (ed.), *The Presidency and the Political System*, 7th edn, Washington, DC: Congressional Quarterly Press, pp. 48–75.

Rockman, Bert A. (2004) 'Presidential Leadership in an Era of Party Polarization', in Colin Campbell and Bert A. Rockman (eds), *The George W. Bush Presidency*, Washington, DC: Congressional Quarterly Press, pp. 319–57.

Rose, Richard (1980) 'British Government: The Job at the Top', in Richard Rose and Ezra N. Suleiman (eds), *Presidents and Prime Ministers*, Washington, DC: American Enterprise Institute for Public Policy Research, pp. 1–49.

Rose, Richard (1991a) *The Postmodern President*, 2nd edn, Chatham, NJ: Chatham House.

Rose, Richard (1991b) 'Prime Ministers in Parliamentary Democracies', in G. W. Jones (ed.), *West European Prime Ministers*, London: Frank Cass, pp. 9–24.

Rose, Richard (1996) 'Politics in England', in Gabriel A. Almond and B. Bingham Powell, Jr. (eds), *Comparative Politics Today*, 6th edn, New York: HarperCollins, pp. 155–209.

Rose, Richard (1998) 'The Sound of One Hand Clapping: The World Moves Away from the White House', *Presidential Studies Quarterly*, vol. 28, pp. 845–50.

Rose, Richard (2001) *The Prime Minister in a Shrinking World*, Cambridge: Polity Press.

Rothwell, Victor (1992) *Anthony Eden: A Political Biography, 1931–57*, Manchester: Manchester University Press.

Rozell, Mark J. (1994) 'President Ford's Pardon of Richard M. Nixon', *Presidential Studies Quarterly*, vol. 24, pp. 121–37.

Rudzio, Wolfgang (1970) 'Mit Koalitionsausschüssen leben?', *Zeitschrift für Parlamentsfragen*, vol. 1, pp. 206–22.

Rudzio, Wolfgang (1991) 'Informelle Entscheidungsmuster in Bonner Koalitionsregierungen', in Hans-Hermann Hartwich and Göttrik Wewer (eds), *Regieren in der Bundesrepublik II*, Opladen: Leske & Budrich, pp. 125–41.

Rudzio, Wolfgang (2000) 'The Federal Presidency: Parameters of Presidential Power in a Parliamentary Democracy', in Ludger Helms (ed.), *Institutions and Institutional Change in the Federal Republic of Germany*, London: Macmillan, pp. 48–64.

Rudzio, Wolfgang (2003) *Das politische System der Bundesrepublik Deutschland*, 6th edn, Opladen: Leske & Budrich.

Saalfeld, Thomas (1995) *Parteisoldaten und Rebellen: Eine Untersuchung zur Geschlossenheit der Fraktionen im Deutschen Bundestag (1949–1990)*, Opladen: Leske & Budrich.

Saalfeld, Thomas (1999) 'Coalition Politics and Management in the Kohl Era, 1982–98', in Stephen Padgett and Thomas Saalfeld (eds), *Bundestagswahl '98: The End of an Era?*, London: Frank Cass, pp. 141–73.

Saalfeld, Thomas (2000) 'Germany: Stable Parties, Chancellor Democracy, and the Art of Informal Settlement', in Wolfgang C. Müller and Kaare Strøm (eds), *Coalition Governments in Western Europe*, Oxford: Oxford University Press, pp. 32–85.

Sanger, David E. and Tyler, Patrick E. (2001) 'Wartime Forges a United Front for Bush Aides', *New York Times*, 23 December, pp. A1, B4.

Sartori, Giovanni (1987) *The Theory of Democracy Revisited*, Chatham, NJ: Chatham House Publishers.

Sartori, Giovanni (1991) 'Comparing and Miscomparing', *Journal of Theoretical Politics*, vol. 3, pp. 243–57.

Savage, Stephen P. and Lynton Robins (eds) (1990) *Public Policy under Thatcher*, London: Macmillan.

Scharpf, Fritz, Reissert, Bernd and Schnabel, Fritz (1976) *Politikverflechtung: Theorie und Empirie des kooperativen Föderalismus in der Bundesrepublik*, Kronberg im Taunus: Scriptor.

Scheele, Henry Z. (1993) 'President Dwight D. Eisenhower and U.S. House Leader Charles A. Halleck', *Presidential Studies Quarterly*, vol. 23, pp. 289–99.

Schickler, Eric (2002) 'Congress', in Gillian Peele, Christopher J. Bailey, Bruce Cain and B. Guy Peters (eds), *Developments in American Politics 4*, London: Macmillan, pp. 97–114.

Schier, Steven E. (2000) 'American Politics after Clinton', in Steven E. Schier (eds), *The Postmodern Presidency*, Pittsburgh, Penn.: Pittsburgh University Press, pp. 255–65.

Schindler, Peter (1999) *Datenhandbuch zur Geschichte des Deutschen Bundestages 1949 bis 1999*, Baden-Baden: Nomos.

Schmidt, Manfred G. (1978) 'Die "Politik der Inneren Reformen" in der Bundesrepublik Deutschland', *Politische Vierteljahresschrift*, vol. 19, pp. 201–53.

Schmidt, Manfred G. (1996) 'Germany: The Grand Coalition State', in Josep M. Colomer (ed.), *Political Institutions in Europe*, London: Routledge, pp. 62–98.

Schmidt, Manfred G. (2000) *Demokratietheorien*, 3rd edn, Opladen: Leske & Budrich.

Schmidt, Manfred G. (2002) 'The Impact of Political Parties, Constitutional Structures and Veto Players on Public Policy', in Hans Keman (ed.), *Comparative Democratic Politics*, London: Sage, pp. 166–84.

Schmidt-Preuss, Matthias (1988) 'Das Bundeskabinett', *Die Verwaltung*, vol. 21, pp. 199–219.

Schmoeckel, Reinhard and Kaiser, Bruno (1991) *Die vergessene Regierung*, Bonn: Bouvier.

Schneider, Andrea H. (1999) *Die Kunst des Kompromisses*, Paderborn: Schöningh.

Schneider, William (2004) 'Bush's Vanished Capital', *National Journal*, vol. 36, p. 580.

Schönbach, Klaus and Semetko, Holli A. (1995) 'Journalistische "Professionalität" versus Chancengleichheit von Regierung und Opposition', in Klaus Armingeon and Roger Blum (eds), *Das öffentliche Theater*, Berne: Haupt, pp. 49–64.

Schöne, Siegfried (1968) *Von der Reichskanzlei zum Bundeskanzleramt*, Berlin: Duncker & Humblot.

Schreckenberger, Waldemar (1994) 'Informelle Verfahren der Entscheidungsvor-bereitung zwischen der Bundesregierung und den Mehrheitsfraktionen', *Zeitschrift für Parlamentsfragen*, vol. 25, pp. 329–46.

Schroeder, Wolfgang and Esser, Josef (1999) 'Modell Deutschland: Von der Konzertierten Aktion zum Bündnis für Arbeit', *Aus Politik und Zeitgeschichte*, no. 37, pp. 3–12.

Schüttemeyer, Suzanne S. (1998) *Fraktionen im Deutschen Bundestag 1949–1997*, Opladen: Westdeutscher Verlag.

Schwarz, Hans-Peter (1989) 'Adenauers Kanzlerdemokratie und Regierungstechnik', *Aus Politik und Zeitgeschichte*, no. 1–2, pp. 15–27.

Searing, Donald D. (1994) *Westminster's World: Understanding Political Roles*, Cambridge, Mass.: Harvard University Press.

Seaton, Janet and Winetrobe, Barry K. (1999) 'Modernising the Commons', *Political Quarterly*, vol. 70, pp. 152–60.

Sebaldt, Martin (2000) 'Interest Groups: Continuity and Change of German Lobbyism since 1974', in Ludger Helms (ed.), *Institutions and Institutional Change in the Federal Republic of Germany*, London: Macmillan, pp. 188–204.

Seldon, Anthony (1987) 'The Churchill Administration, 1951–1955', in Peter Hennessy and Anthony Seldon (eds), *Ruling Performance*, Oxford: Basil Blackwell, pp. 63–97.

Seldon, Anthony (1994) 'Policy Making and Cabinet', in Dennis Kavanagh and Anthony Seldon (eds), *The Major Effect*, London: Macmillan, pp. 154–66.

Seyd, Patrick (1998) 'Tony Blair and New Labour', in Anthony King (ed.), *New Labour Triumphs: Britain at the Polls*, Chatham, NJ: Chatham House, pp. 49–73.

Seymour-Ure, Colin (1984) 'British "War Cabinets" in Limited Wars: Korea, Suez and the Falklands', *Public Administration*, vol. 62, pp. 181–200.

Seymour-Ure, Colin (1996) *The British Press and Broadcasting since 1945*, 2nd edn, Oxford: Basil Blackwell.

Seymour-Ure, Colin (2003) *Prime Ministers and the Media*, Oxford: Basil Blackwell.

Shaiko, Ronald G. (1998) 'Reverse Lobbying: Interest Group Mobilisation from the White House and the Hill', in Alan J. Cigler and Burdett A. Loomis (eds), *Interest Group Politics*, 5th edn, Washington, DC: Congressional Quarterly Press, pp. 255–82.

Shell, Donald (1992) *The House of Lords*, 2nd edn, New York: Harvester Wheatsheaf.

Shell, Donald (1995a) 'The Office of Prime Minister', in Donald Shell and Richard Hodder-Williams (eds), *Churchill to Major*, London: Hurst, pp. 1–29.

Shell, Donald (1995b) 'Prime Ministers and their Parties', in Donald Shell and Richard Hodder-Williams (eds), *Churchill to Major: The British Prime Ministership since 1945*, London: Hurst, pp. 137–68.

Shugart, Matthew Soberg and Carey, John M. (1992) *Presidents and Assemblies*, Cambridge: Cambridge University Press.

Siaroff, Alan (2003) 'Comparative Presidencies', *European Journal of Political Research*, vol. 42, pp. 287–312.

Simonis, Georg (ed.) (1998) *Deutschland nach der Wende*, Opladen: Leske & Budrich.

Sinclair, Barbara (1995) *Legislators, Leaders, and Lawmaking*, Baltimore, Md.: Johns Hopkins University Press.

Sinclair, Barbara (1999) 'Dilemmas and Opportunities of Legislative Leadership in a Non-Parliamentary System', *Journal of Legislative Studies*, vol. 5, no. 3/4, pp. 283–302.

Skowronek, Stephen (1993) *The Politics Presidents Make: Leadership from John Adams to George Bush*, Cambridge, Mass.: Belknap Press of Harvard University Press.

Smith, Gordon (1994) 'The Changing Parameters of the Chancellorship', in Stephen Padgett (ed.), *Adenauer to Kohl*, London: Hurst, pp. 178–97.

Smith, Martin (1998) 'Reconceptualising the British State', *Public Administration*, vol. 76, pp. 45–72.

Smith, Martin (1999) *The Core Executive in Britain*, London: Macmillan.

Spitzer, Robert J. (1998) 'The Item Veto Dispute and the Secular Crisis of the Presidency', *Presidential Studies Quarterly*, vol. 28, pp. 799–805.

Steffani, Winfried (1995) 'Semi-Präsidentialismus? Zur Unterscheidung von Legislative und Parlament', *Zeitschrift für Parlamentsfragen*, vol. 14, pp. 521–41.

Steffani, Winfried (1999) 'Ministerpräsident und/oder Premierminister?', in Tobias Dürr and Franz Walter (eds), *Solidargemeinschaft und fragmentierte Gesellschaft*, Opladen: Leske & Budrich, pp. 223–48.

Stephan, Klaus (1988) *Gelernte Demokraten: Helmut Schmidt und Franz Josef Strauß*, Hamburg: Rowohlt.

Stern, Klaus (1980) *Das Staatsrecht der Bundesrepublik Deutschland. Bd. II*, Munich: Beck.

Stone Sweet, Alec (2000) *Governing with Judges: Constitutional Politics in Europe*, Oxford: Oxford University Press.

Streeck, Wolfgang (2003) 'No Longer the Century of Corporatism', MPIfG Working Paper 03/04, Cologne: Max-Planck-Institut für Gesellschaftsforschung.

Stuckey, Mary (1991) *The President as Interpreter-in-Chief*, Chatham, NJ: Chatham House.

Sturm, Roland (1995) 'How Independent Is the Bundesbank?', *German Politics*, vol. 4, no. 1, pp. 27–41.

Sturm, Roland (1999) 'Party Competition and the Federal System: The Lehmbruch Hypothesis Revisited', in Charlie Jefferey (ed.), *Recasting German Federalism*, London: Pinter, pp. 197–215.

Sturm, Roland (2003) 'Policy-Making in a New Political Landscape', in Stephen Padgett, William E. Paterson and Gordon Smith (eds), *Developments in German Politics 3*, Basingstoke: Palgrave, pp. 101–20.

Stüwe, Klaus (2001) 'Das Bundesverfassungsgericht als verlängerter Arm der Opposition?', *Aus Politik und Zeitgeschichte*, no. 37–38, pp. 34–44.

Tenpas, Kathryn Dunn (2000) 'The American Presidency: Surviving and Thriving amidst the Permanent Campaign', in Norman J. Ornstein and Thomas E. Mann (eds), *The Permanent Campaign and Its Future*, Washington, DC: American Enterprise Institute and the Brookings Institution, pp. 108–33.

Tenpas, Kathryn Dunn and Hess, Stephen (2002) 'The Bush White House: First Appraisals', *Presidential Studies Quarterly*, vol. 32, pp. 577–85.

Thatcher, Margaret (1993) *The Downing Street Years*, London: HarperCollins.

Thomas, Graham P. (1997) *Prime Minister and Cabinet Today*, Manchester: Manchester University Press.

Thorpe, D. R. (1996) *Alec Douglas-Home*, London: Sinclair-Stevenson.

Thunert, Martin W. (2001) 'Germany', in R. Kent Weaver and Paul B. Stares (eds), *Guidance for Governance*, Tokyo: Japan Center for International Exchange, pp. 157–206.

Thurber, James (ed.) (1996) *Rivals for Power: Presidential–Congressional Relations*, Washington, DC: Congressional Quarterly Press.

Tichenor, Daniel J. (2003) 'The Presidency and Interest Groups', in Michael Nelson (ed.), *The Presidency and the Political System*, 7th edn, Washington, DC: Congressional Quarterly Press, pp. 329–54.

Tratt, Jacqueline (1996) *The Macmillan Government and Europe*, London: Macmillan.

Tsebelis, George (1995) 'Decision Making in Political Systems: Veto Players in Presidentialism, Parliamentarism, Multi-Cameralism and Multi-Partyism', *British Journal of Political Science*, vol. 25, pp. 289–325.

Tsebelis, George (2002) *Veto Players: How Political Institutions Work*, Princeton, NJ: Princeton University Press.

Veen, Hans-Joachim (1976) *Opposition im Bundestag*, Bonn: Eichholz.

Vincent, John (1987) 'The Thatcher Governments, 1979–1987', in Peter Hennessy and Anthony Seldon (eds), *Ruling Performance*, Oxford: Basil Blackwell, pp. 274–300.

Wagschal, Uwe (2000) 'Monetary Institutions: Maintaining Independence in Times of Fiscal Stress', in Ludger Helms (ed.), *Institutions and Institutional Change in the Federal Republic of Germany*, London: Macmillan, pp. 143–65.

Walcott, Charles E. and Hult, M. Karen (2003) 'The Bush Staff and Cabinet System', *Perspectives on Political Science*, vol. 32, pp. 150–5.

Walker, David (1987) 'The First Wilson Governments, 1964–1970', in Peter Hennessy and Anthony Seldon (eds), *Ruling Performance*, Oxford: Basil Blackwell, pp. 186–215.

Walker, David B. (1995) *The Rebirth of Federalism*, Chatham, NJ: Chatham House.

Walter, Franz (1997) 'Führung in der Politik: Am Beispiel sozialdemokratischer Parteivorsitzender', *Zeitschrift für Politikwissenschaft*, vol. 7, pp. 1287–336.

Walter, Franz and Müller, Kay (2002) 'Die Chefs des Kanzleramtes', *Zeitschrift für Parlamentsfragen*, vol. 33, pp. 474–501.

Warshaw, Shirley Anne (1996) *Powersharing: White House–Cabinet Relations in the Modern Presidency*, Albany, NJ: State University of New York Press.

Watts, Ronald L. (1999) 'German Federalism in Comparative Perspective', in Charlie Jeffery (ed.), *Recasting German Federalism*, London: Pinter, pp. 265–84.

Webb, Paul (2000) *The Modern British Party System*, London: Sage.

Weber-Panariello, Philippe A. (1995) *Nationale Parlamente in der Europäischen Union*, Baden-Baden: Nomos.

Weisberg, Herbert F. (1980) 'Cabinet Transfers and Department Prestige', Mimeo of paper presented at the 38th annual meeting of the Midwest Political Science Association.

Wengst, Udo (1984) *Staatsaufbau und Regierungspraxis 1948 bis 1953*, Dusseldorf: Droste.

Werz, Nikolaus (2000) 'Helmut Kohl: Auf dem Weg zum Mythos?', in Yves Bizeul (ed.), *Politische Mythen und Rituale in Deutschland, Frankreich und Polen*, Berlin: Duncker & Humblot, pp. 219–34.

Wessels, Bernhard (1999) 'Die deutsche Variante des Korporatismus', in Max Kaase and Günter Schmid (eds), *Eine lernende Demokratie – 50 Jahre Bundesrepublik Deutschland*, Berlin: Sigma, pp. 87–113.

Wewer, Göttrik (1991) 'Das Bundesverfassungsgericht – eine Gegenregierung?', in Bernhard Blanke and Hellmut Wollmann (eds), *Die alte Bundesrepublik*, Opladen: Westdeutscher Verlag, pp. 310–35.

Wewer, Göttrik (ed.) (1998) *Bilanz der Ära Kohl*, Opladen: Leske & Budrich.

Whitehead, Philip (1987) 'The Labour Governments, 1974–1979', in Peter Hennessy and Anthony Seldon (eds), *Ruling Performance*, Oxford: Basil Blackwell, pp. 241–73.

Wildavsky, Aaron (1966) 'The Two Presidencies', *Trans-Action*, vol. 4, pp. 7–14.

Wildenmann, Rudolf (1969) 'Die Rolle des Bundesverfassungsgerichts und der Deutschen Bundesbank in der politischen Willensbildung', *Veröffentlichungen der Universität Mannheim, Bd. 23*, Stuttgart: Kohlhammer, pp. 3–19.

Wildenmann, Rudolf (1986) 'Ludwig Erhard und Helmut Schmidt, die charismatischen Verlierer', in Hans-Dieter Klingemann and Max Kaase (eds), *Wahlen und politischer Prozeß*, Opladen: Westdeutscher Verlag, pp. 87–107.

Wilke, Jürgen (1999) *Mediengeschichte der Bundesrepublik Deutschland*, Cologne: Böhlau.

Wilke, Jürgen and Reinemann, Carsten (2000) *Kanzlerkandidaten in der Wahlkampfberichterstattung*, Cologne: Böhlau.

Wilson, Graham K. and Barker, Anthony (2003) 'Bureaucrats and Politicians in Britain', *Governance*, vol. 16, pp. 349–72.

Winter, Thomas von (2001) 'Verbändemacht im kooperativen Staat', in Andrea Gourd and Thomas Noetzel (eds), *Zukunft der Demokratie in Deutschland*, Opladen: Leske & Budrich, pp. 211–34.

Woldendorp, Jaap, Keman, Hans and Budge, Ian (2000) *Party Government in 48 Democracies (1945–1998)*, Dordrecht: Kluwer.

Woodward, Bob (1999) *Shadow*, New York: Touchstone.

Woodward, Bob (2002) 'A Struggle for the President's Heart and Mind', *Washington Post*, 17 November, p. A1.

Wyszomirski, Margaret Jane (1989) 'Presidential Personnel and Political Capital: From Roosevelt to Reagan', in Mattei Dogan (ed.), *Pathways to Power*, Boulder, Col.: Westview Press, pp. 45–73.

Yalof, David (1999) *Pursuit of Justices: Presidential Politics and Selection of Supreme Court Nominees*, Chicago: University of Chicago Press.

Yates, Jeff and Whitford, Andrew (1998) 'Presidential Power and the United States Supreme Court', *Political Research Quarterly*, vol. 51, pp. 539–50.

Yoder, Amos (1986) *The Conduct of American Foreign Policy Since World War II*, New York: Pergamon Press.

Zastrow, Volker (2004) 'Wessen Opposition?', *Frankfurter Allgemeine Zeitung*, 10 February, p. 1.

Zohlnhöfer, Reimut (1999) 'Die große Steuerreform 1998/99: Ein Lehrstück für Politikentwicklung bei Parteienwettbewerb im Bundesstaat', *Zeitschrift für Parlamentsfragen*, vol. 30, pp. 326–45.

Zohlnhöfer, Reimut (2003) 'Rot-grüne Regierungspolitik in Deutschland 1998–2002', in Christoph Egle, Tobias Ostheim and Reimut Zohlnhöfer (eds), *Das rot-grüne Projekt*, Wiesbaden: Westdeutscher Verlag, pp. 399–419.

Zons, Achim (1984) *Das Denkmal*, Munich: Olzog.

Zuck, Rüdiger (1998) 'Verfassungswandel durch Vertrag?', *Zeitschrift für Rechtspolitik*, vol. 31, pp. 457–9.

Index